THE JOY OF COMPUTERS

THE JOY OF COMPUTERS

PETER LAURIE

DESIGNED BY

BERNARD HIGTON

LITTLE, BROWN AND COMPANY

Boston Toronto

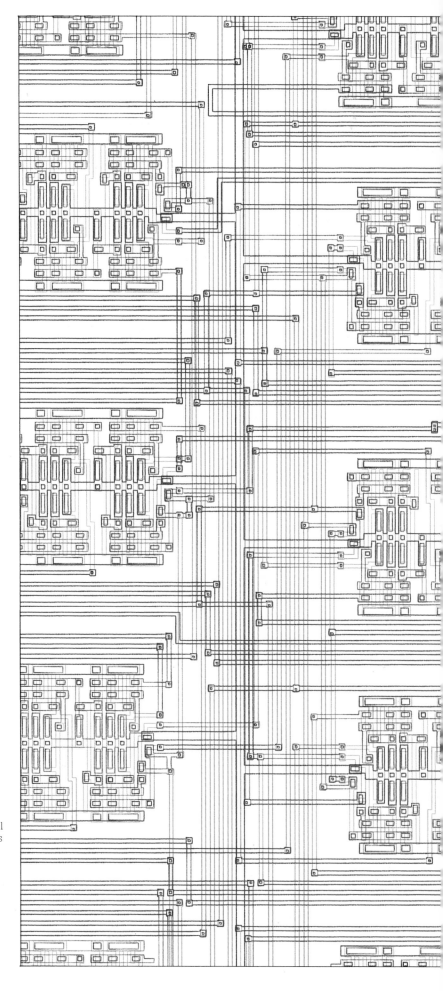

LIBRARY OF CONGRESS CATALOG CARD NO. 83-81331

FIRST AMERICAN EDITION

ISBN 0-316-51636-8

Published in the United Kingdom by Hutchinson & Co.
(Publishers) Ltd

Printed and bound in the UK

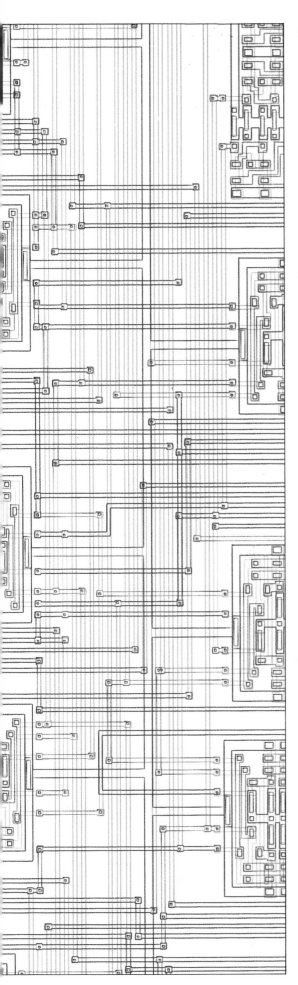

CONTENTS

INTRODUCTION

This book is an attempt to open a few windows into a fascinating new world which has, until the last couple of years, been the preserve of a few thousand highly paid, inbred professionals.

Now the cheapness of small computers has spread them in their hundred thousands all over the world. Millions of people are beginning to worry that they – and perhaps more alarmingly their children – are 'incomputerate', an even worse disadvantage than illiteracy. Certainly, it is true now that the computer sector of many national economies is one of the few that show any signs of life. Young computer scientists straight out of university command substantial salaries as professionals in the hardware and software industries. People with much slighter skills – perhaps no more than a few months' experience of self-taught BASIC – are beginning to be in demand to manage microcomputers in business.

There is a myth, which has been carefully fostered by the giant computer corporations, that there is something magical about computers and the people who run them. The legend has got about that computers are 'electronic brains' and that programmers are some sort of supermen. The facts are that computers are very stupid and the people who program them are normal human beings. Anyone who can count from 0 to 7 on his or her fingers and make 8 can learn to be a programmer. The business is not difficult; it is just tricky.

It is very misleading to imagine that computers can 'think' like people. They cannot. They have no more a mind of their own than a lawnmower. However, they make it possible for people to 'bottle' thought. You work out how to do a particular job or solve a problem, write a program, and the computer will then apply your thinking to that job or problem as long and as often as you like. In this sense computers and programs are half alive because they perpetuate the thinking of their creators. In the trade you often hear people say things like 'How does that subroutine know it ought to do such and such?', as if it were a human. What they ought perhaps to say is: 'How did the person who wrote the subroutine expect information to get to it to make it do such and such?'

The information-processing revolution promises to make profound changes in our way of life, but these changes will be no more difficult than many others which have been successfully assimilated. In recent history we have had the revolutions of printing, industrial production, railways, electricity, telegraph and telephones, flying, radio and television. Computing is merely one more step in the human race's continuous drive to master its environment. We invented machinery to save and surpass our bodies' labour; now we have invented computers to save and surpass the labour of our minds.

In the end, no doubt, computing will take us to places we never dreamed of when we started.

Even though the computing business only started during the Second World War and has been in existence for such a short time, it has produced a very rich and complicated culture all its own. You cannot really understand today's microcomputers without having some notion of what has gone before, because they incorporate all sorts of assumptions and ideas that have built up gradually over the years.

But although history is important, the pace of change is so fast that anyone with a good idea has an excellent chance of making a mark on the industry. Change is happening on two fronts simultaneously. The hardware of computers is getting daily cheaper and more powerful. This means that jobs which a few years ago could only be attempted on huge machines by their dedicated attendants can now be done as routine on tens of thousands of office desks. The second change is that computing is being brought out into the light of every day to be the tool of every man. No longer are these machines used only by a lavishly paid caste of high priests talking their own brand of mumbo-jumbo; they have been joined by perfectly ordinary people who are interested in getting a job done rather than in the intricacies of computing. This is changing computers in just the same way that mass markets changed motorcars.

To begin with, motorcars were the toys of the enthusiast. You could drive one from London to Beijing, but you had to be prepared to rebuild the whole thing several times on the way. As soon as cars began to be sold on the mass market this had to stop. They had to become reliable, standardized, comfortable. Far from being willing to regrind the pistons every twenty miles, the new car owner was upset if the door rattled or the cigarette lighter was faulty. The same thing is happening to computers. A few years ago the typical owner of a home computer was a fanatic, who would happily rebuild the machine twice a night on the kitchen table. Now there are tens of thousands of people who expect to be able to turn on their micros and do their accounts or word processing or play a game, and who would be baffled by the thought of a soldering iron.

You might imagine that the world of computing would be totally orderly, surgically sterile in its logic. I am happy to say that this is not at all the case. In fact the computing business is strangely like the world of high fashion. Computing too has its share of fads and fashions, oddballs, fanatics, charlatans and lunatics – and a large number of hard-working, interesting, sensible people who are fascinated to be at the frontier of human progress, doing whatever seems best at the time to help the whole thing forward.

From another point of view, the computing world is like the Wild West of America in the last century. The territory is so vast, the riches so huge, that no one has time to sit still and brood. The industry sucks people in like leaves. It has a voracious appetite for new hands and new ideas. It demands performance rather than qualifications. In the Wild West, if you could shoot straight and had an honest face, you were made sheriff. In the computer business if you can do the job you have it – no one cares where you learned to do it or what letters you have after your name.

There are several forces that draw people in. One is, no doubt, the fact that the micro industry offers jobs when jobs are scarce. Secondly, it offers a field wide open to all the talents: the whole world is in the process of being computerized, and so the industry needs people who know about everything under the sun. Thirdly, the financial rewards are potentially vast. The growth of mass markets opens up the possibilities of Hollywood-style money. The two teenage founders of Apple Computers, who had to sell a van and a calculator to finance their first machine, were millionaires five years later.

Whether for riches or for excitement, there have always been plenty of people in the industry prepared to follow their ideas wherever they may lead, and the result has been a most amazing wealth of different machines, different languages and different techniques for doing all sorts of things. As a consequence, there is so much that could be described that this book could be rewritten four or five times without duplicating much of the material. I can only open windows onto a multitude of fascinating gardens; I hope my readers will think it worthwhile to go out into them.

PETER LAURIE, 1983

PART ONE / THE COMPUTER

THE MICRO

A micro is a computer – a small one to be sure, but in principle no different from the IBMs and the Crays that fill innumerable computer rooms with clinical grey boxes. The classic definition of a computer is that it is a machine for 'processing data', but that in itself is not much help. Some understanding of what a computer is and what it does will, I hope, emerge from this book, so I shall not bother now with a textbook definition. This is in any case no sort of textbook. It is an evocation, an attempt to get across some of the fascination and fun of these machines.

It might be a good idea to get a grip on what we are talking about. Computers are divided into three rough classes: main-frames, minis and micros. The difference between them used to be purely technical; now it is much more a question of price and marketing.

A main-frame is a big machine costing many thousands in any currency. It needs a staff of professionals to manage it and a specially prepared site – which may cost as much as the computer itself.

A mini is the fruit of the first spasm of cheapening and miniaturization in computer technology. Minis came in about ten years ago to give users – who were usually university departments or fairly large companies – computers that did not need a full-time staff of professional servants or special sites. They cost rather fewer thousands than main-frames, but are still beyond the reach of all but the most affluent and skilled individuals.

The essence of a micro is that it can be afforded and used by virtually anyone. Micros themselves divide (for the moment) into two classes: personal computers, which are cheap and not very powerful, but which perform an essential function in spreading 'computeracy'; and business machines, which often perform many of the functions of minis or main-frames.

This neat classification is now becoming thoroughly confused by the avalanche of computing power pouring into the new chips (see pp. 18-19). The original 8-bit micros were not very powerful. But the newer 16-bit machines are often as powerful as minis; while the very latest generation of micros, such as Hewlett-Packard's 32-bit machine, have the computing power of small main-frames.

But none of this matters terribly, because the interesting and important part of computing does not lie in the hardware – the actual machine – but in the software – the programs.

The most sensible way of thinking about a micro is as a rather complicated electric typewriter. You hit a key on the keyboard. By a surprisingly involved process (which we shall look at in the pages to come) that letter appears on the screen. You can write several letters, or indeed a word, a sentence, a paragraph – even a book like this one – see it on the screen and save it on disk or magnetic tape. You can get the book back and change it. You can automatically alter 'Carter' to 'Reagan' if there has been a shift in America's presidency. You can get a program to index the book – to tell you what page each word falls on. None of this is at all difficult. But it is tedious, and it is much better to have a machine do it than do it yourself.

You might want to do very boring sums. You might be wrestling with the cash flow for your business or your department. What happens if wages go up 5 per cent, sales volume goes up 30 per cent, the cost of materials goes down 6 per cent, interest rates fall 1.1 per cent and you open up a new market in Saudi Arabia? The micro can calculate it all. If you are designing a bridge you will have to make sure that each girder is strong enough to carry the required load plus the weight of traffic on the structure. If one element turns out to be too frail you make it stronger – and that changes the load on all the others, which you have to recalculate. This could take a long time and it would be much better to let a machine do it.

Suppose you are a quantity surveyor, responsible for working out the amounts of materials necessary for a particular building. How many bricks are needed to build a wall 43 feet tall by 166 feet long with openings for sixteen windows and four doors? How much mortar do you need to lay the bricks? How much concrete for the foundations? Your micro can work it all out.

You might even like playing Space Invaders, but prefer not to go out to the amusement arcade. The micro has something for you too.

Microcomputers are good at boring tasks. They free their owners to do more creative things. They are quite hard to get working, and that in itself can be very interesting. But there is, to be honest, nothing very fascinating about a computer just doing its job.

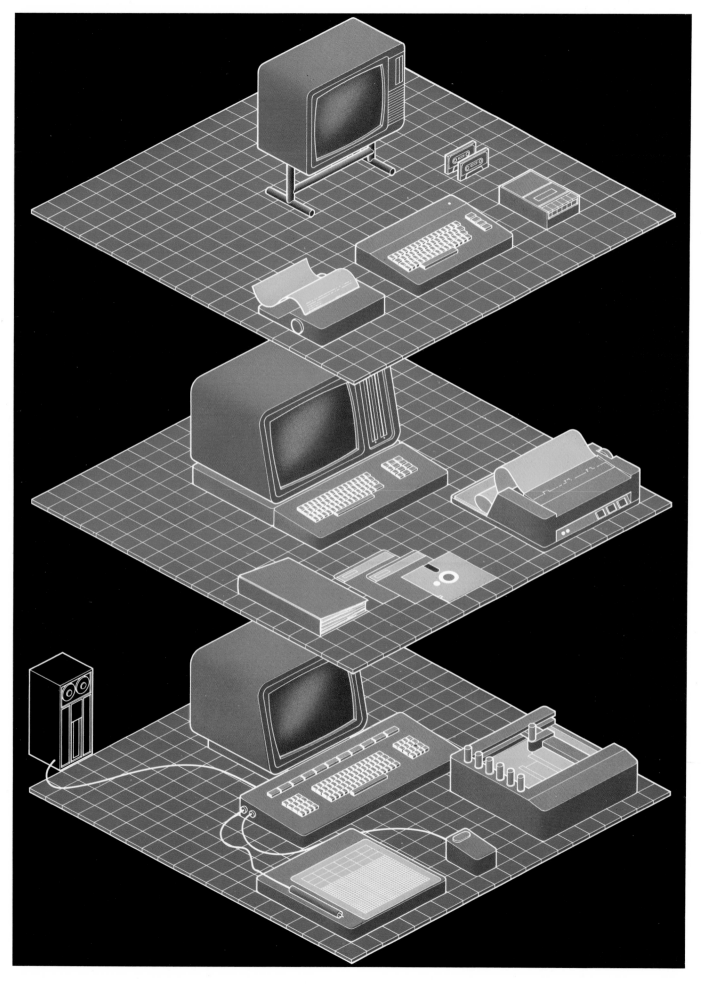

GETTING INSIDE

A computer runs a program that does something to some data and then produces some output. The program might do nothing more riveting than look to see what key you hit at the keyboard and then print the same letter on the screen. The key you hit is data, the letter on the screen is output.

As far as the computer is concerned, you could hit a letter, a number, a punctuation key or a non-printing key. They are all coded in the ASCII (American Standard Code for Information Interchange, see p. 185) character set as numbers ranging from 0 to 127. 'A' is 65, a space between words is 32, '3' is 51 and '+' is 43, and so on.

The computer, however, can understand only one thing: the presence or absence of electric current, which can represent 'yes' or 'no', 'on' or 'off', or '1' or '0'. And so these decimal numbers are converted into their binary equivalents. You do not need to be able to convert decimal numbers into binary; you just have to remember that where decimal numbers run from 0 to 9 and carry into the next column, binary numbers run from 0 to 1 before being carried. Two in binary is therefore 10, four is 100, eight is 1000 and sixteen is 10000. In computing binary digits are known as 'bits', often further abbreviated to 'b'.

In executing the ultra-simple screen-printing program, you hit 'A', the keyboard signals 65 (01000001) to the computer, the computer looks up the shape that corresponds to code 65 in a read-only memory (ROM, see pp. 24-5) and prints 'A' on the screen.

If you had typed '3+4', the keyboard would have sent the codes 51,43,52, and the computer would have printed the three shapes '3','+','4' on the screen. We know that you can evaluate '3+4' to make '7', but if you want the machine to do this, you will need quite a complicated program that will scan along the line you have typed in, looking for the codes of things like '+' (and also '−', '*', '/', i.e. subtract, multiply, divide) and the codes of things for it to add up, '3' and '4'. The BASIC language contains within it just such a program, but it is the program (or rather the programmer who wrote it originally) that makes the computer 'know' that it can add up '3' and '4', but not 'A' and

'B' – unless, of course, 'A' and 'B' are being used as names for numbers in an algebraic program.

If you look at the chart on page 185, you will see that the ASCII scheme does not fit very neatly into multiples of 10. A more suitable multiple turns out to be 16, colloquially known as 'Hex' (short for hexadecimal). Counting in Hex goes: 1, 2, 3, ... 9, A, B, C, D, E, F. The number 16 is important in computing; so is 8. Eight bits make 1 'byte' and a byte has come to be the standard unit of useful information. (The abbreviation for byte is B.) The capacity of a computer's internal memory and its external disks is measured in bytes. The reason the byte is a useful unit is that it gives enough space to store all the keyboard characters.

Since a byte consists of 8 bits, it can take any one of 2^8 values. Two multiplied by itself 8 times is 256, so a byte can be used to code 256 different things. Since the ASCII system runs from 0 to 127, it uses only 7 bits or half the 256 possibilities. (If this seems puzzling, remember that every extra bit on a binary number multiplies the highest number it can represent by 2, just as every extra digit on a decimal number multiplies the highest number represented by 10. One bit means from 0 to 1; 2 bits from 0 to 3; 4 bits 0 to 7...; 7 bits 0 to 127 and 8 bits 0 to 255 – or 256 possiblities.)

The other 128 available codes are used in two different ways. If ASCII characters are to be sent down a long wire such as a telephone line, there is always the possibility of error. The eighth bit is set to 1 or 0 according to whether there is an even or an odd number of 1s in the rest of the byte. At the other end the receiving computer checks to see whether this is right. If any byte has been corrupted the eighth bit will appear wrongly set, and the receiving computer will then ask for a repeat. This is called 'parity checking' and the eighth bit is known as the 'parity bit'.

The other way of using the eighth bit or the upper 127 ASCII charcters is within the computer, where transmission errors are unlikely, to give users a set of 'graphics' characters the same size as letters. These graphics characters can be used by the determined to make up rather crude pictures on the screen.

Below The word 'JOY' stored in ASCII characters. The 8 bits of each of the 3 bytes can be held as switch positions, or '1's and '0's

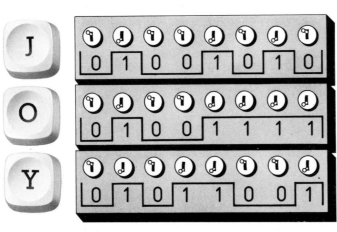

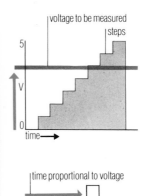

How an analogue-to-digital convertor works. The object is to measure the voltage represented by the horizontal line in the graph. The device produces a comparison voltage that increases in steps at set time intervals. Sooner or later it becomes greater than the voltage to be measured: at that instant a pulse appears on the output. The delay until the pulse is sent is a measure of the voltage

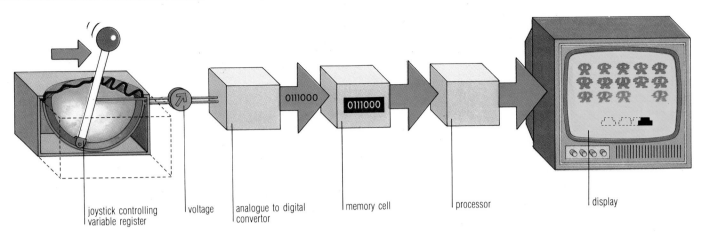

joystick controlling variable register | voltage | analogue to digital convertor | memory cell | processor | display

The joystick used in computer games is only one of the ways in which the computer receives input and translates it into output. As the stick is moved backwards and forwards it alters a variable resistance. The varying voltage coming out of this is proportional to the position of the stick. An analogue-to-digital converter turns the voltage into a number. That number is written into a memory cell in the computer and used by the processor (in this example) to calculate the position of the anti-Space Invader gun on the screen

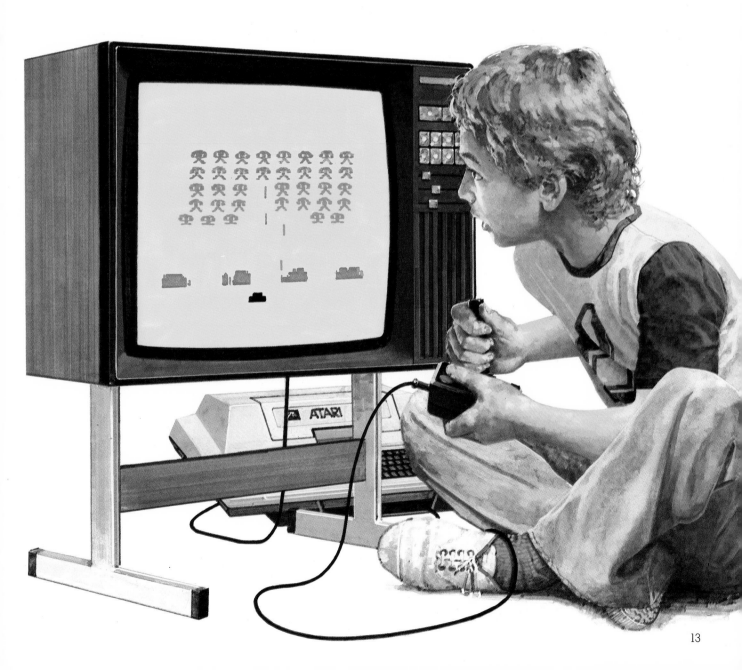

THE COMPUTER BOARD

The world's first proper computer: the Mark 1 at Manchester University, England, in the late forties (top) had several thousand radio valves and could sometimes run for hours at a time before one blew and stopped things dead. It was programmed in 32-base numbers written backwards. Alan Turing (see pp. 162-5), who was responsible for the programming, saw no reason why the computer should pander to its operator's inability to think the way it did. 'User friendliness' has been a bone of contention between programmers and users ever since.
The Mark 1's modern equivalent is the calculator wristwatch, which is almost as powerful as the first computer

If you lever off the case of any computer – from the biggest Cray to the smallest Sinclair – you will find something inside that looks rather like the picture on the right. The black oblongs are commonly called integrated circuit packages – 'IC's for short, or 'chips', though really the chip itself is a tiny ¼-inch square thing sealed inside the black plastic case, which is all you can see from the outside.

These oblongs are called integrated circuits because they combine in a single physical object what used to have to be made up of lots of individual transistors, resistors, capacitors and other circuit components.

The plastic cases have to be much bigger than the actual chip so that clumsy human fingers can handle them and electrical connections can be made to the 'pins' – the shiny metal legs that stick out in a row on each side, and are bent down and soldered into holes in the circuit board to connect the chip into the computer's circuits.

There are hundreds of different sorts of chip which do hundreds of different jobs. There are chips to do the logical functions OR, NOT, AND, XOR (see pp. 20-21). There are chips to pick a single bit out of a flying stream of data and freeze it; chips to remember masses of data, to turn parallel streams into serial streams (see pp. 22-3), to do arithmetic and even to turn written English into spoken English (see p. 120). The type of chip is identified by the number printed on the top.

A chip on its own is not much use. It has to be fed with electrical power, with signals from other chips or external devices, and its outputs have to passed on to the next device in the chain. This is all done by the metallic tracks printed onto the fibreglass circuit board. Another set of tracks is printed on the back of this board; some machines are so complicated that they need three or four layers of tracks to interconnect their chips. Most of the work of designing a computer amounts to picking the chips needed to carry out the specification of the machine, and then laying out a circuit board on which they can be mounted.

This job is made much easier by software packages running on existing computers which will do most of the donkey work of interconnecting the chips and laying out the board.

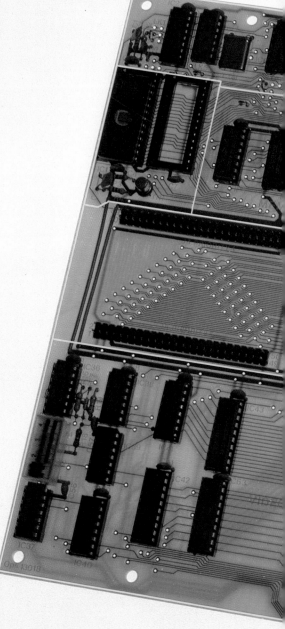

Making the computer then consists simply of printing the board, inserting the right chips in the right holes, soldering the connections and testing the result. All this can be done almost automatically, and makes building a computer more like printing a book than, say, building a house.

Given the right design, it is now very cheap indeed to make up boards like this, and the process is getting cheaper all the time. The casing and power supply are now the only expensive components. The day is coming when most of the cost of a computer will lie in the tin box it lives in – and the delivery charges.

This well-laid-out board shows all the functional parts of a microcomputer. The chips (black rectangles) are linked by metal connectors (bright lines) printed on the board. The connectors on this side run horizontally; on the reverse they run vertically. The small bright circles are rivets connecting the two sides together

1 System clock
2 Bus decoding
3 Z80 processor
4 Direct memory access
5 Input/output
6 Read-only memory
7 64-K random-access memory chips
8 Extra bus sockets
9 Video
10 User clock
11 Floppy disk control

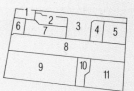

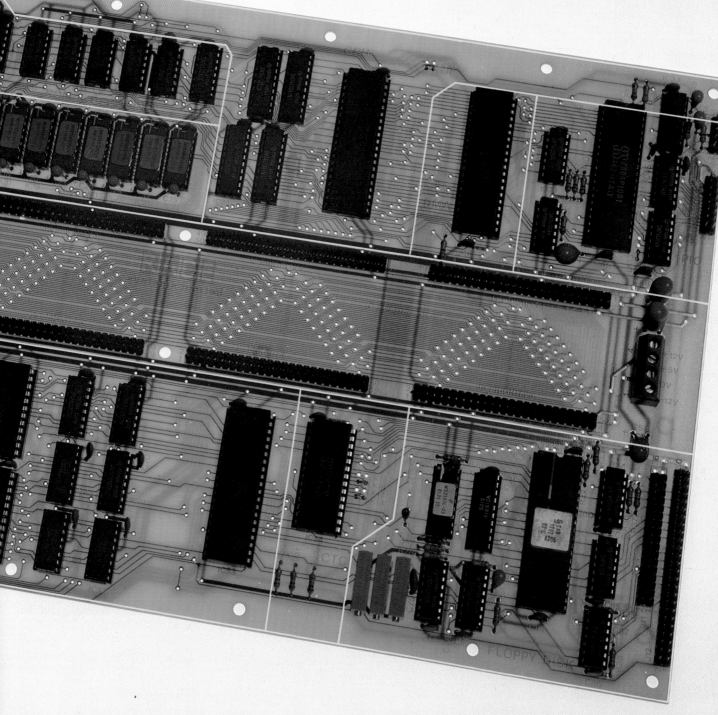

MEMORY AND PROCESSOR

From the user's point of view, a computer's memory may be the most important thing about it. (This is the internal fast memory, not the external disk or tape memory.) All other things being equal, the more memory your computer has the better, because you can run bigger programs and have them working on more data. For reasons we shall come to below, all 8-bit micros – and that includes the vast majority in the world at the time of writing – have a maximum of 2^{16} = 65,536 memory locations that the processor can address at one time. (For some reason, 8-bit pro-

cessors actually use 16 bits for their memory addressing.)

It is thought-provoking to reflect that if the contents of each of the memory locations in a micro were written out on ordinary index cards, and those cards laid end to end, they would stretch for about 6 miles, and the memory in the newer 16-bit machines laid out on cards would cover 100 miles or more. Imagine having to run up and down such an array, picking up a card here, reading it, rushing off over the horizon to read the one it referred to, tearing back, picking up two more and doing the sums they commanded on the trot. This is not an unreasonable analogy because no computer ever does anything that you could not do with pencil and paper. It just does it a lot faster and more accurately – so much so, in fact, that it can give a quantum jump in work possibilities. Many pencil and paper operations that are mundane in themselves become interesting and useful if done on a large enough scale and fast enough.

The heart of any computer is the processor. Like the engine in a car, it is an essential part of the machine, but you need a lot more bits and pieces to make the whole thing work. There are many different types of processor, but they all function in the same basic way. The most important single distinction between them is in the 'word length' they cope with. This 'word' is strictly a chip designer's term and has nothing much to do, for instance, with the words on this page. The 'word' is the basic unit of data that the machine accepts. At the time of writing, most micros in the world used an 8-bit word. That is, they looked at life in 8-bit – or 1-byte – chunks.

At its simplest, a processor is just a chip with three memory locations (just 8 transistors in a row). They are called 'registers' by the experts. One of the locations has a command in it; the

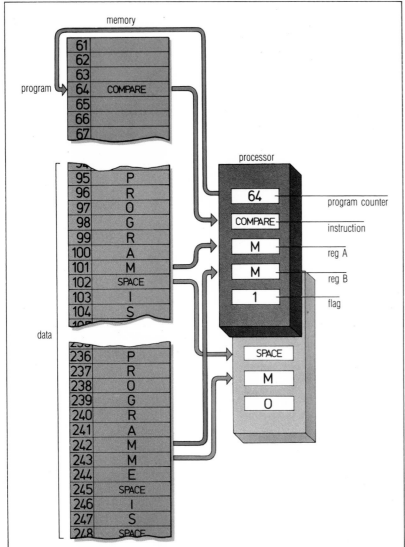

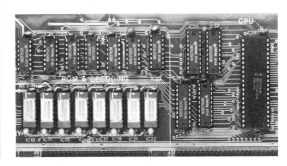

A processor searching memory for the word 'programme' to turn it into 'program'. The instructions are loaded into the top (low numbers) end of memory. The current instruction, 'compare', is loaded in the instruction register, and its number in memory into the program counter. It loads corresponding letters from the pieces of memory that hold the words 'program'

and 'programme' into the A and B registers. The result of the compare instruction is a '1' in the flag register if the letters are the same (foreground) and '0' if they are different (background). The next stage of the program looks at the flag to decide what to do next. In the photograph of the RAM section of the computer board, the memory can be seen as a

row of eight chips. The processor (CPU) is the large chip on the right

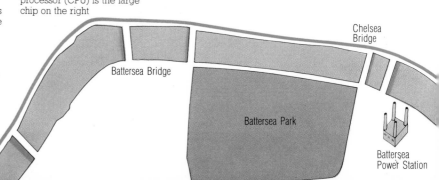

other two contain bytes of data. According to the command, the processor can: add the 2 bytes together; subtract one from the other; or compare them to see if they are the same. And that is all it can do. Of course, even this is far from easy. To do each of these things, the 8 bits in the command register set a whole mass of other transistors, which link the two data locations, to produce the desired effect.

Looking at the short list of apparently useless actions presented above, you might well ask what use they could be. But if you can add and subtract (comparison is just subtraction looking for 0 as the answer), you can do multiplication and division. If you can do addition, subtraction, multiplication and division, you can do calculations such as square roots and logarithms. If you can do that sort of thing, you can do any mathematics at all.

In fact, most of the time the processor is doing much more mundane things, such as looking for the extra letter 'm' in this text where I have written 'programme' instead of 'program', so that my word-processing package can change it. It does this, of course by comparing the code for 'mme' with the codes for various letters in the text until it finds a match and then inserts the codes for 'm'. Since, as we saw on page 12, letters are represented by numbers, that too needs nothing more than comparison of two numbers.

Real processors have a lot more in them than the simplistic three-register one we have just looked at. But in essence they work the same way – and so do the new 16-bit ones, and so do the old 32- and 64-bit processors in the big

main-frames, and so will the new 16-, 32- and 64-bit processors that will be in the computers that we will use in the future. Happily, we ordinary users of micros do not have to wonder how processors are made to do useful things. That has been taken care of by the people who wrote the languages we use – and if, as is even more likely, we do not write programs in BASIC or Pascal, but just run applications packages to do word processing or accounts, or play Space Invaders, we are even further removed, because the people who wrote those packages almost certainly used a high-level language and were themselves very unlikely to know how to make a naked processor do these tricks (see Machine Code and Data Structures, p. 80).

The processor by itself is of no more use than the memory by itself. The two have to work together. Current micros use their memory for two completely different purposes: to store the program, and to store the data the program is to work on. Suppose I am looking for that extra 'm' in 'programme'. What happens is that the ASCII code for 'm' – 109 or 01101101 – is loaded into the A register of the processor. The succéssive ASCII codes representing this text are fed into another register, say B. The processor is then told to compare A with B. If they are the same, an indication appears. The processor gets its instructions from another area of memory, whose contents are fed into the instruction register. The beauty of this scheme is that the programmer can mix up data and program in the same memory in any proportions that he or she needs.

If the contents of each memory location in a micro with 64 K of RAM were written onto an ordinary index card, and the cards laid end to end along the Thames Embankment in London, they would stretch about 6 miles – from Tower Bridge to beyond Battersea

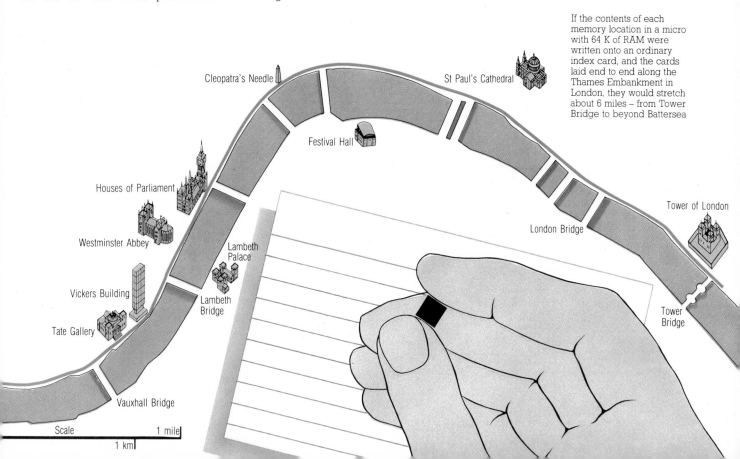

Cleopatra's Needle

St Paul's Cathedral

Festival Hall

Houses of Parliament

Westminster Abbey

Lambeth Palace

Vickers Building

Lambeth Bridge

Tate Gallery

Vauxhall Bridge

London Bridge

Tower of London

Tower Bridge

Scale   1 mile

1 km

CHIPS

This sequence of photographs shows an ordinary integrated circuit package, the ¼-inch square chip inside – with its connecting leads, the circuit on the chip, a group of transistors that make up a 'gate' (see pp. 20-21) and a single transistor

Above A chip in its completed package

Top centre A microprocessor chip inside its casing

Top right Each connector pad on the chip is bonded to one of the external pins by a thin wire

Below left Gates, consisting of several transistors, are the logical building blocks of a chip

Below right Down to the finest detail: these little walls are about a millionth of a metre thick. The whole chip blown up to the scale shown here would be about 4 miles across

Opposite A map of the new world. This processor chip by Texas Instruments – enlarged from about ¼-inch square – shows many recognizable features. Upper left: an area of random access memory (RAM) for the device's storage. Upper right: an arithmetic logic unit. Bottom left: read-only memory (ROM) to encode the processor's instructions. Bottom right: the actual processor, consisting of two banks of eight registers. Round the outside border are the wiring pads (white squares), each with a little knot of buffers and decoders.
A processor chip is actually a miniature computer which mimics many of the features of the machine as a whole. It even has its own language – micro code – into which the machine code produced by the program is translated

It is now time to delve into the tiny chips that do all the tricks described on pages 16-17. As we shall see on pages 165-6, enough transistors can reproduce any logical process. If you can do that, you can imitate any machine at all. Furthermore, you can carry out any procedure that can be logically specified – however complicated and tortuous it may be. For instance, there is no reason in principle why we should not build machines out of transistors that can mine materials from the ground and reproduce themselves – a sort of electronic virus that could be sent forth on a journey through space, making more copies of itself wherever it found a sandy beach. Give such a device fairly rudimentary powers of observation and self-protection and you have a machine to colonize the universe. Later on, of course, we might regret our cleverness.

But enough of technofantasy. It is the transistor we shall concentrate on for the moment. As you can see, it is made up of lines of pillowy stuff; these are the conductors, which carry electricity from place to place. Where they join, some clever physics makes a transistor. Put very simply, a transistor is an electrically operated switch.

To get an idea of the scale of what we are going to be talking about, it is important to realize

that the pillowy lines in the last photograph are about 2 millionths of a metre (2 microns) across. This means that if you used the the technology that is used to make the chips in standard 8-bit micros to print a map, you could get a street plan of the City of London, showing every court and alley, onto that ¼-inch square chip. Alternatively, you could cram some 15,000 words of text onto it. Four chips, fitting into a square inch, would hold the entire text of this book, or a complete daily newspaper. Technology being used to make the new 16- and 32-bit processors would let you put a map of the whole of Greater London or of New York, Paris or Moscow on one of these chips. It is astonishing to realize that you can represent things that are conceptually big enough to get lost in on something small enough to get physically lost in the fluff of a coat pocket.

Technologies still in the laboratory, which will be used to make the computers of the next five years, will be able to put as detailed a map of the whole of southern England or of California from San Francisco to Los Angeles on a ¼-inch chip.

Already, these tiny things are some of the most complicated machines ever built by man; that they can be printed off at a few dollars a time is really extraordinary.

19

TRANSISTORS AND GATES

A transistor does no more and no less than an old-fashioned relay, like the one shown on the right. The relay is an iron bar with a coil around it – an electromagnet. When a voltage is put across the input terminals, a current flows in the coil, the magnet pulls down the iron tab, which pivots on its lever. This then pushes the two springy contacts together so that a current can flow between the output terminals. Consequently a voltage at the input causes a current to flow at the output.

Transistors do just the same, but are very much smaller and can be printed rather than engineered – which makes them much cheaper to manufacture.

A transistor is made by melting some silicon – which can be found in large quantities on any beach – in a furnace and drawing out a single crystal about the size of a bread roll. It is then sliced into nice shiny round wafers.

There are three electrical operations that can be done to silicon: a surface layer can be oxidized to glass to make an electrical insulator (this is easily done by heating it in steam); aluminium lines can be printed on it to conduct electricity as though they were wires; or it can be bombarded with atoms of iodine and other dopants, which sink in and make the silicon itself conduct electricity in some circumstances but not in others. This property gives it the name of 'semiconductor'.

The manufacture of transistors is very simple. It requires the four steps shown on the left. First the silicon is coated with oxide (A). A track is then gouged through the oxide to reveal the silicon again – leaving a bridge in the middle (B). The resist is washed away (C). Then a track of aluminium is printed across the oxide bridge. Finally, the exposed silicon is bombarded with atoms of iodine – the dopant (D).

The transistor has three terminals, known traditionally (and not very meaningfully) as the gate, the source and the drain. The object of the exercise is to control the flow of current between source and drain. Electricity can flow along the doped silicon perfectly well, but there is apparently a snag: the silicon under the aluminium does not get doped, because it is protected from the dopant atoms by the aluminium and oxide bridge. It ought, therefore, to be an insulator. But, in fact, because of the mysteries of semiconductor physics, the little bit of undoped silicon under the bridge will conduct *if* there is an electric field around it. This can be provided very simply by putting a voltage on the gate – on the aluminium

track. Put the voltage on and current will flow from the source to the drain (E). Turn it off and it will not (F).

To make use of this, let us wire the transistor into a simple circuit. The source is connected to a 5-volt supply of current through a resistor. The drain is connected to earth – 0 volts. If we put a voltage on the gate, it will allow a current to flow from the source to the drain. If the whole thing has been correctly designed, current will flow out of the drain faster than it can flow into the source through the resistor, and the source will therefore be at 0 volts.

If we take the voltage off the gate, then the current will not flow, and the source will be at 5 volts. And that is what we set out to do: to make an electrically controlled switch.

Gates

The transistor we have just made may not look a lot of use. But then, a brick is of little use by itself, although given enough you can make a very serviceable pigsty, house or skyscraper. And so it is with transistors.

In order to make use of transistors, they are organized into 'gates' – small groups of devices that do useful logical operations.

We have made the simplest gate already in the drawing (lower left) – an Inverter or NOT gate (so-called because the output is not the input; since it can only be 0 or 1, 1 becomes 0 and 0 becomes 1). You put 5 volts or logical '1' in and get 0 volts or logical '0' out. Conversely, put 0 in and you get 1 out.

That is about all you can do with a single input. If you have two inputs, one output, and all of them can be either 0 or 1, you can do three things. You can AND the inputs; OR the inputs; or Exclusive OR (XOR) the inputs.

These three operations are shown in the 'truth tables' below. In the two left-hand columns are shown the possible combinations of the two inputs A and B. In the right-hand column appears the corresponding output. (The use of the word 'truth' is a hangover from the days when only logicians were interested in such things.)

The stages in making a transistor

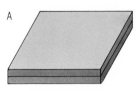
A

B

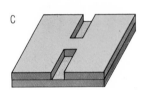
C

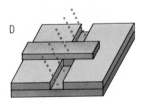
D

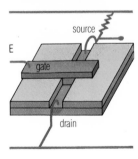
E

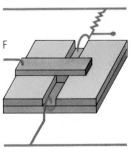
F

NOT	
A	NOT A
1	0
0	1

AND		
A	B	A AND B
1	1	1
1	0	0
0	1	0
0	0	0

OR		
A	B	A OR B
1	1	1
1	0	1
0	1	1
0	0	0

XOR		
A	B	A XOR B
1	1	0
1	0	1
0	1	1
0	0	0

One way of looking at these operations is as a test of the inputs. In the AND gate, for instance, the output is 1 if both the inputs are 1, and 0 otherwise. In the OR gate the output is 0 if both the inputs are 0, and 1 otherwise. In the XOR gate the output is 0 if the inputs are the same, and 1 if they are different.

Since a single transistor inverts the signal, the easiest gates to make are NAND and NOR (AND and OR gates with their ouputs inverted; the tables above apply with 0 and 1 interchanged in their outputs).

The output of the NAND gate can only be 0 if both the inputs are high; otherwise it is 1. The output of the NOR gate is 0 if either or both of the inputs are high; otherwise it is 1.

You could make both gates with some hose and water power, as shown in the drawing on the right. Water only comes out of the AND hose if both taps A and B are on. Water comes out of the OR hose if either tap A or tap B is on.

Again, these operations may not look a lot of use by themselves, but consider the following. On pages 16-17 we were looking at the three things an 8-bit processor does. Essentially, it has two registers and one of the things it can do is compare them to see whether they contain the same 8-bit byte.

REGISTER A: 1 0 1 0 1 1 1 0

REGISTER B: 1 0 1 0 1 1 1 0

XOR A,B
REGISTER C: 1 1 1 1 1 1 1 1

If we make a circuit that Exclusive ORs the bits of the two bytes together in pairs, then ORs the resultant byte pairwise in cascade, we end up with a single bit that is 1 if A and B are different and 0 if they are the same:

A	1	1	0	1	0	1	1	0
B	1	1	0	1	0	1	1	0
XOR	0	0	0	0	0	0	0	0
OR		0		0		0		0
OR			0				0	
OR				0				

Comparison: A and B the same

Let us try this with A and B different:

A	1	1	0	1	0	1	1	0
B	1	1	1	0	0	1	1	0
XOR	0	0	1	1	0	0	0	0
OR		0		1		0		0
OR			1				0	
OR				1				

Comparison: A and B different

So, already we can see a use for even so simple a repertory of gates. We could almost design an

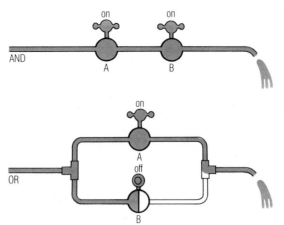

integrated circuit to do the 8-bit comparison function of a processor. Let us try to add two bits together. Often, in logical problems, it helps to start by writing down all the possibilities:

A	B	Ans	Carry
0 + 0 =	0	0
1 + 0 =	1	0
0 + 1 =	1	0
1 + 1 =	0	1

The answer is produced by XORing the inputs, the carry by ANDing them.

We can extend this to add two 8-bit numbers:

CARRIES:		0	1	1	1	1	0	1	0
REGISTER A:		0	0	1	1	1	0	1	0
REGISTER B:	+	0	1	0	1	1	0	1	0
REGISTER C:		1	0	0	1	0	1	0	0

This is slightly more complicated, but still possible. Working from top to bottom, we have *three* bits to add together: the A bit, the B bit and the carry from the previous addition (which is 0 in the right-hand column). However, addition in bits is just like the addition we learned at school: A + B + C is just the same as A + B added to C. So we can use the two-input adder operating the table above twice at each stage, with an OR to sort out the final carry.

And, if your brain is up to it, you can make a circuit to do subtraction. If you can do comparison, addition and subtraction, you can do multiplication and division. If you can do multiplication and division, you can solve equations, do statistics and predict the outcome of complicated events. Going back to the logical functions, if you can do these, you can combine them to perform any operation that can be described as a series of logical steps. The business of computing is really that of trying to reduce useful human operations to rigidly specified steps. As we shall see, it is proving surprisingly difficult. People are cleverer than we think.

The principles of the AND and OR gates can easily be understood in terms of taps and waterpipes. If, in the top diagram, taps A AND B are both on, water flows. If one or both are off it does not. In the lower diagram, if tap A OR tap B is on, the water flows

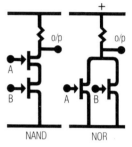

In the left-hand circuit diagram, if transistor A AND transistor B are on, current flows through them to ground, dropping the voltage of the output (O/P) at the bottom of the resistor to 0.
In the right-hand circuit, if transistor A OR transistor B is on, current will flow and the O/P will be 0.
Since in both circuits the O/P is the inverse or NOT of the input (I/P), the gates are called NAND and NOR

BUSSES

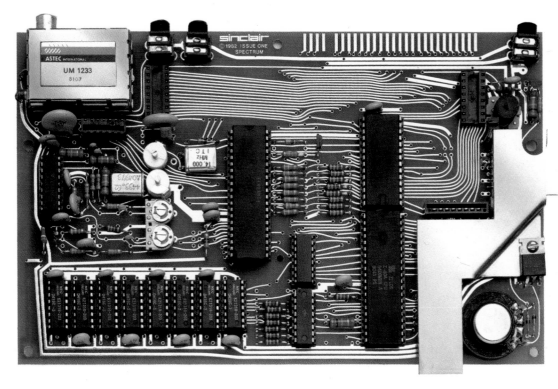

The circuit board of a Sinclair Spectrum home computer. The bus runs mainly on the back of the board, connecting the RAM chips (lower left) to the Z80 processor (lower right), the ROM (upper right), where BASIC and the operating system live, the power (row of contacts, top) and the 'uncommitted logic array' (ULA) (centre). The ULA replaces a great mass of circuitry that would otherwise have to be made of individual integrated circuits on a large board

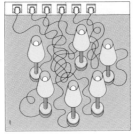

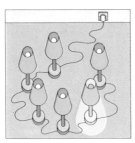

The idea of the 'bus': if a number of electrical devices (top) are connected individually to a source, a jumble of wires results. Much better to run a single wire – the bus (above) – round them all

In computing it is often necessary to connect a lot of devices together. They might be chips on a processor board, boards in a computer, computers in a local network or networks of computers in a national or international system. They might be radars and weapons in a warship, controls in an airliner or robots, machine tools and sensors in an automated factory.

The simpleminded way to make these connections is to take a piece of wire from each subsidiary back to the central controller in a 'star' pattern. There are, however, drawbacks to this scheme: it might need an awful lot of wire and it will certainly need an extra socket on the master for each outlying device. As you add new devices (computing systems always expand), you are sooner or later going to run out of sockets.

The alternative is a 'bus' – a connector that runs around all the subsidiaries in the group in turn. Electrical wiring in the modern house runs in rings – each ring is a simple example of a bus which supplies power to the electrical outlets. Chips on a computer board are connected by a bus which carries power, data and instructions around the machine.

It is clear that there might be a snag here. The peripherals will not all need to act at the same time or do the same thing. If all the chips or devices are connected to the same bits of wire, there has to be a controller of the system, and some way for it to tell the peripherals when each one of them is to wake up. The essence of a bus structure is that although everything is connected to the bus all the time, each device only takes information from the bus, or puts information on it, when it is told to do so.

Busses to run outside the computer are connected to it by 'ports' (see pp. 28-9). They fall into two categories: parallel and serial. The easiest way to look at the problem is in terms of bridging a river. Imagine a regiment of soldiers marching eight abreast (in parallel) reaching a river. The bridge designer has two choices. He can build a wide expensive bridge which will allow the soldiers to march across still eight abreast; or he

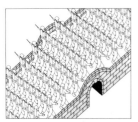

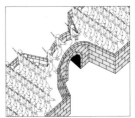

can build a narrow cheap bridge which will carry them in single file (serial). The bus designer has just the same choice. He has a certain number of bits to go from one box to another in a certain time. He can either send them one after the other down a single wire, or provide a number of wires in parallel so that several can make the journey at the same time.

Since data travels inside the computer in parallel, a serial bus has to emerge from a special chip (the SIO – serial input–output) which takes 8 bits in parallel and reads them off one at a time at the right speed to go down the wire – and vice versa. This needs more chips and costs more inside the computer, but less in wire outside it. This is why versions of peripherals such as printers which accept serial data cost more than those which take parallel.

But when a computer designer really needs high-speed data transfer, for instance, between disks and processor, he will use a parallel bus.

Let us look at an electronic office of the not-too-distant future. Helen, the girl in the foreground, wants to get a file off the hard disk for editing. Her station has in it some permanent software that knows how to control the network. She types a message to command what she wants. Her computer waits until the master station finishes what it is doing and starts to 'poll' the work stations. It does this by sending out a series of messages to each work station in turn: 'Number 1 – do you want anything?', 'Number 2 – do you want anything?'... When the other work stations hear the call: 'Number 1 ... ', they shut up, so the master can be sure that any answer comes from Number 1 and no other. Helen is at Number 3 and when its turn comes, it sends her request for a file. The master breaks off its poll to send a message to the hard disk – which might be number 63 – telling it to start reading the contents of the file Number 3 wants out onto the bus. Number 3 is listening and, as the text appears, copies it into memory, where Helen can work on it. When the disk has sent as much text as Number 3 wants, it transmits a 'finished with bus' signal, and the master carries on polling again, which it does all day long, patiently and efficiently. This all sounds rather cumbersome, but in practice it happens so fast that the human users are quite unaware of the process.

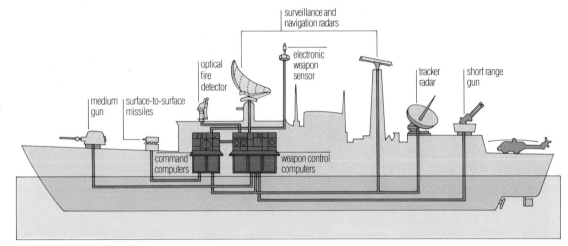

A warship is a good place for a data bus. A single strand of fibre optic – doubled or trebled against battle damage – can link all the ship's sensors, computers and weapons together so that they can all talk to each other as necessary. The bus replaces miles of heavy, vulnerable cable that would otherwise be needed to link all the parts in a star pattern. The fibre optic bus needs much less maintenance and is immune to electrical interference

surveillance and navigation radars

optical fire detector

electronic weapon sensor

tracker radar

short range gun

medium gun

surface-to-surface missiles

command computers

weapon control computers

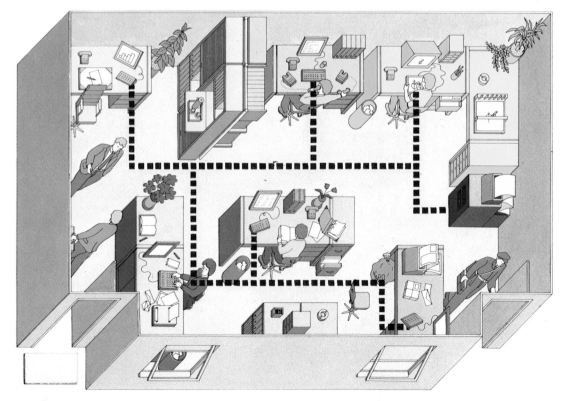

An office of the not-so-distant future, in which people use computers linked together (dotted line) in order to share information

MEMORY

The available RAM in a computer is divided into clearly defined areas that do different things. Different machines and different operating systems work in different ways. In a CP/M disk system, the first area is taken up by some operating system jump tables and various odds and ends. The next area contains the machine's software that prints on the screen – called the monitor. Then comes the TPA – the transient program area, where applications programs run. Here we have shown an interpreted BASIC, a program running under it and BASIC's stack. This area could equally well be taken up by another language or a compiled program. Finally comes the operating system – the code to handle disk, screen and printer interfaces

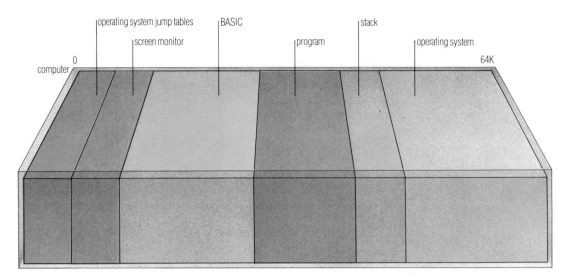

operating system jump tables   BASIC   stack

screen monitor   program   operating system

0   64K

computer

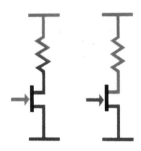

A positive voltage on the gate of a transistor causes the source–drain to conduct and so lets current flow away from the bottom of the resistor. The source then goes to 0 volts. If the gate is at 0 volts, no current flows through the transistor, and the source is high, reading '1'

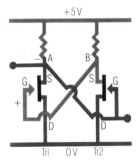

+5 V

A   B

G   S   S   G

+

D   D

Trl   0 V   Tr2

A two-transistor 'static' memory cell. One is on and the other is off at any one time, storing either 0 or 1. (Here, the output at A is blue – low voltage or 0.) They are wired together so that they hold each other in this state until a different value is written into the circuit

If the processor is the engine of a computer, the memory is the saloon – the space in which your programs travel. This alive sort of memory is called 'RAM' – random access memory. 'Random' means that you can read or write any byte of it directly without having to wade through a lot of other stuff first. Memory whose contents are fixed is called 'ROM' – read-only memory. In between the two come various sorts of 'PROM' – programmable read-only memory.

As we have seen, the more memory your computer has the better. As we shall see, the amount of memory you get depends on the price of the computer, and that depends on the density with which the makers of the memory chips can pack circuitry onto their little pieces of silicon.

At the moment we are only concerned with how chips can be made to remember anything. We saw on page 20 that a transistor is essentially an electronic switch: put a voltage on a gate and it allows a current to flow; take it off and the current stops. There is nothing very exciting there. But connect two of them so that each one controls the other and you have what electronic engineers call a 'flip-flop'.

Below left we have two transistors with their sources connected to the 5 V positive rail through two resistors, their drains connected to ground, and each one's gate connected to the other's source. Suppose that Tr 1 is turned on. Current flows through it faster than it can get through the resistor, so its source is pretty well at 0 V. Since Tr 2's gate is connected to Tr 1's source, that turns Tr 2 off, and makes its source high, since current flows through its resistor but cannnot get away. And Tr 1's gate is connected to this high voltage so it is on, so Tr 1's source is low – which is where we started.

The net result of all this is to lock the circuit in its starting state. Point B will always be high and point A will always be low. If either tries to change, the interlocking transistors will restore things. In effect, we have a memory. Other cir-

cuits can look at either A or B – it does not much matter which – the flip-flop will remember either 0 or 1, low or high voltage. Of course, that would not be a lot of use if you could not change what was stored there – if you could not 'write' to it. And in fact, a heavy enough voltage on either of the gates will set up a new 'flip' or a new 'flop'. So, as well as an output from, say, A, we have to have an input onto Tr 2's gate. A low voltage or 0 there will make and keep A low; a high voltage there will make and keep A high. You can easily make such a circuit with individual transistors and resistors. A chip designer would replace each resistor – which is hard to produce – by a transistor with its drain connected to its gate (below).

One flip-flop will remember one bit of information; to remember a useful amount, several thousand of these circuits are printed together on the same piece of silicon and made up into a chip. This sort of RAM is called 'static' because the bits just stay put – in contrast to the 'dynamic' RAM we shall look at in a moment.

Four transistors take up four times as much room as one transistor, which means that the chip manufacturer can only get on a chip one quarter of the memory he would get if he used only one transistor. A memory cell which uses only two transistors would be better, and can be made as follows: a transistor is controlled by its gate. The gate is just a track of aluminium laid on an insulating layer of silicon oxide. Electrically it goes nowhere, so an electrical charge put on it has, in theory, nowhere to leak to. It should stay there for ever doing its job of controlling the flow of current from the source to the drain.

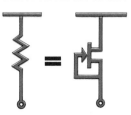

In principle we have a memory again. We can tell what was written onto the gate – 0 or 1 – by looking to see whether current is flowing from the source to the drain.

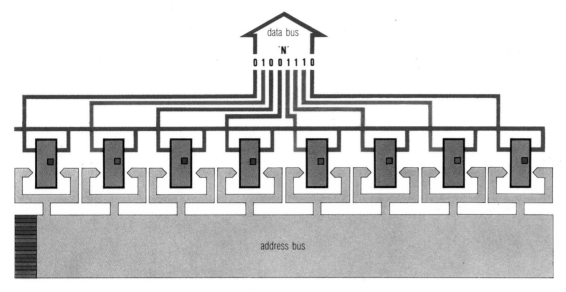

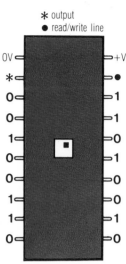

The memory address bus (above left) has sixteen lines. A pattern of 0s and 1s on them (shown by blue and red at the left-hand end of the bus) tells the eight memory chips, which each hold 64-K bits, the right memory cell to open up. Each chip (above right) connects its output to one of the eight data lines so that a complete byte (8 bits) of data appears in the right order on the data bus. Here is 'N': 01001110

In practice the electrons do not stay put on the gate for very long – no more than one thousandth of a second in fact. But that is time enough for several thousand operations of the central processor, plenty of time for useful work. In one thousandth of a second, the processor rushes round all its memory cells, reading what is there and rewriting it so that it will stay put for another thousandth of a second. This is called 'refreshing the memory' and is done by special circuitry attached to the memory chips. It sounds outrageous, but in fact it works very well.

Any memory chip needs a number of pins to connect it to the rest of the computer, and the number depends intimately on the amount of memory it contains. It has to have enough address lines to get at all the memory cells in it; a read/write line to tell it whether data is coming in to be stored, or being read out; and a data line, which is connected to the output of the particular cell. So, if a chip has 2^n memory cells, it needs n address lines. In the illustration above right we show an up-to-date 64-K RAM.* 64 K is 65,536 or 2^{16}, so the chip has to have 16 address pins. The cell being read is at address 0010011001001011.

To remember 1 byte of information, which is the smallest useful unit for most purposes, you need 8 bits, or eight of these circuits. It is probably more convenient to keep each of the 8 bits of the byte in a separate chip, with each chip's data line connected to one of the eight lines in the data bus.

There are several other kinds of memory in common use. 'ROM' – read-only memory – is much simpler; the data is written once when the chip is made and cannot thereafter be altered. Each cell consists of a connection between the data line and the + or − power rail, and this is achieved by printing a mask in manufacture. A ROM chip can store quite large chunks of program or data, and can appear to the processor

* 'K' means a computing thousand, which is, oddly, not 1000, but 1024 – because 1024 is 2^{10}.

just like a piece of RAM into which program or data has been loaded. Most micros have a few kilobits of ROM to control their keyboards and screens – a piece of code usually called the 'monitor' (not to be confused with the actual television-like video monitor on which the screen display appears). Because a ROM is a very simple circuit, you can get an awful lot of it onto a chip. The Japanese have been making 256-Kb ROMs for some time – eight of those could store 40,000 English words, or two thirds of this book.

The drawback to ROM is that you have to order several thousand copies in order to pay for the expensive mask. An alternative that costs more per chip, but lets the small manufacturer make each chip as he goes along, is 'PROM' – programmable read-only memory. This time you buy a blank chip and write your data or program into it by blowing or not blowing a link at each memory location. The blowing is done by applying a high voltage, and is best carried out under the supervision of a computer. A more forgiving, but even more expensive, sort of chip is the 'EPROM' – erasable programmable read-only memory. This is a sort of long-life RAM, which lets you program the cells once and then remembers the data without needing to be refreshed.

Erasable programmable read-only memory (EPROM) chips are to be found in almost every computer, holding firmware. 'Firmware' is software written into hardware, and is used to control basic housekeeping tasks around the machine. By using EPROM rather than read-only memory (ROM) chips, the manufacturer or the user can erase the original program and redo it. Data is erased by shining a powerful ultraviolet light through the glass windows covering the chips

THE KEYBOARD

The average computer user spends most of his or her time in physical contact with the keyboard. With its fifty-odd keys, it allows you to do a wide variety of things. You can type in text as at a typewriter. You can enter numbers for arithmetic. You can control the cursor on the screen – make it go up, down, sideways. You can play Space Invaders or write poetry, do drawings or cast accounts.

There is no absolutely standard computer keyboard. However you can expect to find the following things:

The letters of the alphabet with a shift key to produce upper or lower case and a shift lock

A space bar

The symbols £ $ % & #

A set of brackets () {} []

The arithmetic symbols + − * / ↑ < >, i.e. add, subtract, multiply, divide, raise to the power of, less and greater than

The punctuation marks , ; : . ? !

Two sorts of quotation marks ' and "

Some symbols that are common on computers but rare on typewriters: | \ ~

Four cursor control keys to move the cursor up, down, left and right

In addition to these you will always find at least four special keys: DELETE, CONTROL, ESCAPE, RETURN. These are quite important, so we shall explain each of them.

DELETE does what you would like to be able to do on the typewriter but cannot: erase the character you have just mistyped.

CONTROL or CTRL does not make a character on the screen. You always press it *with another key* and it changes the meaning of that key (see ASCII characters, p. 185). In effect, by holding CTRL down, you get a second keyboard. CTRL characters are usually written like this: '↑ A' means the effect produced by pressing CTRL and A together.

ESCAPE is used by some packages to move from one mode of operation to another.

RETURN (sometimes called NEWLINE or ENTER) is the most used key. It was originally designed to have the effect of hitting the carriage return bar on a typewriter: it moves the cursor on the screen or the print head on the paper to the left-hand margin and down a line. To do this it sends *two* characters: CARRIAGE RETURN followed by LINE FEED. But RETURN has acquired a new meaning: 'go for it' or 'execute'. Very often, when a program asks you to type in a name or a number, it does not think you have finished until you hit RETURN.

Nowadays it is quite common to have a separate numerical keypad like a calculator – more convenient for entering lots of numbers. It is also not unusual to find a row of 'soft keys' along the

top of the keyboard. When you hit one of them you send a string of characters from a little bit of RAM in the keyboard. The soft keys can be programmed to do quite complicated things. For instance, on the word-processing package I used to write this book, you hit 'ESR ↑ R' to start a 'search and replace' operation. If my machine had had a set of 'soft' or 'special function' keys, I could have stored that sequence and just hit one key to send the effect of three. When I stopped doing word processing, I could have shifted to another package and given the soft keys new functions. It is usual for keyboards with soft keys to have a slot to accept slips of cardboard with the current meanings of the prompts written on them. In some systems the keyboard and the screen are fixed together so the program can write the soft key prompts on the bottom line of the screen.

A decent keyboard should have 'type-ahead' or 'rollover', which means that even if the computer cannot accept key strokes because it is doing something else for the moment, the keyboard will store a few in a little bit of RAM and send them when conditions are better. Most keyboards now imitate electric typewriters in repeating a character if you hold the key down for more than half a second or so.

A refinement you do not need (in my view, at least) is key click. Some manufacturers go to great lengths to imitate the clattering of a typewriter by putting a loudspeaker into the keyboard which does little clicks. One good use for it is to signal mistakes – if the computer sends '↑ G' to the screen it should make a little electronic

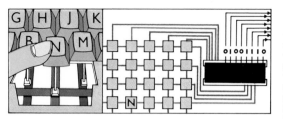

'meep' in the keyboard. This can get the attention of a quick typist.

We saw on pages 12-13 that all these keyboard characters are coded as ASCII characters (the full table can be found on page 185). The ASCII code is one of the computer industry's less half-witted ideas, and has some quite clever features. Notice that 'A' (65) is 32 less than 'a' (97). So too is 'B' (66) 32 less than 'b' (98). To convert letters from upper to lower case you just add 32. ' ↑ A' is 1, so control characters are coded in ASCII by subtracting 64 from the letter code.

Notice that the numbers go up as you go down the alphabet. So to sort into alphabetical order, you just have to sort the ASCII codes into numerical order. The same thing applies to the digits too: '1' (49) is less than '2' (50), so the same program that sorts letters alphabetically will sort digits into order as well.

Above 127 the ASCII character set tends to peter out. Many training micros offer different ranges of 'graphics' characters – squares, blobs and textures, which can be accessed by the keyboard when shifted in some way. The better business machines use this space to cope with special European characters such as å and ü.

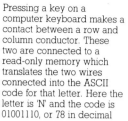

Pressing a key on a computer keyboard makes a contact between a row and column conductor. These two are connected to a read-only memory which translates the two wires connected into the ASCII code for that letter. Here the letter is 'N' and the code is 01001110, or 78 in decimal

The Sinclair ZX Spectrum. Colour and graphics keys are clearly visible on the uppermost row of the keyboard. The circuitry has been ingeniously designed to provide multiple functions for each key, e.g. to produce single letters or numbers or BASIC commands.

The Sinclair Spectrum and its predecessors, the ZX81 and ZX80, must be the most widely used computers in the world, with more than 1 million copies sold. Because they are sold in such huge numbers, they can be made for a fraction of the cost of machines made in smaller quantities. They are bought by vast numbers of people who treat them informally as personal equipment. Because of this, all sorts of new uses and techniques flow out of the newly computerate population

PORTS

A computer on its own is a pretty useless object. It will have an on-off switch and, if you are lucky, a light to show whether it is on or off.

To make it useful you have to connect it at least to a keyboard, a screen and a printer; and very often to other things as well – joysticks for controlling Klingons, roller balls or mice for moving the cursor about, or graphics tablets for drawings. You might want more exotic output than an ordinary printer can provide, so you would need to connect a plotter, a laser, a robot, or whatever device your ingenuity suggests.

Computing would be impossible if all these devices needed their own particular sort of connection. To make things simple the industry has invented another set of (almost) standards for what are called 'ports'. (Probably they are called 'ports' because they are ways to and from the outside world, by analogy with sea- or airports in a country.) There are basically two sorts of port: serial and parallel. As we saw on pages 22-3, a serial port sends or receives the bits of a byte one at a time down a pair of wires; a parallel port sends or receives eight or more at a time down as many wires as it has bits.

What you actually see when you look at a port on the box of computer is a 25-pin socket (usually female, though do not count on it). To make use of it you – or the person who designed the peripheral you want to connect – has to know: whether it is serial or parallel, whether it conforms to one of the standards – RS 232 for serial, Centronics or IEE 488 for parallel (there are other standards as well, and the beginner will probably not be able to cope with the detail of any of them); if the port is serial, what speed it expects data to come at (the 'Baud rate' in bits per second) and whether it does 'handshaking' or expects some other 'protocol'.

If the peripheral is some distance away – perhaps metres, perhaps hundreds of miles – it becomes important to check the integrity of the data when it arrives. This is when the 'parity bit' described on pages 12-13 comes into use, as do far

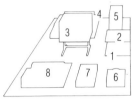

Some of the common devices that can be connected to a computer's (1) ports. The keyboard (2) has its own port, as do the TV (3) and the disk drives (4). The rest use a standard serial or parallel port: adapted electric typewriter (5), printer (6), tape recorder (7) and roller ball – for steering a cursor round the screen (8)

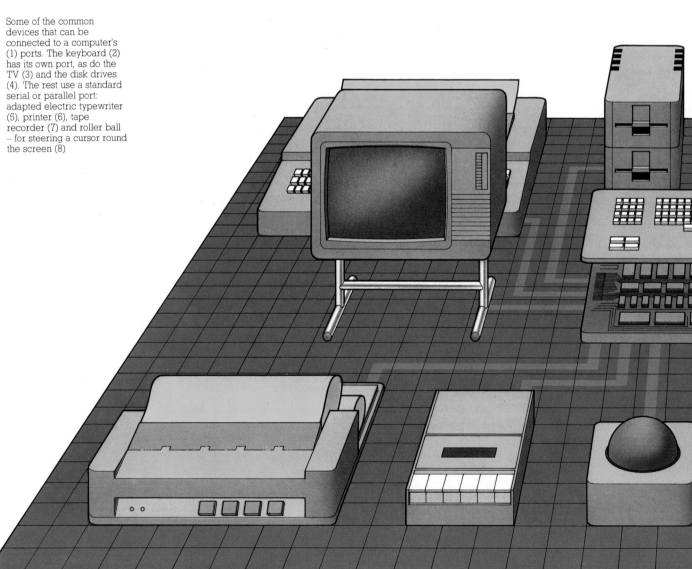

more sophisticated ways of making sure nothing has gone wrong in transmission. The subject of computer communications is a very interesting one in its own right, and books on it fill whole sections of libraries.

Inside the computer each port is arranged to appear to the processor like two memory locations: one for the data to be sent or received and one to tell which way it is going – the 'data' and 'status' bytes. This makes life very simple for the processor. If it is sending data out of a port, it just has to look occasionally at the status byte to see whether more data is needed. If it is, the current program is halted and the processor writes more data to the port. When the outside device signals that it has got enough, the status byte changes, and the processor stops writing data to the port and carries on with the job in hand.

There are two ways of controlling this division of tasks: one is by using the 'interrupt' facility in the processor. The change of a bit in the status byte from 0 to 1 to demand more data puts a signal on a special pin on the processor. This makes it shelve what it is doing and jump to a different program which, in this case, makes it send data to the port. Once that is done, the interrupt is released and the processor goes back to the program it was running. Interrupts can, of course, be used for many other things as well.

The second system of control is 'polling'. In this scheme the main program makes the processor look at the port from time to time to see whether it needs more data. In the process it may go round several peripherals asking each one in turn if it needs attention. In computers that expect a lot of input from the keyboard this is a good scheme, because the user cannot hit keys faster than one every tenth of a second. So long as the processor polls everything (including the keyboard) faster than that, the user will think he or she has got the processor's undivided attention. And since it runs at several million cycles a second, it can get a lot of computing done in that time.

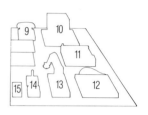

More devices that can be connected to a computer's ports: telephone modem (9), visual display unit (VDU) with screen and keyboard (10), plotter (11), graphics tablet (12), robot (13), joystick or knob (14) and mouse (15). As the mouse is moved about the table a ball under it turns and so moves the cursor on the screen

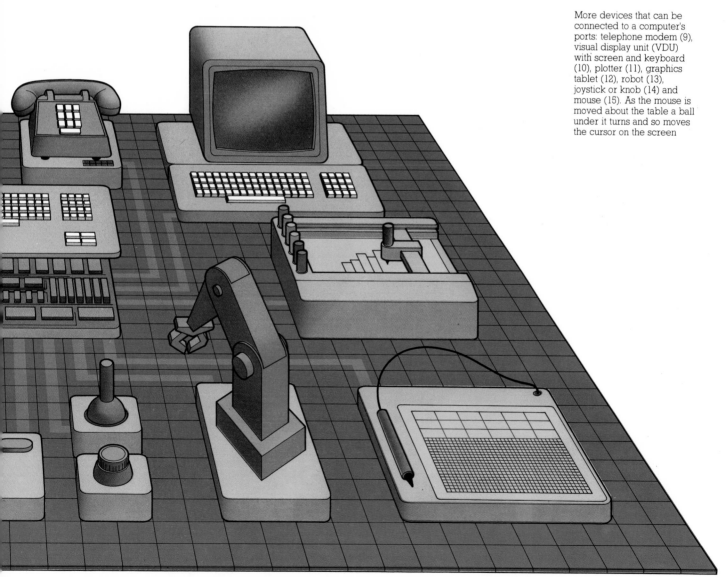

SCREENS

During the lifetime of this book the vast majority of computer screens will still be cathode-ray tubes (CRT) – like a television screen. It is possible in the future that solid state screens may become popular – we shall look at those later. A CRT is a surprisingly complicated object and, if it were not for the enormous popularity of television, would be hopelessly expensive to make.

A CRT consists of a flat-bottomed glass bottle full of vacuum. The flat base is coated with some sort of phosphor salt. At the neck there is a gun which fires a thin beam of electrons at the screen. Where the beam hits the screen, it makes a glowing spot. Control electronics can steer the beam up and down and from side to side by putting appropriate voltages on two pairs of plates. This makes it possible to draw on the screen. Since the phosphor goes on glowing for a few thousandths of a second after the electron beam has moved past, the screen can be drawn and redrawn before the picture has faded. The spot can

be made to move at something like 25,000 m.p.h. across the screen, so this process can be repeated many times a second to give the illusion of a continuous, flicker-free image.

There are two ways of drawing on the screen. In one, called 'vector' graphics, the beam is used like a pencil, and actually draws shapes on the phosphor. This gives high-quality results, but is very slow.

The other method – used in almost all microcomputers – is called 'raster scan', because the beam is made – as in television – to scan across the screen in a raster of parallel lines. As the electron spot crosses lines in the picture it is turned on and off again by the beam-control circuitry. It draws the picture as a series of dots, which on a good-quality screen are close enough together for the eye to see a smooth image.

It would be nice to regard each possible spot as an independent picture unit which could be turned off or on as necessary. In the trade such

Inside a cathode-ray tube (CRT). An electron beam (red) is shot out by the gun – which contains a red-hot wire. The beam passes through a collimator to focus it, and then between two pairs of deflection plates which bend it left or right and up or down by means of electric fields. It then travels through a vacuum until it hits a phosphor coating on the inside of the screen where it makes a bright spot.
The gun can be switched on and off and the beam steered to any point on the screen in order to paint a picture or write text and numbers.
The whole picture must be rewritten every 1/25 second. In a vector scan system the beam is steered like a pencil held in the hand to produce a high-quality picture. In raster scan it travels in parallel lines, being turned on or off as necessary. This is faster but produces a less detailed picture. The vast majority of microcomputers use this system

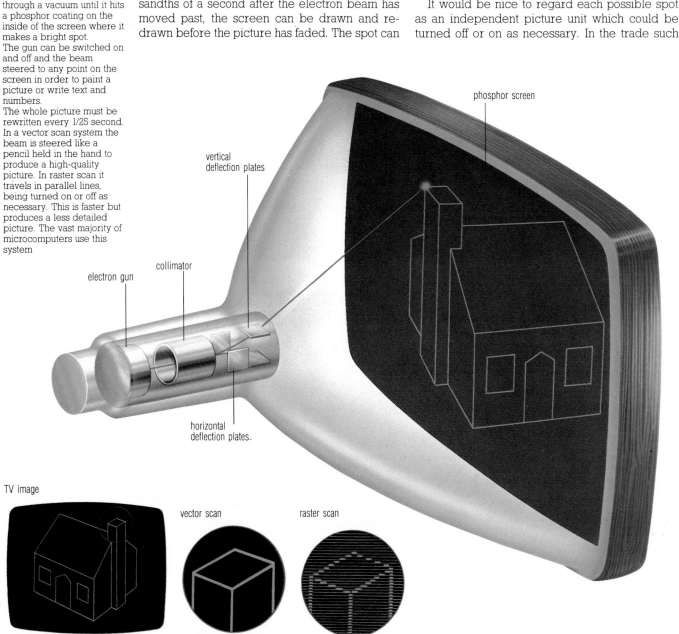

phosphor screen

vertical deflection plates

collimator

electron gun

horizontal deflection plates

TV image

vector scan

raster scan

a unit is called a 'pixel' – a contraction of 'picture cell'. This would mean giving each spot at least a bit of RAM. However, there are about 600 × 600 = 360,000 spots on a television screen – and even that many does not give a particularly sharp picture. But even so, to get decent colour and shade you need at least one byte per pixel. That would need half a megabyte of RAM just to control the screen, which is quite impossible in an 8-bit machine, and would take a big slice out of the affordable memory in a 16-bit machine.

An 8-bit machine controls its screen by dividing it into fewer, larger pixels. The standard scheme is to regard the screen as being 24 lines deep and 80 columns across. In each of these 1920 squares the computer writes one of a preset number of images, each commanded by an ASCII number (see pp. 12-13). Since these ASCII numbers are stored in a single byte, we now need only 2 kilobytes of RAM.

The ASCII code for 'A' is 65, or the byte '01000001'. But it is a far cry from that to the shape 'A'. The machine copes with this by storing the shapes as a pattern of dots, usually 9 deep by 5 across, in a read-only memory.

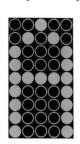

When it is required to draw an 'A', it knows that the first line is to be off, off, on, off, off. The next line is to be off, on, off, on, off. And so on. When the screen has to write a whole line of text, it must know before it starts what the top row of dots will be for all the characters on the line, then the second, and so on. Some screens allow pixels only 7 dots deep, which cannot show the descenders properly in letters like 'y' and 'p'. They are not very satisfactory.

A completely different sort of screen uses solid state technology. It forms its images with light-emitting diodes or liquid crystals. Each dot on it is turned on by control electronics. In a diode display each dot is a tiny source of light which gets turned on or off like an electric light. In a liquid-crystal display, the 'dots' are areas of liquid that are made transparent or dark by putting a voltage across them. Each dot has a pair of transparent electrodes at right angles which can turn it on or off.

In principle these displays should be much better than the old-fashioned CRT because they are smaller, cheaper to make and use less power. In practice, however, to get high resolution you need so many dots, and so much in the way of control electronics, that they are very hard to make. There are also problems about temperature stability and power consumption.

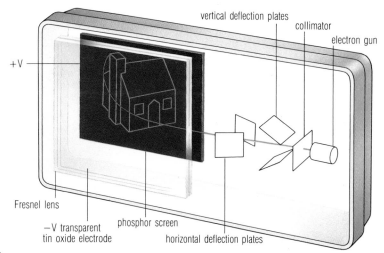

vertical deflection plates   collimator   electron gun

+V

Fresnel lens

−V transparent tin oxide electrode

phosphor screen

horizontal deflection plates

Flat screen

The drawback to the conventional CRT is its bulk. Several manufacturers are working on flat CRTs, where the gun is beside the screen rather than behind it. The electrons have to be made to travel in a complicated curve; it is hard to avoid distortion and defocusing of the picture

A mock-up of a possible design for a portable television set by Sinclair, using a flat-screen CRT. The picture in the photo is, however, pasted on

Liquid-crystal display

Below left There is little reason in principle why liquid-crystal displays should not be used for full screen TVs or computer monitors. So far there have been practical difficulties with stability, temperature sensitivity and the sheer number of logic elements needed to control 600 × 600 pixels

Below right Wristwatches have made liquid-crystal displays familiar. A thin film of transparent organic liquid is sandwiched between glass plates. The shapes of

number segments are put on the front glass as transparent electrodes. When a voltage

is applied to the appropriate segments, the liquid beneath goes dark. Here, the number 5 is being written

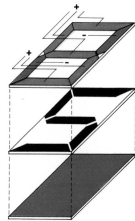

GRAPHICS

The process of writing 'GOOD MORNING' in the middle of a screen 24 lines deep by 40 characters wide is not altogether simple. Positioning it correctly requires arithmetic – which, of course, can be done by a program. First, you must send the cursor 'home' – to the top left-hand corner. Now print 12 line-feeds to bring it to the central line. 'GOOD MORNING' has 11 letters and one space, so you need to print (40−12)/2 = 14 spaces to bring the cursor to the right position to start. At last you can print the phrase and it will appear where it is wanted

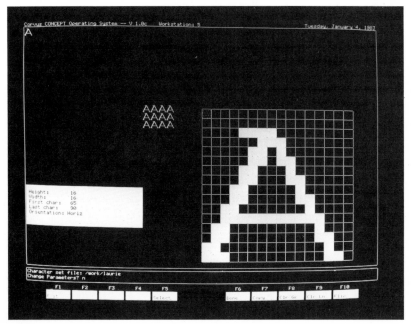

We have seen how shapes get on the screen; the question is: what shapes?

One obvious group is the keyboard letters and numbers. Cheap microcomputers, which are designed to use television sets for their screens, have 40 characters or pixels across the screen; more expensive machines that use a dedicated monitor usually have 80 characters. The quality of the letters tends to be better too.

Whether the screen is 40 or 80 characters across, each letter fills one standard-sized square. This means that – as on a typewriter – 'i's get a lot of air round them, while the 'w's and 'm's are a bit crowded. A well-designed machine will of course have lower- as well as upper-case letters and the lower case will have proper descenders on the 'y' and 'g'. Since the majority of the world's computer users speak and read English, the character set tends to be British or North American (the difference is in the hash and pound signs, which share the same ASCII code). However, markets in northern European countries are now getting big enough to make it worthwhile for manufacturers to provide a number of special characters needed in various languages, such as accented 'e's and 'a's in French and umlauts in

German. These have to be provided as separate characters since the mechanism of the screen does not allow the cursor to go back and add an extra element such as an accent to an existing character. It is quite amusing to open these machines up and find a 'country' switch inside which turns on the appropriate bits of ROM to produce the local speciality.

If you want to produce larger letters than normal, you have to build them up like this:

```
PPPPPPPPPPPP
PPP          PP
PPP           PP
PPP          PP
PPPPPPPPPP
PPP
PPP
PPP
PPP
PPPPP
```

A few machines are beginning to appear with different-sized character sets, so that you can write headlines on the screen as well as body copy. There is no reason in principle why a 16-bit machine, with plenty of memory and processing power, should not produce proportionally spaced text on the screen – that is, printing which gives letters of different widths different amounts of space.

There is nothing sacred about the 120-odd shapes that we recognize as letters, numbers and punctuation. The computer can be made to draw any shape that is not too complicated for the dot structure of its screen. This means that Arabic, for instance, presents no real problem. The shapes are no more complicated than those of the English alphabet and there are actually fewer characters so that they can be held in ROM and addressed with single byte codes as in ASCII. Japanese is more difficult since Katakana, the simpler of the two Japanese systems, has about 2000 characters and many of them are considerably more complicated than English letters. They can, however, be handled, given a screen with over-sized character cells and a 2-byte addressing code (1 byte can only call up 256 different characters).

Letters and numbers are sufficiently standard and necessary to make it worth providing them in ROM. Many hobby computers also provide a 'graphics set' of odd shapes in the same size as letters, which can be used by the resolute to make up pictures and monsters for games. However, the programmer may want to produce more complicated shapes still, and these must be created specially in RAM.

In all graphics operations the screen is repainted – usually 25 times a second – from a special area of memory, which may be part of the main RAM, or may be separate. This area is

Some of the 16-bit machines let users redesign their screen letters. Instead of being permanently stored in ROM as on 8-bit machines, they are kept on disk and read in each time the computer is turned on. Here is a program on the Corvus Concept being used to reshape the letter 'A'

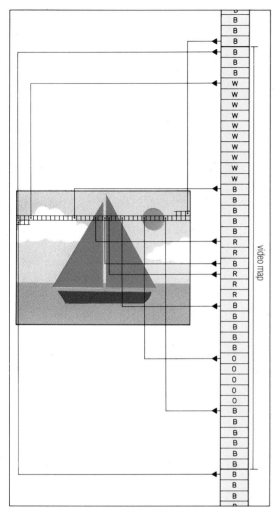

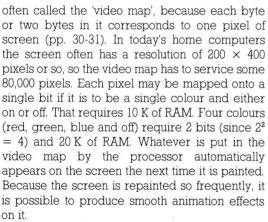

video map

Secondly, the computer must be able to calculate whatever changes are necessary, and write the whole picture out again to the video map in $\frac{1}{25}$ second. Bearing in mind that even a low-quality display may have some 8 KB of video map, this is a drastic limitation and means either that the changes must be simple or that you use a very powerful computer. The third possibility, used in computer-aided film making, is to take much longer than $\frac{1}{25}$ second over the updates, film each frame one by one, and then run the film at the proper speed.

Even so, there are many things that can be done with simple two-dimensional animation on a computer. The main problem is the updating of the video map. Obviously each byte in it could be computed each time. For real three-dimensional animation this is necessary, at great cost in processing power (see pp. 114-15), but for two-dimensional animation on home computers some tricks are available. There are many high-resolution graphics boards about, either available as add-ons or built into particular machines. They work in slightly different ways, but they all tend to offer the same sort of facilities.

One can usually predefine a number of shapes which can be written onto the screen at any given position. The obvious ones, letters and numbers (which may be rotatable), are provided by the manufacturer of the machine. Usually a number of 'graphics characters' are also available – these take up the same space as a standard letter, but consist of light and dark squares in various com-

often called the 'video map', because each byte or two bytes in it corresponds to one pixel of screen (pp. 30-31). In today's home computers the screen often has a resolution of 200 × 400 pixels or so, so the video map has to service some 80,000 pixels. Each pixel may be mapped onto a single bit if it is to be a single colour and either on or off. That requires 10 K of RAM. Four colours (red, green, blue and off) require 2 bits (since $2^2 = 4$) and 20 K of RAM. Whatever is put in the video map by the processor automatically appears on the screen the next time it is painted. Because the screen is repainted so frequently, it is possible to produce smooth animation effects on it.

The thing to bear in mind is that the whole screen is painted afresh each time. This has two consequences. First, to produce animation effects the new screen must be just like the old screen except for those details that have 'moved'. For instance, if the picture shows Donald Duck talking, then everything stays the same except for his beak. Every $\frac{1}{25}$ second a new picture is drawn with the beak in a slightly different position. This is exactly the principle of film animation, but for the fact that all the 'frames' are drawn on the same piece of 'celluloid' – the screen.

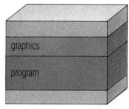

low resolution

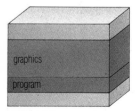

high resolution

binations. An ingenious and hardworking person can mate these together to do rudimentary drawings.

There may be a graphics language like Logo (p. 77), some graphics commands as an extension to the resident BASIC (pp. 58-61), which give commands to spot the cursor anywhere on the screen, draw a line between two points, draw circles, or fill areas with tone. Sometimes a special drawing package is provided to do this.

If the hardware supports colour, there is usually some way of defining a palette of 16 or 256 colours which can then be called by number. This palette can usually be set up at the beginning of a program, chosen from a much wider range of colours. Suppose that all the people's faces in a particular animation were coloured 6. To begin with a pink tone would be assigned to 6. At some point a ghost appears and everyone goes grey with horror. This effect can be produced in one move simply by changing 6 from pink to grey. Another method uses three colour planes, each corresponding to red, green and blue, which can either be on or off, giving eight colours.

There are two main systems for helping the animator. The first is 'paging', in which there are two or more video maps. A picture is drawn on one – taking longer perhaps than the $\frac{1}{25}$ second nominally available. When it is ready the next video output is taken from it, while a new picture is prepared in one of the other areas. This is expensive in terms of RAM.

The second system involves 'sprites', a number of hardware areas which accept smaller pictures that can be transferred into the main area at any given point. In some systems they are arranged in depth so that the pictures on the 'nearer' levels overwrite those farther away. The effect is very like the transparent overlays used by film-animation technicians.

As an example, let us imagine an animation scene which consists of a man walking on some grass behind a tree. Behind him there are clouds moving in a blue sky.

In many systems each sprite must consist of image parts of the same colour, so to make a multicoloured image we have to use more than one sprite. The tree then needs two sprites: one on plane 0 for the brown trunk, and one on plane 1 for the green leaves. These two will be painted on the screen at the right relative positions to make them appear to move – if we decide to track with the walking man – as one. The man's body (assuming it is all one colour) is drawn on sprite 2, and three sets of legs and arms in different walking positions on sprites 3, 4 and 5. As he walks, these three sprites will be called in order to animate the movements of his limbs. The points where they join his body are stationary so that the three sprites merely have to be called at the same position as the body to appear to join onto it. The clouds are painted on sprite 6, the grass and sky on the backdrop plane – which does not move.

These pictures can be drawn by using a digitizing board (pp. 110-11) by steering the cursor round the screen with cursor control keys or a joystick, by writing little programs in BASIC or Logo to create the shapes, or by combining shapes that have been created earlier and stored on disk or tape.

The business of animation is now easy. A program is written which calls the various sprites in their correct positions. Imagine to start with that we want the tree and the clouds stationary and the man walking. Sprites 0, 1 and 6 are called in their final positions. The program then loops with the man's body on sprite 2 at the left-hand edge of the screen, with the first set of legs and arms. It may be necessary to wait for a while so that his

A more sophisticated colouring process than the one shown on page 33 uses two stages. This time the code numbers written into the video map select colours from a 'palette' – another area of RAM which contains a list of colours which may be blends of several cruder tints. This is useful if you want to be able to change all the areas painted in one colour to another. Here the pig is coloured by making colour 6 point to a pink. When he sees the ghost, he is turned grey by making colour 6 point to a grey tint

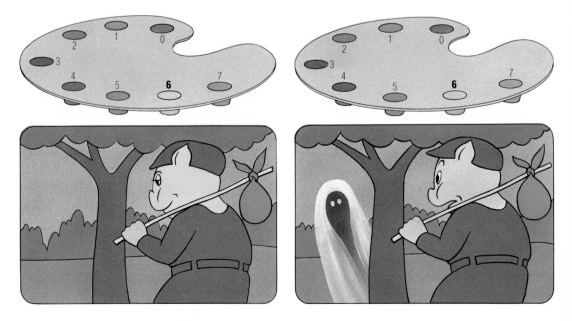

Although you can steer the cursor around the screen with a keyboard, it is not the most artistic drawing tool. A graphics tablet is an improvement. The user draws with an electronic stylus – which may have a pen built into it. The stylus emits low-power radio pulses which are detected by a fine grid of wires moulded into the tablet. Circuitry in the tablet converts the position of the stylus tip into X and Y coordinates, which are sent to the computer. Its graphics are then used to display the picture on the screen

How sprites are used for animation. Certain computers, such as the Atari, provide several picture areas which can be printed in any desired position on the screen. The lower-number areas overwrite the higher so that, in this sequence, the boy can be made to walk behind the tree but in front of the moving clouds and the grass. The three versions of his arms and legs are called in sequence at different positions across the screen to animate him walking

Far right Sprites can be used for more serious tasks too. Here three sprites are used to produce moving pointers, while the background paints the dials. The computer translates three different measurements into the proper positions of the pointers

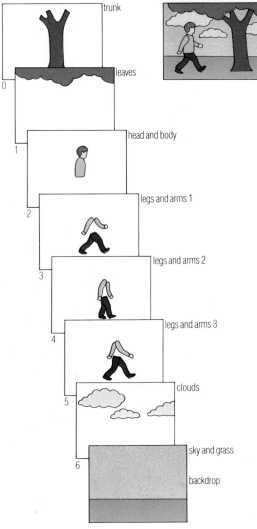

trunk
leaves
0
head and body
1
legs and arms 1
2
legs and arms 2
3
legs and arms 3
4
clouds
5
sky and grass
6
backdrop

walk is not too fast, before moving him forward a pixel to the right and calling the second set of limbs in that position. And so on for the third set, then back through the loop. He will now 'walk' across the screen. When he comes to the tree trunk he will appear to pass behind it since lower number sprites paint over higher numbers. Conversely, he will pass in front of the clouds, which have a higher number than any of the sprites making up his body.

If the clouds are to move – say from right to left – then the sprite-calling loop in the program must call them at appropriate positions, starting at the right-hand edge and moving left.

The sprite concept can be used for more serious matters too. The animated image shows a computer simulation of three different types of instrument, and might be used in place of conventional instruments in an industrial control system. The sprites consist of a dial pointer (0), a vertical scale pointer (1) and a horizontal scale pointer (2). The two scale pointers are simply called with appropriate Y and X coordinates to indicate the quantities they are to measure; the dial pointer needs to be called with an X,Y coordinate calculated to fall on the circumference of a circle. It would be possible to simulate a hand on a dial, but it would obviously be harder to do it with sprites – which can only move from side to side and up and down.

This kind of animation can only produce crude effects, even by two-dimensional standards. Images can only be two-dimensional and they cannot rotate. A real animation system would need facilities for doing these things automatically, plus some help for the artist in preparing all the images he or she needs (see pp. 112-15).

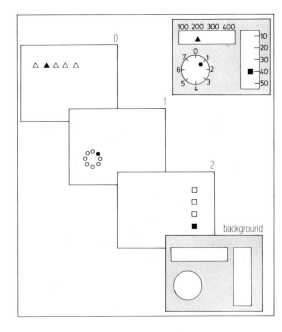

0
1
2
background

ABCDE
ABCDE

Enlarged printout by
daisywheel (top) and by
dot-matrix

Right The principle of the
Olivetti ink-jet printer. Solid,
electrically conducting ink is
stored in a glass tube whose
small, open end is near the
paper. To print a dot, a high
voltage is connected across
the ink and a conductor just
outside. The spark blows
some ink out of the tube and
onto the paper

Not many things about
computers are beautiful in
themselves, but a
daisywheel (below right),
with its fragile spokes and
tiny elegant letters, is one of
them.
Below is a close-up of one of
the spokes of a Qume
daisywheel

Very often we want to produce words and pictures on paper rather than on the screen. The machine to do this is called, fairly logically, a printer. In many ways it works like an electric typewriter. Paper is fed in around a cylindrical rubber platen and typed on. But, unlike typewriters, computer printers seldom write by hitting a ribbon with little type heads on the ends of metal arms. This is because the mechanism is too fragile for the greater speed of operation. Instead they use one of two methods. In the 'daisywheel' system the letters are made by raised metal or plastic shapes on the ends of the petals of a plastic wheel as shown in the photograph below right. The correct letter is spun into position in front of the ribbon, and then is hit by a little hammer to print the letter.

The second method is called 'dot matrix'. This produces letters on paper in exactly the same way as they are written on the screen: by rows of dots. These dots are produced by the print head which contains a vertical row of rods hit by hammers. Again, these hit a ribbon to mark the paper (in some new machines the dots are written by ink jets or lasers – see below).

Generally, daisywheel printers are expensive, noisy and slow but produce very nice-looking text. The more sophisticated machines can do proportionately spaced letters – like the letters on this page, where 'i' is narrower than 'w'.

Dot-matrix printers are quicker and quieter, but generally produce rougher-looking print. However, if the hammers are small enough and close enough together, the result can look very like typing. Dot-matrix printers have improved enormously in the last couple of years, and it seems likely that eventually they will oust the daisywheel.

The great advantage of the dot-matrix printer is that it can print any shape its software tells it to print. This means that you can switch from roman to italic, to narrow, to bold face, all in the same line of a document. If necessary it is equally easy to switch back and forth between Russian, Arabic, Japanese and English characters. They can all be held in ROM in the machine, or sent to it by the host computer.

The more advanced new daisywheel and dot-matrix printers usually offer a 'graphics' mode, in which the print head will print small single dots. The head and the platen will move in such small steps that the dots can be overlapped to produce lines or areas of continuous black on the paper. Greys are made by spacing the dots out. This can produce attractive pictures, but the software necessary to drive the printer can only be called daunting since every one of tens of thousands of dots must somehow be individually programmed.

The drawback to all printers is that they are mechanically complicated, highly stressed and apt to break down. There is an energetic search for simpler methods of making marks on paper, and two solutions are coming on the market. One is 'ink jet' printing, in which dots are made not by hitting a ribbon with a hammer, but by firing a drop of ink at the paper. In the most elegant system seen yet, the Olivetti ink-jet printer fires

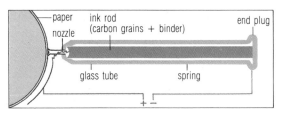

the dot by an electric spark inside a simple capsule of ink. This is quiet and fast, and there is hardly anything to wear out. When the ink capsule runs out, you just slide in a new one.

A more expensive system steers a laser beam to write the text, and then prints marks by some sort of xerographic process. This is much more expensive, but, since nothing mechanical touches the paper, it can be extremely fast. It is being used to produce enormous quantities of 'personalized mail' for direct selling campaigns.

However, while all this technology is very nice, it does raise some horrific problems for the end-user. Suppose you would like to print your

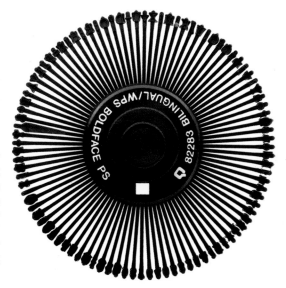

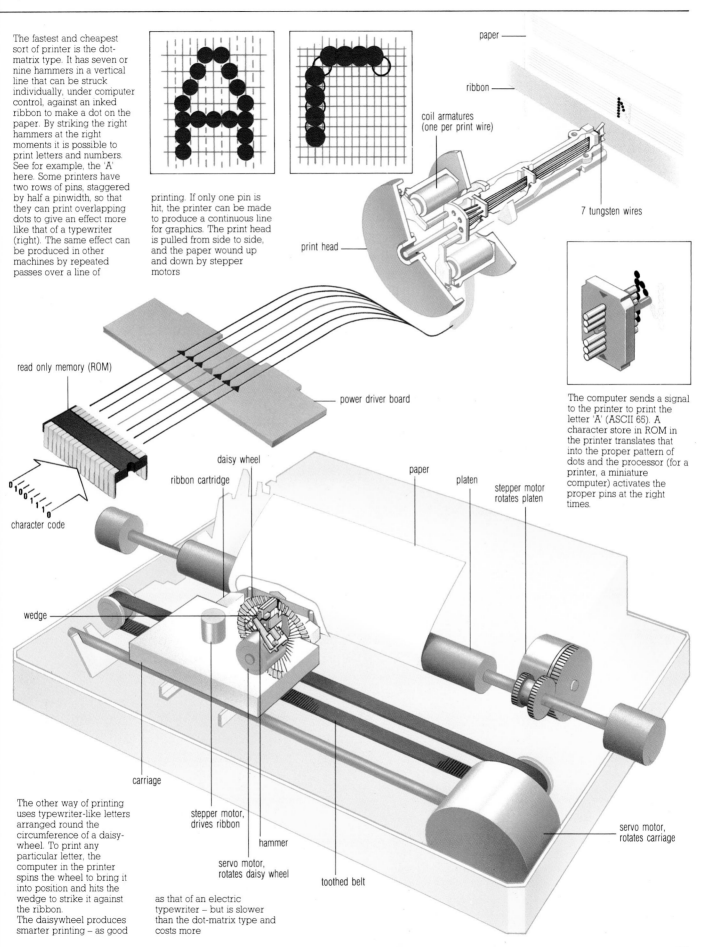

The fastest and cheapest sort of printer is the dot-matrix type. It has seven or nine hammers in a vertical line that can be struck individually, under computer control, against an inked ribbon to make a dot on the paper. By striking the right hammers at the right moments it is possible to print letters and numbers. See for example, the 'A' here. Some printers have two rows of pins, staggered by half a pinwidth, so that they can print overlapping dots to give an effect more like that of a typewriter (right). The same effect can be produced in other machines by repeated passes over a line of printing. If only one pin is hit, the printer can be made to produce a continuous line for graphics. The print head is pulled from side to side, and the paper wound up and down by stepper motors

paper

ribbon

coil armatures
(one per print wire)

7 tungsten wires

print head

read only memory (ROM)

character code

power driver board

The computer sends a signal to the printer to print the letter 'A' (ASCII 65). A character store in ROM in the printer translates that into the proper pattern of dots and the processor (for a printer, a miniature computer) activates the proper pins at the right times.

daisy wheel

ribbon cartridge

paper

platen

stepper motor
rotates platen

wedge

carriage

The other way of printing uses typewriter-like letters arranged round the circumference of a daisy-wheel. To print any particular letter, the computer in the printer spins the wheel to bring it into position and hits the wedge to strike it against the ribbon.
The daisywheel produces smarter printing – as good

stepper motor,
drives ribbon

hammer

servo motor,
rotates daisy wheel

toothed belt

servo motor,
rotates carriage

as that of an electric typewriter – but is slower than the dot-matrix type and costs more letters – or, if you are a writer, your articles – proportionately spaced with a justified right-hand margin (just as this text is set). You can buy the hardware and software to do the job, but it may be agony to get it all to work together. The first problem is that the word-processing software has to calculate how many words it can get on a line. It has to 'word-wrap' the last word down to the next line. Then it must calculate how much spare space is left by the words it can get on the line. To fill the line out and bring the last letter of the last word to the right-hand margin, it must insert spaces. In proper proportional spacing these spaces are minute fractions of an inch spread evenly about between all the letters. The computer can do the calculations easily enough, and if the printer knows about these small spaces, it can receive the appropriate codes. The snag is, however, that the software must know in advance the width of each of the printer's letters and punctuation marks so that it can make the proper allowances. Since you, the innocent user, may well have bought the printer and the word-processing package from two quite different sources, it is up to *you* to tell the word processor how much space on the line is needed by each letter. This can be a complicated business.

We are at the stage of computing where there are many bright ideas and very little cohesion between them. The user's problems are often caused as much by manufacturers' ingenuity as anything else. Although in principle computers can do anything, in practice making them do anything remotely useful is often so complicated that it is not worth the effort. It is better to settle for something modest and useful that you can get

working, rather than something perfect that you cannot.

Phototypesetters

Documents produced by computer printers – which are no more than smart electric typewriters – are one thing; documents produced by proper printing are another.

There are several differences. First, one expects a very much higher standard of evenness and accuracy in proper printing. Because the letters are more accurate they can be denser; the text in a newspaper, for example, is set far more closely than that of a typewritten letter. Secondly, the typesetter has at his disposal a far greater range of typefaces, spaces between letters, and lines and borders of various sorts. In fact, there are so many possibilities in typesetting that a separate profession is needed to control them – that of the typographer – and there are many things that worry typographers which few of us consumers of printing could explain, although we would very soon know if they got them wrong. An ordinary computer printer is quite incapable of producing properly typeset documents, so a 'phototypesetter' is needed.

There are three common types of phototypesetter, which differ in how they produce the letter-shaped images that embody the text typed into them. One keeps its library of letters and symbols – in many different sizes and typefaces – on a glass disk in photographic negative. It produces output on photographic printing paper by moving the right image on the disk to the right place on the paper and then shining a light through the disk.

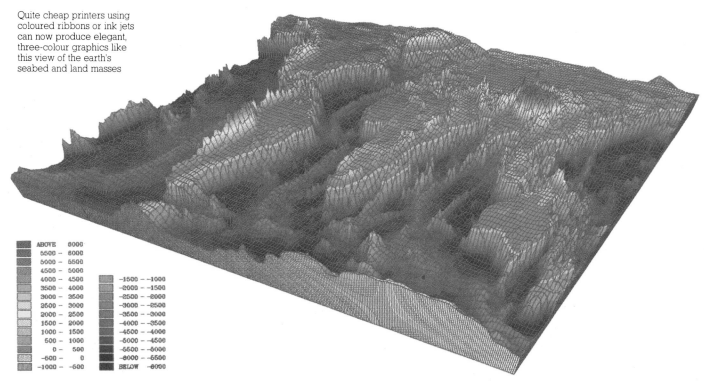

Quite cheap printers using coloured ribbons or ink jets can now produce elegant, three-colour graphics like this view of the earth's seabed and land masses

ABOVE	6000
5500 –	6000
5000 –	5500
4500 –	5000
4000 –	4500
3500 –	4000
3000 –	3500
2500 –	3000
2000 –	2500
1500 –	2000
1000 –	1500
500 –	1000
0 –	500
–500 –	0
–1000 –	–500

–1500 –	–1000
–2000 –	–1500
–2500 –	–2000
–3000 –	–2500
–3500 –	–3000
–4000 –	–3500
–4500 –	–4000
–5000 –	–4500
–5500 –	–5000
–6000 –	–5500
–6500 –	–6000
BELOW	–6000

The second sort of phototypesetter draws each letter on a high-resolution CRT screen, and photographs that in the correct position on a piece of light-sensitive paper. A third sort draws each letter with a laser under software control.

Making it work is far from easy, and quite a lot of skill is needed at the keyboard to get a good result. A big problem is the hyphenation of long words that stretch over the right-hand margins of short lines. There are programs to do this automatically, but they seldom work satisfactorily, and there is no real substitute for a good operator.

Recently people have started using microcomputers as 'front ends' to phototypesetters to insert the necessary control characters into word-processing text. This makes it possible for documents produced on micros to go direct to typesetting without having to be re-keyed – a great saving of useless labour, though one that is not popular with the print unions.

Plotters

We saw on page 36 that a printer could be made to produce rather rough-looking pictures. The smarter approach to graphics is to build a separate machine altogether, a plotter which uses a pen and draws rather as a human does.

In essence, you have a pen controlled by two motors which move it in small steps both horizontally and vertically. By moving the pen an appropriate number of steps at a time both up and across, it can be made to go in any direction.

If the pen is moved with no vertical steps, it draws a horizontal line. If it is moved with no horizontal steps, it draws a vertical line. If the vertical and horizontal steps are equal, it draws a line at 45 degrees. If the size of each step is about one tenth of the width of the pen line, the steps will be pretty well invisible, and the effect will be one of smooth drawing.

The more you pay for a plotter, the nearer it approaches this ideal, but the good ones are very expensive. They now use a range of pens of different colours, and it is very amusing to see the head go off and pick up a green pen from the rack, write some green, then go and get a red one to add some finishing touches.

However, the cost is not terribly important because these machines are used to produce engineering drawings for very large and expensive projects. By holding the instructions for the plotter in a central database, it is relatively easy to coordinate the work of many engineers; by producing the finished drawings using a plotter, the work of many draftsmen is saved.

The engineer who designs a plotter has some pretty tough problems to tackle. If the machine could take all year to do a drawing things would be easy, but the whole point is to do the job as quickly as a draftsman can. The designer therefore has to contend with problems like overshoot in the stepping motors, which makes the pen

wobble around its new position unless he waits for a millisecond or two before writing. The designer has to contend with slop in the gears and cords that move the pens, because they will make the pen settle at different positions depending on where it came from.

If the plotter is to work fast, the head has to be accelerated quite drastically. The biggest engineering flat-bed plotters use cables as thick as a finger to withstand the mechanical loads needed for such acceleration, and when in operation they have to be covered by a glass lid to keep hands from being sliced off by the flying hardware.

Quite a lot of the marks on an engineering drawing are letters or standard figures such as circles, squares and ellipses. So the software in the plotter which controls the head has some of the functions of a printer. To write the name of a part you do not have to steer the pen round the letters as if they were bits of machinery, you can just type in 'PRINT "Sprocket hole ¼"' or 'PLOT CIRCLE 2.6,3.56,6.1' – the numbers being the coordinates of the centre and the radius. A plotter by itself is no more use than a printer by itself: you need software to drive it, which does the same sorts of operations as word-processing software does for a printer. However, software to create and manage 3D engineering images is not simple. Nor does it make trivial demands on hardware. We get some idea on pages 102-3 what these might be.

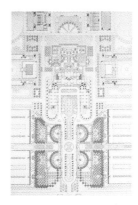

Top A high-speed plotter drawing land contours for a map. The pens move so fast that they would take off your hand if you put it in the way

Centre The four-colour plotter of this Sharp portable computer is more restricted in its capabilities. However, this little gem of engineering design combines the functions of calculator and computer

Above 'Computer Garden' by Scott, Brownrigg and Turner, supposedly the first computer-generated work of art to be shown at the Royal Academy. Think what Louis XIV would have done at Versailles with the help of such a machine!

MAGNETIC MEMORY

A typical office computer system, including dual disk drive. The girl is holding two floppy disks

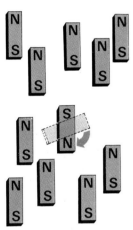

Data is written onto magnetic medium by magnetizing small areas: up for '1' and down for '0'. Once magnetized, they hold their data because the little magnets in the recording material lock one another in position. Here the miniature magnet in the centre has rotated out of line. The north–north repulsion from its nearest neighbours will spin it back again

Right, top Cassette tape is the cheapest way of storing computer data, but it suffers from slow access. Of the three files shown here, A is way upstream of the head, B is within a second or so of being read, and C is a long way downstream

Below Data is recorded on disk as tiny areas of magnetism on circular tracks in pie-shaped sectors. The read/write head can be placed over any track; the rotating disk brings the required sector under the head. This gives very fast access to data

On pages 24-5 we were looking at electronic memory to be used within the computer and directly connected to the processor for fast access. Because this is still quite expensive (64 K costs about £150 or $230 with all the chips to refresh it and control its busses), we need much cheaper backup memory which can work quite slowly. These two sorts of memory are rather like the few papers you have out on your desk, which you can search quite fast, and the great mass of papers you have in your filing cabinet in which it takes longer to find anything.

All you need for a memory is some sort of physical effect which can be caused electrically so that a computer can write it, and will itself cause some electrical effect so the computer can read it. In principle it does not matter what the effect is, and over the years people have used many strange things. One of the earliest computer memories, built for the Mark 1 computer in Manchester, England, in the late 1940s, used little dollops of charge written onto a cathode-ray tube. A simple, slow, but very reliable method is to use holes in paper tape. They can be made by an electrically operated punch and read by light beams or little electrical contacts. Many big computer installations still use paper tape – and indeed I have a complete English dictionary on about 5 miles of it under my bed.

Since the inventor of a cheap computer memory would become rich beyond the wildest dreams, there has been a considerable incentive to explore possible technologies. It is interesting that, of all the methods proposed, the one that has stood the test of time and is now almost universally used is magnetic recording. This is done by coating some suitable surface with magnetic goo and then magnetizing little areas of it in one of two directions to record either a '1' or a '0'. (In practice it is a little more complicated: what records the 1 is a *change* from north to south magnetization; 0 is recorded by south followed

by north.) The beauty of magnetic recording is that each little area is self-locking. The tiny magnets that make up an area all point up or down depending on whether they are recording 1 or 0, and if one of them feels the urge to get out of line, the others push it back.

The well-behaved magnets all lie so that each one's north pole is next to another one's south pole, which is just what they like. Any error results in a magnet that has somehow turned itself around so that its north is next to all the other norths and its south to the souths. As anyone who has played with a couple of magnets knows, this causes strong repulsions, and the offending magnet gets spun the right way round. This feature means that data written on magnetic media can be left for quite a long time (by computing standards, in which time is measured in millionths of a second) without decaying. It is generally reckoned that data ought to be re-recorded every two years, otherwise it suffers the mysterious and fatal 'byte rot'.

There are very few other physical processes which have this self-locking, self-maintaining ability. The world, therefore, relies on magnetic recording. There are some other ideas on the horizon (see pp. 42-3) but as yet nothing has replaced magnetism.

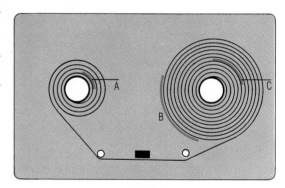

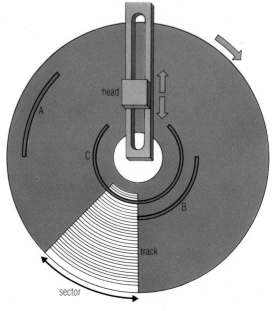

For want of anything better, this technique was used for many years for storing computer data as well – the distinctive tape machines have become a standard visual symbol in films and television for 'computer', even though they are now obsolete. What makes tape good for music – its serial nature – makes it bad for computing, as any owner of a micro which uses a cassette recorder will tell you. The trouble is that you almost certainly do not want to read your data from one end of a file to the other.

On the tape shown opposite, Jack the Giant Killer (A) is about half a mile upstream of the head, while a program for playing noughts and crosses (B) is several hundred yards downstream, and Tom Thumb's Record (C) is as far away as childhood. This is not much good. To do better, some bright spark had the idea of combining the best features of magnetic tape and gramophone records. The magnetic goo is spread out on the disk surface, which spins round, while the head which reads and writes the little magnetic areas moves in and out from the centre to the rim. This vastly reduces the amount of time needed to get to any particular spot on the disk, though it does result in a complicated piece of gear.

The data is written on 'sectors', which are segments of a circle and 'tracks', which are circles of differing radius. The tracks do not go in a spiral, as they would on a record. A small hole in the disk near the centre lets a beam of light through on every revolution, so circuitry in the disk drive can work out where the head is in relation to all the sectors. This is the 'soft sector' scheme, where the sectors are set up electronically using a timing signal from the single hole. A few machines use 'hard sector' disks, which have a hole in the disk for each sector. Reading the three bits of data that were so inaccessible on the tape is now easy. We just have to drive the head in or out to get it on the right track and then wait for the right sector to come round. The average time taken to run the head to any track from any other is called the 'seek time', and the average time to wait while the sector you want comes round is called the 'latency'.

In real life a floppy disk with reasonably well-written systems software to drive it (see pp. 44-7) should take between $\frac{1}{3}$ and $\frac{1}{5}$ second to find any particular thing; a hard disk should be at least twice as fast. Practically all medium-priced micros nowadays have disk drives, and they are

Having got a method of making indelible marks (very like ink on paper), you then need some way of getting to any particular mark easily and quickly. In a tape recorder for voice or music the magnetic goo is coated on thin flexible plastic tape and pulled steadily past a read/write head. Since music is essentially a serial entertainment, where one thing comes after another and you do not want to dive rapidly into the middle of a piece, this works very well.

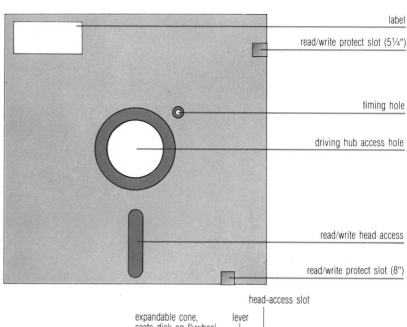

label
read/write protect slot (5¼")
timing hole
driving hub access hole
read/write head access
read/write protect slot (8")

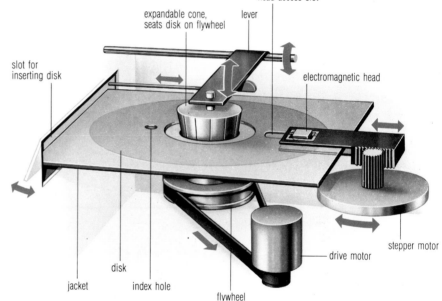

head-access slot
expandable cone, seats disk on flywheel
lever
slot for inserting disk
electromagnetic head
disk
jacket
index hole
flywheel
drive motor
stepper motor

spreading down into the training machines. Most of these drives are for 'floppies', in which the recording material is coated onto a thin, flexible disk of plastic which lives inside a square envelope. There are four sizes in common 8-, 5¼, 3- and 3¼-inch

What makes a disk drive expensive is the accurate engineering necessary to put the tiny read/write head reliably on the same track time after time. Attempts have been made fairly regularly to produce devices which combined the cheapness of tape drives with the speed of access of disks. One such was called 'The Stringy Floppy', but I do not recall that it made a great impression on the world. At the time of writing, Sir Clive Sinclair in Britain about to bring something called the 'Micro-Drive' onto the market. It is said to look like a disk, but to have a mechanism that winds the head spirally into the centre and out again. This makes for cheap hardware but will be slow.

Top A floppy disk. The disk itself – a thin, flexible circle of plastic, coated with magnetic material – lives inside a square plastic sleeve. It cannot be removed from the sleeve. You must never touch the surface of the disk itself; do not bend, heat, staple or write on it with a biro. Do not leave it under a telephone either, because the magnetic field of the bell can ruin the disk. To use, you slide it into the opening of the disk drive with the label towards the door

Above The parts of the drive mechanism

single-density disks are best. But once a program or data file is established on your machine, you can safely use the quad option because the head errors will be the same on read and write and the thing will work.

The floppy disk drive is connected to the main computer board by a multi-way cable. It usually reads from and writes to memory through a direct memory access (DMA) chip – a sort of dedicated processor that does nothing but read and write to memory in parallel with the main processor. Data transfer to and from the disks is usually at something like 250 KB/s.

Although hard disks are becoming much more common as their price drops, there are still many merits to the floppy. The disk itself is very cheap; it can store quite a lot of data – up to 500 KB on each side – though some, like the Apples, hold only 90 K. You can make a copy of your programs and data and keep it safely under the bed. You can send it through the post with great ease. On the other hand, it gets a lot of wear and tear and tends to die at unpredictable intervals. For the sake of your sanity, always take backup copies of your important files.

The really infuriating thing about mini-floppies is that a disk written in one machine will very probably not read in another, because each manufacturer makes up his own way of writing data to the disk. Although everyone knows the aggravation this causes, the new $3\frac{1}{4}$-inch disks seem to suffer from the same problem.

There *is* a standard in 8-inch floppies – a single-sided, single-density disk (SSSD) will work in pretty well *any* machine. This is why software is distributed so often on 8-inch SSSD. To get software from a machine that reads 8-inch disks to one that writes the particular $5\frac{1}{4}$-inch format you want necessitates bringing them physically together and pumping the data across through an RS 232 interface (see pp. 28-9).

The good news over the last couple of years has been from the manufacturers of hard disks. The argument is that the smaller you can make the magnetic patches that store data, the more of them you can get onto a given area of disk. That gives the end-user greater capacity with no increase in recovery time because the head moves just the same distances.

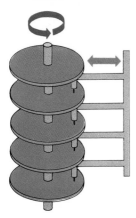

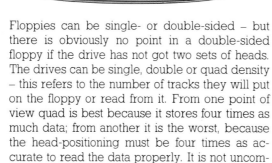

Top A hard-disk data-storage unit must be one of the most precisely engineered devices any of us are likely to own. The heads fly so close to the disk surface that even a particle of cigarette smoke will cause them to crash. They must therefore operate in a totally clean, sealed chamber. (Here, the lid has been removed)

Above Many hard-disk drives actually contain several disks mounted on the same spindle and accessed by multiple read/write heads. This increases storage without greatly increasing cost

Right The read/write head of a disk is a very small electromagnet. When it is being used to write data onto the disk, a current flows through the coil

Floppies can be single- or double-sided – but there is obviously no point in a double-sided floppy if the drive has not got two sets of heads. The drives can be single, double or quad density – this refers to the number of tracks they will put on the floppy or read from it. From one point of view quad is best because it stores four times as much data; from another it is the worst, because the head-positioning must be four times as accurate to read the data properly. It is not uncommon for a quad-density disk written in one machine not to work in a second, identical, machine. For data transfer between machines

causing a magnetic field to appear at the gap. This field passes through the disk's surface, magnetizing the particles in it. When the head is being used to read, the magnetism of data areas in the disk induces minute electrical currents in the coil which are amplified and fed to the computer

The way to make the areas smaller is to put the magnetic recording head closer to the disk surface. That means that the old flexible floppy has to be replaced by a firm, smooth, hard disk. The rubbish that flies around in the air – dust, hairs, even particles of cigarette smoke – must be excluded if the thing is to work; so the disk lives inside its own little air-conditioned space. Moreover, the clearance between the head and the disk is so small – about 18 millionths of an inch – that it cannot be held accurately enough by machinery. The head actually flies on the wind carried by the spinning disk – held down against the air pressure by a light spring. When the disk stops, the head 'lands' on a special track where there is no data. The whole thing is a marvel of ingenuity and will put up to 50 MB of storage in a box the size of a 5¼-inch floppy-disk drive. A good typist can keep up an average of nearly a thousand words an hour, so 30 MB would take 623 working days to fill up – more than two years.

But the quest for even greater storage capacity goes on. The fashionable scheme is to move from horizontal recording – where the little magnetic areas lie in the surface of the disk – to vertical recording, where they run from one side of the disk to the other. This is thought to increase the recording density by a factor of perhaps 40, so a mini-floppy could hold 20 MB of data, and a hard disk 1200 MB, or eighty years' typing.

Magnetic bubbles

It seems very silly that data storage has to depend on motors and whirling disks when, one would think, there must be much more elegant and compact mechanisms available. The problem with disks is not just that they are not very elegant, but that it is almost always the moving parts that fail. The head in particular easily becomes dirty or damaged – with drastic consequences for the data stored on the disks. An apparent solution, which was much touted in the later seventies, was magnetic bubble storage. The idea was to encode data in little 'domains' of magnetism – small volumes in which the magnetically encoded information locked itself in place as usual – and instead of moving these domains physically past a read/write head, to make them ripple through the magnetic material. You would then have a

high-volume memory without any moving parts.

The result was 'bubble memory', in which small magnetic 'bubbles' were pushed through a thin layer of magnetic material by externally applied magnetic fields. The material was patterned in various subtle ways to make the bubbles behave properly. A piece of data was encoded by magnetizing a string of bubbles either north–south (to represent binary 1) or south–north (to represent 0). The string of bubbles was formed in a loop – which might be folded over to fill up the available material – and shunted around the loop to bring each bubble in turn past a read/write head built into the magnetic material. It was essentially an endless tape, though one in which the tape stood still and the data moved. It proved possible to move the data quite fast through the material, so the main disadvantage of a tape store – slowness – was avoided. However, this required quite elaborate and power-consuming magnetic coils which were not easy to make. No doubt if bubble memory had caught on commercially, it would have become cheap. However, because conventional disks sell in such huge volumes, they are already very cheap; bubbles could never compete. Now they are used mostly for computers in military aircraft and ships, where disks would not work reliably because of dust and gunfire, and where expense is relatively unimportant.

A data-storage technology that never quite made it: magnetic bubbles. Instead of writing data magnetically onto the recording medium on a whirling disk, the magnetic bubble storage device moves the data through a stationary magnetic medium. The rows of chevrons make a path along which the little magnetized regions are moved by powerful exterior coils. The parallel bars make up the system's version of the read/write head

Below The head and disk surface of hard disk, vastly enlarged. The magnetic material (bottom of page) is brown, the head white (rest of page) and the 18 microns between them blue. This is such a tiny distance that only a part of a human hair to the same scale (shaded area) can be shown

FILES AND OPERATING SYSTEMS

A disk by itself offers raw storage space. It is like an empty filing cabinet – not much use without drawers and file pockets. The file pockets have to be labelled and indexed somehow, so that people can find whatever documents they have stowed away. In a computer this job is done by the 'operating system', a program which manages all the computer's internal housekeeping tasks. In many ways, as far as the user is concerned, it *is* the computer.

At the lowest level, an operating system does a variety of mundane but essential jobs. When you write in BASIC:

10 INPUT"Enter next number";N

BASIC – which is just a program for understanding what people mean by this sort of remark – hands the string 'Enter next number' over to the operating system with a command to print it on the screen. The command then expects input from the keyboard, and waits for the operating sytem to provide it. When the user has typed in a number and hit RETURN, that number is handed back to BASIC.

A close-up of a disk with data written onto it. The data is arranged in concentric tracks broken into radial sectors. Each file is shown as a different colour. As files are written and erased, the free space on the disk gets fragmented. The files shown here rarely have two sectors together. The directory track (shown enlarged) records where all the files are. 'CALC', for instance, is on track 4, sector 7; track 12, sector 6; etc.

The code to do these operations could, of course, be written into BASIC. The reason it is not is that you might want to run other languages or programs written in machine code. They too must be able to print messages on the screen and accept input from the keyboard, so simply to save effort it makes sense to write the routines once and let everyone use them. Furthermore, the way information is passed to and from the operating system can be made standard, guaranteeing that standard software packages can print on the screen and get text from the keyboard.

An operating system will also handle the printer, sending it text at the right speed and recognizing its 'handshaking' signals (see pp. 28-9).

It will also carry out the whole tricky business of storing information on, and recovering it from, the disk. The problem here is to make the best use of the available space. Starting out with an empty platter, this is easy enough. You write the first file and then the second and then the third. When you get to the centre the disk is full and you stop. However, long before that you have almost certainly taken the first file, made some changes, erased the first version and recorded the new one. The new version will probably not fill the old space up neatly: it will be too big or too little. Quite soon the disk will be in a terrific mess with great chunks of space not quite big enough for complete files.

The standard scheme is to split the disk up into small chunks of storage – usually called 'records' (not to be confused with 'Records' in a database, pp. 94-7). The operating system keeps a directory, usually written on the outermost couple of tracks of the disk, to show which chunks are in use by which file. So, File 1 may be written onto records 34, 35, 36, 47, 53, 96, 97, 98, 99, 100, File 2 may be on 2, 3, 4, 5, 6, 7, 26, 29, 39, 126, File 3 on others, while a whole lot more are blank. When a file is erased, its records are marked as empty in the directory; when a file n records long is written, it is put onto the first n blank records in the directory. This simple scheme makes efficient use of the disk at the cost of keeping a directory, and having to jump the head about a lot if the disk has been well used.

The users do not have to know anything about this. As far as they are concerned, they ask the operating system to write and read files and that is what it does. How it sets about it is its own affair.

Before we go any further, it might be a good idea to look at the important idea of a 'file', because so much serious computing revolves around it. A file is simply a long string of bytes (what else could it be?) written on a disk. It has a name, a beginning and an end. The name is kept in the directory with a number to show which record begins the file. To show precisely where the file stops in its last record, there is an end-of-file (EOF) marker. Whenever a file is read, the operating system checks each byte that comes off the disk, looking for the EOF marker. When it finds one, it stops reading. If by some accident you get an EOF in the middle of a file, you have a problem.

The bytes in a file can be looked at in two ways: as data of some sort or as a program. The data might be a text file, which can be translated to and from alphabetic characters by a word-processing package; or a string of bytes representing numbers – the output of a payroll or stock-control package – with some bytes representing text mixed in amongst them; or even bytes which represent the coordinates of dots in a picture drawn on the computer screen. Very often you cannot tell by looking at the file what it is – it has to be read by the right program to make sense.

If the file is a program, its bytes will be interpreted as machine code instructions (see pp. 80-85) and memory addresses. There will almost certainly be some data mixed in amongst the program, but the program bits of the file will know what is data and what is not. The 'interpreting' is done by the operating system, and it is guided by the name of the file. Tradition says that file names should consist of two parts: a name and an extension, to identify the file and tell the operating system which sort it is.

The crucial difference between the two sorts of files is that when you give the operating system the name of a program file it knows what to do with it, which is to read it from the disk, load it into memory with its start at the place where programs start and set it going. All other files need to be accessed by programs since the operating system on its own does not know what to do with them.

A good operating system does much more than this. It should have simple programs – usually called 'utilities' to distinguish them from programs that do something useful in the real world – to report on the disk space left, the sizes of the files, to rename files and copy them from one disk to another. It should allow the user to set up printer types and speeds. If the system allows multiple users (see pp. 146-9), it should prevent one user from messing with another's files. It should control how users write to and read from shared files, so that someone does not try to read from a file that is being written to. It should allow one user to send messages to another, and to the outside world.

In the real micro world there are several groups of operating systems whose manufacturers inherited the main-frame scheme in which each manufacturer automatically provides his customers with his own operating system. This is partly to prevent them shopping around for the most profitable part of the computer package – the software.

Although they do on each individual machine

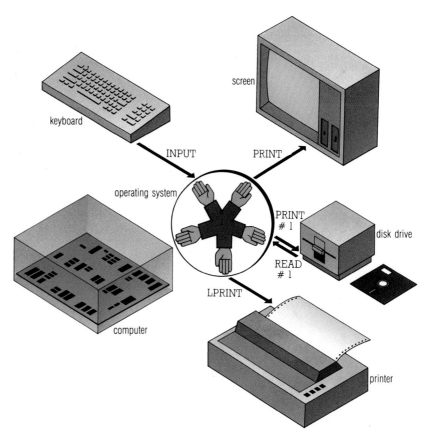

what an operating system should do, systems that are peculiar to one manufacturer do not not fully realize the advantage of the basic idea: that a common operating system makes machines of different design appear to be the same.

This is a discovery that was made by the microcomputing community almost by accident in the mid-seventies, when Gary Kildall wrote some software to get data on and off the disk of a microcomputer. He called the software 'Control Printer/Monitor'. The result was CP/M, which was a huge success, used by dozens and then hundreds of manufacturers of 8080 and Z80 microcomputers. In the course of time, history was rewritten to make 'CP/M' stand for 'Control Program for Microcomputers'.

A common operating system like CP/M provides the software market with a very much larger community of customers than it would otherwise have. Using a system specific to one machine – even if it were more efficient than CP/M – would be like printing a book in Finnish rather than English because the logic of the language suits its particular subject better. Unfortunately there are far fewer readers who know Finnish than English. The development of a mass market in computer software would be impossible without common operating systems.

Unfortunately, the ownership of a widely used operating system is so profitable that several people are trying to get in on the act, with consequent fragmentation of the market.

An operating system is a program (which runs inside the computer, though here it is shown schematically outside it) which links processor, keyboard, screen, disk files and printer together. All machines that use the same operating system should appear identical to the programs they run.
The words in capital letters are the commands in Microsoft BASIC to perform various functions. Because they can rely on a standard operating system they can be the same on many different machines

Fragmentation of the operating system market is a bad idea for several reasons. First, a general operating system creates a large market, which in turn attracts many software products. Competition forces cheapness and good performance, and this benefits the user. Secondly, if several manufacturers provide the same operating system, no single one of them can dominate the market. One manufacturer decided a few years ago that he did not like outsiders selling software to his customers. To prevent this, he changed his operating system. It turned out that the manufacturer suffered as much as anyone, because users reacted badly to this bullying. But if, say, a dozen other manufacturers had made machines which used that operating system and accepted the same software, then any one of them would have been unable to make this move without damaging himself far more than anyone else.

Looked at in this way, there are at the moment only two – or perhaps one and two bits – systems in the micro market. The main contender is CP/M (and its upwards derivatives and improvements such as MS-DOS). It has grown up – just – with the market, and is an adequate, simple system. By main-frame standards it is bare to the point of imbecility, but it does pretty well all that the single user wants, and seems to be adapting to micros in small networks under the guise of CP/Net. There are a number of similar, 'CP/M look-alike', network operating systems such as Turbodos, MacNos, MMost (see pp. 148-9).

The rival to CP/M and MS-DOS in their various formats is UNIX, an operating system originally devised for multi-user minis some ten years ago by Bell Laboratories in America. If CP/M is too bare, UNIX seems almost too lavish. In its present form it is a professional programmer's tool which allows users to set up whole processes of programs set in train by a single keystroke. The output of one program can be 'pipelined' into the input of another. It has a wonderful mechanism called the 'shell', which allows any program to run any other program as if it were the operating system.

UNIX suits professional programmers very well, but in its complete form would drive most ordinary computer users crazier than they are already. But this is not really important since it is so easy for the programmer to tailor the way the end-user sees it. By the time this book is published, there is likely to be a cross between UNIX and CP/M or MS-DOS on the market. Certainly, however it works, it will be possible to make it behave like CP/M if the users wish so that they can run CP/M software under it.

Smalltalk

So far we have been looking at the operating system's work at the lowest level of the machine – housekeeping tasks between the disks, keyboard, screen and printer. The operating system

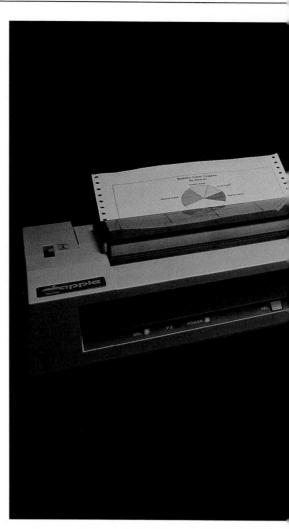

also has a responsibility at the highest level, for it is only through it that the user can run programs.

One solution is to create new operating systems which will automatically load whole series of programs – feeding into them, if necessary, commands that the user would otherwise have to read out of the manual and type in at the keyboard. Another approach called Smalltalk, developed by Xerox at its Palo Alto research centre and taken up by Apple with its new Lisa machine, is to throw out the alphabetic listing of programs and data files, and give the users something they feel more at home with. The Smalltalk solution is to give people pictures of things they can make sense of: a picture of a paper folder means a data file; a printer means the printer; and a dustbin is where you put things you want to get rid of.

To make these pictures operate you have a cursor controlled by a 'mouse' (see pp. 28-9). As you move the mouse about your desk top, so the cursor moves around the screen. When the mouse is on the picture of the thing you want to execute, you press a button. If you want to print a particular file, you steer the cursor onto it, press the button, then steer the cursor to the picture of the printer. Press the button again, and the file will be printed out. If you want to edit another

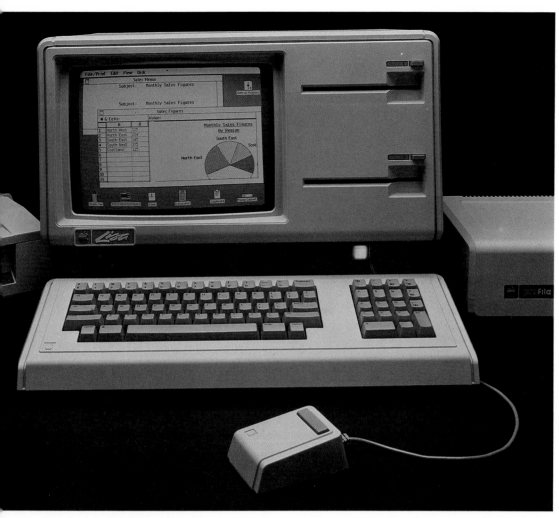

The widespread use of computers creates tremendous problems in explaining them to people who are used to pen and paper. It is rather like taking the driver of an ox-cart and trying to tell him about freeways, interchanges, traffic lights, parking restrictions, gear boxes, petrol, tyres, spark plugs and a hundred other things. On his first drive he is likely to become an accident statistic and lose interest in motors. Apple are attempting to solve this problem by pretending that their auto is an ox-cart. Their Lisa tries to duplicate a desk on its screen

file, you put the cursor on the picture of the editor to load it, and then on the file you want to get loaded and presented on the screen.

Naturally, all this takes a lot of processing power. The screen has to have very high resolution if it is to present usefully detailed pictures. Moreover, the Lisa implementation lets you have multiple pages of documents on the screen, with one lying on top of another as paper documents would on a desk. You can pull bits of one document into another – a piece of spread sheet (see p. 100) can be lifted and 'pasted' into a report being prepared with the word processor. There is a drawing package that lets the user draw sketches, save them, get them back and incorporate them into documents. There is also a graph-drawing package, and a rudimentary database manager among other things.

This makes heavy demands on the hardware. Lisa has a 68000 processor – the most powerful of the 16-bit machines, and 2 MB of RAM. This in turn makes it an expensive machine. To judge by the crowds round any demonstration of Lisa, it speaks loudly to the naive computer user. It remains to be seen how long people will be happy to pay what will always be a heavy extra price for the hardware necessary to mimic paper,

rather than spend a few hours learning to do things in a more economical way. More seriously, it may turn out that although paper metaphors for computational ideas make it easier to sell machines to inexperienced users, in the long run it may be a sterilizing influence. As I have tried and will try again to show in this book, there are many aspects of computing which have no parallels in the familiar world of paper information. Sooner or later people who want to be 'computerate' will have to buckle down to the fact that computing is actually *different* from paper.

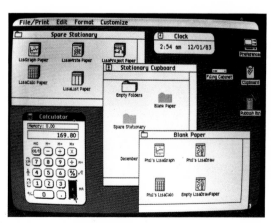

Here Lisa is offering the user 'blank paper', a calculator, a dustbin and other familiar objects. In the author's opinion, this can only lead to confusion later on

HOME SOFTWARE

By the nineties this will be a familiar scene, as husband and wife do their accounts on their home computer and wonder where all the credits went

The boom in cheap chips has produced an even more surprising boom in cheap, small computers – 'home' or 'personal' computers, as the market seems to have decided to call them.

At the time of writing (mid-1983) these machines tended to have fairly simple hardware. Their processors were Z80s or 6502s, and they tended to have 40 × 20 screens or even less in some cases. Sometimes they only had upper-case letters on the screen, with some pretty primitive graphics. They did have colour – provided you had a colour television to interface the machine to and no one else in the family wanted to watch 'Dallas'. They often had less than 64 K of RAM – amounts ranging from 16 K to 48 K were common. Most unsatisfactory of all from the point of view of commercial microcomputing, they had no disks. Their backup storage was on audio tape recorders. If the tape recorder did not work properly, you had no backup at all. Furthermore, even when it did work, it meant that you could only access your data files serially (see pp. 22-3). A microcomputer is really only useful when it can get at a lot more than 20 K or so of data in memory (after a language has been loaded), and in any order.

These constraints meant that users of home computers were limited to programs that would run completely in memory. Nevertheless, an astonishing market sprang up overnight, supplying software for the small machines. It consisted chiefly of games. Chess was the most intellectual, and (but it is hard to pick among so many) Molar Mauler the least. A long way after games in popularity came educational programs which attempted to teach – in a gamelike setting – the elements of algebra, physics or a (human) language.

For a while in the development of the micro it looked as though teaching would be a very important job for these machines. The argument was that, just as a textbook spreads an expert teacher among tens of thousands of pupils, rather than the couple of hundred he or she could teach face to face in a year, so computerized lessons would be even more valuable. They could involve the pupil, test him, grade themselves to his progress and abilities. The drawback so far is that students are almost by definition not very well off – either personally, or in terms of the equipment which society is prepared to buy for them. They can therefore only afford cheap com-

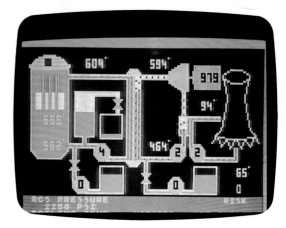

puters and these impose all the limitations we have noted above. The result is very crude software, which cannot yet imitate the content and richness of even an ordinary textbook.

A more serious problem is that teaching consists of more than pupils reading through a text and being tested on their comprehension. A good teacher has a much more intimate relationship with the class than that. He or she understands what they think they know as well as what they do know. The teacher understands what problems each pupil has in learning and adjusts the lesson accordingly. A good teacher is learning about the pupils as fast as they are learning about the subject. Imitating this demands far more sophisticated artificial intelligence software than we begin to know how to write, so it is not surprising that computers play only a minor role in teaching ordinary classroom subjects.

Of course, computeracy itself is beginning to be thought of as a desirable subject for children

to learn, and cheap computers are just the thing for teaching it. Curiously enough, there are teachers who resist them passionately. I suspect the reason is that children do not need much formal instruction in computing. The instant feedback they get from the machine entrances them and stimulates them to try more and more, so the teacher is reduced to the role of occasional adviser to people who know what they are doing. Some teachers find this a rather humiliating role.

Almost all small machines have a version of BASIC supplied with them, and users who get tired of pre-written games move naturally to writing their own. A third category of software for personal computers that comes right in the 'computeracy' class is versions of big machine languages such as Lisp and Forth.

Finally there are attempts to provide business software such as word processing, spread sheet calculation, accounting and database management (see pp. 94-101).

All these suffer from the necessity of having to keep data in serial files on tape. The least promising application must be the database managers – imitating card indexes – that use a serial file on tape. This means that a single search through the database could take up to fifteen minutes, and that relational searches which involve using information from one Record as the starting point for a further search could take days to run.

Notwithstanding the hardware limitations, this market continues to thrive. Within three years of the first really cheap micro – the Sinclair ZX80 – there were some million personal computers in the United Kingdom alone, which was said by enthusiastic journalists to be the most densely computerized country in the world. By the middle of 1983 one home in five was thought to have a microcomputer, and the software market was beginning to rival that for pop music or video

tapes. In fact a leading music company, Virgin Records, launched into the computer games business as an area it could not afford to ignore. As a further result, pictures of teenage millionaires who had dropped out of school but were now making fortunes from their monster games became a routine feature of the daily papers. As with any mass consumer market, the emphasis shifted to advertising and presentation and away from technical perfection.

It is a far cry from the population of inarticulate computer freaks who were wrestling with heaps of circuit boards, machine code and spaghetti back in 1979.

It is quite clear that before very long the personal micro will be a 16-bit machine with disks. It should have high-resolution graphics and masses of RAM. The huge volumes that will be sold will make the cost hardly more than today's machines. We can expect the personal software market to convulse itself once again, drawing in large amounts of what we now think of as high-priced professional software (see pp. 94-101) and issuing it at tens rather than hundreds of dollars or pounds.

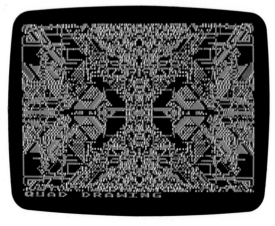

COMPUTER GAMES

Would Babbage, Turing or von Neumann ever have guessed that the destruction of Space Invaders by teenage boys would be the major use for computers?

For a great number of people microcomputers exist only to play games. This may be a rather limited viewpoint. For many others, the phrase 'computer games' brings a great sinking of the spirits. But they too may be guilty of tunnel vision.

Computers offer an excellent vehicle for certain sorts of games because one can easily build very complicated machines on them. Perhaps fortunately, when one thinks of the sadistic tendencies of games authors, they can only offer minimal physical involvement, but when it comes to the hand and eye they are as taxing as the most dramatic ball games.

There is a whole spectrum of computer games, ranging from the mindless reflex entertainments of arcade games like Space Invaders, up to the intellectual heights of chess. In between are some interesting entertainments which not only demand quick reflexes but also quite deep thought. These games often put the player in the position of a military commander who must make strategic and tactical decisions against time, without – as so often in real life – being in full possession of the facts.

If a history of computer games were ever written, it might be said that they descended from two roots. The first is the illicit entertainments of programmers on big commercial and academic systems who, to relieve the drudgery of routine work, wrote games in their lunch hours. The venerable Startreck package is possibly the ancestor of them all, and there can hardly be a big computer in the world that has not such a program lurking somewhere in its files. Sensible managements tend to encourage gaming at a cost of thousands of dollars a minute, because it interests programmers in the tools of their trade and encourages them to experiment.

The other, and more respectable, ancestor of the computer game is the simulation or model (see pp. 88-9). Modelling techniques are much used by the miltary to predict the outcome of new weapons and strategies. In many of these models the computer is used simply as a large, fast book-keeper, to calculate the results of possible strategic decisions.

The danger with simulations is that people tend to believe them, even though somewhere in the logic a shortcut has been taken that makes nonsense of the whole thing.

A prime example is a computer simulation of the world's economy commissioned by the Club of Rome (a group of big businessmen, politicians and civil servants) in the 1970s. It resulted in a report called *Limits to Growth*, which predicted a sudden collapse of the world economy round about the year 2000. Starvation and anarchy would be the lot of all, rich and poor alike. Because this dire prediction emerged from a group with considerable prestige, made even more impressive by using a computer, many people believed it.

Later on it emerged that there was a fatal flaw in the computer model. It had an important section on the price and supply of crude oil. As we all know, there is a limited amount of crude in the ground, and before very long we must think about using some other source of energy. The program reflected this fact, but failed to model what would happen to the price of oil as supplies dried up. It assumed that oil would go on costing what it did in the early 1970s until, one day, there was no more. Naturally, this threw the world economy into confusion.

In real life, as reserves of oil dry up, the oil-producing nations will raise the price to compensate for the lack of income in the future. The increasing price of oil will automatically stimulate developments in alternative energy sources. Given only moderate efficiency in the mechanisms of the market, we should make the transition from oil to whatever comes next with only moderate dislocation, not the complete disaster predicted by the computer model.

Games for microcomputers fall into three main classes: the nervous, the romantic and the intellectual.

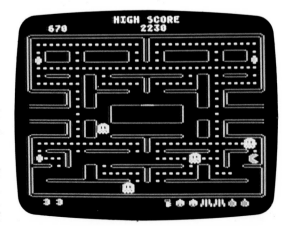

The nervous games are often called 'arcade' games – they demand quickness of hand and eye and offer little to think about. They have a unique fascination because of instant feedback – the eye–hand nervous loop extends outside the body into the machine, locking arcade-game devotees into an addiction that is sometimes as powerful as heroin's.

The romantic games derive from a genre of fiction based on J. R. R. Tolkien's *The Lord of the Rings*. They extended into board games and have now been automated in a class of computer game generally called 'adventure'. The core of an adventure game is some sort of invisible land-scape (which may be three-dimensional) divided into cells. Each player assumes a character – Wizard, Warrior, Warlock, Troll – collects more or less useful tools – lantern, magic sword, key, flask of water – and sets off on his quest. At each stage he can go up, down, east, west, south or north into another cell. The way into the cell may be through a narrow door which will not admit the bag of gold the player is 'carrying', or needs a key that he has not got.

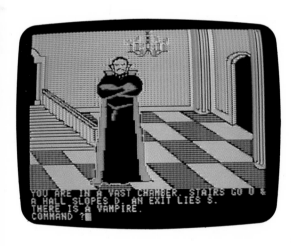

When he gets into the cell, it may contain a man-eating griffin or a charming young lady. Adventure games can last for days and modern ones have striking graphics, some with attempts at animation.

A third sort of game is the intellectual, where little emphasis is placed on creating atmosphere and a lot on strategy. A typical example would be Eastern Front, a war game in which the player has to command tank armies fighting against the Nazis. These games tend to set emphasis on dy-namic behaviour; it takes time and effort to get a Panzer division moving, but once it is, it takes some stopping. Concepts like the servo loop (see pp. 130-31) come in very handy to the authors of intellectual games.

Hammurabi is an interesting game in which the player is given a feudal country to rule. At the start of each year he has so many peasants left over from last year – less those that have died,

starved or run away, plus those who have been born. He has so much corn in store – less what the rats have eaten. He has so many soldiers, castles, markets and palaces. He has to make decisions about the levels of taxation and corrup-tion in the civil service, the amount of corn to be allocated to the peasants or saved for seed. He can hire soldiers or build palaces. Then his neighbours (played by the computer) can attack. Depending on his provision of soldiers he may win and gain land, or lose and lose land. Decisons made in one year throw their effects forward for many years after. The whole business gets very complicated and quite fascinating.

These games would be much more interesting if they could present a moving picture of the world they represent. But, as we will see on pages 112-15 lifelike graphics make huge de-mands on computer power, and 8-bit machines do not have anything like enough. The advantage given by 16-bit processing power is clearly apparent in games and simulations. Microsoft's light aeroplane simulation on the IBM Personal Computer is very striking, giving a view of the aircraft's instruments – which all work realistically

– and the scenery outside the cockpit. It is so realistic that it is just as boring as flying a light aircraft . . . unless you run out of fuel and crash.

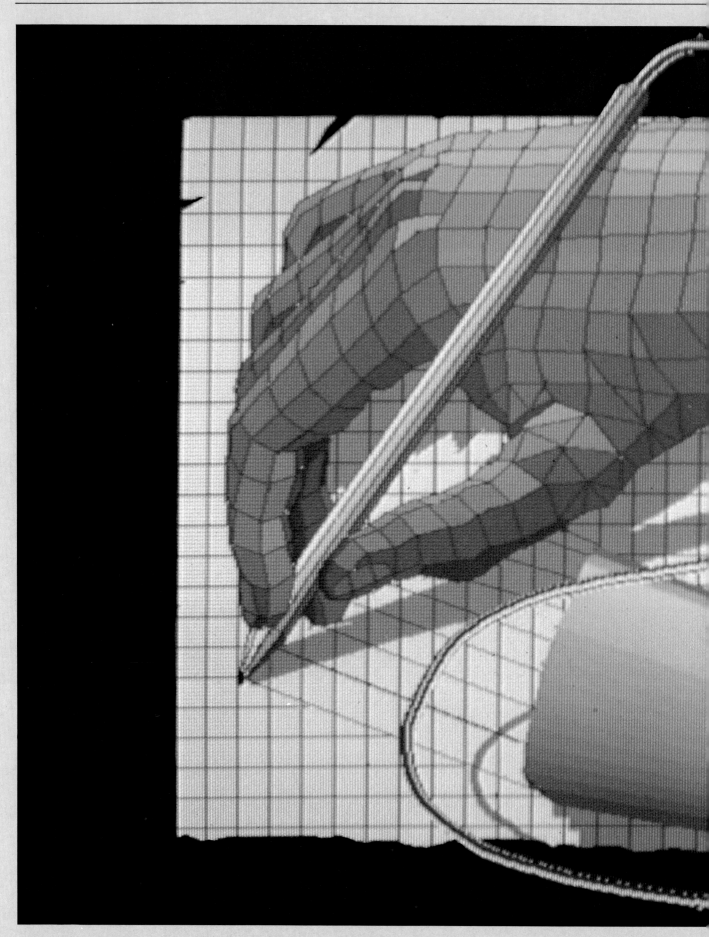

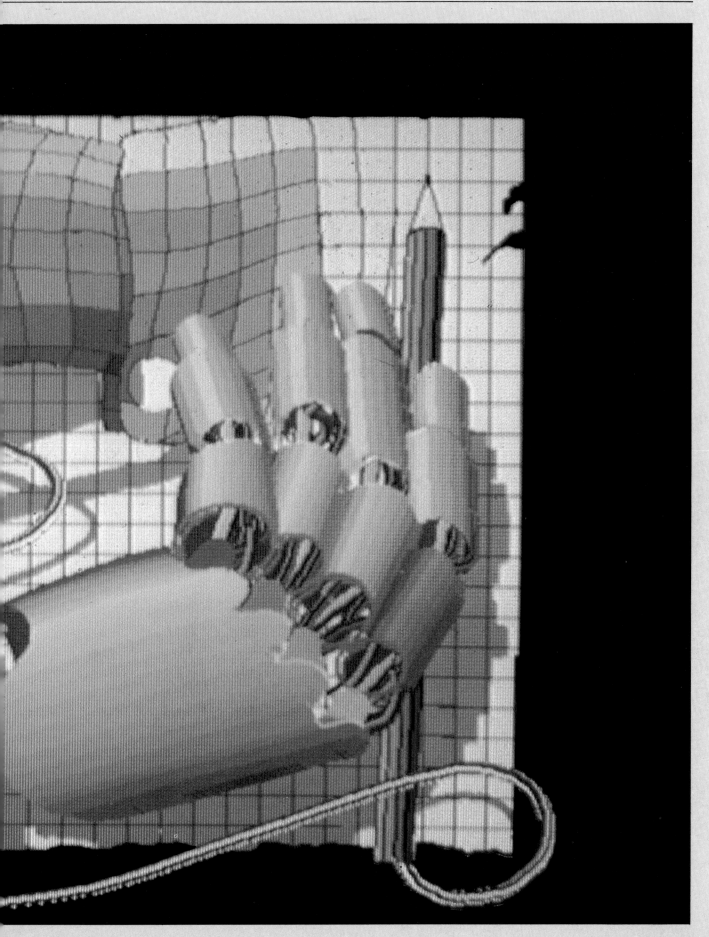

PROGRAMMING

There is an old story that schoolmasters used to tell their pupils – and may do still – about Alexander the Great. When he was a young man, handsome, powerful, monarch of all he surveyed, he was taught mathematics by Aristotle. One day, tiring of the business of learning geometry, he asked if there was not some easier method? And Aristotle told him that there was no royal road to geometry: everyone, rich or poor, strong or weak, had to learn it in just the same way.

So it is with computing. My own belief is that as the 1980s continue it will become more and more necessary to be computerate – just as after the introduction of printing it was essential to become literate. If you were illiterate you were handicapped, and, as is nature's way, the handicapped went under.

'Computeracy' means first of all familiarity with the machine, the keyboard and the conventions of the business – for example, hitting 'RETURN' to make things happen. Secondly, it means understanding a whole lot of new concepts to do with things inside the machine that you cannot see, things like memory locations, files, programs and data. The trouble is that you only find out what you are doing wrong by your mistakes.

Computers can do only a limited range of things, and most of what they do is internal. As far as the outside world goes, the vast majority will only write letters and pictures on a screen or paper. To communicate with them you have to use a keyboard or a joystick.

In human terms a computer is a cripple who can write and draw but cannot move about, pick anything up or even see what is around it. So the first task in programming is to be realistic about

what it can cope with. People often think that a computer would be useful in the home, managing things like menus. It is a nice idea, but it is unrealistic. You would like it to look in the larder and the fridge and report that you had three tins of sardines, a half-used jar of mayonnaise and some rice, so the best supper you could manage would be a sort of salad. 'What about the lettuce?' you would ask, and the machine would observe that the cat had done something nasty in it.

But all this is what the computer cannot do. The poor, legless, eyeless thing cannot go poking about in the larder. To get the information into it, *you* would have to be its eyes and legs and then type in the data. While you were doing that, your own perfectly good menu-producing computer – driven by hunger as the silicon one is not – would have planned a meal and have it half ready.

A current computer's practical sphere of action is limited to handling symbols on screen and paper. This is wide enough since it covers a large chunk of intellectual life – in business, science and amusement.

The second step in writing a program is to find some data that you and the computer can both make some sense of. Space Invaders is an excellent example – people see the little shapes on the screen as alien monsters that have to be killed; the computer sees them as neat little shapes that can be drawn here and there as the player wants. When the coordinates of the missile coincide with the coordinates of the monster the machine replaces the monster by a different picture of exploding rubbish and outputs a tone to the loudspeaker.

In business people can feed the thing lists of numbers which to them mean cash in and cash out – profit and loss – fun or disaster; to the computer they are just numbers, which it knows very well how to manipulate. If the debts are bigger than the takings, then the profit has the symbol '−' in it; that is all, and it is nothing to the machine if its owner goes out and commits suicide.

So, having settled on some mutually convenient symbols, you then have to ask whether the computer's commands can do anything useful to them. Languages that will run on micros are quite clever in some ways and very stupid in others. They can do logarithms and sines and cosines, which many intelligent adults cannot do, but they cannot work out how to organize a problem at all.

Even though there are many things that a computer cannot do, there are still plenty that it can – if you take enough trouble. Let us look at what you would have to do to get a computer to work out the number of days between any two dates. It sounds easy. But in fact it requires a pretty clever program.

To begin with, we have to remember that Americans write dates in the old English way as month, day, year; the more modern Europeans, as day, month, year. Once you tell the program which you want, it has to be able to cope with either. (You have to tell it, because '4.3.84' means 3 April to an American, but 4 March to a European and there is no way the machine can deduce which is which.)

It ought to be able to cope with dates like '3 April 1982' or '16/5/79'. It should not care if you use spaces, dots, dashes or slashes between the numbers. If the month has been named – remembering that the program should be able to handle the minimum number of letters, in either upper or lower case, necessary for unique identification: 'Au' for August, 'Jul' for July – it has to turn the name into a number. It then has to know how many days the first of that month is from the start of the year. In the process it should detect invalid dates such as '31/4/1983', or '30 Feb 1600'. It should be able to guess that '83' means '1983' and not some moment in Roman history.

Then it has to calculate the number of days from each of the dates to some arbitrary date in the long-distant past. To be quite safe some people make this date the start of the current calendar in 1582. This process has to take into account the varying numbers of days in the months, an extra day in a leap year (divisible by 4) and the cancelled extra day in a super-leap year (divisible by 400). Then each date has to be converted into a day number.

Once these two day numbers have been calculated for the two dates, it is easy to see which comes first by looking at which day number is the smaller, and to find how many days there are between the two dates by subtracting one from the other. The whole business involves going to the library to check up on leap years, and about two days' hard programming. Yet you and sometimes I can do it in our heads. Computers are very, very stupid.

It is beyond the scope of this book to write such a program, so let us look at a much easier task, using a hitherto unknown language which I have made up called 'FOODGOL'. Its purpose is to illustrate the basic programming concepts of steps, tests and loops.

Steps, loops and subroutines

As a simple example, let us look at the steps needed to eat your dinner:

Eating Program 1

1. Pick up knife and fork
2. Cut off a morsel of food
3. Stick it with fork
4. Put in mouth
5. Cut off a morsel of food
6. Stick it with fork
7. Put in mouth
8. Cut off a morsel of food
9. Stick it with fork
10. Put in mouth
11. Cut off a morsel of food
12. Stick it with fork

This looks sensible enough, if a bit tedious to write. But we could make the program much simpler by incorporating a loop:

Eating Program 2

1. Pick up knife and fork
2. Cut off a morsel of food
3. Stick it with fork
4. Put in mouth
5. Goto 2

Now, each time you have put some food in your mouth the program makes you go to step 2: 'Cut off a morsel of food', followed by 'Stick it with fork', etc. Hold on - what will happen when the food on your plate is all eaten up?

Eating Program 3

1. Pick up knife and fork
1a Is there any food on plate? If not, put knife and fork down, stop
2. Cut off a morsel of food
3. Stick it with fork
4. Put in mouth
5. Goto 1a

What was missing was a test to see whether the actions should continue. This is now a complete programming loop. It will make you start eating, continue eating and stop eating when there is nothing left. In fact, it is difficult to see how you would write the program without using a loop. Look at Eating Program 1 again. How do you know in advance how many times to repeat the cycle? Do you write 10 of them and hope you do not get served any banquets? Or 100, and put up with scraping an empty plate, maybe dozens of times? There has to be a test to see if you have finished.

We can enlarge the program to let you have some pudding:

Eating Program 4

1. Pick up knife and fork
1a Is there any food on plate? If not, put knife and fork down, goto 6
2. Cut off a morsel of food
3. Stick it with fork
4. Put in mouth
5. Goto 1a
6. Ask for pudding
7. Is there any food on plate? If not, put knife and fork down, stop
8. Cut off a morsel of food
9. Stick it with fork
10. Put in mouth
11. Goto 7

We have changed the program in three ways. First, when the first course is finished, step 1a takes us to step 6 which makes us ask for pudding. There is a new loop to cope with eating the pudding, with a new test to see if it has been finished.

However, lines 8,9,10 are exact copies of 2,3,4. Lines 11 and 5 are very similar. We can make the same chunk of program control eating both courses with a 'subroutine'.

Eating Program 5

1. Pick up knife and fork
1a Is there any food on plate? If not, put knife and fork down, goto 6
2a Gosub 100
5. Goto 1a
6. Ask for pudding
7. Is there any food on plate? If not, put knife and fork down, stop
8. Gosub 100
11. Goto 7

100. Cut off a morsel of food
101. Stick it with fork
102. Put in mouth
103. Return

'Gosub' is a computing command borrowed from BASIC (see pp. 58-61) which means 'Goto the step ordered (in this case, 100), do the steps that follow, and come back when you meet the command RETURN.' Having jumped from step 2a to the subroutine at step 100, executed the steps there and returned, the program does the next step, which is 5, just as before. When the test at 1a shows there is no more first course, the program jumps – as before – to step 6, and uses the subroutine at step 100 to eat the pudding.

What is the point? First, it saves program space. Secondly, it means that all the eating is carried out by the same bit of program. If eating is to be done in a different way, say, by using chopsticks rather than a knife and fork, it is easy to change the way the program works. In this case we have to, because we have forgotten to tell the unfortunate eater to chew and swallow. As the program stands, he will stuff his mouth with food until he suffocates:

Eating Program 6

1. Pick up knife and fork
1a Is there any food on plate? If not, put knife and fork down, goto 6
2a Gosub 100
5. Goto 1a
6. Ask for pudding
7. Is there any food on plate? If not, put knife and fork down, stop
8. Gosub 100
11. Goto 7

100. Cut off a morsel of food
101. Stick it with fork
102. Put in mouth
102a Chew
102b Swallow
103. Return

It would have been much more difficult to alter Eating Program 1 – we would have had to add two new steps every three steps. A mistake would have been easy. We have also just fixed a 'bug' – a bit of the program which did not do what it was meant to. Professional programmers spend most of their time doing that.

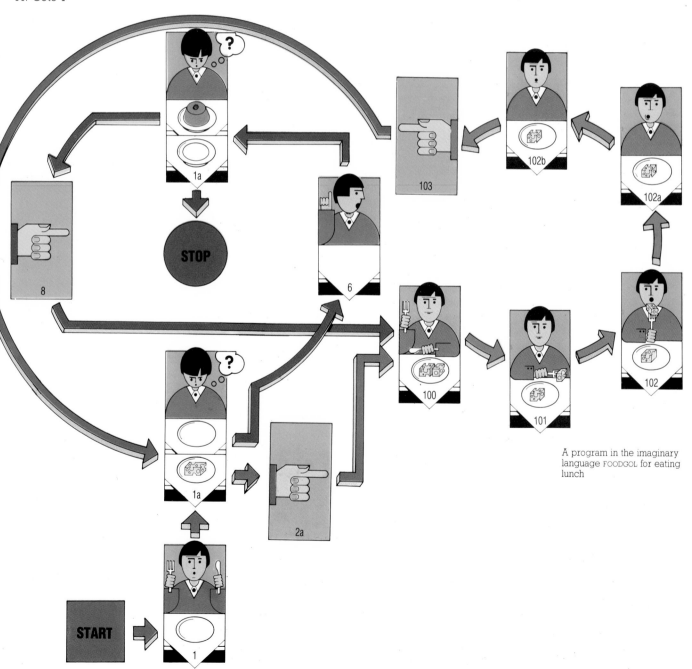

A program in the imaginary language FOODGOL for eating lunch

BASIC

On the last page we looked at the way programs in many languages get written: by giving a list of commands which are to be executed one after the other; by compacting similar actions into single subroutines, which are called from different places in the program; and by testing to see whether various stages have been achieved.

This kind of program structure is used by a large range of languages: Fortran, Algol, COBOL, Pascal, 'C', among many others, and also BASIC. BASIC is likely to be the first language most readers of this book will come across, because dialects of it are installed in the vast majority of personal computers. It has disadvantages, which we will come to, but it has several great advantages too.

The best of them is that it is simple to get started with BASIC. Almost anyone can write some sort of program within a few minutes of meeting a computer – even if it does no more than print 'Hi' on the screen. Secondly, BASIC is interpreted. This means that you can write a bit of program and run it immediately to see if it works. More serious languages have to be compiled each time before they can be run. This is a process which can take between minutes and hours, and is very discouraging for the beginner. If your BASIC program does not work (as it will not most of the time), you edit it and try again.

On the down side, there is no 'standard' BASIC. A list of the commands in one of the more popular versions is given on pages 186-7; I suggest that you put a finger in those pages to help you follow what we are going to do here.

The BASIC language consists of three sorts of things: commands, variables and functions. Commands are easy to understand – they are verbs: 'PRINT', to print something on the screen; 'LPRINT', to print on the printer; '+', to add two numbers together and so on. Variables are very like variables in algebra, except that instead of 'x' and 'y', in many dialects of BASIC you can give them more helpful names such as HOURSPER-WEEK or KLINGONSKILLED. There are two sorts of variable, one to represent a number and another to represent text. If the program were to ask the user his or her name and age you would write the lines:

```
10 PRINT"Please type in your name"
20 INPUT NAME$
30 PRINT"and your income"
40 INPUT INCOME
```

This is, in fact, a tiny program. There are several things to notice about it. First, the lines are numbered, and the program will execute the commands in them in order of the numbers. Secondly, the numbers are (by convention) 10 apart, so that you can insert extra lines if you want later on. The PRINT command expects to be followed by a 'string' – that is, some characters in quotation marks, or a variable (see below). The INPUT command waits for the user to type something at the keyboard, followed by a RETURN. When this program runs, you will see on the screen:

Please type in your name
?

(INPUT puts up a '?' to show that it expects you to do something.)

You type in Chris or whatever it is, and hit RETURN. BASIC now knows that the 'value' of the variable NAME$ is 'Chris'. The '$' after the variable NAME is to tell BASIC that what follows is to be treated as text and not a number – the two are handled quite differently inside.

The program will then write on the screen:

and your income
?

and you type in 14 or 14000 or whatever it is, followed by RETURN; that number is now the value of the variable INCOME. Since BASIC began as a language for doing mathematics it assumes that a variable without any distinguishing '$' is a number.

Because programs need to do so much of this sort of thing, the language provides a more compact method – you can build a 'prompt' into the INPUT command:

10 INPUT"Please enter your name and income, separated by a comma";NAME$,INCOME

The string in quotes after INPUT gets printed on the screen. It is followed by ';' to tell BASIC not to move the cursor to a new line, which it would otherwise do after printing anything. It then expects the user to type:

Chris,14000

It is sensible to tell people about the comma that INPUT expects, since they might otherwise forget and BASIC would complain by producing an 'Error message'. If you try to enter: "Chris. 14000" or "Chris – 4000", BASIC will not understand.

We have now fed two variables into our program: one string and one numeric. Having got them inside, we can now do things to them, and, in keeping with the two different data types, there are two different sorts of operation we can carry out.

First, let us look at string operations. It might be nice to make the computer respond gracefully by greeting the person who had just typed in a name. We could make it say:

Good morning Chris. I am pleased to make your acquaintance.

There are several ways we could do this trick. One is just to print the whole thing on the screen with a program like this:

```
20 ?"Good morning";
30 ?NAME$;
40 ?".I am pleased to make your acquaintance"
```

The '?' is a shorthand in many BASICS for 'PRINT'. Originally it was used to print unknown variables, so it made sense from the user's point of view: "What is (?)variable so and so"– as used here in line 30. The full stop after 'Chris' has to go in the third line. Remember the ';' prevents new lines after each program line. Without it you would see:

Good morning
Chris
.I am pleased to make your acquaintance

Another way to do this would be to 'concatenate' these three strings together into a single string and then print that:

```
20 B$="Good morning"+NAME$+".I am pleased
to make your acquaintance."
30 ?B$
```

We are making up a new variable, B$, out of the three bits we have on hand. The sign '+' when used with strings simply means 'glue together'. You will notice too that '=' is being used oddly – certainly by the standards of school algebra. It is unfortunate that BASIC uses '=' in two quite different senses, and it can be very puzzling to beginners.

As used here, '=' means 'move the right-hand side into the left-hand side', or 'make the left-hand side equal to the right-hand side'. It would have been better perhaps to use a symbol like '←'to suggest leftwards movement – though it would mean typing an extra character each time. Some languages use ':=' to distinguish this sort of equals from a real equals:

```
IF A=B THEN ...
```

We could do that here. There might be a particular person that you did not like, so you could put a new line in (see the usefulness of numbering lines 10 apart?):

```
15 IF NAME$="John" THEN ?"Beat it":GOTO 10
```

This is a real equals and will test to see whether the hated John is at the keyboard. (In practice you would have to test for 'JOHN' and 'john' as well.) The 'IF' command works the way you would expect. If NAME$ is John then the program executes the commands after 'THEN', otherwise it ignores this line and 'falls through' to line 20 as before.

There is a new symbol here, ':'. This introduces a second command after the command to print 'Beat it' – to jump to line 10, which asks for someone else to type in his or her name and income.

Arrays

You cannot get far in BASIC – or indeed any other computer language – without bumping into the idea of an array. An array is a variable with several slots so it can hold several strings or numbers instead of just one.

The simpler sort of array, called a 'vector', has only one row of variable positions. Suppose we are interested in the weather and we want to record the total rainfall for each day of the week. A vector is just the thing we need. At the beginning of the program we have to set up the array with the dimension command – because BASIC has to reserve some space for it:

```
DIM RAIN(7)
```

That tells the program we want a variable called 'RAIN' with seven slots in it, which we can access by calling (quite naturally) for RAIN(1), RAIN(2), etc. So, we can write a little program to run on Sunday which will let us enter the rainfall we recorded during the week:

```
10 DIM RAIN(7)
20 for K=1 to 7
30 INPUT"Rainfall for today";RAIN(K)
40 NEXT K
```

This program uses a loop set up by lines 20 and 40. The loop starts with the variable K set to 1, and increases it by 1 each time until it reaches 7. When the program runs, it asks "Rainfall for today?" and you type in 2.3 or .006 or whatever it was, and that value gets stuck into the appropriate slot of RAIN.

From this illustration we see that Monday was wet, while on Saturday and Sunday the rain was torrential.

	1	2	3	4	5	6	7
Rain	.9	.01	.04	.6	1.2	4	2

	Mon	Tues	Wed	Thurs	Fri	Sat	Sun
Day	Mon	Tues	Wed	Thurs	Fri	Sat	Sun

		1	2	3	4	5	6	7
rain	1	.9	.01	.04	.6	1.2	4	2
max T	2	14	22	24	20	17	16	18
min T ▶	3	6	9	10	8	7	7	7
humidity	4	.7	.6	.5	.55	.6	.8	.7
rain	5	1	8	9	5	1	0	0
wind	6	10	2	2	15	20	25	20

You can also have string arrays in BASIC. It might be nice to make this little program ask you for the rainfall by naming the days of the week. To do that we need to set up a corresponding string array called DAYS, in which we store 'Monday', 'Tuesday', ... 'Sunday'.

```
10 DIM RAIN(7),DAYS$(7)
20 DATA Monday, Tuesday, Wednesday, Thursday, Friday, Saturday, Sunday
30 for K=1 to 7
```

```
40 READ DAY$(K)
50 NEXT K
60 FOR K=1 TO 7
70 ?"Rainfall for;"DAY$(K):INPUT RAIN(K)
80 NEXT K
```

Line 20 holds the days of the week as data, separated by commas. The command READ in line 40 puts them one at a time into DAY$(K), so we now have a second array.

The second loop, in line 60, prints the appropriate name of the day in line 70, and asks for the rainfall to be typed in, as before. We could have combined the two loops, but it is easier to see what is happening like this.

There is a grander kind of array which holds several rows of variables, either string or numeric. We might have a meteorological station, and want to store half a dozen different numbers about each day: rainfall, maximum and minimum temperatures, humidity, hours of sunshine and wind speed. This would have to be dimensioned at the beginning of the program with:

```
1 DIM MET(7,6)
```

and accessed in the same way. For instance, the minimum temperature on Friday is stored at MET(7,3) and is 7.

Numbers

On the previous pages we saw some of the things that BASIC can do with strings. Now we will look at numbers. We asked the person at the keyboard to type in his or her name and income, and these two things were put into variables. We have the income in the numeric variable INCOME, and we can do arithmetic with it.

```
10 INPUT"Please enter your name and income,
separated by a comma";NAME$,INCOME
15 IF NAME$="John" THEN ?"Beat it":GOTO 10
20 B$="Good morning"+NAME$+".I am pleased
to make your acquaintance."
30 ?B$
40 MINE=INCOME*.8
50 INCOME=INCOME−MINE
60 ?MINE;"of that should be mine;";INCOME;"of
that should be yours"
```

We have added three new program lines here: 30, 40 and 50, which may seem to be rather puzzling. Line 40 calculates a new variable, MINE, as 80 per cent (or .8 times) the variable INCOME. The symbol '*' is used for multiply since 'x' could be confused with a variable.

Line 50 makes sense if you remember that '=' means 'put right-hand side into left-hand side'. This line says: 'make the new value of INCOME the old value, less MINE'. Line 60 prints out the greedy little computer's view of the economic situation:

'11200 of that should be mine; 2800 of that should be yours'

There are many other things that BASIC lets you do to numbers. You can subtract and divide, raise to powers, take logarithms and antilogarithms, calculate sines and cosines and from them all the other trigonometrical functions. You can generate random numbers – well, numbers that are produced by a sufficiently complicated procedure that they look random to the casual observer. Of course, a computer, being a completely logical machine, cannot produce a truly random number, that is, one selected completely by chance. The best they can do is to start the series of random-looking numbers with a 'seed' input by the operator. Each time the randon number generator is run with the same seed it will produce the same series. When a truly random number is needed – as in the draw for Britain's National Savings Premiun Bond winners – it is necessary to count some unpredictable subatomic events like the decay of radioactive atoms. This has interesting philosophical implications on the differences between humans – as a source of randomness – and machines (see p. 183). Most of these operations are done by 'functions', the third sort of thing in the BASIC menagerie.

To calculate the logarithm of a number, say A, you simply write:

```
70 B=LOG(A)
```

using the LOG function. There are functions to use on strings as well:

```
70 B=INSTR(B$,"I")
```

would work out how far into B$ (as defined in line 20 of our little program) the letter 'I' came, and would turn out to be 20.

Graphics

More and more small computers now come with fairly high-resolution screens and some primitive (by CAD standards, see pp. 102-7) graphics. The minimum scheme is to give commands to draw a point, a straight line or to fill a space with colour. The colour of what is drawn is commanded by a number. For instance, to draw a point at the position X,Y (coordinates starting at the bottom left-hand corner with 0,0), you would say:

```
PLOT POINT (C,X,Y)
```

To draw a line of colour 5 from the point 34,56 to the point 121,444, you would say:

```
PLOT LINE (5,34,56,121,444)
```

The command:

```
PLOT FILL (3,34,56,121,444)
```

would fill the rectangle defined by the two points as opposite corners with the colour 3.

In some BASICs with graphics capabilities, one does not have the luxuries of PLOT, LINE or FILL. To draw a line under program control it is necessary to work out where the dots are to come. For instance, to draw a line five units long sloping downwards at 45 degrees from the point X,Y, one would write:

```
100 FOR K=1 TO 5
110 FOR J=1 TO 5
120 PRINT AT X+K, Y−J, "*"
130 NEXT J
140 NEXT K
```

to produce this effect:

```
*
  *
    *
      *
        *
```

By changing the signs in line 120, the line can be made to any of the four orientations. By leaving out either the X or the Y coordinate, the line can be made to go vertically or horizontally. Lines at other angles are more difficult and come out looking like this:

```
                    * * * * * *
                * * * * * *
            * * * * * *
    * * * * * *
```

The programe has to calculate how many steps along are needed for each step up, or vice versa.

There are many machines, particularly the more serious ones built for business use, that have no graphics commands at all. To print a character at position X,Y on the screen, they have to do it the hard way. Every machine has a command to send the cursor "Home", so that is where it goes. It is then moved down Y lines and across X spaces, and the appropriate character printed. The process then repeats for the next character.

None of this looks a very promising way of drawing a Hyperon Battle Station for your next game. The easiest method is to use a digitizing pad (see pp. 110-11) – if you have one. If you have not, there is a way of drawing in BASIC using DATA statements. This program will draw a ship at any position on the screen:

```
10 HOME$=CHR$(29) REM YOUR HOME
   CHARACTER
20 DOWN$=CHR$(10) REM CURSOR DOWN
30 RT$=CHRS(32) REM CURSOR RIGHT
40 W=79:H=23' REM WIDTH AND HEIGHT OF
   YOUR SCREEN
200 INPUT "POSITION"; X,Y
210 INPUT "WHICH SHIP TO PRINT"; I
220 ON I GOSUB 5000, 6000, 7000
230 A$=INPUT$(1)
240
'REM* * * * * * * * * * * * * * * * * * * * * * * *
900 READ HT
910 IF Y+HT>H THEN HT=H−Y
920 FOR I=1 TO HT
```

```
930 READ D$
1000 PRINT HOME$
1010 PRINT STRING$ (Y+I, DOWN$);
1020 PRINT STRINGS (X,RTS);
1030 PRINT LEFT$ (D$, W−X);
1035 NEXT I
1040 RETURN
4998 'REM
4999 'REM * * * * * * * * * * * * * * * * * * * * * * *
5000 RESTORE 10000:GOSUB 900: RETURN
6000 REM JUMP TO ANOTHER DRAWING
10000 DATA 7
10010 DATA"        *              *
10020 DATA"        *              *
10030 DATA"        *      * * * * * * *
10040 DATA"        *      * * * * * * *
10050 DATA" * * * * * * * * * * * * * * * * * *
10060 DATA'    * * * * * * * * * * * * * * * *
10070 DATA"      * * * * * * * * * * * * * * * *
```

The picture is drawn, just as it will appear on the screen in the DATA statements of lines 10010–10070. Line 10000 has a numeric DATA statement telling the program how many lines of picture to expect. This would let you add other pictures with more or less lines. Lines 10–50 set up the screen for your machine.

Line 200 asks for the position on the screen, and the lines following expect that there might be more than one picture to draw – which we haven't room for here. The ON . . . GOSUB statement sends execution to the first, second or third subroutine specified. Here only the first is included, but you could add more.

Subroutine 5000 sets the DATA mechanism to read from line 10000. If you had another picture at line 11000, then subroutine 6000 would be RESTORE 110000. . . . Execution then jumps to line 900. Lines 900 and 910 calculate how much to leave out of the picture if it should overlap the edge of the screen – this will not happen automatically. The loop from lines 920 and 1040 prints each data line of the picture at the right place on the screen, truncating it if it overflows.

Given these rather meagre BASIC commands, the ingenious can (and resolutely do) soon write programs to display a circular clock face with moving hands on the screen.

If you look at pages 186-7, you will see there are many commands and functions we have not touched on. However, if you want to learn BASIC, the only way to do it is to buy a small computer and actually do it. Trying to learn to program without a computer is like trying to learn to ride a bicycle without a bike. In the process of learning BASIC you will also (and that will be the hardest part) learn what I call 'computish' – the incredibly stupid way in which computers 'think'. And in the process of learning that, you will probably come to a sensible evaluation of what these machines can and cannot do.

These programs have been selected from the many published in the British magazine *Practical Computing* while the author was editor. My thanks are due to IPC Electrical and Electronic Press Ltd for permission to reproduce them here.

They have been chosen to present some variety and to illustrate various basic techniques. I have had to keep off programs that make very specific demands on screen handling.

Most of these listings would be improved by inserting your machine's screen clearing command.

Code

Since the history of computing started with code-breaking, it seems reasonable to give a little program, here to encrypt and decrypt messages – though do no expect to fool the National Security Agency.

In essence encryption is very simple. You take your message letter by letter, and turn it into numbers. The ASCII codes will do fine. You then change each number in a way that only you and the person who is to read it know. The simplest way is to pre-arrange a list of random numbers, and add them to the corresponding numbers of the letter code. This is the principle of the 'one-time pad' which produces an unbreakable coding scheme. The drawback is that the lists of random numbers have to be as long as the total length of all the messages to be exchanged. The Second World War cryptologists achieved their results by painstaking correlation of every scrap of information they could glean, and this meant decoding vast amounts of signals traffic about the most mundane subjects.

Conversely, modern armies and diplomats have to encrypt vast amounts of material to defeat such analysis, and therefore would have to distribute mountains of one-time files to do their coding in this way. This is hardly practical, so the search is for a way of generating a list of random numbers that is random enough not to be predictable by the other side, but can still be duplicated by your friends. This is not easy, because any mechanical process will sooner or later start generating the same list again. When that happens, the code-breaker has a chance to crack it. Furthermore, there may be regularities within the list that he can also exploit.

A simple way of generating a list of numbers (a 'key') which is random enough not to be easily predicted by outsiders, but regular enough to be remembered by your friends, is to use a codeword. Each letter of the codeword is used to code the corresponding letter of the message. If the codeword is shorter than the message, it is recycled. This is done by the program below.

```
10 '*****CODE2******
20 KEY$="ZEBRA"
30 INPUT"String to be coded";I$
```

```
40 FOR K=1 TO LEN(I$)
50 L=L+1
60 IF L>LEN(KEY$) THEN L=1
70 K$=MID$(KEY$,L,1)'GET THE L'TH LETTER
  OF KEY$
80 J$=MID$(I$,K,1)
90 O=ASC(K$) XOR ASC(J$)
100 PRINT O;" ";
110 NEXT K
```

The decode is carried out by CODE 2:

```
10 '*****DECODE2******
20 KEY$="ZEBRA"
25 INPUT "Length of code";LC
40 FOR K=1 TO LC
50 L=L+1
60 IF L>LEN(KEY$) THEN L=1
70 K$=MID$(KEY$,L,1)'GET THE L'TH LETTER
  OF KEY$
80 INPUT"Next code number";J
85 LPRINT J;" ";
90 O=ASC(K$) XOR J
100 LPRINT CHR$(O);
110 NEXT K
```

Both programs could easily be changed so that the codeword was entered when they were run.

This simple scheme would not give a serious codebreaker much difficulty, because the key repeats at the end of the codeword. You could make the repeat longer by re-enciphering the output with a second codeword, which would make the repeat the length of the two words multiplied together. The process could be continued with as many keywords as you liked: six words each eight letters long would give a repeat of 8^6 – more than 250,000 characters. Providing you changed the codewords before sending that much text, you would be fairly safe. What defeats the professional code-user is the need to send millions of characters using the same key. Rubbish keys would be better still because that would deny the cryptanalyst the help of regularities in the keywords (see Markov, p. 68).

Anagram

These programs tend to focus on text handling because that is what computers do easiest. Anagrams are a problem everyone has had to wrestle with at some time or another. This program takes a string of letters to be anagrammed, asks if any letters are known in the output, and then prints out all the possibilities. In this example, it was given the letters 'AARAS' to be rearranged, and the letters –N–G—M– as what was known. The results are shown below:

```
100 'ANAGRAM PROGRAM
110 'M G PRITCHARD, PC APRIL 1980
120 PRINT"ANAGRAM"
130 PRINT"----------"
140 INPUT"Type only the letters to be re
arranged";A$
150  PRINT
160 L=LEN(A$)
170 INPUT"Are there any letters known (Y
/N)";Q$
```

```
ANAGRAMS   ANAGSRMA
ANRGASMA   ANAGASMR
ANSGARMA   RNAGAAMS
ANAGASMR   ANAGSAMR
ANSGRAMA   RNAGAAMS
RNAGAAMS   RNAGSAMA
RNAGSMA    RNSGAAMA
ANAGASMR   ANAGSAMR
ANAGRSMA   ANRGSAMA
ANSGAAMR   ANSGRAMA
SNAGRAMA   SNAGAAMR
SNRGAAMA   SNRGAAMA
SNAGARMA   ANAGSAMR
ANAGRSMA   ANAGRAMS
ANRGSAMA   ANSGARMA
ANAAGSMR   ANAGSRMA
ANAGSAMR   RNAGAAMS
ANSGARMA   SNAGRAMA
SNAGARMA   SNRGAAMA
SNRGAAMA   ANRGAAMS
SNAGRAMA   ANAGSRMA
ANAGASMR   ANAGARMS
ANAGRAMS   ANSGRAMA
ANSGRAMA   RNAGSAMA
ANRGAAMS   RNAGAAMS
ANAGRSMA   RNAGAAMS
RNAGASMA   RNSGAAMA
RNSGAAMA   ANRGSAMA
ANAGRSMA   SNAGARMA
ANRGAAMS   SNAGARMA
ANAGASMR   SNAGARMA
SNAGARMA   ANRGASMA
SNRGAAMA   ANAGSAMR
ANAGAMS    ANAGRSMA
ANRGSAMA   ANSGAAMR
ANSGRAMA   RNAGAAMS
ANAGSAMR   RNAGAAMS
ANAGRSMA   ANAGRSMA
ANSGAAMR   SNAGAAMR
ANSGAAMR   SNAGARMA
SNAGARMA   ANRGASMA
SNRGAAMA   ANAGRSMA
SNAGRAMA   ANAGRAMS
ANAGARMS   ANRGASMA
ANRGASMA   ANSGARMA
SNAGARMA   RNAGSAMA
SNAGRAMA   RNAGAAMS
SNAGAAMR   RNSGAAMA
```

```
180 IF Q$="N" OR Q$="n" THEN 240
190 IF Q$<>"Y" AND Q$<>"y" THEN 170
200 PRINT:PRINT:INPUT"Type the known let
ters, eg `-B--D-`";K$:W=L
201 FOR J=1 TO LEN(K$)
203 IF MID$(K$,J,1)="-" THEN T=T+1
205 IF LEN(K$)<>L THEN PRINT"Wrong lengt
h; try again":GOTO 200
206 NEXT J
210 T=0:FOR J=1 TO LEN(K$)
212 IF MID$(K$,J,1)="-" THEN T=T+1
215 NEXT J
230 GOTO 270
240 K$="":FOR J=1 TO L:K$=K$+"-":NEXT J
250 PRINT:INPUT"Number of letters to beg
in";W
260 IF W<1 OR W>L OR W<>INT(W) THEN PRIN
T"Error":GOTO 250
270 DIM B$(L),C$(L),Q(L)
280 PRINT:PRINT
290 GOSUB 5000
300 FOR J=W TO L
310 K=1
320 Q(K)=1
330 IF B$(Q(K))="" THEN 440
340 C$(K)=B$(Q(K)):B$(Q(K))=""
350 K=K+1
360 IF K<=J THEN 320
370 A=1
380 FOR S=1 TO LEN(K$)
390 IF MID$(K$,S,1)="-" THEN PRINT C$(A)
;:A=A+1:GOTO 410
400 PRINT MID$(K$,S,1);
410 NEXT S:PRINT,
420 K=J
430 B$(Q(K))=MID$(A$,Q(K),1)
440 Q(K)=Q(K)+1
450 IF Q(K)<=L THEN 330
460 K=K-1
470 IF K>=1 THEN 430
480 NEXT J
490 END
5000 FOR N=1 TO L
5010 B$(N)=MID$(A$,N,1)
5020 NEXT N
5030 RETURN
```

Cloze

This program arises out of research into teaching English. It allows the teacher to enter a piece of text in lines 100–200. He or she might type in:

WHEN I CAME BACK FROM MY HOLIDAY, I RAN STRAIGHT OUT INTO THE GARDEN TO SEE MY RABBIT WILLIAM

Cloze then asks for the number of words to skip before printing a set of dashes. If the teacher asked for two, it would clear the screen and print this:

WHEN I —— BACK FROM — HOLIDAY, I —— STRAIGHT OUT —— THE GARDEN — SEE MY —— WILLIAM

It then asks the student to enter the missing words one at a time. If the first one matches, it prints the sentence again up to the second space and asks again.

From the technical point of view, it is interesting mainly for the improvement to the BASIC INPUT statement in lines 100–200. Letters are taken from the keyboard one at a time with I$=INPUT$(1) and added to the current word with line 180. This means that the programmer has to cope with deletions (line 130) but also means that he can test the input for an 'end of entry' character – in this case '*', and act accordingly. In a more sophisticated program that needs full cursor control over the screen, this sort of input can test for characters used to move the cursor up, across, down, and print the appropriate code to the screen. For instance, you might want users of the program to type in CONTROL D (^D) to move the cursor down. When the input routine detects ASCII 4, it would go into a subroutine and PRINT CHR$(8), which would make the cursor go down a line. An improvement to the whole thing would be to match either upper- or lower-case letters in line 310.

It is worth puzzling over lines 270–277 to work out how Cloze rather neatly prints dashes for the letters in the hidden words.

```
10 GOSUB 1000
15 M=0
20 PRINT "CLOZE"
30 'REM    BY CHRIS HARRISON, PC JUNE 198
2
40 FOR I=1 TO 1000:NEXT
49 'REM A$ = WORDS OF TEXT; R$= STUDENT'
S RESPONSE TO FIRST AVAILABLE BLANK
50 DIM A$(200), R$(200)
59 'REM ASTERISK REQUIRED TO SHOW END
60 PRINT"WRITE YOUR TEXT IN HERE WITHOUT
 COMMAS. WHEN YOU HAVE FINISHED, ENTER A
 SPACE AND AN ASTERISK.
80 M=M+1:N=1'REM N SETS LETTERS IN THE W
ORD COUNTER
90 'REM TEXT INPUT ONE LETTER AT A TIME
100 I$=INPUT$(1) 'REM EQUIVALENT TO INKE
Y$ OR GET$
120 'REM NOW WE ALLOW FOR ERASURE. IF N<
1 WE START THE WORD AGAIN.IF BACKSPACE I
S USED THEN REVERSE THE CURSOR AND IGNOR
E THE PREVIOUS LETTER.
130 IF N<1 THEN 90 ELSE IF I$=CHR$(8) TH
EN A$(M)=LEFT$(A$(M),N-2)):N=N-1:PRINT C
HR$(8):GOTO 100
140 IF I$="" THEN 100
149 'REM SPACE NOT COUNTED AS A WORD
150 N=N+1:IF I$=" " THEN PRINT" ";:GOTO
80
159 'REM IF I$="*" THEN END TEXT
160 IF I$="*" THEN 210
169 'REM IF RETURN KEY HIT NO ACTION TAK
EN
170 IF I$ = CHR$(13) THEN 100
179 'REM EACH WORD BUILT UP FROM LETTERS
180 A$(M)=A$(M)+I$
189 'REM NOW PRINT OUT EACH LETTER
190 PRINT I$;
199 'REM REPEAT THE PROCESS
200 GOTO 100
209 'REM S IS USED FOR SPACING
210 PRINT:PRINT:PRINT:INPUT" WHAT INTERV
AL DO YOU WANT";S
219 'REM   AN ENTRY OF 3 MEANS 2 WORDS AN
D THEN A BLANK
220 S=S+1
229 'REM NOW WE'RE READY. CLEAR SCREEN O
N LINE 240
240 GOSUB 1000
269 'REM NOW PRINT A SPACE BEFORE EACH W
ORD ,THEN THE WORDS EXCEPT FOR THOSE EVE
RY S-1 WHEN WE PRINT AS MANY DASHES AS T
HERE ARE LETTERS
```

```
270 PRINT" ";:FOR I=1 TO M STEP S
272 FOR J=I TO I+S-1
275 PRINT A$(J);" ";:NEXT J
277 PRINT STRING$(LEN(A$(J)),"-");" ";:I
=I+1:NEXT I
279 'REM NOW ALLOW FOR AS MANY ANSWERS A
S THERE ARE BLANKS
280 FOR I=S+1 TO M STEP S+1
299 'REM NOW BLANK OUT THE FIRST PART OF
 THE SCREEN - WE WILL USE FOR MESSAGES A
ND ALLOW FOR ANSWERS
300 PRINT"NOW FILL IN THE BLANKS";:INPUT
 R$(I)
309 'REM IS THE ANSWER CORRECT?
310 IF R$(I)=A$(I) THEN 350
325 IF V>1 THEN PRINT"BAD LUCK. THE WORD
 IS ";A$(I); ELSE 330
326 FOR L=1 TO 300:NEXT L:GOTO 350
329 'REM IF WRONG REPLY, GIVE ANOTHER TR
Y
330 PRINT"NO, BAD LUCK, TRY AGAIN";V=V+1
:GOTO 300
349 IF THE REPLY CORRECT, REPRINT THE OR
IGINAL TEXT UP TO THE POINT REACHED
350 FOR K=1 TO I:PRINT A$(K);" ";:NEXT K
:PRINT
370 V=0:NEXT I
380 PRINT"THE  WHOLE SENTENCE WAS:":FOR
I=1 TO M:PRINT A$(I);" ";:NEXT I:PRINT
389 'REM ALLOW FOR A RERUN
390 PRINT"ANOTHER GO? (Y/N)";:INPUT R$
410 PRINT"FINISH"
1000 'REM CRUDE WAY OF CLEARING SCREEN
1010 FOR K=1 TO 24:PRINT:NEXT K
1020 RETURN
```

Life

A computer never does anything you could not do with pencil and paper – given time; but it can sometimes do it so fast that it seems to take on a life of its own. A beautiful example of this is the game of Life, invented by the British mathematician John Conway.* It is not a game in the ordinary sense because once you have set it going it 'plays' itself, but it is none the less fascinating for that.

The idea is extremely simple. The game is played on a large board of squares – held in the computer as memory bits or bytes. Each square can either be empty or hold a 'living' cell – it is 0 or 1. It has eight neighbours:

```
0  0  0
0  x  0
0  0  0
```

At each turn the computer examines each square on the board, and the following rules apply:

a cell that is dead becomes alive if it has exactly *three* live neighbours (these cells have three sexes, not two);

a cell that has four or more live neighbours is suffocated to death;

a cell with only one live neighbour – or none – dies of exposure.

*Elwyn R. Berlekamp, John H. Conway, Richard K. Guy, *Winning Ways*, Academic Press, 1982.

The player only has to start the game going with some initial arrangement of cells and stand back in amazement as 'life' takes over.

```
10 W=40:H=24:CLR$=CHR$(29)'REM YOUR SCRE
EN WIDTH, HEIGHT AND HOME
15 W=W-1:H=H-1
20 DIM A(W+2,H+2),B(W+2,H+2)
30 'REM INPUT START PATTERN ENDED BY ""
40 PRINT"Input lines of cells. Hit RETUR
N alone to finish"
45 L=0
50 INPUT A$:L=L+1
60 IF A$="" THEN 200
65 IF ML<LEN(A$) THEN ML=LEN(A$)'GET LON
GEST LINE
70 IF LEN(A$)>W THEN PRINT"too long":GOT
O 50
80 IF L>H THEN 200
90 FOR K=1 TO LEN(A$)
100 C$= MID$(A$,K,1):IF C$<>" " THEN A(K
,L)=1
110 NEXT K
115 GOTO 50
200 'REM, NOW SHIFT START PATTERN TO MID
DLE OF SCREEN
210 SW=INT((W-ML-1)/2)
220 SH=INT(H-L-1)/2)
230 FOR K=1 TO ML
240 FOR J=1 TO L
250 B(K+SW,J+SH)=A(K,J)
260 NEXT J
270 NEXT K
280 GOSUB 10000
300 'REM NOW DO A GENERATION FROM B TO A
310 POP=0
320 FOR K=1 TO H
330 FOR J=1 TO W
340 N=0:C=B(J,K)'REM ZERO NEIGHBOUR COUN
T, SAVE CELL VALUE
370 N=B(J-1,K-1)+B(J,K-1)+B(J+1,K-1)+B(J
-1,K)+B(J+1,K)+B(J-1,K+1)+B(J,K+1)+B(J+1
,K+1)'REM COUNT UP NEIGHBOURS
410 GOSUB 30000
420 A(J,K)=NXT:POP=POP+1'REM PUT NEXT GE
NERATION INTO A
430 NEXT J
440 NEXT K
450 IF POP=0 THEN STOP
460 GOSUB 20000
490 'REM NOW PUT GENERATION INTO B
500 POP=0
510 FOR K=1 TO H
520 FOR J=1 TO W
530 N=0:C=B(J,K)
540 N=A(J-1,K-1)+A(J,K-1)+A(J+1,K-1)+A(J
-1,K)+A(J+1,K)+A(J-1,K+1)+A(J,K+1)+A(J+1
,K+1)
550 GOSUB 30000
555 B(J,K)=NXT:POP=POP+1
560 NEXT J
570 NEXT K
580 IF POP=0 THEN STOP
590 GOSUB 10000
600 GOTO 300
10000 'REM SUBROUTINE TO DISPLAY ARRAY B
10005 PRINT CLR$;
10010 FOR K=1 TO H
10020 FOR J=1 TO W
10030 IF B(J,K)=1 THEN PRINT"*"; ELSE PR
INT" ";
10035 'PRINT B(K,J);
10040 NEXT J
10050 PRINT
10060 NEXT K
10070 RETURN
20000 'REM SUBROUTINE TO PRINT ARRAY A
20005 PRINT CLR$;
20010 FOR K=1 TO H
```

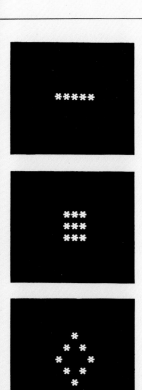

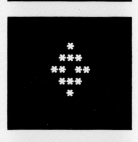

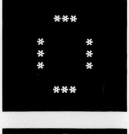

```
20020 FOR J=1 TO W
20030 IF A(J,K)=1 THEN PRINT"*"; ELSE PR
INT" ";
20035 'PRINT A(J,K);
20040 NEXT J
20050 PRINT
20060 NEXT K
20070 RETURN
30000 'REM DO DECISION
30010 IF N<2 OR N>3 THEN NXT=0:GOTO 3010
0'REM DEATH BY LONELINESS OR OVERCROWDIN
G
30020 IF C=0 AND N=3 THEN NXT=1:GOTO 301
00'REM BIRTH
30030 NXT=C'REM NO CHANGE
30100 RETURN
```

Let us examine a sequence (right) more closely. What happened was this:

1. The two end cells in 1 died, but three more arose on each side because they each had three live neighbours.

2. The corners survive because they have three neighbours, but everything else dies of overcrowding.

3–6. The ring succeeds too well, and all the cells in the middle die off. Four sets of 'blinkers' are left. A blinker is three cells in a line: the end two die off from exposure, but two more are born on each side, so the line switches from vertical to horizontal to vertical again – for ever. The configuration of four blinkers is called a 'traffic lights'.

Fans of Life have identified a number of patterns like this which repeat cyclically. A more interesting shape is the 'glider', a pattern that walks, moving a square up and a square along every four generations. To make this easier to see, we've made it move horizontally:

```
X . .      . X .      X X .      . X .      . X
. X . .    X X . .    . . X .    . . X .    . . X
. X .      . X .      . X .      X X .      . . X
X X .      . X .      . X .      . X .      X X
 0          1          2          3          4
```

There is a rather complicated pattern called a 'glider gun', which will shoot a stream of gliders out, one every thirty generations. In what seems at first a most perverse intellectual exercise, Conway has made use of this to design a computer which uses, not electrical pulses running along wires as its raw material, but gliders moving inside a computer. A glider represents a 1, the absence of a glider represents a 0. If they bang into one another in the right way they eliminate each other, so it is possible to make a NOT gate. More complicated arrangements can make two streams of gliders interact as if there were AND and OR gates. Another configuration will 'eat' gliders, so that surplus bits can be disposed of.

Given all this, one has the raw material for a computer – albeit a computer made of symbols operating inside a hardware computer, but a computer none the less.

Noughts and Crosses

'NANDC' = Noughts AND Crosses – simple when you know. The training robot shown on pages 140-41 can be regarded as a 'display routine' for this sort of program. Instead of painting Os and Xs on the screen, the robot manipulates draughts pieces on a real board.

```
10 REM *************************
20 REM NOUGHTS AND CROSSES
30 REM *************************
40 DIM T(8,3)
50 DIM U(9,4)
60 DIM C(9),B(9)
70 PRINT CHR$(12)
80 PRINT "*** NOUGHTS AND CROSSES ***"
90 PRINT
100 PRINT "YOU ARE 'X', THE COMPUTER IS
'O'"
110 PRINT "BELIEVE IT OR NOT, YOU CAN WI
N!"
120 X1=0:X2=0
130 REM INIT TABLES P AND U
140 FOR P=1 TO 8
150 FOR I=1 TO 3
160 READ T(P,I)
170 NEXT I
180 NEXT P
190 DATA 1,2,3
200 DATA 8,9,4
210 DATA 7,6,5
220 DATA 1,8,7
230 DATA 2,9,6
240 DATA 3,4,5
250 DATA 1,9,5
260 DATA 7,9,3
270 FOR S=1 TO 9
280 FOR J=1 TO 4
290 READ U(S,J)
300 NEXT J
310 NEXT S
320 DATA 1,4,7,0
330 DATA 1,5,0,0
340 DATA 1,6,8,0
350 DATA 2,6,0,0
360 DATA 3,6,7,0
370 DATA 3,5,0,0
380 DATA 3,4,8,0
390 DATA 2,4,0,0
400 DATA 2,5,7,8
410 REM HERE FOR A NEW GAME
420 LET N=0
430 FOR S=1 TO 9
440 LET C(S)=0
450 LET B(S)=0
460 NEXT S
470 REM FLIP COIN FOR WHO STARTS
480 IF RND(1) < .5 THEN 510
490 PRINT "YOU HAVE THE FIRST GO"
500 GOTO 530
510 PRINT "THE COMPUTER HAS FIRST GO"
520 GOTO 760
530 REM PLAYER'S MOVE
540 GOSUB 1230
550 INPUT "YOUR GO";M
560 LET F=-1
570 IF M=INT(M) THEN 600
580 PRINT "ILLEGAL MOVE--TRY AGAIN"
590 GOTO 530
600 IF M<1 OR M>9 THEN 580
610 IF B(M) <> 0 THEN 580
620 REM UPDATE LISTS C, CHECK FOR WIN
630 LET B(M)=F
640 FOR J=1 TO 4
650 LET P=U(M,J)
660 IF P=0 THEN 700
```

```
670 LET C(P)=C(P)+F
680 IF C(P)=-3 THEN GOSUB 1230:GOTO 900
690 IF C(P)=3 THEN GOSUB 1230:GOTO 800
700 NEXT J
710 LET N=N+1
720 IF N=9 THEN GOSUB 1230:GOTO 930
730 IF F=1 THEN 530
740 REM COMPUTER'S MOVE
750 GOSUB 1230
760 GOSUB 950
770 PRINT "THE COMPUTER'S MOVE IS:"
780 LET F=1
790 GOTO 620
800 REM GAME OVER
810 PRINT "AND THE COMPUTER WINS"
820 X2=X2+1
830 PRINT
840 PRINT"SCORE NOW--COMPUTER";X2;", YOU
    ";X1
850 INPUT "TYPE 'YES' FOR ANOTHER GAME";
    A$
860 IF A$<>"YES" THEN STOP
870 PRINT
880 PRINT "NEW GAME"
890 GOTO265
900 PRINT "YOU BEAT THE COMPUTER"
910 X1=X1+1
920 GOTO 830
930 PRINT "THE GAME IS A DRAW"
940 GOTO 830
950 REM SELECT A MOVE
960 FOR P=1 TO 8
970 IF C(P)=2 THEN 1030
980 NEXT P
990 FOR P=1 TO 8
1000 IF C(P)=-2 THEN 1030
1010 NEXT P
1020 GOTO 1070
1030 FOR I=1 TO 3
1040 LET M=T(P,I)
1050 IF B(M)=0 THEN 1220
1060 NEXT I
1070 FOR S=1 TO 9
1080 LET V(S)=0
1090 IF B(S)<>0 THEN 1150
1100 FOR J=1 TO 4
1110 LET P=U(S,J)
1120 IF P=0 THEN 1140
1130 LET V(S)=V(S)+1+ABS(C(P))
1140 NEXT J
1150 NEXT S
1160 LET V=0
1170 FOR S=1 TO 9
1180 IF V(S)<=V THEN 1210
1190 LET V=V(S)
1200 LET M=S
1210 NEXT S
1220 RETURN
1230 REM PRINT BOARD
1240 PRINT
1250 PRINT" 1  2  3"; TAB(15);
1260 FOR A=1 TO 3
1270 GOSUB 1410
1280 NEXT A
1290 PRINT:PRINT
1300 PRINT " 8  9  4";TAB(15);
1310 A=8:GOSUB 1410
1320 A=9:GOSUB 1410
1330 A=4:GOSUB 1410
1340 PRINT:PRINT
1350 PRINT " 7  6  5";TAB(15);
1360 FOR A=7 TO 5 STEP -1
1370 GOSUB 1410
1380 NEXT A
1390 PRINT:PRINT
1400 RETURN
1410 IF B(A)=0 THEN PRINT".  ";:RETURN
1420 IF B(A)=-1 THEN PRINT"X  ";:RETURN
1430 PRINT"O  ";:RETURN
```

Zombies

Zombies is a very silly game. You try to sidestep the horrid creatures so that they run into pillars, knock themselves out and self-destruct; otherwise they get you, a protein lunch.

```
10 REM ********************
20 REM      ZOMBIES
30 REM ********************
40 REM 'GRAPH1' TURNS PLOTTING ON
50 REM 'GRAPH0' TURNS IT OFF
60 REM 'PLOT X,Y,Z' PUTS THE CHARACTER W
   ITH ASCIII CODE Z AT X,Y
70 CLEAR 1000
80 PRINT CHR$(12):GOSUB 640
90 GRAPH1
100 CLEAR
110 DIM B(12,22),Z(25,2),P(8),Q(8)
120 FOR N1=1 TO 8
130 READ P(N1),Q(N1)
140 NEXT N1
150 DATA 1,-1,1,0,1,1,0,1,-1,1,-1,0,-1,-
    1,0,-1
160 PLOT 74,57,53
170 PLOT 76,57,52
180 PLOT 78,57,51
190 PLOT 74,54,54
200 PLOT 76,54,88
210 PLOT 78,54,50
220 PLOT 74,51,55
230 PLOT 76,51,56
240 PLOT 78,51,49
250 FOR N1=1 TO 25
260 FOR N2=1 TO 2
270 Z(N1,N2)=0
280 NEXT N2
290 NEXT N1
300 Z1=0
310 FOR N1=1 TO 12
320 FOR N2=1 TO 22
330 B(N1,N2)=4
340 PLOT N2*2,N1*3,143
350 NEXT N2
360 NEXT N1
370 FOR N1=2 TO 11
380 FOR N2=2 TO 21
390 R =20*RND(10)
400 IF R>18.5 THEN GOTO 500
410 IF R<17.95 THEN GOTO 480
420 Z1=Z1+1
430 Z(Z1,1)=N1
440 Z(Z1,2)=N2
450 B(N1,N2)=2
460 PLOTN2*2,N1*3,ASC("Z")
470 GOTO 500
480 B(N1,N2)=1
490 PLOTN2*2,N1*3,ASC(" ")
500 NEXT N2
510 NEXT N1
520 X=5+INT(10*RND(15))
530 Y=3+INT(5*RND(15))
540 B(Y,X)=3
550 PLOTX*2,Y*3,ASC("X")
560 FOR N1=Y-1 TO Y+1
570 FOR N2=X-1 TO X+1
580 IF ABS(Y-N1)+ABS(X-N2)=0 THEN GOTO 6
    10
590 B(N1,N2)=1
600 PLOTN2*2,N1*3,ASC(" ")
610 NEXT N2
620 NEXT N1
630 GOTO 770
640 PRINT"You have just landed on ZOMBIE
    ISLAND"
650 PRINT
660 PRINT" Your only hope of survival i
   s to lure"
```

```
670 PRINT"all the ZOMBIES into potholes.
 You may"
680 PRINT"indicate the direction of your
 move"
690 PRINT"as follows:"
700 PRINT
710 PRINT"543"
720 PRINT"6X2"
730 PRINT"781":PRINT:PRINT
740 INPUT"Hit RETURN to continue";AA$
750 PRINT CHR$(12)
760 RETURN
770 REM
780 FOR N1=1 TO Z1
790 IFB(Z(N1,1),Z(N1,2))=2 THEN GOTO860
800 FOR N2=N1 TO Z1
810 Z(N2,1)=Z(N2+1,1)
820 Z(N2,2)=Z(N2+1,2)
830 NEXT N2
840 Z1=Z1-1
850 GOTO 780
860 NEXT N1
870 PRINT
880 PRINT"  Your move";
890 INPUT A
900 IF A>8 THEN GOTO 920
910 IF A>=1 THEN GOTO 940
920 PRINT"Please use a number between 1
and 8"
930 GOTO 880
940 B(Y,X)=1
950 PLOTX*2,Y*3,ASC(" ")
960 Y=Y+Q(A)
970 X=X+P(A)
980 ON B(Y,X) GOTO 990,1020,990,1040
990 B(Y,X)=3
1000 PLOTX*2,Y*3,ASC("X")
1010 GOTO 1060
1020 PRINT"MMMMM TASTY!--Munch Munch--PR
OTOPLASM!"
1030 GOTO 1430
1040 PRINT"aaaaargh KASPLUTCH Right into
 the pit---";
1050 GOTO 1430
1060 Z2=1
1070 Z8=Z(Z2,1)
1080 Z9=Z(Z2,2)
1090 B(Z8,Z9)=1
1100 PLOT Z9*2,Z8*3,ASC(" ")
1110 Z8=Z8+SGN(Y-Z8)
1120 Z9=Z9+SGN(X-Z9)
1130 ON B(Z8,Z9) GOTO 1320,1280,1210,114
0
1140 PRINT"KERSPLOSH---Goes a ZOMBIE"
1150 FOR Z3=Z2 TO Z1
1160 Z(Z3,1)=Z(Z3+1,1)
1170 Z(Z3,2)=Z(Z3+1,2)
1180 NEXT Z3
1190 Z1=Z1-1
1200 GOTO 1370
1210 PLOT X*2,Y*3,42
1220 FOR MN=0 TO 150
1230 NEXT MN
1240 PLOT X*2,Y*3,32
1250 PLOT X*2,Y*3,ASC("Z")
1260 PRINT"The ZOMBIES get lunch after a
ll!"
1270 GOTO 1430
1280 PRINT"EEK!--Here come the ZOMBIES!!
";
1290 B(Z(Z2,1),Z(Z2,2))=2
1300 PLOTZ(Z2,2)*2,Z(Z2,1)*3,ASC("Z")
1310 GOTO 1360
1320 B(Z8,Z9)=2
1330 PLOT Z9*2,Z8*3,ASC("Z")
1340 Z(Z2,1)=Z8
1350 Z(Z2,2)=Z9
1360 Z2=Z2+1
1370 IF Z2<=Z1 THEN GOTO 1070
1380 IF Z1>=1 THEN GOTO 870
1390 PRINT
1400 PRINT"Well done!---You escaped---Th
e"
1410 PRINT"ZOMBIES are extinct."
1420 GOSUB 1550
1430 PRINT" Another game ";
1440 REM
1450 INPUT A$
1460 IF A$="Y" OR A$="YES" THEN PRINT CH
R$(12): GOTO 90
1470 IF A$="N" OR A$="NO" THEN 1520
1480 PRINT"Please answer YES or NO":GOTO
 1430
1490 GRAPH0
1500 RUN
1510 GOTO 1430
1520 GRAPH0
1530 PRINT CHR$(12)
1540 END
1550 FOR J=X+1 TO 79
1560 FOR HJ=0 TO 1
1570 PLOT J*2,Y*3,ASC("X")
1580 PLOT (J-1)*2,Y*3,ASC(" ")
1590 IF J*2>=78 THEN 1620
1600 NEXT HJ
1610 NEXT J
1620 PLOT J*2,Y*3,ASC(" ")
1630 RETURN
```

Star Voyage

This version of a venerable space adventure program is so big that it will almost certainly need at least a 56-K machine.

```
1 CLEAR 1000
10 REM
20 LQ=1000
30 INPUT"NUMBER(1 TO 2500)";I
40 IFI<1ORI>25000ORI<>INT(I)THEN30
50 I1=IMOD97:IFI1=0THENI=I+199
60 I=RND(-I1):FORI1=1TOI:X=RND(1):NEXT
70 DIM G1$(16),V$(5,5),C$(20),G(8,8),D$(
12),Q$(10,10),D4(12),D9(106)
80 DIM S2(8,8):Q$="?"
90 DATA S.R. SENSORS,L.R. SENSORS,PHASER
S,PHOTON TUBES,LIFE SUPPORT
100 DATA WARP ENGINES,IMPULSE ENGINES,SH
IELDS,SUBSPACE RADIO
110 DATA SHUTTLE CRAFT,COMPUTER,TRANSFER
 PANEL,ABANDON,CHART,COMPUTER
120 DATA DAMAGES,DESTRUCT,DOCK,IDLE,IMPU
LSE,LRSCAN,NAVIGATE,PHASERS,QUIT
130 DATA SHIELDS,SOS,SRSCAN,STATUS,TORPE
DO,TRANSFER,VISUAL,WARP,SHORT
140 DATA MEDIUM,LONG,BEGINNER,NOVICE,SEN
IOR,EXPERT,COURSE,WCOST,ICOST
150 DATA PEFFECT,OUT,ANTARES,SIRIUS,RIGE
L,MERAK,PROCYON,CAPELLA
160 DATA VEGA,DENEB,CANOPUS,ALDEBARAN,AL
TAIR,REGULUS,BELLATRIX,ARCTURUS
170 DATA POLLUX,SPICA,10.5,12,1.5,9,0,3,
7.5,6,4.5
180 DEF FNA(X)=INT(8*RND(X))+1:DEF FNB(X
)=INT(10*RND(X))+1
190 DEF FND(X)=X/60
200 DEFFNR(X)=INT(X*10+.5)/10:DEFFNS(X)=
INT(X*100+.5)/100
210 FORI=1TO12:READD$(I):NEXT:FORI=1TO20
:READC$(I):NEXT
220 FORI=1TO3:READT$(I):NEXT:FORI=1TO4:R
EADS$(I):NEXT:FORI=1TO5
230 READC2$(I):NEXT:FORI=1TO16:READG1$(I
):NEXT:FORI=1TO9:READC5(I):NEXT
240 GOSUB9760:S7$(1)="":S7$(2)="  ":S7$(
3)=" ":S7$(4)=""
250 IFA2<>0THEN760
260 J4=0:T1=0:INPUT"COMMAND";A$:?:?:GRAP
```

```
H1:GRAPH0:IF A$="ST" THEN AL=1:AL(1)=1:G
OSUB11150:AL(1)=0:AL=0:GOTO260ELSEIF LEN
(A$)>1 THEN 280
270 ?"2 LTRS":GOTO260
280 FORI=1TO20
290 IFA$=LEFT$(C$(I),LEN(A$))THEN350
300 NEXT
320 ?:FORI=1TO20STEP4
330 ?C$(I);TAB(12);C$(I+1);TAB(22);C$(I+
2);TAB(32);C$(I+3)
340 NEXTI:?:GOTO250
350 ONIGOTO370,380,390,400,410,420,430,4
70,490,500
360 ONI-10GOTO530,760,550,580,590,600,61
0,620,660,670
370 GOSUB 12310:GOTO250
380 GOSUB 2020:GOTO250
390 GOSUB2540:GOTO250
400 GOSUB3540:GOTO250
410 GOSUB12550:GOTO250
420 GOSUB3430:GOTO250
430 GOSUB11700:IFJ3=0THEN250
440 IFA2<>0THEN760
450 IFG(Q1,Q2)=1000THEN720
460 GOSUB790:GOTO250
470 GOSUB5390:IFJ3=0THEN250
480 GOTO680
490 GOSUB5650:GOTO250
500 GOSUB11830
510 IFJ3=0THEN250
520 GOTO680
530 GOSUB8270:IFJ3=0THEN250
540 GOSUB790:GOTO250
550 GOSUB10370:IFJ3=0THEN250
560 IFA2<>0THEN760
570 GOSUB790:S9=0:GOTO250
580 GOSUB4720:GOTO250
590 GOSUB11090:GOSUB5650:GOTO250
600 ?:GOSUB12770:GOTO250
610 GOSUB8660:IFJ3=0THEN250ELSE680
620 GOSUB11560:IFJ3=0THEN250
630 IFA2<>0THEN760
640 IFG(Q1,Q2)<>LQTHEN250
650 GOTO720
660 ?"NO VIS":GOTO 260
670 GOSUB10210:GOTO250
680 IFA2<>0THEN760
690 IFT1<>0THENGOSUB3640
700 IFA2<>0THEN760
710 IFG(Q1,Q2)<LQTHEN750
720 GOSUB1580:IFA2<>0THEN760
730 IFA2<>0THEN760
740 GOTO710
750 GOSUB790:GOTO250
760 INPUT"AGAIN";A$
770 IFLEFT$(A$,1)="Y"THEN240
780 ?CHR$(26):END
790 IF(C3<>0)AND(J4=0)THENGOSUB6620
800 IFK3=0THENRETURN
810 IFA2<>0THENRETURN
820 P2=1/I8
830 J5=0
840 ?
850 IFC5$="DOCKED"THEN1530
860 H2=0:H3=0:C6=1
870 IFS9=1THENC6=.5+.5*RND(1)
880 A3=0
890 FORL=1TOK3
900 IFK6(L)<0THEN1320
910 A3=1
920 D6=.8+.05*RND(1)
930 H4=K6(L)*D6^K8(L)
940 IF(S4=0)AND(S9=0)THEN1000
950 P3=.1:IFP2*S3>P3THENP3=P2*S3
960 H5=P3*C6*H4+1
970 IFH5>S3THENH5=S3
980 S3=S3-H5:H4=H4-H5
990 IF(P3>.1)AND(H4<5E-03*E1)THEN1320
1000 J5=1
1010 ?FNR(H4);"HIT ON ";S5$;" FROM ";
1020 J6=K4(L):J7=K5(L)
1030 IFQ$(J6,J7)="K"THEN?"KLING AT";
1040 IFQ$(J6,J7)="C"THEN?"CMNDR AT";
1050 ?J6;"-";J7
1060 IFH4>H2THENH2=H4
1070 H3=H3+H4
1080 IFH4<(275-25*S8)*(1+.5*RND(1))THEN1
310
1090 N4=1+INT(H4/(500+100*RND(1)))
1100 ?"CRIT. HIT";
1110 K9=1
1120 FORW4=1TON4
1130 J9=INT(12*RND(1))+1
1140 C5(W4)=J9
1150 E3=(H4*D5)/(N4*(75+25*RND(1)))
1160 IFJ9=6THENE3=E3/3
1170 D4(J9)=D4(J9)+E3
1180 IFW4=1THEN1250
1190 FORV=1TOW4
1200 IFJ9=C5(V-1)THEN1260
1210 NEXTV
1220 K9=K9+1
1230 IFK9=3THEN?
1240 ? " AND ";
1250 ?D$(J9);
1260 NEXTW4
1270 ? " DMGED."
1280 IFD4(8)=0THEN1310
1290 IFS4<>0THEN?"SHLDS DOWN."
1300 S4=0
1310 E1=E1-H4
1320 NEXTL
1330 IFA3=0THENRETURN
1340 IFE1<=0THEN1510
1350 P4=100*P2*S3+.5
1360 IFJ5<>0THEN1390
1370 ?"SHLDS DWN TO ";
1380 GOTO1430
1390 ?"ENRGY:";FNS(E1);"   SHLDS ";
1400 IFS4<>0THEN?"UP,";
1410 IF(S4=0)AND(D4(8)=0)THEN?"DWN, ";
1420 IFD4(8)>0THEN?"DMGD, ";
1430 ?INT(P4);"%"
1440 IF(H2<200)AND(H3<500)THEN1540
1450 J8=INT(H3*RND(1)*.015)
1460 IFJ8<2THEN1540
1470 ?
1480 ?"SUFED ";J8;"CAS."
1490 C4=C4+J8
1500 GOTO1540
1510 F9=5
1520 GOSUB4710:RETURN
1530 ?"BASE HELPS ";S5$
1540 FORW4=1TOK3
1550 K8(W4)=K7(W4)
1560 NEXTW4
1570 GOSUB10980:RETURN
1580 ?:IFJ4=0THEN1610
1590 ?"R ALERT"
1600 ?S5$;" NEAR SPNOVA"
1610 ? "TRYING TO MOVE ";S5$;" ELSEWHERE
"
1620 S2(Q1,Q2)=1
1630 GOSUB7260
1640 IFD4(6)=0THEN1830
1650 ?
1660 ?"WARPS DMGD."
1670 ?"IMPULSE"
1680 IFD4(7)=0THEN1730
1690 ?"IMP DMGED."
1700 F9=8
1710 GOSUB4710
1720 RETURN
1730 P2=.75*E1
1740 D6=4E-03*(P2-50)
1750 D7=1.4142+1.2*RND(1)
1760 D1=D6
1770 IFD6>D7THEND1=D7
1780 T1=D1/.4
1790 D2=12*RND(1)
```

```
1800 J4=0
1810 GOSUB5590
1820 GOTO1940
1830 W1=6+2*RND(1)
1840 W2=W1*W1
1850 P2=.75*E1
1860 D6=P2/(W1*W1*W1*(S4+1))
1870 D7=1.4142+2*RND(1)
1880 D1=D6
1890 IFD6>D7THEND1=D7
1900 T1=10*D1/W2
1910 D2=12*RND(1)
1920 J4=0
1930 GOSUB12040
1940 IFJ4<>0THEN1980
1950 F9=8
1960 GOSUB4710
1970 RETURN
1980 IFR1<>0THENRETURN
1990 F9=1
2000 GOSUB4710
2010 RETURN
2020 ?CHR$(12):?"        1   2   3   4   5
   6   7   8"
2030 ?"        --- --- --- --- --- --- ---
---"
2040 FORI=1TO8
2050 ?I;" ";
2060 FORJ=1TO8
2070 ONSGN(S2(I,J))+2GOTO2080,2100,2120
2080 ?" .1.";
2090 GOTO 2170
2100 ?" ...";
2110 GOTO2170
2120 IFS2(I,J)>LQTHEN2160
2130 IFG(I,J)<LQTHEN?S7$(LEN(STR$(G(I,J)
)));STR$(G(I,J));
2140 IFG(I,J)=LQTHEN?" ***";
2150 GOTO2170
2160 ?S2(I,J)-LQ;
2170 NEXTJ:?:?:NEXTI:GOSUB7550:?:?
2180 ?S5$;" IN ";G2$;" (";Q1;"-";Q2;")"
2190 RETURN
2200 ?CHR$(26)
2210 S8=0:L2=0
2220 ?"MISSION LENGTH";
2230 INPUTA$
2240 FOR I=1TO3
2250 IFA$=LEFT$(T$(I),LEN(A$))THEN2290
2260 NEXTI
2270 ?"SHORT,MEDIUM OR LONG";
2280 GOTO2230
2290 L2=I
2300 ?"BEGINER,NOVICE,SENIOR OR EXPERT";

2310 INPUTA$
2320 FORI=1TO4
2330 IFA$=LEFT$(S$(I),LEN(A$))THEN2360
2340 NEXTI
2350 GOTO2300
2360 S8=I
2370 INPUT"MISSION PASSWORD";X$:?
2380 ?CHR$(12)
2390 J=RND(1)
2400 D5=.5*S8:I2=INT(L2+1+RND(1)*3)
2410 IFI2>5THENI2=5
2420 R3=I2
2430 I5=7*L2
2440 R5=I5
2450 R7=(S8-2*RND(1)+1)*S8*.1+.1
2460 IFR7<.2THENR7=R7+.1
2470 I1=INT(2*R7*I5)
2480 R1=I1
2490 I4=INT(S8+.0625*I1*RND(1))
2500 R2=I4
2510 I3=(I1+4*I4)*I5
2520 R4=I3
2530 RETURN
2540 IFD4(11)=0THEN2570
2550 ?"NO COMP"
2560 RETURN
2570 ?"COMP OK"
2580 INPUT"PROG NME";B$
2590 FORI=1TO6
2600 IFB$=LEFT$(C2$(I),LEN(B$))THEN2660
2605 IF B$="OU" THEN 260
2610 NEXT
2620 ?"PROGS:"
2630 ?"  COURSE    WCOST    OUT"
2640 ?"  PEFFECT   ICOST"
2650 GOTO2580
2660 ON IGOTO2670,2910,2980,3040,2580,31
10
2670 INPUT "QUAD,SECT";A3,A4
2680 IF(A3<>INT(A3))OR(A4<>INT(A4))THEN3
120
2690 IFA3<0THEN2580
2700 IFA3=0THENA3=10*Q1+Q2
2710 A3=A3+.5
2720 K=INT(A3/10)
2730 IF(K<1)OR(K>8)THEN3120
2740 C6(1)=K:K=INT(A3-C6(1)*10)
2750 IF(K<1)OR(K>8)THEN3120
2760 C6(2)=K:A4=A4+.5
2770 K=INT(A4/100)
2780 IF(K<1)OR(K>10)THEN3120
2790 C6(1)=C6(1)+(K-1)/10:K=INT(A4-K*100
)
2800 IF(K<1)OR(K>10)THEN3120
2810 C6(2)=C6(2)+(K-1)/10
2820 X=Q1+((S6-1)/10)-C6(1):Y=Q2+((S7-1)
/10)-C6(2)
2830 D1=0:D2=0:IF(X=0)AND(Y=0)THEN2890
2840 D1=SQR(X*X+Y*Y)
2850 IFX<0THENZ7=SGN(Y)*(3.1416-ATN(ABS(
Y/X)))
2860 IFX=0THENZ7=SGN(Y)*1.5708
2870 IFX>0THENZ7=ATN(Y/X)
2880 D2=12-Z7*1.9098593:IFD2>12THEND2=D2
-12
2890 ?"COURSE: ";FNS(D2);" FOR";
2900 ?FNS(D1);"QUADS.":GOTO2580
2910 INPUT"DIST,WARP";D1,A4
2920 IF(D1<0)THEN2580
2930 C7=D1*A4*A4*A4
2940 T1=(10*D1)/((A4*A4)+1E-05)
2950 ?"TIME: ";FNS(T1);"DATES"
2960 ?"ENRGY: ";FNR(C7);"UNITS (";FNR(C7
+C7);"IF SHLDS UP)"
2970 GOTO2580
2980 INPUT"DIST";D1
2990 IFD1<0THEN2580
3000 C7=250*D1+50:T1=D1/.4
3010 ?"TIME: ";FNR(T1);"DATES"
3020 ?"ENRGY: ";C7;"UNITS"
3030 GOTO2580
3040 INPUT"RANGE IN QUADS";A3
3050 IFA3<0THEN2580
3060 A3=A3*10:C7=(.9^A3)*100
3070 ?"PHSRS ";LEFT$(STR$(C7),5);"% EFFE
CTIVE AT THAT RANGE"
3080 GOTO2580
3090 GOSUB9750
3100 GOTO2580
3110 RETURN
3120 ?"FORM IS MN,XXYY...MN IS QUAD"
3130 ?"XXYY IS SECT...E.G. 64,0307 REFER
S"
3140 ?"TO QUAD 6-4, SECT 3-7."
3150 GOTO 2580
3160 IFT2$<>"C"THEN3250
3170 C3=0:?"CMNDR AT";
3180 FORF=1TOR2:IF(C1(F)=Q1)AND(C2(F)=Q2
)THEN3200
3190 NEXTF
3200 C1(F)=C1(R2):C2(F)=C2(R2):C1(R2)=0:
C2(R2)=0
3210 R2=R2-1:F1(2)=1E+30
3220 IFR2<>0THENF1(2)=D0-(I4/R2)*LOG(RND
(1))
```

```
3230 K2=K2+1
3240 GOTO3270
3250 ?"KLING AT";
3260 K1=K1+1
3270 ?A5;"-";A6;"DEAD"
3280 Q$(A5,A6)=".":R1=R1-1
3290 IFR1=0THENRETURN
3300 R5=R4/(R1+4*R2)
3310 G(Q1,Q2)=G(Q1,Q2)-100
3320 FORF=1TOK3
3330 IF(K4(F)=A5)AND(K5(F)=A6)THEN3350
3340 NEXTF
3350 K3=K3-1
3360 IFF>K3THEN3410
3370 FORG=FTOK3
3380 K4(G)=K4(G+1):K5(G)=K5(G+1):K6(G)=K
6(G+1)
3390 K7(G)=K7(G+1):K8(G)=K7(G)
3400 NEXTG
3410 K4(K3+1)=0:K5(K3+1)=0:K7(K3+1)=0:K8
(K3+1)=0:K6(K3+1)=0
3420 RETURN
3430 IFC5$="DOCKED"THEN3520
3440 IFB6=0THEN3460
3450 IF(ABS(S6-B6)<=1)AND(ABS(S7-B7)<=1)
THEN3480
3460 ?S5$;" NOT NEAR BASE."
3470 RETURN
3480 C5$="DOCKED"
3490 ?"DCKD"
3500 E1=I7:S3=I8:T4=9:L1=J1
3510 RETURN
3520 ?"ALREADY DCKD!"
3530 RETURN
3540 J=0:?:FORI=1TO12
3550 IFD4(I)<=0THEN3600
3560 IFJ<>0THEN3590
3570 ?"     DEVICE";SPC(12);"-REPAIR TIM
ES-"
3580 ?SPC(21);"IN FLIGHT    DOCKED":J=1
3581 ?SPC(21);"---------    ------"
3590 ?"  ";D$(I);TAB(23);FNS(D4(I));TAB(
33);FNS(D3*D4(I))
3600 NEXTI
3610 ?TAB(23);"VIS PERM DMGED"
3620 IFJ=0THEN?"ALL DEVS (EXPT VIS) FUNC
T"
3630 RETURN
3640 M=0:D7=D0+T1:FORL=1TO5
3650 IFF1(L)>D7THEN3670
3660 M=L:D7=F1(L)
3670 NEXTL
3680 X6=D7-D0:D0=D7
3690 R4=R4-(R1+4*R2)*X6
3700 R5=R4/(R1+4*R2)
3710 IFR5>0THEN3750
3720 F9=2
3730 GOSUB4710
3740 RETURN
3750 IF(D4(5)=0)OR(C5$="DOCKED")THEN3810
3760 IF(L1>=X6)OR(D4(5)<=L1)THEN3790
3770 F9=3:GOSUB4710
3780 RETURN
3790 L1=L1-X6
3800 IFD4(5)<=X6THENL1=J1
3810 R=X6
3820 IFC5$="DOCKED"THENR=X6/D3
3830 FORL=1TO12
3840 IFD4(L)<=0THEN3890
3850 D4(L)=D4(L)-R
3860 IFD4(L)<0THEND4(L)=0
3870 IFD4(L)<>0THEN3890
3880 ?"DMGE CONTROL ";D$(L);" NOW OK"
3890 NEXTL
3900 IFM=0THENRETURN
3910 T1=T1-X6
3920 ONMGOTO3930,3970,4190,4280,4450
3930 X2=0:Y2=0:GOSUB10520
3940 F1(1)=D0-.5*I5*LOG(RND(1))
3950 IFG(Q1,Q2)=LQTHENRETURN
3960 GOTO3640
3970 IFR2=0THEN4180
3980 IFC5$="DOCKED"THEN4160
3990 I=INT(RND(1)*R2)+1
4000 Y6=(C1(I)-Q1)^2+(C2(I)-Q2)^2
4010 IFY6=0THEN4160
4020 Y6=SQR(Y6):T1=.17778*Y6
4030 ?S5$;" CAUGHT IN L.R. TRACT BEAM--"
4040 Q1=C1(I):Q2=C2(I)
4050 S6=FNB(1):S7=FNB(1)
4060 ?"PULLED TO QUAD";Q1;"-";Q2;", SECT
";S6;"-";S7
4070 IFR6<>0THEN?"(IDLE CNCLD)"
4080 R6=0
4090 IFS4<>0THEN4150
4100 IF(D4(8)=0)AND(S3>0)THEN4130
4110 ?"(SHLDS OUT)"
4120 GOTO4150
4130 GOSUB10390
4140 S9=0
4150 GOSUB7260
4160 F1(2)=D0+T1-1.5*(I5/R2)*LOG(RND(1))
4170 GOTO3640
4180 F1(2)=1E+30:GOTO3640
4190 D9(1)=D0:D9(2)=R1:D9(3)=R2:D9(4)=R3
:D9(5)=R4:D9(6)=R5
4200 D9(7)=S1:D9(8)=B1:D9(9)=K1:D9(10)=K
2
4210 FORI=1TO8:FORJ=1TO8:D9(I-1+8*(J-1)+
11)=G(I,J):NEXTJ:NEXTI
4220 FORI=75TO84:D9(I)=C1(I-74):NEXT
4230 FORI=85TO94:D9(I)=C2(I-84):NEXT
4240 FORI=95TO99:D9(I)=B2(I-94):NEXT
4250 FORI=100TO104:D9(I)=B3(I-99):NEXT
4260 D9(105)=B4:D9(106)=B5
4270 S0=1:F1(3)=D0-.3*I5*LOG(RND(1)):GOT
O3640
4280 IF(R2=0)OR(R3=0)THEN4330
4290 FORI=1TOR3:FORJ=1TOR2:IF(B2(I)=C1(J
))AND(B3(I)=C2(J))THEN4340
4300 NEXTJ:NEXTI
4310 F1(4)=D0+.5+3*RND(1)
4320 F1(5)=1E+30:GOTO3640
4330 F1(4)=1E+30:F1(5)=1E+30:GOTO3640
4340 B4=B2(I):B5=B3(I)
4350 IF(B4=Q1)AND(B5=Q2)THEN4310
4360 F1(5)=D0+.5+3*RND(1)
4370 F1(4)=F1(5)-.3*I5*LOG(RND(1))
4380 IFD4(9)>0THEN3640
4390 ?"BASE";B4;"-";B5;" UNDER ATTACK-"
4400 ?"RESIST TIL";FNR(F1(5))
4410 IFR6=0THEN3640
4420 INPUT"CANCEL IDLE";B$
4430 IFLEFT$(B$,1)="Y"THENR6=0
4440 GOTO3640
4450 F1(5)=1E+30:IF(R2=0)OR(R3=0)THEN364
0
4460 K=INT(G(B4,B5)/100):IFG(B4,B5)-K*10
0<10THEN3640
4470 FORI=1TOR2:IF(C1(I)=B4)AND(C2(I)=B5
)THEN4490
4480 NEXT:GOTO3640
4490 IFS2(B4,B5)=-1THENS2(B4,B5)=0
4500 IFS2(B4,B5)>999THENS2(B4,B5)=S2(B4,
B5)-10
4510 IF(B4<>Q1)OR(B5<>Q2)THEN4600
4520 FORI=1TOK3:K=K4(I):L=K5(I)
4530 IFQ$(K,L)="C"THEN4550
4540 NEXT
4550 IFK6(I)<25+50*RND(1)THEN3640
4560 Q$(B6,B7)=".":B6=0:B7=0
4570 GOSUB7230
4580 ?"BASE DEAD"
4590 GOTO4640
4600 IF(R3=1)OR(D4(9)>0)THEN4640
4610 ?
4620 ?"BASE QUAD";B4;"-";B5
4630 ?"DEAD"
```

```
4640 G(B4,B5)=G(B4,B5)-10
4650 IFR3<=1THEN4690
4660 FORI=1TOR3:IF(B2(I)=B4)AND(B3(I)=B5
)THEN4680
4670 NEXT
4680 B2(I)=B2(R3):B3(I)=B3(R3)
4690 R3=R3-1
4700 GOTO3640
4710 ?"GAME OVER":GOTO760
4720 IFC5$<>"DOCKED"THEN4750
4730 ?"ALREADY DCKD!"
4740 RETURN
4750 IFD4(9)=0THEN4770
4760 ?"SUBSPACE OUT":RETURN
4770 IFR3<>0THEN4790
4780 ?"NO REPLY FROM BASE":RETURN
4790 N1=N1+1:IFB6=0THEN4810
4800 GOTO4870
4810 D1=1E+30
4820 FORL=1TOR3:X=10*SQR((B2(L)-Q1)^2+(B
3(L)-Q2)^2)
4830 IFX>D1THEN4850
4840 D1=X:K=L
4850 NEXTL
4860 Q1=B2(K):Q2=B3(K):GOSUB7260
4870 Q$(S6,S7)="."
4880 ?
4890 ?"BASE QUAD";Q1;"-";Q2;"RESPONDS";
4900 ?"  ";S5$;" DEMATERIALIZES."
4910 P2=(1-.98^D1)^.333333
4920 FORL=1TO3
4930 IFL=1THEN?"1ST ";
4940 IFL=2THEN?"2ND ";
4950 IFL=3THEN?"3RD ";
4960 ?"RE-MAT THE ";S5$;". . . . .";
4970 IFRND(1)>P2THEN5000
4980 ?"FAILS.":NEXTL
4990 F9=11:GOSUB4710:RETURN
5000 FORL=1TO5:I=B6+INT(3*RND(1))-1
5010 IF(I<1)OR(I>10)THEN5050
5020 J=B7+INT(3*RND(1))-1
5030 IF(J<1)OR(J>10)THEN5050
5040 IFQ$(I,J)="."THEN5060
5050 NEXTL:?"FAILS.":GOTO4990
5060 ?"OK":S6=I:S7=J:Q$(I,J)=LEFT$(S5$,1
)
5070 GOSUB3430:?"SAFE":RETURN
5080 P4=2:L5=K3:N=1
5090 FORK=1TOL5
5100 IFH3(K)=0THEN5360
5110 D6=.9+.01*RND(1):H2=H3(K)*D6^K7(N)
5120 P3=K6(N)
5130 P=ABS(P3):IFP4*H2<PTHENP=P4*H2
5140 K6(N)=P3-SGN(P3)*ABS(P)
5150 X8=K4(N):Y8=K5(N)
5160 IFH2>4.99THEN5180
5170 ?"MINOR HIT":GOTO5190
5180 ?FNR(H2);"HIT ON ";
5190 M$=Q$(X8,Y8)
5200 IF M$="K"THEN?"KLING AT";
5210 IFM$="C"THEN?"CMNDR AT";
5220 ?X8;"-";Y8
5230 IFK6(N)<>0THEN5270
5240 A5=X8:A6=Y8:T2$=Q$(X8,Y8):GOSUB3160

5250 IFR1<>0THEN5370
5260 F9=1:GOSUB4710:GOTO5370
5270 IFK6(N)<0THEN5360
5280 IFRND(1)<.9THEN5360
5290 IFK6(N)>(.4+.4*RND(1))*P3THEN5360
5300 ?
5310 ?"SHIP AT SECT";
5320 ?X8;"-";Y8
5330 ?"LOST GUN"
5340 ?
5350 K6(N)=-K6(N)
5360 N=N+1
5370 NEXTK
5380 RETURN
5390 J3=0
```

```
5400 IFD4(7)<>0THEN5640
5410 IFE1<=75THEN5470
5420 INPUT"COURSE";D2
5430 IFD2<.01ORD2>12THENGOSUB12780ELSE54
50
5440 RETURN
5450 P3=50+250*D1
5460 IFP3<E1THEN5540
5470 ?
5480 ?"IMPULSE"
5490 ?"REQ 50 UNITS 250 PER ";
5500 IFE1>75THEN5520
5510 ?"QUAD.NO GOOD NOW.'":RETURN
5520 ?"QUAD.MAX OF ";
5530 ?FNR(4E-03*(E1-50)-.05);"QUADS.'":R
ETURN
5540 T1=D1/.4
5550 IFT1<R5THEN5590
5560 ?"MAX. IMPULSE 4 SECTS PER DATE"
5570 INPUT"AUTHORIZE ";B$
5580 IFLEFT$(B$,1)<>"Y"THENRETURN
5590 GOSUB5850:J3=1
5600 IFA2<>0THENRETURN
5610 E1=E1-P3
5620 IFE1>0THENRETURN
5630 F9=4:GOSUB4710:RETURN
5640 ?"IMPULSE OUT":RETURN
5650 N$="     £"
5660 ?
5670 IFD4(2)<>0THEN5840
5680 ?"L.R. SCAN QUAD";Q1;"-";Q2:?
5690 I=Q1-1:J=Q1+1:K=Q2-1:L=Q2+1
5700 FORM=ITOJ:FORN=KTOL
5710 IF(M<=0)OR(M>8)THEN5770
5720 IF(N<=0)OR(N>8)THEN5770
5730 IFD4(11)=0THENS2(M,N)=1
5740 IFG(M,N)>=LQTHEN ?"  ***";" ";
5750 IFG(M,N)<LQTHEN?SPC(5-LEN(STR$(G(M,
N))));G(M,N);
5760 GOTO5780
5770 ?N$;" ";
5780 NEXTN:?
5790 ?
5800 NEXTM
5810 IFD4(11)=0THENRETURN
5820 ?"SCAN NOT KEPT"
5830 RETURN
5840 ?"LR SENSORS OUT":RETURN
5850 A5=(15-D2)*.523599:D4=-SIN(A5):D6=C
OS(A5):B8=ABS(D4)
5860 IFABS(D6)>B8THENB8=ABS(D6)
5870 D4=D4/B8:D6=D6/B8:T5=0:T6=0
5880 IFD0+T1<F1(2)THEN5910
5890 T5=1:C5$="RED":D1=D1*(F1(2)-D0)/T1+
.1
5900 T1=F1(2)-D0+1E-05
5910 Q$(S6,S7)=".":X7=S6:Y7=S7:H9=INT(10
*D1*B8+.5)
5920 IFH9=0THEN6020
5930 FORL=1TOH9
5940 X7=X7+D4:X1=INT(X7+.5):Y7=Y7+D6:Y1=
INT(Y7+.5)
5950 IF(X1<1)OR(X1>10)THEN6190
5960 IF(Y1<1)OR(Y1>10)THEN6190
5970 IFQ$(X1,Y1)="O"THEN6000
5980 IFQ$(X1,Y1)<>"."THEN6070
5990 NEXTL
6000 D1=.1*SQR((S6-X1)^2+(S7-Y1)^2)
6010 S6=X1:S7=Y1
6020 F4=S6:F5=S7
6030 IFQ$(X1,Y1)<>"O"THEN6520
6040 T2=FNA(1):T3=FNA(1)
6050 Q1=FNA(1):Q2=FNA(1):S6=FNB(1):S7=FN
B(1):?
6060 ?"SPACE PORTAL ENTERED":GOTO6490
6070 T6=1:K=50*D1/T1+1E-03:D1=.1*SQR((S6
-X1)^2+(S7-Y1)^2)
6080 IF(Q$(X1,Y1)="K")OR(Q$(X1,Y1)="C")T
HEN6180
6090 ?S5$;" BLOCKED BY ";
```

71

```
6100 IFQ$(X1,Y1)="*"THEN?"STAR AT";
6110 IFQ$(X1,Y1)="B"THEN?"BASE AT";
6120 ?" SECT";X1;"-";Y1;"...."
6130 ?"EMERG STOP REQD";FNR(K);"UNITS"
6140 E1=E1-K
6150 S6=INT(X7-D4+.5):F4=S6:S7=INT(Y7-D6
+.5):F5=S7
6160 IFE1>0THEN6520
6170 F9=4:GOSUB4710:RETURN
6180 S6=X1:S7=Y1:GOSUB9600:F4=S6:F5=S7:G
OTO6520
6190 IFK3=0THEN6250
6200 FORL=1TOK3
6210 F3=SQR((X1-K4(L))^2+(Y1-K5(L))^2)
6220 K8(L)=.5*(F3+K7(L)):NEXTL
6230 IFG(Q1,Q2)<>LQTHENGOSUB790
6240 IFA2<>0THENRETURN
6250 X7=10*(Q1-1)+S6:Y7=10*(Q2-1)+S7
6260 X1=INT(X7+10*D1*B8*D4+.5)
6270 Y1=INT(Y7+10*D1*B8*D6+.5):L6=0
6280 L5=0
6290 IFX1>0THEN6310
6300 X1=-X1+1:L5=1
6310 IFY1>0THEN6330
6320 Y1=-Y1+1:L5=1
6330 IFX1<=80THEN6350
6340 X1=161-X1:L5=1
6350 IFY1<=80THEN6370
6360 Y1=161-Y1:L5=1
6370 IFL5=0THEN6390
6380 L6=1:GOTO6280
6390 IFL6=0THEN6460
6400 ?"MESSAGE...DATE";FNR(DO)
6410 ?"CAN'T EXIT GAL."
6420 ?"ENGINES DOWN AT ";
6430 Z1=INT((X1+9)/10):Z2=INT((Y1+9)/10)
6440 ?"QUAD";Z1;"-";Z2;",  ";
6450 ?"SECT";X1-10*(Z1-1);"-";Y1-10*(Z2-
1);"!"
6460 IFT5<>0THENRETURN
6470 Q1=INT((X1+9)/10):Q2=INT((Y1+9)/10)
6480 S6=X1-10*(Q1-1):S7=Y1-10*(Q2-1)
6490 GOSUB7550:?:GOTO6510
6500 ?CHR$(26):?"ENTERING ";G2$;" QUAD
(";Q1;"-";Q2;")"
6510 Q$(S6,S7)=LEFT$(S5$,1):GOSUB7260:GO
SUB11090:GOSUB5650:RETURN
6520 Q$(S6,S7)=LEFT$(S5$,1)
6530 IFL6=1THENRETURN
6540 IFK3=0THEN6610
6550 FORL=1TOK3
6560 F3=SQR((F4-K4(L))^2+(F5-K5(L))^2)
6570 K8(L)=.5*(K7(L)+F3)
6580 K7(L)=F3
6590 NEXTL
6600 GOSUB10980
6610 GOSUB7230:RETURN
6620 A=1:B=1
6630 FORK=1TOK3
6640 C=K4(K):D=K5(K)
6650 IFQ$(C,D)="C"THEN6670
6660 NEXTK
6670 N=0:F=K6(K)+100*K3
6680 IFF>LQTHENN=INT(RND(1)*K7(K)+1)
6690 IF((C5$="DOCKED")AND((B4<>Q1)OR(B5<
>Q2)))THENN=-S8
6700 IFN=0THENN=INT(((F+200*RND(1))/150)
-5)
6710 IFN=0THENRETURN
6720 IF(N>0)AND(K7(K)<1.5)THENRETURN
6730 IFABS(N)>S8THENN=SGN(N)*ABS(S8)
6740 T=ABS(N):P=S6-C:Q=S7-D
6750 IF2*ABS(P)<ABS(Q)THENP=0
6760 IF2*ABS(Q)<ABS(P)THENQ=0
6770 IFP<>0THENP=SGN(P*N)
6780 IFQ<>0THENQ=SGN(Q*N)
6790 R=C:S=D:Q$(C,D)="."
6800 FORL2=1TOT:L=R+P:M=S+Q
```

```
6810 IF(L>0)AND(L<=10)THEN6830
6820 ONSGN(N)+2GOTO7060,6920,6920
6830 IF(M>0)AND(M<=10)THEN6850
6840 ONSGN(N)+2GOTO7060,6860,6860
6850 IFQ$(L,M)="."THEN6980
6860 IF(Q=B)OR(P=0)THEN6920
6870 M=S+B
6880 IF(M>0)AND(M<=10)THEN6900
6890 ONSGN(N)+2GOTO7060,6910,6910
6900 IFQ$(L,M)="."THEN6980
6910 B=-B
6920 IF(P=A)OR(Q=0)THEN6990
6930 L=R+A
6940 IF(L>0)AND(L<=10)THEN6960
6950 ONSGN(N)+2GOTO7060,6970,6970
6960 IFQ$(L,M)="."THEN6980
6970 A=-A:GOTO6990
6980 R=L:S=M
6990 NEXTL2
7000 Q$(R,S)="C"
7010 IF(R=C)AND(S=D)THENRETURN
7020 K4(K)=R:K5(K)=S:K7(K)=SQR((S6-R)^2+
(S7-S)^2)
7030 K8(K)=K7(K):IFN>0THEN?"CMNDR ADVANC
ES TO";
7040 IFN<0THEN?"CMNDR RETREATS TO";
7050 ?" SECT";R;"-";S:GOSUB10980:RETURN
7060 I=Q1+INT((L+9)/10)-1:J=Q2+INT((M+9)
/10)-1
7070 IF(I<1)OR(I>8)THEN7220
7080 IF(J<1)OR(J>8)THEN7220
7090 FORL3=1TOR2
7100 IF(C1(L3)=I)AND(C2(L3)=J)THEN7220
7110 NEXTL3:?"CMNDR ESCAPES TO ";
7120 ?"QUAD";I;"-";J;"   (REGAINS STRENGT
H)"
7130 K4(K)=K4(K3):K5(K)=K5(K3):K7(K)=K7(
K3):K8(K)=K8(K3)
7140 K6(K)=K6(K3):K3=K3-1:C3=0
7150 IFC5$<>"DOCKED"THENGOSUB7230
7160 GOSUB10980
7170 G(Q1,Q2)=G(Q1,Q2)-100:G(I,J)=G(I,J)
+100
7180 FORL3=1TOR2
7190 IF(C1(L3)=Q1)AND(C2(L3)=Q2)THEN7210
7200 NEXTL3
7210 C1(L3)=I:C2(L3)=J:RETURN
7220 A=-A:B=-B:GOTO6990
7230 C5$="GREEN":IFE1<LQTHENC5$="YELLOW"
7240 IFG(Q1,Q2)>99THENC5$="RED"
7250 RETURN
7260 J4=1:B6=0:B7=0:K3=0:C3=0:U=G(Q1,Q2)
:IFU>999THEN7530
7270 K3=INT(.01*U):FORA=1TO10:FORB=1TO10
:Q$(A,B)=".":NEXTB:NEXTA
7280 Q$(S6,S7)=LEFT$(S5$,1):U=G(Q1,Q2):I
FU<100THEN7400
7290 U=U-100*K3:FORA=1TOK3
7300 S=FNB(1):K4(A)=S:T=FNB(1):K5(A)=T
7310 IFQ$(S,T)<>"."THEN7300
7320 Q$(S,T)="K":K7(A)=SQR((S6-S)^2+(S7-
T)^2):K8(A)=K7(A)
7330 K6(A)=RND(1)*150+325:NEXTA
7340 IFR2=0THEN7390
7350 FORA=1TOR2
7360 IF(C1(A)=Q1)AND(C2(A)=Q2)THEN7380
7370 NEXTA:GOTO7390
7380 Q$(S,T)="C":K6(K3)=LQ+400*RND(1):C3
=1
7390 GOSUB10980
7400 IFU<10THEN7440
7410 U=U-10
7420 B6=FNB(1):B7=FNB(1):IFQ$(B6,B7)<>".
"THEN7420
7430 Q$(B6,B7)="B"
7440 GOSUB7230:IFU<1THENRETURN
7450 FORA=1TOU
7460 S=FNB(1):T=FNB(1):IFQ$(S,T)<>"."THE
N7460
```

```
7470 Q$(S,T)="*":NEXTA
7480 IF(T2<>Q1)OR(T3<>Q2)THENRETURN
7490 S=FNB(1):T=FNB(1):IFQ$(S,T)<>"."THE
N7490
7500 Q$(S,T)="O":?
7510 ?"S.R. SENSORS SPACE-WARP IN QUAD"
7520 RETURN
7530 FORA=1TO10:FORB=1TO10:Q$(A,B)=".":N
EXTB:NEXTA
7540 Q$(S6,S7)=LEFT$(S5$,1):RETURN
7550 G4$="III":L=2:IFQ2>=5THEN7570
7560 L=1
7570 G2$=G1$(2*(Q1-1)+L):L=Q2
7580 IFL<=4THEN7600
7590 L=Q2-4
7600 G3$="IV":IFL=4THEN7620
7610 G3$=LEFT$(G4$,L)
7620 G2$=G2$+" "+G3$:RETURN
7630 IFRND(1)>.1THEN7650
7640 GOSUB10520:RETURN
7650 Q$(A5,A6)=".":?"STAR AT SECT";A5;"-
";A6;"NOVAS."
7660 G(Q1,Q2)=G(Q1,Q2)-1:S1=S1+1
7670 B9=1:T6=1:T7=1:K=0:X1=0:Y1=0
7680 H4(B9,1)=A5:H4(B9,2)=A6
7690 FORM=B9TOT6:FORQ=1TO3:FORJ=1TO3
7700 IFJ*Q=4THEN8140
7710 J5=H4(M,1)+Q-2:J6=H4(M,2)+J-2
7720 IF(J5<1)OR(J5>10)THEN8140
7730 IF(J6<1)OR(J6>10)THEN8140
7740 IFQ$(J5,J6)="."THEN8140
7750 IFQ$(J5,J6)="O"THEN8140
7760 IFQ$(J5,J6)<>"*"THEN7820
7770 IFRND(1)>=.1THEN7790
7780 X2=J5:Y2=J6:GOSUB10520:RETURN
7790 T7=T7+1:H4(T7,1)=J5:H4(T7,2)=J6:G(Q
1,Q2)=G(Q1,Q2)-1
7800 S1=S1+1:?"STAR AT SECT";J5;"-";J6;"
NOVAS."
7810 GOTO8130
7820 IFQ$(J5,J6)<>"B"THEN7890
7830 G(Q1,Q2)=G(Q1,Q2)-10:FORV=1TOR3
7840 IF(B2(V)<>Q1)OR(B3(V)<>Q2)THEN7860
7850 B2(V)=B2(R3):B3(V)=B3(R3)
7860 NEXTV:R3=R3-1:B6=0:B7=0:B1=B1+1:GOS
UB7230
7870 ?"BASE AT SECT";J5;"-";J6;"DEAD"
7880 GOTO8130
7890 IF(S6<>J5)OR(S7<>J6)THEN7990
7900 ?"SHIP BUFFETED BY NOVA.":IFS4<>0TH
EN7920
7910 E1=E1-LQ:GOTO7950
7920 IFS3>=LQTHEN7970
7930 D6=LQ-S3:E1=E1-D6:GOSUB7230:S3=0:S4
=0
7940 ?"SHIP SHLDS OUT.":D4(8)=5E-03*D5*(
RND(1))*D6
7950 IFE1>0THEN7980
7960 F9=7:GOSUB4710:RETURN
7970 S3=S3-LQ
7980 X1=X1+S6-H4(M,1):Y1=Y1+S7-H4(M,2):K
=K+1:GOTO8140
7990 IFQ$(J5,J6)<>"C"THEN8120
8000 FORV=1TOK3
8010 IF(K4(V)=J5)AND(K5(V)=J6)THEN8030
8020 NEXTV
8030 K6(V)=K6(V)-800:IFK6(V)<=0THEN8120
8040 N5=J5+J5-H4(M,1):N6=J6+J6-H4(M,2)
8050 ?"CMNDR AT SECT";J5;"-";J6;"DMGED";

8060 IF(N5<1)OR(N5>10)OR(N6<1)OR(N6>10)T
HEN8110
8070 ?" BUFFETED TO SECT";N5;"-";N6
8080 Q$(N5,N6)="C":K4(V)=N5:K5(V)=N6
8090 K7(V)=SQR((S6-N5)^2+(S7-N6)^2):K8(V
)=K7(V)
8100 Q$(J5,J6)="."
8110 ?:GOTO8140
8120 A5=J5:A6=J6:T2$=Q$(J5,J6):GOSUB3160
:GOTO8140
8130 ?:Q$(J5,J6)="."
8140 NEXTJ:NEXTQ:NEXTM
8150 IFT6=T7THEN8170
8160 B9=T6+1:T6=T7:GOTO7690
8170 IFK=0THENRETURN
8180 D1=K*.1
8190 IFX1<>0THENX1=SGN(X1)
8200 IFY1<>0THENY1=SGN(Y1)
8210 I=3*(X1+1)+Y1+2
8220 D2=C5(I)
8230 IFD2=0THEND1=0
8240 IFD1=0THENRETURN
8250 ?"NOVA DISPLACES SHIP."
8260 GOSUB5850:RETURN
8270 P=2:J3=1
8280 IFC5$<>"DOCKED"THEN8300
8290 ?"CAN'T FIRE THRU SHLDS.":GOTO8370
8300 IFD4(3)=0THEN8320
8310 ?"PHASERS DMGED.":GOTO8370
8320 IFS4=0THEN8340
8330 ?"SHLDS NOT DOWN":GOTO8370
8340 IFK3>0THEN8380
8350 ?
8360 ?"S.R. SENSORS ` NO ENEMY"
8370 J3=0:RETURN
8380 ?"PHASERS LOCKED; ENERGY=";
8390 ?.01*INT(100*E1)
8400 INPUT"TO FIRE";P1:IFP1<E1THEN8420
8410 ?"ENERGY=";:GOTO8390
8420 IFP1>0THEN8440
8430 J3=0:RETURN
8440 E1=E1-P1
8450 IFD4(11)=0THEN8480
8460 P1=P1*(RND(1)*.5+.5)
8470 ?"PHASER ACCURACY!!!":?
8480 E=P1:IFK3=0THEN8650
8490 E=0:T5=(K3*(K3+1))/2
8500 FORI=1TOK3:H3(I)=((K3+1-I)/T5)*P1
8510 H5(I)=ABS(K6(I))/(P*.9^K7(I))
8520 IFH3(I)<=H5(I)THEN8540
8530 E=E+(H3(I)-H5(I)):H3(I)=H5(I)
8540 NEXTI
8550 IFE=0THEN8620
8560 FORI=1TOK3:R7=H5(I)-H3(I)
8570 IFR7<=0THEN8600
8580 IFR7>=ETHEN8610
8590 H3(I)=H5(I):E=E-R7
8600 NEXTI:GOTO8620
8610 H3(I)=H3(I)+E:E=0
8620 GOSUB5080
8630 IF(E<>0)AND(A2=0)THEN8650
8640 J3=1:RETURN
8650 ?FNR(E);"WASTED":J3=1:RETURN
8660 J3=1:IFD4(4)=0THEN8680
8670 ?"TORPS DMGED.":GOTO8720
8680 IFT4<>0THEN8700
8690 ?"NO TORPS":GOTO8720
8700 INPUT"TORP COURSE";C6
8710 IFC6<.01ORC6>12THENGOSUB12780ELSE87
30
8720 J3=0:RETURN
8730 INPUT"BURST OF 3";B$:N=1
8740 IFLEFT$(B$,1)="N"THEN8830
8750 IFLEFT$(B$,1)<>"Y"THEN8730
8760 IFT4>2THEN8780
8770 ?"NO BURST.";T4;"TORPS LEFT.":GOTO8
720
8780 INPUT"SPREAD(3 - 30)";G2
8790 IFG2<0THEN8720
8800 IF(G2<3)OR(G2>30)THEN8780
8810 G2=FND(G2)
8820 N=3
8830 FORZ6=1TON
8840 IFC5$<>"DOCKED"THENT4=T4-1
8850 Z7=Z6:R=RND(1)
8860 R=(R+RND(1))*.5-.5
8870 IF(R>=-.4)AND(R<=.4)THEN8940
8880 R=(RND(1)+1.2)*R:IFN=3THEN8900
8890 ?"TORP MISFIRES":GOTO8910
8900 ?"TORP";Z6;"MISFIRES"
```

73

```
8910 IF RND(1)>.2THEN8940
8920 ?"TORPS DMGED BY MISFIRE."
8930 D4(4)=D5*(1+2*RND(1)):GOTO9580
8940 IF(S4<>0)OR(C5$="DOCKED")THENR=R+1E
-03*S3*R
8950 A3=C6+.25*R:IFN=1THEN8980
8960 A8=(15-A3+(2-Z6)*G2)*.523599:?
8970 ?"TRACK TORP";Z7;"--":GOTO8990
8980 ?"TORP TRACK --":A8=(15-A3)*.523599

8990 X4=-SIN(A8):Y4=COS(A8):B8=ABS(X4)
9000 IFABS(Y4)>ABS(X4)THENB8=ABS(Y4)
9010 X4=X4/B8:Y4=Y4/B8:X5=S6:Y5=S7
9020 FORL9=1TO15:X5=X5+X4:A5=INT(X5+.5)
9030 IF(A5<1)OR(A5>10)THEN9560
9040 Y5=Y5+Y4:A6=INT(Y5+.5)
9050 IF(A6<1)OR(A6>10)THEN9560
9060 IF(L9=5)OR(L9=9)THEN?
9070 ?FNR(X5);"-";FNR(Y5);"--->"
9080 IFQ$(A5,A6)<>"."THEN9100
9090 GOTO9550
9100 ?:IFQ$(A5,A6)="K"THEN9150
9110 IFQ$(A5,A6)<>"C"THEN9370
9120 IFRND(1)>.1THEN9150
9130 ?"CMNDR AT SECT";A5;"-";A6;"USES AN
TI-PHOTON DEVICE !"
9140 ?"TORP NEUTRALIZED.":GOTO9570
9150 FORV=1TOK3
9160 IF(A5=K4(V))AND(A6=K5(V))THEN9180
9170 NEXTV
9180 K=K6(V):W3=200+800*RND(1)
9190 IFABS(K)<W3THENW3=ABS(K)
9200 K6(V)=K-SGN(K)*ABS(W3):IFK6(V)<>0TH
EN9220
9210 T2$=Q$(A5,A6):GOSUB3160:GOTO9570
9220 IFQ$(A5,A6)="K"THEN?"KLING AT";
9230 IFQ$(A5,A6)="C"THEN?"CMNDR AT";
9240 ?A5;"-";A6
9250 A7=A8+2.5*(RND(1)-.5)
9260 W3=ABS(-SIN(A7)):IFABS(COS(A7))>W3T
HENW3=ABS(COS(A7))
9270 X7=-SIN(A7)/W3:Y7=COS(A7)/W3
9280 P=INT(A5+X7+.5):Q=INT(A6+Y7+.5)
9290 IF(P<1)OR(P>10)OR(Q<1)OR(Q>10)THEN9
360
9300 IFQ$(P,Q)<>"."THEN9360
9310 Q$(P,Q)=Q$(A5,A6):Q$(A5,A6)=".":?"D
MGED"
9320 ?"PUSHED TO SECT";P;"-";Q
9330 K4(V)=P:K5(V)=Q:K7(V)=SQR((S6-P)^2+
(S7-Q)^2)
9340 K8(V)=K7(V)
9350 GOSUB10980:GOTO9570
9360 ?"DMGED,NOT DEAD":GOTO9570
9370 IFQ$(A5,A6)<>"B"THEN9450
9380 ?"BASE DEAD"
9390 IFS2(Q1,Q2)<0THENS2(Q1,Q2)=0
9400 FORW=1TOR3
9410 IF(B2(W)<>Q1)OR(B3(W)<>Q2)THEN9430
9420 B2(W)=B2(R3):B3(W)=B3(R3)
9430 NEXTW:Q$(A5,A6)=".":R3=R3-1:B6=0:B7
=0
9440 G(Q1,Q2)=G(Q1,Q2)-10:B1=B1+1:GOSUB7
230:GOTO9570
9450 IFQ$(A5,A6)<>"*"THEN9530
9460 IFRND(1)>.15THEN9490
9470 ?"STAR AT SECT";A5;"-";A6;"UNAFFECT
ED BY PHOTON"
9480 GOTO9570
9490 X2=A5:Y2=A6:GOSUB7630:A5=X2:A6=Y2
9500 IFG(Q1,Q2)=LQTHENRETURN
9510 IFA2<>0THENRETURN
9520 GOTO9570
9530 ?"TRUCE-MONITOR DEAD":Q$(A5,A6)="."
:?
9540 T2=0:T3=0:GOTO9570
9550 NEXTL9
9560 ?"TORP MISSED!"
9570 NEXTZ6
9580 IFR1<>0THENRETURN
```

```
9590 F9=1:GOSUB4710:RETURN
9600 ?"R ALERT":?
9610 ?"COLLISION IMMINENT":?
9620 ?S5$;" RAMS ";:W7=1:IFQ$(S6,S7)="C"
THENW7=2
9630 IFW7=1THEN?"KLING AT ";
9640 IFW7=2THEN?"CMNDR AT ";
9650 ?"SECT";S6;"-";S7:A5=S6:A6=S7:T2$=Q
$(S6,S7)
9660 GOSUB3160:?S5$;" HEAVILY DMGED."
9670 K=INT(5+RND(1)*20):?"SICKBAY REPORT
S";K;"CASUALTIES!"
9680 C4=C4+K:FORL=1TO12:I=RND(1)
9690 J=(3.5*W7*(RND(1)+I)+1)*D5
9700 IFL=6THENJ=J/3
9710 D4(L)=D4(L)+T1+J:NEXTL:D4(6)=D4(6)-
3
9720 IFD4(6)<0THEND4(6)=0
9730 S4=0:IFR1<>0THENRETURN
9740 F9=1:GOSUB4710:RETURN
9750 RETURN
9760 A2=0:G1=0:GOSUB2200:S5$="ENTERPRISE
"
9770 I7=5000:E1=I7:I8=2500:S3=I8:S4=0:S9
=S4:J1=4:L1=J1
9780 Q1=FNA(1):Q2=FNA(1):S6=FNB(1):S7=FN
B(1):I9=10:T4=I9
9790 W1=5:W2=25:FORI=1TO12:D4(I)=0:NEXT
9800 J2=100*INT(31*RND(1)+20):D0=J2:K1=0
:K2=0:N1=0:N2=0:R6=0:C4=0
9810 A1=1:D3=.25:FORI=1TO8:FORJ=1TO8:S2(
I,J)=0:NEXTJ:NEXTI
9820 F1(1)=D0-.5*I5*LOG(RND(1)):F1(5)=1E
+30
9830 F1(2)=D0-1.5*(I5/R2)*LOG(RND(1)):I6
=0
9840 F1(3)=D0-.3*I5*LOG(RND(1)):F1(4)=D0
-.3*I5*LOG(RND(1))
9850 FORI=1TO8:FORJ=1TO8:K=INT(RND(1)*9+
1):I6=I6+K
9860 G(I,J)=K:NEXTJ:NEXTI:S1=0
9870 FOR I=1TOI2
9880 X=INT(RND(1)*6+2):Y=INT(RND(1)*6+2)
9890 IFG(X,Y)>=10THEN9880
9900 IFI<2THEN9940
9910 K=I-1:FORJ=1TOK:D1=SQR((B2(J)-X)^2+
(B3(J)-Y)^2)
9920 IFD1<2THEN9880
9930 NEXTJ
9940 B2(I)=X:B3(I)=Y:S2(X,Y)=-1:G(X,Y)=G
(X,Y)+10:NEXTI
9950 B1=0:K=I1-I4:L=INT(.25*S8*(9-L2)+1)

9960 M=INT((1-RND(1)^2)*L):IFM>KTHENM=K
9970 N=100*M
9980 X=FNA(1):Y=FNA(1):IFG(X,Y)+N>999THE
N9980
9990 G(X,Y)=G(X,Y)+N:K=K-M:IFK<>0THEN996
0
10000 FORI=1TOI4
10010 X=FNA(1):Y=FNA(1):IF(G(X,Y)<99)AND
(RND(1)<.75)THEN10010
10020 IFG(X,Y)>899THEN10010
10030 IFI=1THEN10060
10040 M=I-1:FORJ=1TOM:IF(C1(J)=X)AND(C2(
J)=Y)THEN10010
10050 NEXTJ
10060 G(X,Y)=G(X,Y)+100:C1(I)=X:C2(I)=Y:
NEXTI
10070 I=INT(D0):?:S0=0
10080 T2=FNA(1):T3=FNA(1):IFG(T2,T3)<100
THEN10080
10090 ?"STARDATE.............";I
10100 ?"NUMBER OF KLINGONS....";I1
10110 ?"NUMBER OF STARDATES...";INT(I5)
10120 ?"NUMBER OF STARBASES...";I2
10130 ?"STARBASE LOCATIONS....";
10140 FORI=1TOI2:?B2(I);"-";B3(I);
10150 IFI<>I2THEN?", ";
10160 NEXTI:?
```

```
10170 GOSUB7550
10180 ?"THE ";S5$;" IS IN THE ";G2$;" QU
AD."
10190 GOSUB7260
10200 INPUT"CONT";NL$:?CHR$(26):GOSUB110
90:GOSUB5650:RETURN
10210 INPUT"WARP";K
10220 ?
10230 IFK<1THEN10340
10240 IFK>10THEN10350
10250 J=W1:W1=K:W2=W1*W1
10260 IF(W1<=J)OR(W1<=6)THEN10290
10270 IFW1<=8THEN10300
10280 IFW1>8THEN10310
10290 ?"WARP";W1:RETURN
10300 ?"MAX SPEED 6":RETURN;
10310 IFW1=10THEN10330
10320 RETURN
10330 ?"TRY":RETURN
10340 ?"MIN. WARP 1":RETURN
10350 ?"MAX. WARP 10"
10360 RETURN
10370 J3=0:IFD4(8)<>0THEN10490
10380 IFS4<>0THEN10420
10390 INPUT"SHLDS DOWN.UP";B$
10400 IFLEFT$(B$,1)="Y"THEN10450
10410 RETURN
10420 INPUT"SHLDS UP.DOWN";B$
10430 IFLEFT$(B$,1)="Y"THEN10480
10440 RETURN
10450 S4=1:S9=1:IFC5$<>"DOCKED"THENE1=E1
-50
10460 ?"SHLDS UP":IFE1<=0THEN10500
10470 J3=1:RETURN
10480 S4=0:S9=1:?"SHLDS DOWN":J3=1:RETUR
N
10490 ?"SHLDS DMGED,DOWN. ":RETURN
10500 ?"SHLDS USE ALL ENERGY."
10510 F9=4:GOSUB4710:RETURN
10520 IFX2<>0THEN10620
10530 N=INT(RND(1)*I6+1):FORX=1TO8:FORY=
1TO8
10540 N=N-(G(X,Y)-INT(G(X,Y)/10)*10):IFN
<=0THEN10560
10550 NEXTY:NEXTX:RETURN
10560 IF(X<>Q1)OR(Y<>Q2)THEN10680
10570 IFJ4<>0THEN10680
10580 N=INT(RND(1)*(G(X,Y)-INT(G(X,Y)/10
)*10))+1
10590 FORX3=1TO10:FORY3=1TO10:IFQ$(X3,Y3
)<>"*"THEN10610
10600 N=N-1:IFN=0THEN10620
10610 NEXTY3:NEXTX3
10620 ?"R ALERT"
10630 X3=X2:Y3=Y2
10640 ?"SUPERNOVA DETECTED SECT";X3;"-";
Y3
10650 X=Q1:Y=Q2:K=(X2-S6)^2+(Y2-S7)^2
10660 IFK>1.5THEN10720
10670 ?"EMERG AUTO-OVERRIDE JAMMED":A2=1
:GOTO10720
10680 IFD4(9)<>0THEN10720
10690 ?"MESSAGE..DATE";INT(D0)
10700 ?"SUPERNOVA IN QUAD";X;"-";Y;
10710 ?" CAUTION"
10720 N=G(X,Y):R=INT(N/100):Q=0
10730 IF(X<>Q1)OR(Y<>Q2)THEN10750
10740 K3=0:C3=0
10750 IFR=0THEN10810
10760 R1=R1-R:IFR2=0THEN10810
10770 FORL=1TOR2:IF(C1(L)<>X)OR(C2(L)<>Y
)THEN10800
10780 C1(L)=C1(R2):C2(L)=C2(R2):C1(R2)=0
:C2(R2)=0
10790 R2=R2-1:R=R-1:Q=1:IFR2=0THENF1(2)=
1E+30
10800 NEXTL
10810 IFR3=0THEN10850
10820 FORL=1TOR3:IF(B2(L)<>X)OR(B3(L)<>Y
)THEN10840
```

```
10830 B2(L)=B2(R3):B3(L)=B3(R3):B2(R3)=0
:B3(R3)=0:R3=R3-1
10840 NEXTL
10850 IFX2=0THEN10890
10860 N=G(X,Y)-INT(G(X,Y)/100)*100
10870 S1=S1+(N-INT(N/10)*10):B1=B1+INT(N
/10)
10880 K1=K1+R:K2=K2+Q
10890 IF(S2(X,Y)<>0)AND(D4(9)<>0)THENS2(
X,Y)=LQ+G(X,Y)
10900 IF(D4(9)=0)OR((Q1=X)AND(Q2=Y))THEN
S2(X,Y)=1
10910 G(X,Y)=1000
10920 IF(R1<>0)OR((X=Q1)AND(Y=Q2))THEN10
960
10930 ?CHR$(26):?"SUPERNOVA IN QUAD";X;"
-";Y;"DESTROYED"
10940 ?"ENEMY FLEET"
10950 F9=1:GOTO4710
10960 IFA2=0THENRETURN
10970 F9=8:GOTO4710
10980 IFK3<=1THENRETURN
10990 Z4=0:FORO=1TOK3-1:IFK7(O)<=K7(O+1)
THEN11060
11000 K=K7(O):K7(O)=K7(O+1):K7(O+1)=K
11010 K=K8(O):K8(O)=K8(O+1):K8(O+1)=K
11020 K=K4(O):K4(O)=K4(O+1):K4(O+1)=K
11030 K=K5(O):K5(O)=K5(O+1):K5(O+1)=K
11040 K=K6(O):K6(O)=K6(O+1):K6(O+1)=K
11050 Z4=1
11060 NEXTO
11070 IFZ4<>0THEN10990
11080 RETURN
11090 IFD(1)<>0THEN11330
11100 ?:?"    1 2 3 4 5 6 7 8 9 10"
11110 FORI=1TO10:IFI<10THEN?" ";
11120 ?I;:FORJ=1TO10:?Q$(I,J);" ";:NEXTJ

11130 ONIGOTO11150,11160,11180,11190,112
40
11140 ONI-5GOTO11250,11260,11270,11300,1
1310
11150 IF AL=1 THEN ?" STARDATE      ";FN
R(D0) ELSE ?:GOTO 11320
11160 IF C5$<>"DOCKED"THENGOSUB7230
11170 IF AL=1 THEN ?" CONDITION     ";C
5$ ELSE ?:GOTO 11320
11180 IF AL=1 THEN ?" POSITION      ";Q1
;"-";Q2;" : ";S6;"-";S7 ELSE ?:GOTO 1132
0
11190 IF AL=1 THEN ?" LIFE SUPPORT   ";:
IF D4(5)<>0 THEN 11210
11200 IF AL=1 THEN ?"ACTIVE":GOTO 11240
ELSE ?:GOTO 11320
11210 IF C5$<>"DOCKED" THEN 11230
11220 IF AL=1 THEN ?"DMGED, SUPPORTED BY
 BASE"GF AL=1 THEN ?"DMGED, RESERVES=";F
NS(L1)GOTO 11240 ELSE ?:GOTO 11320
1OR      ";FN
R(W1) ELSE ?:GOTO 11320
11250 IF AL=1 THEN ?" ENSE ?:GOTO 11320
11260 IF AL=1 THEN ?" TORPEDOES     ";T4
EN ?" SHIELDS        ";:
B$="DOWN,":IF S4<>0 THEN B$="UP,"
11280 IF D4(8)>0 T B$="DAMAGED,"
1129 FAL1 HN B$IT(00S3I8+5";R1
 ELSE ?:GOTO 11320
11310 IF AL=1 THEN ?" TIME LEFT     ";FN
S(R5):?:?:?:AL=1:GOSUB 11150:AL=0:
RETURN
11330 ?"S.R. SENSORS DMGED.":RETURN
11340 ?"T350 IFS0<>0THEN11390
11360 T1=-.5*I5*LOG(RND(1))
11370 ?"FORWARD IN TIME0
11390 M=D0:D0=D9(1)
11400 ?"BACK IN TIME";FNR(M-D0);"DATES."
:S0=0
):R3=D9(4):R4=D9(5
):R5=D9(6)
11420 S1=D9(7):B1=D9(8):K1=D9:FORJ=1TO8:G
```

```
(I,J)=D9(I-1+8*(J-1)+11):NEXTJ:NEXTI
11440 FORI=85TO94:C2(I-84)=D9(I):NEXT
11460 FORI=95TO99:B2(I-94)=D9(I):NEXT
11470 OR=1=D9(106)
11480 F1(1)=D0-.5*I5*LOG(RND(1))
11490 IFR2<>0*LOG(RND(1))
11510 FORI=1TO8:FORJ=1TO8:IF1<S2(I,J)THE
NS2(I,J
11530 ?
11540 ?"SPOCK KNOWS CHART"
11550 GOSUB7260:RETURN
11560 J3=0:IFD4(12)<>0THEN1169 TO SHLDS"
;Z3
11580 IFZ3<0HNRTUN159 FE1S3Z;"UNITS LEFT.
'"
11610 RETURN
11620 E1=E1+S3-Z3:S3=Z3:?"TRANSFER"
11630 ?"(SHIP ENERGY=";FNR(E1);"    SHLD
 ENERGY=";FNR(S3);")"
11640 J3=1
11650 T1=.1:P5=(K3+4*C3)/48:IFP5<.1THENP
5=.1
11660 IFP5>RND(1)THENGOSUB790
11670 IFA2<>0THENRETURN
11680 GOSUB3640:RETURN
11690 ?"TRANSFER PANEL DMGED.":RETURN
11700 J3=0:INPUT"DATES";Z5:IF(Z5<R5)AND(
K3=0)THEN11720
11710 INPUT"SURE";B$:IFLEFT$(B$,1)<>"Y"T
HENRETURN
11720 R6=1
11730 IFZ5<=0THENR6=0
11740 IFR6=0THENRETURN
11750 T1=Z5:Z6=Z5
11760 IFK3=0THEN11790
11770 T1=1+RND(1):IFZ5<T1THENT1=Z5
11780 Z6=T1
11790 IFT1<Z5THENGOSUB790
11800 IFA2<>0THENRETURN
11810 GOSUB3640:J3=1:IFA2<>0THENRETURN
11820 Z5=Z5-Z6:GOTO11730
11830 J3=0:IFD4(6)<>0THEN12300
11840 INPUT"COURSE";D2:IFD2<.01ORD2>12TH
ENGOSUB12780
11850 INPUT"DIST";D1
11860 P=(D1+.05)*W1*W1*W1*(S4+1):IFP<E1T
HEN11980
11870 J3=0
11880 IF(S4=0)OR(.5*P>E1)THEN11910
11890 ?"ENERGY SHORT";
11900 ?"WITH SHLDS UP.":RETURN
11910 W=INT((E1/(D1+.05))^.333333):IFW<=
0THEN11960
11920 ?"ENERGY-TRY";W
11930 IFS4<>0THEN11950
11940 RETURN
11950 ?"LOWER SHLDS.":RETURN
11960 ?"ENERGY SHORT"
11970 RETURN
11980 T1=10*D1/W2:IFT1<.8*R5THEN12040
11990 ?"THAT TRIP";
12000 ?"REQRS APPRX";FNR(100*T1/R5);
12010 ?"%":?" OF TIME.SURE ";
12020 INPUT B$:IFLEFT$(B$,1)="Y"THEN1204
0
12030 J3=0:RETURN
12040 Q4=0:W=0:IFW1<=6THEN12200
12050 P=D1*(6-W1)^2/66.6667:IFP>RND(1)TH
ENQ4=1
12060 IFQ4<>0THEND1=RND(1)*D1
12070 W=0:IFW1<10THEN12090
12080 IF.25*D1>RND(1)THENW=1
12090 IF(Q4=0)AND(W=0)THEN12200
12100 A=(15-D2)*.5236:X1=-SIN(A):X2=COS(
A)
12110 B8=ABS(X1):IFABS(X2)>ABS(X1)THENB8
=ABS(X2)
12120 X1=X1/B8:Y1=Y1/B8:N=INT(10*D1*B8+.
5):X=S6:Y=S7
12130 IFN=0THEN12200
12140 FORL=1TON
12150 X=X+X1:Q=INT(X+.5):IF(Q<1)OR(Q>10)
THEN12200
12160 Y=Y+Y1:R=INT(Y+.5):IF(R<1)OR(R>10)
THEN12200
12170 IFQ$(Q,R)="."THEN12190
12180 Q4=0:W=0
12190 NEXTL
12200 GOSUB5850:IFA2<>0THENRETURN
12210 E1=E1-D1*W1*W1*W1*(S4+1):IFE1>0THE
N12230
12220 F9=4:GOSUB4710:RETURN
12230 T1=10*D1/W2:IFW<>0THENGOSUB11340
12240 IFQ4=0THEN12290
12250 REM
12260 ?"WARPS OUT"
12270 ?"SHUTTING DOWN"
12280 D4(6)=D5*(3*RND(1)+1)
12290 J3=1:RETURN
12300 ?"WARPS DMGED.":RETURN
12310 ONSGN(D4(10))+2GOTO12320,12340,123
30
12320 ?"QUEENE-NO SHUTTLE":RETURN
12330 ?"SHUTTLE DMGED.":RETURN
12340 REM
12350 ?"ABANDON SHIP!"
12360 ?"ESCAPE-GALILEO."
12370 ?"REST BEAM DOWN"
12380 ?"TO NEAR PLANET.":IFR3<>0THEN1240
0
12390 F9=9:GOSUB4710:RETURN
12400 ?"CAUGHT BY KLINGS`RELEASED TO"
12410 ?"FED."
12420 ?"IN COMMAND"
12430 ?"QUEENE"
12440 N=INT(RND(1)*R3+1):Q1=B2(N):Q2=B3(
N)
12450 S6=5:S7=5:GOSUB7260:Q$(S6,S7)="."
12460 FORL=1TO3:S6=INT(3*RND(1)-1+B6)
12470 IF(S6<1)OR(S7>10)THEN12500
12480 S7=INT(3*RND(1)-1+B7):IF(S7<1)OR(S
7>10)THEN12500
12490 IFQ$(S6,S7)="."THEN12510
12500 NEXTL:GOTO12450
12510 S5$="FAERIE QUEENE":Q$(S6,S7)=LEFT
$(S5$,1):C5$="DOCKED"
12520 FORL=1TO12:D4(L)=0:NEXT:D4(10)=-1:
E1=3000:I7=E1
12530 S3=1500:I8=S3:T4=6:I9=T4:L1=3:J1=L
1:S4=0:W1=5:W2=25
12540 RETURN
12550 IFD4(11)=0THEN12580
12560 ?"COMP OUT-NO DESTRUCT"
12570 RETURN
12580 ?"OK"
12590 ?"ID-OK"
12600 ?"DESTRUCT-ON":J=3
12610 FORI=10TO6STEP-1:?SPC(J);I:GOSUB12
760:J=J+3:NEXT
12620 ?"PASSWORD";
12630 REM
12640 REM
12650 INPUTB$:IFB$<>X$THEN12740
12660 ?"PASSWORD-OK":J=10
12670 FORI=5TO1STEP-1:?SPC(J);I:GOSUB127
60:J=J+3:NEXT
12680 ?"ENTROPY OF ";S5$;" MAXIMIZED"
12690 ?:IFK3=0THEN12730
12700 W=20*E1:FORL=1TOK3:IFK6(L)*K7(L)>W
THEN12720
12710 A5=K4(L):A6=K5(L):T2$=Q$(A5,A6):GO
SUB3160
12720 NEXTL
12730 F9=10:GOSUB4710:RETURN
12740 ?"PASSWORD-BAD"
12750 ?"CONTINUITY-EFFECTED":RETURN
12760 K=12345:FORM=1TO90:K=K+1:NEXTM:RET
URN
12770 FORI=1TO10:GOTO11130:RETURN
12780 ?"COURSE 01-12 ONLY":RETURN
```

STRUCTURED PROGRAMMING

Young children learn the elements of programming techniques with the help of a 'turtle', which draws pictures on a large piece of paper, under the control of the Logo language

You will not spend much time in the world of computing before you hear or read the phrase 'structured programming'. A great deal of temper is expended over the question of whether children – and indeed adults – should or should not be taught to program in this way.

The essence of the problem is BASIC. BASIC is easy to learn but, say the proponents of 'real' programming languages, this is an illusion. It is easy to learn because it is not really computing – it is like a pond which you can walk into safely and comfortably, but which has no depth. You cannot swim in it.

Proper languages – known as 'structured languages' – are harder to learn because they behave unlike ordinary, noncomputing experience. The essence of them is that you can keep on building. You write programs by writing little logical building blocks called 'procedures'. At the first level, these are just like the 'eating' subroutine on pages 56-7, in our Foodgol program for eating a meal. BASIC makes you work like the builder of a cottage, who gets all the materials delivered to the site, stands back and starts to put them together. He does not need a plan, he just gets on with it, simply and naturally.

However, you cannot build a cathedral in the way you build a cottage. You have to think as an architect rather than as a jobbing builder. You start with notional stones, combine them into pillars and arches and then forget them; combine the pillars and arches into vaults and forget them; the vaults into naves and the naves into a cathedral. The architect could not possibly do this if the way he worked forced him to keep thinking

of individual stones at every stage. And that is what BASIC does.

There is a mass of structured languages. They divide into two groups. The most common are Fortran, Pascal, 'C' and Algol. These are often known as von Neumann languages after the distinguished mathematician who was associated with early computer development. Then there are the list-processing languages like Lisp, and the teaching languages Logo and Prolog.

Logo is interesting mainly because of the passionate fervour of its enthusiasts. It is usually presented on a micro which drives something called a turtle. This is a simple, but precisely made, device which draws with a pencil. The point of drawing is to make the computer suitable for the classroom. The turtle crawls around a big sheet of paper on the floor. It has a pencil at its centre which can be pressed down or picked up. It can run forward or turn on its centre. The turtle is connected to the computer by a cable and responds to commands like:

FORWARD:X (go forward the distance X)
RIGHT:A (turn right A degrees)
DRAW (put the pencil down)

You write a program by defining words. To draw a square you might start by defining the command HOOK which consists of moving the turtle X units FORWARD, and then turning RIGHT. Do this four times and you have a SQUARE.

After a while the energetic Logo programmer (the same sort of thing applies in Lisp and Forth) will have built up a mass of verbs which he or she can combine.

TRADITIONAL LANGUAGES

A language is simply a way of communicating with a computer, using precise instructions. The language has to be a compromise between what machines recognize and what people understand.

The first language was machine code (see pp. 80-85), and very tough it was too. The struggles to do decimal arithmetic in binary code were so intense that they have left a deep scar on the psyche of people in computing, with the result that up to now every book on the subject has informed its baffled readers how to do this recondite task. A knowledge of binary arithmetic is no more necessary for everyday computing than astro navigation is for an airline passenger.

Machine code programmers soon found that they were repeating pieces of code and invented the idea of subroutines (pp. 56-7) and 'macros'. A macro is a bit of code which is used as the equivalent of a single statement. If you had a piece of code to add two decimal numbers, every time you needed two decimal numbers added, you would insert it as a macro. After a while you would not even think of it as code: it would just be 'ADD'. In time you would have written all the common functions and have a library of macros which could be thrown into action by writing a list of their names as a 'program':

ENTER NUMBER
ADD NUMBER,6,ANSWER
PRINT ANSWER

is how it might look, calling the macros 'ENTER', 'ADD' and 'PRINT'. The variables they need – NUMBER for ENTER; NUMBER, 6 and ANSWER for ADD; ANSWER for PRINT – are put in standard positions and are known in the trade as 'arguments'.

This is not really a high-level language yet, but it is getting on that way, and anyone who writes a lot of machine code will be used to thinking of programs at two levels: lines of actual machine code that he or she is working on, and great chunks of code – that are used as units – that work and do not need fiddling with.

Thinking of programs like this produced two stages of work. There was the actual coding, or 'assembly' of the instructions, and then the 'linking' of chunks together to make a program. Often the linker or assembler would look in a library for its macros – on big machines these macros might well have been written by other hands long ago. This is the scheme that still applies in traditional languages such as assembler, Fortran, Algol and COBOL.

Algol was originally not a computer language at all. It was a standard way of writing down mathematical formulae so that there was no doubt about who was doing what to which. Later on someone recognized that if you could write macros corresponding to the mathematical commands in Algol and, secondly, if all the macros worked in a compatible way, you could have a

language – provided that, thirdly, you had some piece of program that would read the names of the macros you wanted, get them out of the library, and hurl them at the data. This program is called a 'compiler'. One of the beauties of this scheme was that the differences between the then (and even more now) rapidly growing number of machines could be hidden behind the compiler.

This was a point of view forced on the designers of European languages by the multiplicity of small computer builders. They produced incompatible hardware that had to be smoothed over and made to look as if it were the same machine by the language itself. In America things were different. There IBM dominated the scene and all computers were the same.

A number of progams for writing machine code appeared in the 1950s, called generically 'autocodes', and out of those two languages emerged: Fortran and PL/I. Fortran (Formula Translation language) worked pretty well and is still in use today. PL/I was intended to be the great answer to all language problems. However, since it was built piecemeal by engineers, rather than designed as an architectural whole, it has never really been popular.

A development of the autocodes for commercial use was COBOL. COBOL was invented by Captain Grace Hopper of the United States Navy in the 1950s, and no one seems to have loved it from that day to this. The designers of COBOL tried to make a language that would understand English. After a time this was abandoned, and it was hoped that its programs could be understood by people who understood English. What emerged was stuff like this:

000480 IF CRT–STOCK–CODE = SPACE GO TO END–IT
000490 IF CRT–UNIT–SIZE NOT NUMERIC GO TO CORRECT ERROR
000500 MOVE   CRT–PROD–DESC   TO PRODUCT–DESC

Algol improved Fortran by allowing more flexible subroutines, which could have their own internal variables that were not seen by anything outside them. However, the committee which designed it was made up of such purists that they refused to countenance any way in which an Algol program might get data from the outside world to work on, or pass its results back to its waiting audience. They conceived of a program as something that happened totally inside a computer with no reference to the outside world. This unhappy omission somewhat hampered Algol's development.

However, if Algol was never much of a success in terms of numbers of programs, it did make a great theoretical step forward. It made the mathematical idea of 'recursion' available to the programmer. The idea in Fortran is that one subroutine could 'call' or use another, but it could not call itself. Algol removed this restriction, so that you could set a subroutine burrowing down into a great heap of data and it would wriggle back on its own tail as many times as it had to. Recursion does for the subroutine what we saw the subroutine doing for the individual command on pages 56-7: it makes it possible to apply it an indefinite number of times.

The next step forward was BASIC. The problem with compiled languages is that they take a long time for the compiler and then the linker to process the program you write. If – as is almost always the case – it does not work, you have to go back to the original code, change it and re-compile. This can take a discouragingly long time for beginners. The idea of BASIC is to interpret and execute each line as you go along. This is very handy for the user because he or she can write some program, run it, see what went wrong, and change it. This facility has proved so popular that BASIC has – in terms of numbers of machines on which it is used – swept the world. It is not so good for the compiler because it has to spend most of its daily work interpreting (which is why such software is called an 'interpreter') what the user has offered up by way of program statements, and only a small amount of time executing them.

Because an interpreter has to do so much to work out what is wanted, it runs very slowly. There is, in fact, a compiled version of BASIC which runs about ten times faster than interpreted; but assembler doing the same thing would run perhaps five times faster again.

Pascal, which was designed by Niklaus Wirth, attempts to combine the best features of Algol and BASIC. In Pascal you have to declare all your variables – not make them up as you go along, as you can in BASIC – and the system does a lot of checking of variables as it runs. Moreover, subroutines are a lot more civilized than in BASIC, and a subroutine can call itself – recursively – which it cannot in most versions of BASIC.

After all these 'high-level' languages had been around for a while, people found they were still spending a lot of time writing machine code and assembler and other migraine-inducing stuff. They had to do this because the high-level programs did not compile small enough to get into the available memory or, when there, they did not run fast enough. In order to speed things up, people invented languages that were improved machine code. Although these were more difficult to write than ordinary high-level languages, they ran faster and compiled smaller. Forth is one of these – an odd beast that insists, for instance, that you do not write '3 + 4', but '3 4 +' as you had to with the early calculators.

Another language, which gives speed and compactness at the expense of simplicity, is 'C'. It works very like Pascal except that it has fewer safeguards and direct access to things like the processor's registers. 'C' looks like this:

```
compare (p1, p2, n)
    char *p1, *p2;
    int n;{
        register int m;
        for (m = 0; m<n && *p1==*p2 &&
            *p1 !='\0'; ++p1, ++p2, ++m);
        return (m==n ||*p2 ==* p1);}
```

Hardly flowing, romantic stuff, but useful.

However, there is another world in computing. People working in artificial intelligence are really doing something quite different from the mathematicians and engineers who invented the classical languages. In artificial intelligence they start with a sentence in, say, English: 'Pick up the knife.' They know what is wanted but not how to do it. How does the human eye and brain 'see' a knife and pick it up? Which knife anyway?

To cope with this they invented 'list-processing' languages, of which the first was Lisp. In Lisp you start with some grand overall statement such as:

MEANING UNIVERSE(GODS,MEN)

and then try to flesh it out with some subsidiary statements such as:

NATURE(MEN,MORTAL)
NATURE(GODS,IMMORTAL)

and hope to arrive, in due course, at a program that will work out the Meaning of the Universe by making statements about MORTAL, IMMORTAL and whatever you can think of that might be relevant to them. You hope eventually to work down to something the language knows about, written in machine code. If you succeed, you have a working program. If not, not.

This ability to build up your own verbs seems at first sight a great improvement on the rigidity of the von Neumann languages. However, the very flexibility of the list-processing languages soon overwhelms the programmer with a mass of verbs that he or she has invented – and as quickly forgotten. The more conventional languages have only a limited number of verbs that are clearly defined in their manuals. It is less exciting but much more practical, and this is probably why list-processing languages have never caught on in commercial data processing.

A third trend is emerging now, under our feet. It is stimulated by the vast number of people who could be drawn into computing if only it could be made intelligible to them. There is in consequence a frenzied search, urged on by huge commercial pressures, to find ways of presenting computing operations to them in terms that they can understand without (apparently) having to put themselves to the trouble of learning anything new. This work was pioneered by Xerox in their Star machine, and has seen the light of day in Apple's Lisa (see pp. 46-7).

MACHINE CODE AND DATA STRUCTURES

We can now see that a high-level language is just a tool for arranging and feeding chunks of pre-written machine code to the processor. In order to get to grips with machine code we need to give the processor more attention than we did on pages 16-17. A real processor has a number of registers to store data for manipulation. It has many more than the three commands of the earlier description – though they do not really do many more things.

To fix our ideas, let us look at the Z80 processor – which is installed in more different types of computer than any other. The Z80 has two complete sets of registers – it is, in fact, a dual processor – and the programmer can switch to and fro just as a clever knitter can keep two sets of needles on the go at once. The Z80 has, in each set, a special 1-byte register, called the accumulator or A. It has three 2-byte registers, and a fourth intended to hold addresses. It has a second special register, F, for 'flags'.

A flag is a particularly computerish idea, which has no real counterpart outside. It is a signal that something has or has not happened. For instance, we might be comparing one byte with another to see if they are identical. The Z80 has a special instruction to do this – 'CP B' compares the byte in B with the byte in A. If they are the same the zero flag – the second bit in the flag byte – is set to 0. Other instructions, such as 'jump', can also make use of this, so that the programmer can jump to another bit of program if the bytes in A and B are the same, or go back, load another byte into B and try again if they are not.

The Z80 command set, in addition to the add, subtract and compare functions that are at the heart of a micro, will also:

load bytes from memory into registers – and the reverse;

exchange the contents of registers with each other;

copy data from one part of memory to another;

search a block of memory for a particular byte;

do the logical functions AND, OR, EXCLUSIVE OR (see pp. 20-21) on two bytes in registers;

carry out some rather exotic functions that make it possible to do decimal arithmetic with binary tools;

do jumps from one program line to another. These jumps can be controlled by the contents of some of the registers. This makes it possible, say, to look for the letter 'a' in an area of memory with an instruction – if found do one thing, if not do another;

rotate the bits in a register left and right, test them individually, set or reset them. (To 'set' a bit means to make it '1'; to reset it, make it '0');

get bytes from an input port and send bytes to an output port;

call subroutines and return from them;

interrupt current program execution and jump to another line.

A cursory glance at this list will show few things that look useful or even comprehensible. The truth of the matter is that programming at the level of assembly language is very slow, very hard work. It would take a whole book to give an adequate idea, so we can do no more than touch on the flavour of it here. It is, however, worth doing if just for the experience and confidence it gives one to work at the most fundamental level of the machine.

Assembler

As we saw on pages 24-5, the program lives in one part of memory, the data it works on in another. Let us write a tiny program to search for the word 'Peter' in memory. We might want to do this as part of a word-processing operation – perhaps to change 'Peter' in the last document we wrote to 'John'. First we have to find 'Peter'.

There are several ways of doing this job, but the simplest is to start at the left-hand end of the part of memory to be searched and run along it looking for 'P'. If it is not found, the next letter is tested; if it is found, the next one is tested against 'e'. If that fits, the next is tested for 't'; if it is not found, the processor goes back to 'P'.

Many of the actual commands that the Z80 recognizes consist of a byte of instruction followed by two bytes of address. 'Jump to memory location m n' is '11000011(m)(n)'. Even the hardiest professional programmer cannot remember a hundred of those, so machine code is actually written in 'assembler', a sort of language in which mnemonics replace bytes. 'Jump to m n' is 'JP mn'.

Assembler also allows the programmer to give names to particular memory locations. This again helps the programmer's brain, but also makes it possible to write code without knowing just

A simplified diagram of the inside of the Z80 processor chip. Each Z80 actually contains two complete processors, which is why the A to L registers are shown twice. Execution can shift from one register set to the other under program control.
The 8-bit accumulator (A) register is shown connected to the arithmetic logic unit (ALU), which takes its other input from the data bus, sends an output to the bus and to the flag register (F). The other registers come in pairs and can be treated for some purposes as 16-bit registers. IX and IY are 16-bit registers that can be incremented by the data bus and used to address data in memory. SP is the 16-bit stack pointer program. PC points to the next instruction to be executed. Buffers are temporary storage areas

where in memory it will end up. Most assembly-language programs are written without specifying any particular memory addresses. They come out in 'relocatable format', which means they can be loaded into memory anywhere, and work. This is useful because a complete program is usually made up of lots of little machine code segments, each of which was written and tested on its own. Their positions in memory for test and their positions when they finally run may be quite different.

These segments are stuck together by the 'linker', a program that links chunks of code into a seamless whole, adjusting the memory locations as it goes. So, having established these preliminaries, let us look for 'Peter'. We shall assume that 'Peter' is stored in an area of memory whose first byte is called 'NAME'; and that the text we are searching is in an area called 'TEXT'.

Example of machine code

```
DSEG
NAME:    DB     'Peter/'
TEXT:    DB     'We shall be sending
                 someone to Paris – probably
                 Peter./'

CSEG
START:   LD     HL,TEXT
L0:      LD     DE,NAME
         LD     A,(DE)
         LD     B,A
L1:      LD     A,(HL)
         CP     '/'            ;look for end of
                                text
         JR     Z,NOTFND       ;jump if end
         CP     B              ;look for next
                                character
         INC    HL
         JR     NZ,L1
         PUSH   HL
L2:      INC    DE
         LD     A,(DE)
         CP     '/'
         JR     Z,FOUND
         CP     (HL)
         INC    HL
         JR     Z,L2
         POP    HL
         JR     L3
NOTFND:                        ;program to
                                cope with the
                                not-found case
                                goes here
FOUND:                         ;program to
                                cope with the
                                found case
```

As you can see, this is pretty complicated, and you might not want to write it for a living. Sensible people only write machine code when they have to, and that is when they need code that is small and runs fast. It is usually used for languages and systems software, or bits of programs in high-level languages that get used often – and would otherwise slow things down.

Professional software houses hate machine code, because it is very expensive to write, very hard to maintain – that is, mend when bugs appear – and usually has to be completely rewritten if the program is to run on another machine, or if the original programmer changes jobs.

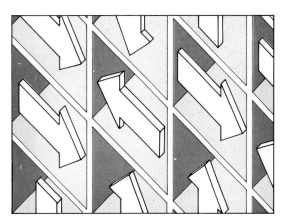

Pointers

At its simplest, a pointer is an address where something is stored. A variable in BASIC may well be stored as a name in a list of possible names, each one with a pointer next to it which indicates another piece of memory where the value is. For instance, in the diagram below we have a variable called 'FRUITS' pointing to an actual fruit 'apple'. Pointers are extensively used in advanced programming, and indeed the language 'C', currently used for most serious programming, seems to be largely about manipulating pointers. (The '*'s in the sample of 'C' on page 79 indicate pointers to the variables that follow.) In it you can have pointers to pointers to pointers and get in a tangle quite quickly. But the beauty of pointers is that you can aim routines at different things in memory without having to move the data to the scene of operations. Programming with pointers is rather like going rabbit shooting at night with a powerful light.

The disadvantage of using pointers to indicate the things you want to work on is that the memory – and the disk – eventually gets full up with things that are no longer pointed to, like 'quince' in the diagram overleaf. To stop the memory getting full of this sort of rubbish, programs that use pointers have to have 'garbage collection' routines that go about like rather bossy dustmen, checking every bit of memory to see whether it is pointed to, and if not, restoring it to a list of free memory for the next routine to use when it wants to store something.

Many BASICs store text by having a list of pointers and lengths. The pointer '111' indicates the start of the string 'apple', and the length shows how long it is – five characters. This makes it easier to store data items of widely different sizes

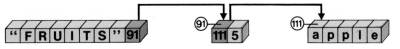

Stacks

The word 'stack' in computing has a special and very important meaning. It is an area of memory that is handled in a special way. It usually stores data in fixed-length chunks – 2 bytes in an 8-bit machine – to cope with memory addresses. It has a pointer to the next vacant stack address that lives in a special register in the processor. Of course, a program can have its own stack as well. A piece of data is 'pushed' onto the stack to store it, and 'popped' off again when it is wanted. Most assemblers have commands 'PUSH' and 'POP' to do these things automatically. The custom is to reserve a few hundred bytes of memory at the top of the program area for the stack. The chief use of stacks is in subroutines. At the end of the subroutine the stack sets the address to which the program must return.

Arithmetic and floating point (the faint-hearted can skip this)

If we write a program statement that contains the message 'C=2+3' to the machine, we want it to do some arithmetic and store the result under the variable name 'C'. '2+3' is, to the computer, a string of three ASCII symbols: '00110010', '00101011', '00110011'. It has a piece of program called a 'parser' that recognizes strings with the form 'number', 'operator', 'number'. When it sees something like that it goes away and wrestles with it. The operator '+' tells it to take the two numbers and do a particular sort of operation on them by using the appropriate chunks of machine code. The operators '−', '*' or '/' (subtract, multiply or divide) would each command different chunks doing different things.

Things are not too bad when we try to do a sum like '2+3' because 2 and 3 can be turned from their ASCII codes directly into bytes 00000010 and 00000011 and then added by the processor's built-in add command. Since an 8-bit processor has some double registers, numbers up to 65,536 can be handled in this way. There is a command to subtract as well. However, the result may be a negative number, and this is normally handled by using the first bit in the first byte to signal + or −. This limits the numbers 2 bytes can represent to the range −32,766 to +32,767 and often shows up in high-level languages which have a special way of handling 'integers' – numbers that are represented internally by 2 bytes.

The numbers '2' and '3' are easy enough, and '2345' presents no great problem, but bigger numbers such as '10,078,489.56472' are a different proposition. They can hardly be put into byte form. They could be stored as strings, with each digit represented either by its ASCII code byte or its value in bits. However, this gets very wasteful since each byte is capable of storing up to 255 numbers, but we would only want it to hold the ten digits in the range 0–9. We would only be using a twenty-fifth of its capacity.

The answer that has evolved over many years of agonizing machine code programming is 'floating point arithmetic'. The essence of this scheme is that numbers are represented in scientific format: '2345' would be stored as 2.345 E 3. The first part of this is the 'mantissa', the second the 'abscissa'. A fixed number of bytes is allocated to each and the effect is that a floating point number can consist of a fixed number of significant integers, though the decimal point can come anywhere. For instance, 2345.678, 23.45678 and .00002345678 are essentially the same floating point number with the points in different places – commanded by different values for the abscissa. This makes the job of writing a high-level language somewhat easier because the amount of memory needed for each number used in arithmetic is known in advance – which it would not be if string representations were allowed. In Microsoft BASIC, for instance, the programmer has a choice of three ways of representing numbers – each giving a higher accuracy for the numbers: 'integer', represented by 2 bytes and covering the range −32,766 and +32,767; 'single precision', which is stored as 4 bytes and gives seven decimal digits; and 'double precision', stored as 8 bytes, giving fourteen significant digits. The programmer needs to be able to choose which he or she wants in order to save space in a big program and speed up execution. A routine that loops through some bit of arithmetic will run some ten times faster if its numbers are integers rather than double precision.

Machine code programs to do floating point arithmetic are very tough indeed, and it is lucky for the contemporary programmers that they can buy the routines ready made in any respectable high-level language.

There are several tricks or – to put a smarter name on them – basic methods which are used by professional programmers. The novice can benefit from knowing about them because they are used in the languages he or she uses, and because he or she may want to use them directly.

Flags

We saw on page 80 how flags are used in machine code programming; they are also very useful in higher-level languages.

You will often want to make note of some condition for general access throughout a program. For instance, you might be writing a program that talked about a third person, and you want it to say 'he' or 'she' appropriately. You would find out which is right to begin with and set a flag variable to 'M' or 'F'. All the routines that talked about the person can then adjust themselves accordingly. You might be writing a multilingual package. By setting a 'language' flag, you could make it go and get the prompts from the appropriate file.

Data Storage

As I cannot repeat too often, all that gets stored inside a computer is masses of 0s and 1s. They have no intrinsic meaning – you cannot really tell whether one set of 0s and 1s is a program to fight the Third World War or data to produce weight-watchers' menus. All programmers face the problem of wrenching the outside world into some representation by bits.

The nearest part of the outside world to the computer is the keyboard. We saw on pages 12-13 how each possible keystroke turns into a single byte. That is fine as far as it goes, but it does not do much for more human chunks of information like words and numbers.

A 'word' is a string of characters. Although in ordinary English words usually consist of up to forty or so letters with vowels and consonants roughly alternating to make syllables, there is no reason not to allow 'words' to consist of any typable characters, and indeed of any bytes (remember that ASCII characters have 0 as the most significant bit; most computers have a set of 'graphics' characters which correspond to bytes with 1 as their most significant bit).

This means that we can store real words such as 'apple', part numbers such as '34thg89/45' or even more exotic things. The way these are normally stored is by keeping the string of ASCII bytes with a byte at the front whose value is interpreted as the length of the string: 5apple934thg89/4.

The length bytes are underlined, and the point of them is that any program which comes to read one of these 'strings' of bytes just looks at the length number, and reads that many bytes. The next byte is another length byte. There is a consequence to keeping the length as a single byte: no string can be more than 255 characters long – since 255 (FF Hex) is the biggest value a byte can have (see pp. 12-13).

In a more sophisticated application, the length byte might be kept somewhere else, with a pointer to the actual text. The pointer is, of course, just the address of the start of the string. If you wanted to change 'apple' to 'pear' you would just alter the pointer from the address of 'apple' to the address of 'pear', altering the length byte from 5 to 4.

After a few more changes – from 'pear' to 'grapefruit' and then to 'plum' – the system still works perfectly well, but the area where the strings are kept – the 'string space' – is getting a little full of discarded fruit. It is very much the same problem that we had with storing things on disks on pages 44-5 – but it is solved in a different way. The 'garbage collector' runs when there is no longer any clear space at the top of the string space to add a new fruit. It runs through the string space looking for areas that are *not* pointed to by the list of string names and lengths. It then moves all the strings down, and readjusts the pointers. In this way the odd bits of free space in the middle of the strings reappear at the top, free for new use.

Imagine now that we want to keep a list of possible fruits which we are going to access in a more controlled way than as separate strings. They might be: apple, pear, quince, orange, avocado.... We may want to alter, add or delete fruit in the list. A reasonably simple way of doing the job is to give each entry an extra two bytes which point to the next one. The usefulness of this is that if you want to change 'quince' to 'lemon', you just have to alter the bytes that point to 'quince' so that they point to 'lemon', and then make 'lemon' point to 'orange'. This makes what is called a 'linked list'.

People often want to make more ambitious lists with branches, called 'tree' structures, where one choice leads to others. For example, you might have a list of continents, countries, cities. Each connection in this list is called a 'node' and points to the nodes that follow. So we start with a 'world' node, which points to the continents: world a, b, c, d.... The pointer 'a' leads to: Asia e, f, g, h.... 'e' leads to: China j, k, l,... and j leads to Beijing.

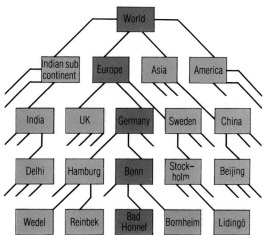

A scheme for storing a large list of countries and towns in a computer. Each entry (apart from the first, 'World') is pointed to by another, and points to a varying number of other entries. This makes it easy to run down: World–Europe–Germany–Bonn–Bad Honnef (a village near Bonn). However, it is hard to implement in the machine since each entry points to a varying number of further entries

This is relatively simple to store – just write, say, 'China,j,k,l', where j,k,l are pointers to the towns in that country – wherever they are kept in string space. However, it is not terribly easy to program because the number of pointers depends on the number of towns in each country, or the number of countries in each continent. It

Below A linked list is a way of storing a simple list of data. Each entry has an extra byte which gives the start of the next entry. To change an entry – from 'lemon' to 'quince' – alter the byte at the end of 'pear' so that it points to 'quince'. Nothing now points to 'lemon' so it has disappeared from the list

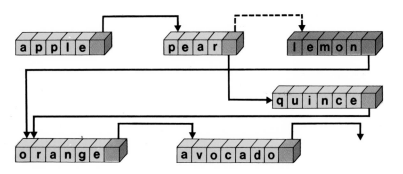

A better scheme than the one shown on the previous page: each entry points to only two others. Inside the machine (below), each entry has two 2-byte addresses after it which store the beginnings of the next items on the list. At the front of each entry is the address of the item that points to it, so that the list can be searched from the bottom up – to find out, for example, what country Bad Honnef is in. This is called a 'tree'

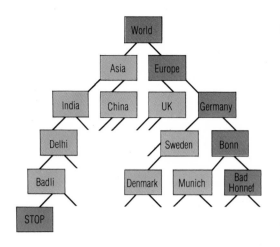

is easier to store this kind of stuff in a tree whose nodes have only two branches.

Now, the nodes and their pointers have a standard format: 'China,a,b'. The drawback is that, for instance, all the continents do not appear at the same level, so you cannot deduce what something is from where it is. One way of coping with this might be to make things of the same sort chain to the left, with a marker to say when they change. You can store a vast amount of information like this, because the number of nodes doubles at each level. A full tree ten nodes deep will store 1024 items, one twenty deep will store a million. This is fine if you just want to know, say, what villages there are in Asia, but if you want to go back up the tree to find out what country contains the village of Bad Honnef (West Germany, near Bonn), you have a rather difficult task: your program has to roam about plaintively asking: 'Is anyone pointing to Bad Honnef?' in order to find the town it hangs off. This could take an awful lot of processing.

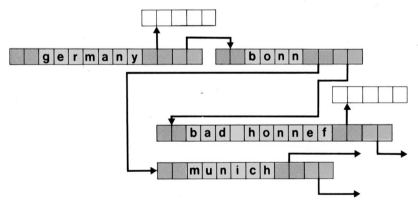

The answer is backwards as well as forwards pointers. The things at the nodes could be many other things besides places. They could be materials needed in manufacture, companies in an industry, or in expert systems (see p. 86) rules for handling information at other nodes: 'If the patient foams at the mouth, has a fever and has been bitten by a mad dog, then....'

Sorting

It has been said that at any one moment 20 per cent of all the computers in the world are sorting data. That was said in the days before the Sinclair ZX81 was the most widespread computer, but it illustrates the curious fact that people have an often irrational passion for seeing their data sorted into some sort of order. As Wilhelm Knuth observes: 'Data that has been sorted into alphabetical order often looks quite authoritative even when the associated numerical information has been incorrectly computed.'

The other thing it shows is that sorting takes a very long time.

'Sorting' a file means taking the records in it and arranging them in some sort of order. It might be records of employees, sorted alpabetically:

Able, Tom
Baker, John
Baker, William

Notice that the Bakers have been sorted by their first names as well. You might want to sort by people's earnings:

Lucas, Andrew, £345.26
Baker, William, £122.87
Baker, John, £45.20

You might want to sort things in a much more complicated way. For instance, the British Post Office allows you a reduced rate on large mailings if you sort your mail by post code to save them the trouble. You would need a specially written program that knew about post (zip) codes.

But, for the moment, let us stay with an alphabetical sort. We have a number of records (see pp. 44-5), and we want to sort them alphabetically on the first word. There are dozens of different ways of doing the job. Knuth devotes 379 dense pages to the subject, so we cannot really do it justice here. He writes of sorting by: insertion, exchanging, selection, merging and distribution. There are two conflicting objectives in writing a program to sort: you want the thing to run in the minimum amount of memory – or, at least, not more than the memory you have available; and you want it to run in the minimum time – or, at least, not longer than the working life of your computer. The key activity in sorting is comparing two things together: should this name come below or above this other name? Any sorting program has to do a lot of comparing and that takes time. Much of the art of sorting is in devising algorithms, clever methods which involve the fewest possible comparisons between one thing and another.

Just to get grip on the problem, let us write a little program in BASIC to sort words into alphabetic order. These words are going to be held in a string array W$ in memory. ('REM' means that the text following is an explanatory remark.)

```
1    REM FIRST ENTER SOME WORDS
10   DIM W$(100)
20   INPUT"Enter a word and hit Return –
     Return alone to quit";W$(N)
30   IF W$(N)=" " THEN 50 REM EXIT IF NO
     WORD
40   N=N+1:GOTO 20 REM N COUNTS
     WORDS
50   PRINT N;"words entered – sorting"
60   SWP=0 REM FLAG TO SHOW IF
     ANOTHER PASS NEEDED
70   FOR K=0 TO N-1
80   IF W$(K)>W$(K+1) THEN SWAP
     W$(K),W$(K+1):SWP=1 REM SEE TEXT
90   NEXT K
100  IF SWP=1 THEN PSS=PSS+1:?"Pass";PSS:
     GOTO 60 REM COUNT PASSES, DO
     ANOTHER IF ANY SWAPS ON LAST
110  REM NOW PRINT THE RESULTS
120  FOR K=0 TO N
130  PRINT W$(K);" ";
140  NEXT K
```

This little program first asks you to enter some words to sort – it could, of course, get them from a file or a data statement. It then runs through them in line 80, comparing each word – W$(K) – with the one to its right – W$(K+1) – to see if it is 'bigger'. BASIC allows you to use the symbol '>' with strings – it compares the ASCII values of the first, second, third, etc., characters in both words. If any of them *is* bigger then the test succeeds. This produces telephone-book sorting. Suppose we are comparing 'banana' with 'banal'. Both words are the same until we get to the second 'n' in 'banana'. This is ASCII 110, and is greater than ASCII 108 – the value of 'l' in 'banal'. The test would therefore succeed, and we would want to move 'banal' to the left of 'banana'. This is done with the command 'SWAP'. If your BASIC does not have it, you will need a subroutine like this:

```
1000 N$=W$(K)
1010 W$(K)=W$(K+1)
1020 W$(K+1)=N$
1030 RETURN
```

and you will have to change line 80 to:

```
80 IF W$(K)>W$(K+1)THENGOSUB1000:SWP=1
```

Notice that line 80 needs all the words to be in the same case. The test will work with either 'banal' and 'banana' or 'BANAL' and 'BANANA' or 'Banal' and 'Banana'. But it will not work with 'banal' and 'BANANA' because all the capital letters have lower ASCII codes than their small equivalents (see pp. 12-13). A proper sorting routine would have to convert all the words to either upper or lower case before comparing them.

This is a 'bubble' sort because the words float to the left as the sort proceeds. It is the easiest sort to write but, as you will see when you run it, it is very inefficient to run because on average we have to make N passes through the list, making N comparisons each time, so the running time is proportional to N^2. Knuth says of it: 'The bubble sort seems to have nothing to recommend it, except a catchy name.'

A decent sort should run in a time proportional to $N*Log(N)$. What this means in practice is seen by comparing the two criteria:

Records	N^2	$N*LOG(N)$
10	100	23
100	10,000	460
1000	1,000,000	6908
10,000	100,000,000	9,2103

A well-written sort will take as long to run over 10,000 records as a bubble sort over 100.

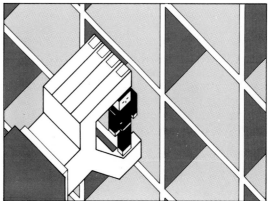

Hashing

Another 'big computer' technique worth being aware of is hashing. The name suggests a fairly brutal procedure and it is just that. The idea is to take things like words, people's names, amounts of money – recognizable entities from the real world – and do something to them to produce unique index numbers. To make this plainer, let us suppose we are filing a stack of bills from different companies. We want to put them into folders in some way so that we can find any of them again. One way of proceeding might be to take the ASCII value of the first letter of the name, add it to the ASCII value of the second divided by 10, add it to the third divided by 100 and so on:

Name	Hash
john	119.25
fred	115.51
harrods	115.966
maceys	120.804

In this way, each word gets assigned to a number which is guaranteed to be unique, but will, at the same time, fall into a small area. There are, of course, millions of different ways of producing hashes. Part of the fun of computing is trying to invent methods that will produce unique values without taking up too much space.

EXPERT SYSTEMS

Top There are a number of routine problems that can only be solved by applying a huge number of rules to the information available. One of them is geological prospecting: 'If there is schist on top of granite and surface streams show high magnesium content and . . . then there is ore underground.' Here is a computer-generated display that, taking all the information into account, shows where it might be best to start digging

Above One of the most tedious, but essential, laboratory tasks is classifying and counting small particles in samples of blood, medicines, mineral products, and so on. A TV camera mounted on a microscope provides a simple two-dimensional image for a specialized vision system that recognizes particles by shape and size and counts them

When people start computing, it seems as if writing programs is the difficulty. But what they really find hard is not the unfamiliar code but the range of new concepts which programming creates and allows you to manipulate. As we shall see on pages 94-7 when looking at relational searches in databases, the computer opens up intellectual difficulties that simply do not arise in a world of pens and paper. By learning to program you also – without realizing it – learn to understand some of these things.

To help the incomputerate, what is wanted is not so much a programming aid as a thinking aid. Very crudely, this is what the class of software called 'expert systems' – or 'knowledge-based' systems – is all about.

The crudest expert system is a database manager (see pp. 94-7). It indexes various sorts of knowledge and lets you call information out of it. 'I sold something to Binks & Co. on 14 January 1982. What was it?' A system that only answers that sort of question cannot be considered 'expert' even though it knows a lot. The next level up is a system that can index and cross-reference information supplied to it by a human 'oracle' or expert, and give it back to the user in an intelligent way. It can cope with a good deal of uncertainty in the user's view of what is happening. Imagine a database that tells you how to mend your car. You might have a conversation with it like this ('Y' is you, 'X' is the expert system):

Y: It won't start
X: Is there petrol in the tank?
Y: Yes
X: Is the battery flat?
Y: I don't think so
X: What certainty?
Y: 80%
X: Take a look at the plugs

The expert system can cope with uncertain answers. You do not have to say that the battery is or is not flat; you can give a percentage. The system might go on to ask if the spark plugs were all right – you might be only 50 per cent sure about those. At the end of its questions it will possibly deliver a range of possible troubles, with the likelihood of each one being the cause of the problem.

Now, to make such a system requires an oracle who can tell the embryo program that is to become expert in car mending that if you are 80 per cent sure that the battery is functioning, and if the engine does not fire and if there is petrol in the tank and if the spark plugs are better than 50 per cent in order then there is probably a loose wire under the bonnet. The difficulty is that the program is not just dealing with mechanics: it is dealing with what non-mechanical people think about mechanics. To make such a program work properly you would have to do a huge survey of unmechanical owners of nonoperative cars

to find out how likely they were to be right when they said they were 80 per cent sure the battery was all right. Still, there are said to be situations in which there are oracles around who can give these sorts of judgements.

A more useful thing still would be a learning system. You would show it a whole mass of facts and ask it to deduce some rules. Of course, the facts must be in the computer somehow, and since computers cannot walk round cars, peering under the bonnet and into the petrol tank, this means text or numbers that are held on disk.

Imagine you asked such a system to look at the stock and staff records for your business over the last two years. It would go away and brood over the files and come back and say: 'It seems to me that whenever you run out of blue buttons in the winter months, you hire two extra workers.' And you say 'Land's mercy!', and save on your wages bill by ordering plenty of blue buttons as soon as you come back from your summer holiday.

Such a system, written by Richard Forsyth of the North London Polytechnic, was set to look at the hospital records of heart attack patients. It was asked to look at what was known about the patient on admission, and to discover the best indicator of survival. It found that if the patient's mean arterial pressure (in mm of mercury) is greater than 61 less the urine output (in ml/hr), the patient will probably live; otherwise he will die. This surprised the doctors, who had watched plenty of people dying of heart attacks, but had not noticed the indications with the precision that the computer had.

In principle such a program could do what the 'program generators' were supposed to do. To write a book-keeping program, you would not have to sit down and work out just what went on in your books and how to get the computer to do it; you would just show it the books from the last couple of years and let it deduce what was going on. Of course, there would be places where you could explain what you meant, but it would do the bulk of the brain work.

You could use the program in situations where you did not know what the rules were. Suppose you were an ecologist, doing a survey of the habits of urban foxes. You could divide the city up into 100-metre (300-yard) squares and enter into the computer a list of all the foxes in these squares, and the things you thought might have a bearing on their behaviour. And when you run the program over it, the machine might report: 'Did you know that dog foxes like garages provided there's a bread shop within 100 metres, otherwise they like rose bushes; while vixens like libraries, hat shops and rose bushes?'

This sort of software is beginning to filter out of the artificial intelligence laboratories. One such system is the Analog Concept Learning System from Edinburgh University, which runs on machines as small as the Apple.

ZIPF'S LAW

Most of the problem – and the challenge – and the fun of computing is that it lets you deal with very much greater volumes of information much faster than you can using paper. You can handle more things in more different ways; and, not surprisingly, new kinds of behaviour emerge.

One of the most interesting insights into the behaviour of masses of information was discovered by an American sociologist named George Zipf back in the 1940s.* Although the work has great relevance to a computerate view of the world, it was done – with immense labour – using paper and pencil. Zipf started out looking at the frequency of words in English text. He went through large chunks of prose, counting how often each word was repeated. He then arranged the results in order of rank, so that the most frequently used word came first, then the next and so on. Then he drew a graph of the results.

This looks much as you would expect: as words get rarer, they are used less often. However, the graph does not dive straight into the bottom axis because there are always rare new words coming in to trickle the curve out to the right.

The next thing he did was to plot rank against the *logarithm* of the frequency. Now this looked altogether more intriguing. He got a straight line. To the nonmathematical, this may not be very interesting, but it meant that frequency and rank were connected by an equation like this:

$$\log F = -k(\log R) + l$$

where k and l are constants. Now, we can look at l as the log of some other constant, say m, so this equation becomes:

$$\log F = -k(\log R) + \log m$$

or:

$$\log F = \log ((m/R)+(k))$$

It turned out that k was pretty well 1, so, taking antilogarithms:

$$F = m/R$$

which, in plain English, meant that the frequency of a word was proportional to 1 over its rank. The third most common word, for instance, was found just one third as often as the most common word. The hundredth most common word, one hundredth as often as the most common.

All we need to know now is: how common is the most common word? And we do not have to spend weeks counting words in Shakespeare to find out. If we add up: $1/1 + 1/2 + 1/3 + ... 1/n$, we find that although the sum gets big quite rapidly to begin with, it soon starts to level out. You can do it with this program:

```
10 K=0:N=0
20 N= N+1/K
30 ? K; N;" ";
40 K=K+1
50 GOTO 20
```

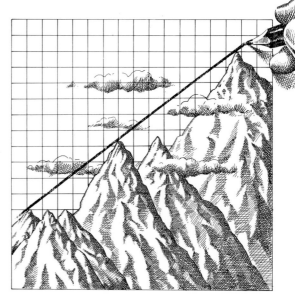

While I was writing this I had the program running on another machine, and got these results:

K	N
10	2.929
100	5.187
1000	7.485
10000	9.788
100000	12.091

As k gets bigger, n stops growing so fast, and when it gets very big, n tends to about 12. You can, of course, carry on running the program until k is 1 million, 10 million and so on, but it will take an awfully long time and will not tell you much more than you knew already.

This is interesting, odd and useful. Zipf found that the same rule, or something very like it, applied all over the place. It applied to the sizes of cities and towns: in any country the second largest city was roughly half the size of the largest; the third one third the size, right down to the tiny villages. So, if you knew the number of people in a country, you could calculate, say, how many towns there ought to be with between 100 and 200,000 inhabitants.

Records of people's addresses in grid-patterned American cities showed that half as many people had walked two blocks to find their spouses as those who discovered love on the block in which they themselves lived; one third as many had walked three blocks, and so on.

Zipf's law also applied to the sizes of businesses – if you know the total value of microcomputers sold in a year, you can use Zipf's Law to work out roughly the turnovers of the different companies in the industry. The biggest company should sell twice as many as the second, and so on down the line. If there are already a hundred companies, and you want to start another, you can work out how many computers you ought to sell each year.

*G. K. Zipf, *Human Behavior and the Principle of Least Effort*, Addison-Wesley, 1949.

MODELLING

One of the most useful jobs computers can do is to 'model' situations that have not yet happened. Computer modelling is used to forecast the outcome of scientific experiments, businesses, economies, weapons systems and wars. It is used for forecasting tomorrow's weather, tomorrow's bank rate and the number of children born in the next five years.

People have, of course, been making mathematical models for centuries. Newton's Laws of Motion are a tool which makes it easy to build mathematical models of systems such as the moon, sun and earth and how they move together. The model works by creating a series of equations which can be solved to give the positions of the three bodies at any time. In this way, for instance, astronomers can predict eclipses many years ahead and – more usefully – produce tables for use by navigators at sea so that they can calculate the position of their ship or aircraft.

There are, however, few systems in real life that can be completely described by equations simple enough to solve on paper. Anyone who has done elementary mechanics can solve the equations that describe the movement of a shell fired from a gun *in a vacuum* – they are the same as for the earth and moon; but no one can easily solve the equations that describe a shell's motion in the atmosphere, where the air drags it backwards in proportion to the square of its speed.

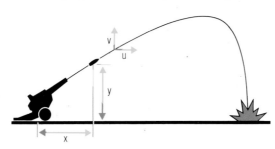

The easiest way to find out how it moves is to use a computer model. You divide the shell's flight up into a large number of small jumps, each taking a short length of time – say a thousandth of a second. You consider the shell at the beginning of one time interval. You know its speed, so you can calculate the air drag on it. You know how much that will slow it down over the time interval. You know the average speed for the interval and therefore how much it will move upwards against gravity, and how much along. You add these two small distances to the previous totals up and along, and start again with a new speed and position. A simple program to calculate the flight of a shell is as follows:

```
10    K=.01:DT=.1
20    INPUT 'Muzzle velocity';W
30    INPUT 'Angle of elevation';AN
40    AN=AN*3.14/2/90
50    U=W*COS(AN):V=W*SIN(AN)
100   FOR T=0 TO 1000 STEP DT
105   PRINT X;Y
110   X=X+U*DT:Y=Y+V*DT
116   IF Y<0 THEN STOP
120   Z=U↑2+V↑2
130   W=W-K*DT*Z
140   U=W*U/Z↑.5
150   V=W*V/Z↑.5-32*DT
160   NEXT T
```

Line 10 sets up two constants: K determines how much the air drag slows the shell down – in real life it would depend on the shape and weight of the shell; DT is the time interval for each step, here set to .1 second. Lines 20 and 30 ask for the muzzle velocity in feet per second and the angle of elevation. Line 40 turns degrees into the radians that BASIC's sine and cosine functions use. Line 50 calculates the initial velocities: U parallel to the earth, V upwards.

The loop that calculates the flight of the shell in each instant starts at 100. (If 1000 is not large enough to cover the whole flight, make it bigger.) Line 105 prints the position of the shell along (X) and up (Y). Line 110 calculates the next position by adding the distance the shell moves horizontally (U*DT) to X and (V*DT) to Y.

Remember that V will be negative once the shell has passed the peak of its flight and starts to fall to earth again, so Y can get less than 0 – i.e. it has hit the earth. Line 116 tests for this and stops the program. Line 120 calculates the square of the speed of the shell through the air – which is, as Pythagoras's Theorem tells us, the sum of the squares of its velocities horizontally and vertically. Line 130 calculates the change in the air-speed W of this shell caused by air drag.

Line 140 calculates the new horizontal speed U from W, proportioned by the old horizontal speed over the square root of Z; and 150 does the same thing for V, with the help of a factor (32*DT) to account for the downward acceleration caused by gravity. Line 150 calculates the new vertical velocity, taking into account air resistance and gravity.

In several steps the calculations are much too simple to describe what is actually happening. But because the steps are so short we can ignore complications such as gravity and air drag working together, which would make the equations

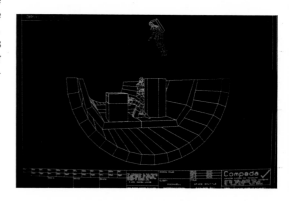

impossible to solve. Ballistic calculations like this were one of the first tasks given to electronic computers during the Second World War.

If you run this program you get a printout of the X and Y positions of the shell. It would not be too hard to make the computer draw the shell's path on the screen or the printer. Notice, though, how inaccurate the computer's results are. Because of the method of small steps, small errors in each calculation soon build up into big ones. Try firing the shell vertically upwards (angle of elevation = 90°). It should go straight up and down again (X=0), but actually it lands quite a way down range – X is a long way from 0.

The Solar Sail

An interesting subject for a model would be the motion of a solar sail moving from planet to planet. The people in the film *Tron* had such a thing, but the film makers obviously had no idea how it might work, for they showed it flying above the earth, driven by a straight light beam.

The idea is to power a space ship with a huge sail of very light, reflecting material. At any moment the ship is in orbit around the sun. You, as skipper of this astronautical barque, can steer it by tilting the sail at different angles to the sun's rays. The sail is several square kilometres in area and has a mirrored surface. The sunlight is reflected from it, and the radiation pressure (even photons have momentum) produces a force at right angles to the sail. This force can accelerate or decelerate the ship along its orbital path, so pushing it away from or towards the sun.

If you set the sail so that it makes your ship move faster in its orbit, the ship flies away from the sun, overcoming gravity. If you tilt it the other way, the ship slows down and falls inwards. Since gravity and the pressure of the sun's rays are both inversely proportional to the square of the ship's distance from the sun, you can 'sail' equally well anywhere in the solar system.

Step-by-step models like this are used for many calculations that are too complicated to cope with all at once. A good example is weather prediction: meteorologists know (or think they do) the laws of physics that control the behaviour of the atmosphere, and they have an idea, from reports of hundreds of weather stations all round the world, what state the atmosphere is in at any one time. Using a step-by-step calculation they can work forwards and predict roughly what the weather will be in a few hours' time. However, to do these calculations fast enough they need the largest possible computers.

Economies are just as complicated and hard to forecast as the weather, so another use for computer modelling is in combining many small, simple sums about economic behaviour to come up with a forecast of economic behaviour at the national level. Unfortunately, none of these economic models has been very successful. The prob-

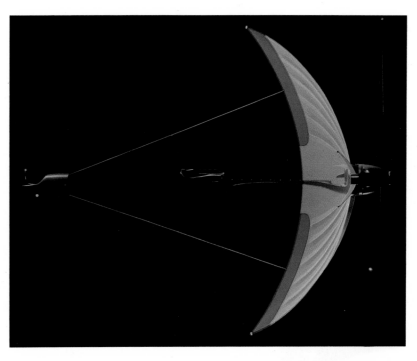

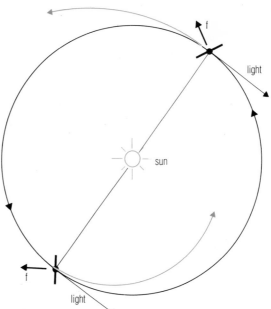

Disney's film *Tron* had some spectacular computer-generated graphics, including the solar sail shown here. Unfortunately the producers of the film seemed to have little idea how such a device would work

Left A solar sail in orbit. The helmsman steers it by angling his mirror-sail so that the force of the reflected light speeds him up along his orbit (top). Centrifugal force flings him farther from the sun. Alternatively (bottom) he slows himself down and so falls towards the sun. By angling the sail up and down he can steer out of the plane of his orbit. The dynamics are tricky: he would need patience and a computer to get anywhere in particular

lem seems to be that economies are not made up of mindless bodies which blindly obey physical laws. On the contrary, they consist of very alert and intelligent beings who are constantly trying to outguess each other about economic events, and adjusting their own behaviour in consequence. This makes the sums vastly more complicated and since no one has any real idea how to write the equations, it is not surprising that the computer models are not very successful.

Economics is just one example of a 'science' that seemed to work wonderfully as long as it was confined to paper and pencil methods on small amounts of data. Then computers came along and made it possible to test predictions on whole economies. Alas – the fatal flaws were revealed.

FRACTALS

Part of the business of computing is to find sim-
plifications of real life so that we can make our
machines behave in reasonably lifelike ways.
One of the great drawbacks to computers is that
the pictures they make are so obviously the work
of machines and not of nature. Natural objects
have a roughness and complexity which is quite
different from the smooth, regular shapes we
usually get from our screens and printers.

Happily, a way forward has recently opened
up, through the work of the mathematician Benoit
Mandelbrot, who has found a simple mathematical way to describe and reconstruct the shapes
of mountains, coastlines, trees – and even the
incredibly fine convolutions of the veins and ar-
teries in our bodies.

Mandelbrot calls this the study of 'fractals' –
things that are broken or irregular. He starts from
a simple question that must have intrigued every
student of geography and plagued every teacher:
'How long is a coastline?' Take an atlas showing
the eastern seaboard of the United States and a
pair of dividers opened to the scale equivalent of
400 miles. Walk the dividers down the coast from
St Stephen on the Bay of Fundy to Key Largo in
Florida. The length of the coastline comes to
about 1685 miles. Now close the dividers to 100
miles and try again. The length increases to 1750
miles – and this a relatively straight coast.

If you had the patience to get larger scale maps
and continue the exercise with the dividers set
to 50, 25, 10, 5, 1 – ever finer measures – the
length of the coast would go on increasing dramatically. Soon you would be measuring in
inches, round every rock. When the scale comes
down to tenths of inches, the length of the coast
shoots up again as you measure your way round
billions of pebbles. If you bring the scale down
once more to thousandths of an inch, you are
measuring the surface roughness of the rocks,
pebbles and grains of sand. Reduce the scale
again and you are inside the crystalline structure
of the rocks. Where precisely is the coast now?

Go down to the atomic scale and the 'coast' increases dramatically again as you measure from
atom to atom. A further reduction in scale takes
you inside the nucleus of the atom, where 'matter'
consists almost entirely of empty space. The
'length of the coast' – if such an idea has any
meaning – is now billions of miles.

When you think about it, the 'coastline' is not
really a line at all. If it were, it would have a
definite length. It is more like an area – a sort of
fuzzy band running along the large-scale coast –
but it is not an area either because not all the
'coast' has coastline in it. The mathematics of
dimensions tells us that a straight line has one
dimension, an area has two and a volume has
three. Mandlebrot and other mathematicians propose that a coast should have a dimension somewhere between 1 and 2.

We can make something similar by a recursive
process. Start with a big shape (top right) which
sits on a line n units long. Shrink it by the appropriate factor and use it to replace the straight
lines in itself. Do the same again, and again. Be-

Above A regular fractal can be made by starting with, say, a simple three-sided figure (top). Replace each line in it by a miniature version of itself (second). Do the same thing again with a still smaller version (third), and again (fourth). Quite soon the whole paper will be covered by something that is neither a line nor a surface, but has some of the properties of both

Left At first sight this looks like a photo from a moon mission; a second look shows continents and islands that never were by sea or land. Richard F. Voss of IBM Research, using rules developed by Benoit Mandelbrot, made the computer play god, inventing and portraying a planet and its satellite that are like – but yet not like – our own

fore long the whole paper area is covered with a dense mass of line. We *know* that each little version of the starting shape is just a line and therefore the pattern is one-dimensional; yet when you stand back, you can see that eventually there will be no bit of paper that has no line on it, and therefore the pattern is *two*-dimensional. We may have been brought up to think that dimensions have to be one or two or three, but there is no mathematical necessity for this. 1.3 does nicely for a fractal. If your computer has graphics it is not hard to write a program to do a few stages of this process.

So far so good, but although this pattern has the bumpiness of a coastline, it is too regular and it needs straightening out. The regularity can be got round by a process like a random walk. One of the earliest programs anyone ever writes on a computer is a version of Drunken Duncan. The idea is to plot the wanderings of a drunk who starts at a lamppost and staggers random distances in random directions. In time he goes everywhere – like a fractal or a ball of wool.

To make something that looks like a coast, this ball of wool needs straightening out. One example Mandelbrot found was a coin-tossing match. Mary and Thomas take turns to toss a coin. Each time it comes up heads, Thomas gives Mary one penny from his stock; each time it comes up tails, Mary gives a penny to Thomas. The graphs of their individual wealth wander up and down, sometimes higher and sometimes lower, and are strangely reminiscent of a section through a piece of land.

Mandelbrot takes this idea and extends it to make a more convoluted coast. The coastline is random but still urged in a general direction, and not made so convoluted that it overlaps itself (as Drunken Duncan's walk does). Mathematically, this means controlling the dimensionality of the coast between 1 and 2. The same thing in three dimensions produces the surface of a landscape, and with a bit of extra logic to set things going on a planet, he gets this spectacular picture which he calls: 'Planetrise over Labelgraph Hill (souvenir from a space mission that never was)'.

BUSINESS SOFTWARE

The most popular types of packaged software mimic in their results the standard sorts of paper document. If you walk into any office in the world and pick up a piece of paper, you can almost certainly classify it into one of four types, each of which has a computer equivalent:

Form – Database manager
Tabulated list – Database manager
Text – Word processors
Spread sheets and accounts – 'Visicalc' type

Databases

There is not a lot of point to computing unless you have information to compute. Historically, big computers started as machines to do complicated calculations on quite small amounts of numerical data, such as calculating the path of an artillery shell, or the conditions in an A-bomb explosion.

At the beginning, microcomputers followed the same path – the first machines had primitive storage devices and were suited to more or less elaborate manipulations of simple data. In real life, however, people need to do relatively simple operations on large amounts of information. That, after all, is what goes on in the majority of offices. The detail of most people's jobs is not complicated – it is just done on an awful lot of bits of paper. Consequently, the revolution that has made micros useful in commerce has been the development of the cheap mass storage devices that are described on pages 176-7.

Storage in itself, however, is not enough. You need a structure in order to find the information you want. A filing cabinet by itself is not much use without drawers and pockets in which to put documents, and some sort of scheme to label these containers so that you can find things again. In a sophisticated paper filing system there will be an index and a register to regulate papers coming in and out, to control who is allowed to see documents, who may amend them and who may not. Much the same sort of thing is necessary in a computerized information storage system, and providing this structure in a usable form is in itself quite a major programming task.

A structured mass of information is generally known as a 'database'. Along with the database will go a 'manager', a program to carry out the scheme used to index and sort the information for the user.

'Database' and 'database manager' are in fact terms inherited from 'big computing', and do not (for reasons we will look at below) sit altogether happily in the micro world. Database managers for micros are now often called 'information managers' – and, I suppose, we shall eventually talk about 'infobases'. Modern micro information managers tend to concentrate more on information in a form that ordinary people would recognize than on the elaborate structures that make up a conventional database manager.

The starting point for any database design is that there is a big gulf between the files managed by the operating system and information as users understand it. Think of the sort of thing that you might write in an office. You might take an index card and write on it the name, address and telephone number of one of your customers. You might scribble a few words about him or her.

You could store this as a complete computer file, but there are two disadvantages: you could only find it by referring to the file's name, when you might want to look for it by the customer's name, the date, the order number or the thing sent. Secondly, most operating systems allocate quite large chunks of disk to each file and restrict you to a limited number of files. After very few delivery notes you would have to start a new disk.

What is needed is some more detailed file structure that lets you store the information that went on the index card in much the same way as it went on the paper, but with the advantage that you can look directly for anything on the index card rather than only being able to find it from the name of the customer if the cards are filed alphabetically. There are several database managers available for micros which all differ in detail. The scheme described here is used by one British product called Superfile.*

Superfile tackles the retrieval of information by allowing the user to create a 'Record'. A Record is a chunk of information – a number of things that you would expect to find together. It consists of one or more 'Items'. Each Item consists of a 'Tag' and a 'Value'. The Tag (which has to be a single word) tells you what sort of information is in the Item, and the Value is the information itself. For instance you might have a personnel Record:

```
XNAME=Tom
XNAME=Cholmondeley
SNAME=Thumb
    ADD=Garden Cottage
    ADD=Beanstalk Drive
    ADD=Fantasyland
    PAY=50
```

The Tag in the first Item is 'XNAME' – a convenient, one-word abbreviation for 'Christian name'. It is necessary to distinguish 'Tom', the Value of 'XNAME', from 'Tom' as the Value, say, of 'CATSEX' in a Record describing cats.

The Record can have any amount of information in it. Tags can be repeated any number of times – as 'XNAME' (Christian name) and 'ADD' (address) are repeated in this example. You do not have to specify the length of the Items, nor do you have to tell Superfile before you start what is to go in a Record. If, after operating your computerized card index for a while, you decide you need to record how many children your employees have, you can add a Tag,'CHILDNUM'.

*Superfile is published by my own company, Southdata Limited.

A typical Record displayed using the screen forms package of Southdata's Superfile.
1 The square brackets separate the 'Fields', where information is entered and displayed, from the rest of the screen, which carries prompts and explanations – just like a form on paper. A Record can be found by typing anything the user knows about it into any of the Fields.
2 'Williams' typed into the Surname Field would find this Record and any others with the same name in the database – but you could also search for 'sounds like Willans'. This might be useful for receptionists and telephone salespersons.
3 Superfile lets the user define a number of Fields as

logically equivalent. This Record could have been found by typing the town, 'Newton Burrows', into any one of the four address Fields.
4 Each Record has a unique reference code.
5 Remarks can be added to Records when necessary. This one could have been found by looking for the

word 'snack' somewhere in Remarks.
6 This form was set up to prevent users entering invalid dates by mistake.
7 This Record could have been found by looking for anyone with a credit rating greater than 250.
8 The form can do arithmetic – here it totals Ms Williams's spending

A small business might want to record its customers, what they have ordered, what they have paid for (not necessarily the same thing at all). A garage might want to keep lists of spare parts, their descriptions, their part numbers, where they are kept and how many are in stock. A hospital might keep records of patients, their diseases, their wards, their doctors, and their diet. With a database manager any part of this information would be immediately accessible.

Like most database managers Superfile has 'utilities' – special programs – to allow users to create Forms on the screen to input the information they need, to find it, alter it and so on, and Report Generators to produce tabulated extracts of information from the database.

A good Forms package lets you draw a form on the screen as you would on paper, and then do calculations on the information as it is entered on or extracted from the database. For instance, you might decide to write a program to calculate your employees' weekly pay. You would add a new Tag to the Tom Thumb Record above, say, 'HOURATE', which stores the hourly rate of pay for each member of your staff. At the end of the week you would use a Form to input the hours they had worked. The Form has a calculation facility, which works out each person's rate of pay and prints a slip.

You can control the validity of information entered, because experience shows people typing in lots of records often make very silly mistakes. You should be able to build in controls to make sure that numbers are numbers – for instance, Tom's pay is not carelessly typed in as 'XXw', which could cause the payroll program some difficulty. If it is very important that things are typed in correctly, you can force verification on the users – that is, they have to type it twice, and both entries must be identical before the information will be accepted.

The second standard utility that comes with most database managers is the Report Generator. Just as the Forms package mimics the well-known style of paper document called a 'form', the Report Generator mimics tabulated reports. It allows the user to design a standard kind of report – for instance, to list everyone who owes the company more than a certain amount, or whose debt has been outstanding more than a certain length of time. In a hospital, a standard report might be produced once a week to show how many patient-bed-days were utilized in each ward with the number of nurse-hours employed and the value of the medical stores used.

Whatever the users of the system want to know, the Report Generator should allow them to find out. Thinking what you want to know and what information you have to collect in order to get it is very much more difficult than actually designing the forms or the reports to do the job. Paradoxically, the power of the computer is often oppressive because it throws open doors which did not even exist in a paper system. For instance the report on ward utilization would need so much sifting in a paper system that the hospital would have to employ a couple of clerks to do nothing else. Their wages and overheads would be a substantial expense and the project would not even be started unless the hospital felt sure that the information was worth having at that price. But in a computer system the cost of collecting and analysing is so small that there are no constraints beyond the administrator's desire to know or reluctance to burden himself with more paper. The natural consequence of cheap information extraction in big computer systems has often been a blizzard of paper, containing so much information that no one could make any sense of it.

Increasingly one finds in dealing with computers that the main constraint on what is done is not cost but human time, and that is often the time of the chief people in the orgnization. This is a natural consequence of automating routine tasks. What is left is creative thought. It comes as a shock to many people in small businesses that installing a computer removes the time-consuming but soothing tasks they used to do. There are no excuses any more for not getting on with the real problems such as 'Why am I doing this at all?'

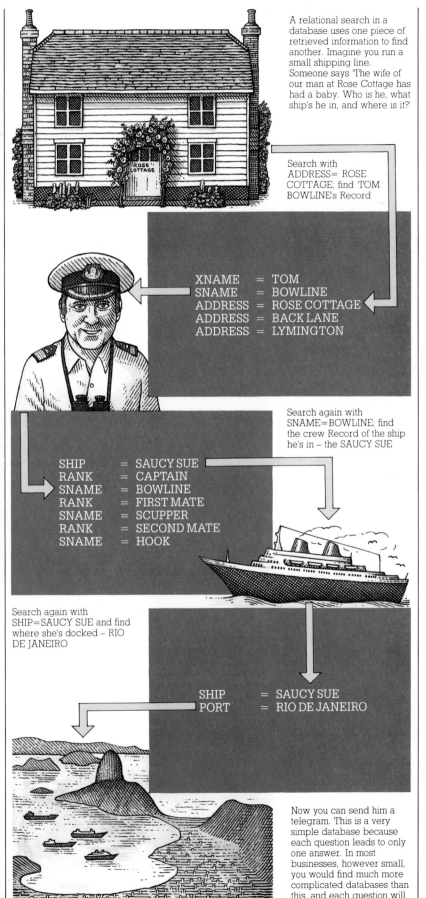

A relational search in a database uses one piece of retrieved information to find another. Imagine you run a small shipping line. Someone says 'The wife of our man at Rose Cottage has had a baby. Who is he, what ship's he in, and where is it?'

Search with ADDRESS= ROSE COTTAGE; find TOM BOWLINE's Record

XNAME   = TOM
SNAME   = BOWLINE
ADDRESS = ROSE COTTAGE
ADDRESS = BACK LANE
ADDRESS = LYMINGTON

Search again with SNAME=BOWLINE; find the crew Record of the ship he's in – the SAUCY SUE

SHIP   = SAUCY SUE
RANK   = CAPTAIN
SNAME = BOWLINE
RANK   = FIRST MATE
SNAME = SCUPPER
RANK   = SECOND MATE
SNAME = HOOK

Search again with SHIP=SAUCY SUE and find where she's docked – RIO DE JANEIRO

SHIP = SAUCY SUE
PORT = RIO DE JANEIRO

Now you can send him a telegram. This is a very simple database because each question leads to only one answer. In most businesses, however small, you would find much more complicated databases than this, and each question will lead to many answers

Relational database

So far so good, and a simple database manager can do a lot in situations where you want to store and retrieve chunks of information. However, as so often in real life, things are more complicated. As soon as you start recording business transactions you run into a complication straight away. Most businesses deal many times with the same people (see Zipf's Law, p. 87, for an idea of how many times). You would need to know, say, the name, address and telephone number of your customers, but for several reasons you would not want to have to record all this information each time you dealt with them. You might get it wrong some of the time. If you sold ten things to Mr Smith and got him into the database as 'Smith', the eleventh time you might make a mistake and put him in as 'Smythe'. The next time you wanted him the computer would not be able to find him. If Mr Smith changed his address or some other detail of himself, you would want to make the alteration in only one place.

This means that your database should be able to link different Records together so that the Record of one particular sale to Smith can be tied to the Record containing Smith's name and address. Furthermore, you might not want to keep all the details of the things you sold him in each transaction Record. Imagine that on 15 January you sold him a dozen of your health shoe type 46. There is a lot of information to go with 'type 46' – they are carved out of beechwood, have leather uppers, brass nails round the welt and weigh 15 lb a pair. You do not want to have to write all that down every time you sell one. So the transaction Record should point to a stock Record which tells you all about type 46: how many you have in stock, how many are on order and from whom. You might have a lot of other Records about the factories that make shoes for you.

This may sound simple, but many books have been written and reputations made by working out ways to do it. In the Superfile package we have been discussing, you link two Records together by including the same Item in each of them. For instance, you might want to link a customer's address Record to his transactions. You could do this by giving him an identification number under the Tag, say, 'ID': ID=34. The same Item would go in each of his transaction Records too, so that you could find Mr Smith's transactions by finding his address Record, extracting his ID, and then searching again with that to get out the Records of what he had bought. Similarly, you could move from those Records to find out who had made the things he bought.

This is what is known in the trade as a 'relational database'. With it you could ask questions like: 'In which towns were shoes sold that were made for us by factory X?' This means in practice that you would look at the factories' Records to pick out X. You would then look to see what types of shoes they made, then at the transactions with these type numbers to find out which customers bought them, and then at the customers' address Records to see what towns they live in.

This can all become quite complicated. In the case of the shoe factory there are not likely to be very many answers at each stage. But imagine that you are a crusading journalist investigating a fraud in a database of incorporated companies. You start with one company, Dirty Deals Inc., and ask: 'What companies share directors with Dirty Deals?' 'What other companies share directors with those companies?'

You are hoping to find that there is a chain of shared directorships back to a single holding company in Panama. But to find it you may have to search many thousands of companies, and you will have to take great care about what you look for. Think what has to happen. Dirty Deals has five directors: A, B, C, D and E. A is also a director of Fictions Inc., Under the Counter Inc. and Feel the Width Inc. Each of those has between three and ten directors, who are all directors of several other companies. So you search on A and find Fictions, which has directors F, G, H and I. You remember A and Fictions and start searching to see what F is up to. He is a director of five more companies – any one of which might be where the fraud all comes together. You have to remember them all, and check them against the results for all the other directors of all the other companies that share a director with Dirty Deals. This is only a two-deep search. The company you want may be ten away from Dirty Deals.

This example demonstrates that the common statement 'It's all in the computer' may be true, but is not necessarily any more useful that if 'it' were on the moon and the Space Programme had been cancelled. This could easily turn into a 'computational explosion' (which we shall meet again on page 175), which quite quickly produces more information than the machine or its users can handle.

On the other hand, the database can easily accumulate more information than you want. 'Mr A. Smith' of '16 High Street' may creep in as 'Andrew Sythe' of 'The Lindens, High St.' Purging a database of duplications is a fearful task.

Moving from paper, where information stayed nice and still and inaccessible, to computers, where it can whizz around and multiply itself, makes you realize that a lot of apparently simple business procedures conceal very taxing intellectual problems, which are only not seen as problems because the rigidity of paper information-handling systems makes it impossible to tackle them. For instance, you could ask a relational database to work backwards from your supplies to your customers to recall purchases of faulty goods.

Word Processors

The next standard sort of document is one that contains mainly text: letters, articles, reports, books and memoranda. Packages to produce this material are called 'word processors'. Since text is, although fairly complicated, well-understood stuff and has been about in the world for many hundreds of years, there is not much scope for originality in the way word processors work.

They all do three main things. They let the user create and edit a document on the screen, print it nicely laid out on paper and, when he or she has finished, store it away on disk ready for next time.

The effect is that a document (such as this book) can be written on the screen, edited, printed out, re-edited and so on without having to go through the agony of retyping it each time. Standard letters, reports and contracts (or chunks of them) can be stored on disk and pulled in with items changed to make up the finished document.

Let us look at these three phases in turn. The first is being able to create text on the screen. Users want to be able to type at the keyboard as if at a typewriter. They need to be able to go back and change bits of text, to move a paragraph from here to there and so on. So, every word-processing system allows users to jump the cursor around, to find particular words, to find a word all through the text (say 'programme') and change it to another (say 'program'). They can go to the disk and pull in some different text from another file – so building up, perhaps, a complicated legal contract by adding standard paragraphs. The paragraphs might be stored with the two parties' names typed as 'N1' and 'N2': a find-and-change facility lets users convert these throughout the document into 'Dr Jekyll' and 'Mr Hyde', the two parties to the agreement. The next time the system is used they might become 'Mr Boswell' and 'Dr Johnson'. If you do not think that is a good idea, ask any typist.

Particularly smart software packages will let you edit several documents at once – well, not absolutely all at once, but they will hold them in the machine and you can switch from one to another at will. Some systems split the screen into two or more parts that behave like independent word-processing screens. You can hop from one to the other, display this document on that screen, and move pieces of text around between them.

Different systems offer different facilities, but these are the usual ones. Dedicated word-processing machines have special keys and screens; microcomputers running word-processing packages have to use the keys they have already got. Often commands to move the cursor around are given by holding down the 'CONTROL' key and a letter. On one machine CTRL C moves the cursor forward a character, CTRL L moves it forward a line.

It would be nice if the text appeared on the screen exactly as it will on the page: 'what you see is what you get', in the language of some optimistic advertisers. Unfortunately this is seldom possible since the better printers give proportionally spaced type while screens can only give mono spacing. In other words, 'i' takes up about a quarter of the space of 'm' on paper, but the same amount of space on the screen. Furthermore, few computer screens have lines longer than 80 characters (40 on the cheaper machines), while most printers give 132 or more characters on the page. However much word-processor manufacturers like to say that 'what you see is what you get', unfortunately it is not true.

There is an argument in favour of regarding the word-processing screen on which one can move the cursor about, creating and erasing text, as a more natural arena for most people than the 'drawing board' simulation of Lisa (see pp. 46-7).

The second phase is storing what you have typed on the screen on disk. This should be done almost automatically so that the user is unconscious of disk operations. In well-written word-processing packages, as users move the cursor through the text, it is pulled on and off disk so that they can work on documents that may be several million characters long if they want. Furthermore, the package should automatically make backup copies of their work so that if disaster strikes – the power is turned off while they are working – all the work is not wasted.

The third phase is turning what users have typed on the screen into printed text on the page. As we have seen, what appears on the screen may not – cannot – look anything like what arrives on the page. For example, when I typed this book on the screen, I had no idea how wide the typographer would want to make the lines, the margins or how many lines there would be on a page. I did not know how may lines he would leave between sections, or how deeply he would indent the first letters. My word-processing system lets me set all these things by putting commands into the text. The way it works is to look for a full stop followed by two capitals at the beginning of a line: .LL49 commands a line length of 49 characters – about the width of these columns. When the package is printing text and comes to that command, it sets 49 into its line-length counter. When it comes to the beginning of a word that will carry the line over 49 characters, it sends a line feed, carriage return to start a new line. If the text is to be printed justified right and left (like this book), then it has to store the line in memory, and add spaces to pad it out to 49 characters wide.

There is no reason why formatters should not be more intelligent, and cope with other ways of presenting text than merely word-wrapping it or leaving it exactly as it appeared on the screen. For instance, you might want your paragraphs

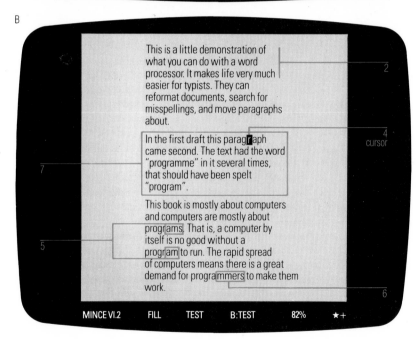

A word-processing package for a micro lets you use the screen as typing paper. Its great advantage over paper is that you do not have to retype the entire text in order to correct or revise it.
1 The line length has been changed from 55 characters in A to 35 in B.
2 'Word wrapping' has been switched on, so lines are turned before the first word that would go past the new line length (e.g. 'what' in the second line of B).
3 The cursor is over a spelling mistake.
4 The incorrect letter has been deleted and replaced.
5 The user has done a 'search and replace' operation on the wrongly spelt word 'programme' to turn it in to 'program' thoughout the text. However, 'programmers' (**6**) is still correct and stays.
7 The last paragraph in A has been brought into second place in B. Once a text is finished it can be saved on disk and recalled for printing or re-editing. The package can be made to pull pieces out of existing files on disk, so that the user can build up one document (say a contract) out of standard items. A second part of the software, called the 'formatter', controls how documents are printed onto paper. It can control the printer's proportional spacing, produce justified right-hand margins, number clauses, subclauses and sub-subclauses, produce indexes and contents lists. These examples were produced using Mark of the Unicorn's Mince package

numbered in order, or printed out as poetry, or arranged in lists. The machine should be able to arrange text just as a good secretary would.

The bit of the program that does this work is called the 'formatter'. In older systems and on main-frames, it is a separate piece of software that prints text files created by the editor. Writing either of these packages is not a simple job, so people almost always buy in programs to do it.

Spread Sheets

The remaining sort of standard document is an accountant's spread sheet. People first started doing double-entry book-keeping in Italy in the 1200s, and no doubt they would have recognized the spread sheets shown here in a trice.

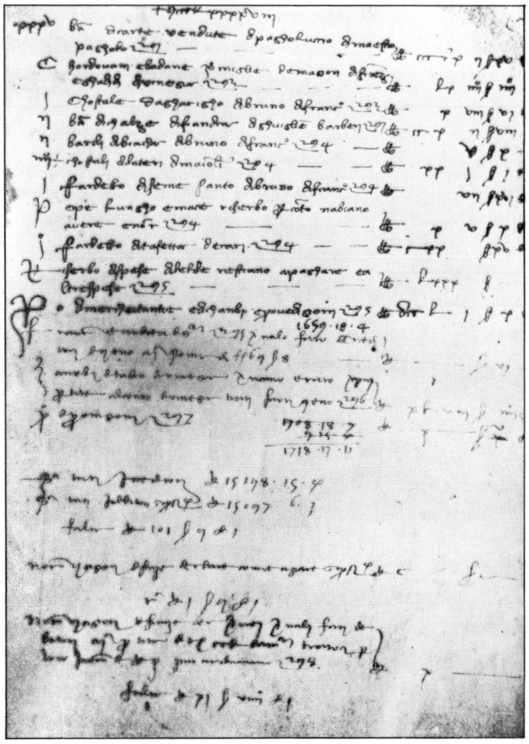

A balance sheet from the Italian firm of Francesco Datini operating in Barcelona in 1399

There is now a piece of software which imitates this bit of paper. With it you can set up rows and columns, enter figures in the boxes – say for sales in March – and then have calculations which work out the tax, the salesman's commission and the overheads, and print at the bottom how much is left for you. These things are useful for routine calculations on past business; and to let managers experiment with future conditions. What happens

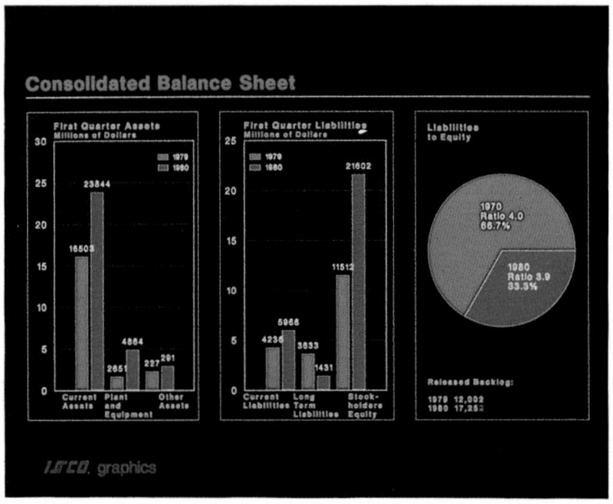

Many people find pie and bar charts easier to understand than columns of figures. Computers with high-resolution colour screens can run software to show business trends in graphic form

if tax goes up 3 per cent? Suppose our petrol bill goes down £10,000 (or $20,000), but wages go up 4.9 per cent? Instead of having to wade through hundreds of calculations with a pocket calculator, they can enter one figure and let the software recalculate all the others.

Again, these software packages let other people create more sophisticated things. If bankers, for instance, all want to do some rather involved set of calculations to produce what is essentially the same sort of sheet, then someone can sit down with the standard software package and build in his own calculations to make a new, more specialized standard package. More and more people are selling their skills in this way; when data links (see pp. 178-9) are really working well, it may become a big new industry.

A spread sheet is one way of presenting numerical information, but not always the best way, particularly if you are looking for correlations between two different sets of figures. A manufacturer, for instance, might want to look at the effect of increased advertising on his sales. The figures might all be there, but presented in such a way that they are hard to understand. So more and more people are using standard software packages to produce graphs from their spread-sheet figures. You simply have to nominate two variables – spending up the vertical axis, say, and time along the horizontal one – and the package should go off, find out the greatest and the smallest amounts, scale the graph appropriately and produce it on the screen or printer. If you want two or more quantities graphed together, you nominate them as well.

Another way of presenting information about money is in the form of a 'pie chart'. Here again, it is not difficult for standard software to take a series of numbers that add up to 100 per cent and display them in this manner. As screen hardware gets better and cheaper – with more pixels and colour (see pp. 30-31) – so graphical methods will become more common.

Accounts

Since computers are so good at handling numbers and many people are not, an obvious application for micros has been the keeping of accounts. A computer will not – or should not – make mistakes in arithmetic or procedure or forget things it has been told. Well, that is not quite true, but there is enough truth there to make accounting packages very popular.

What in principle should such a piece of software do? A business is in essence very simple. It buys things like peanuts or programmers' time, and it sells peanut brittle or software packages. The difference between the money it spends and the money it makes is what the owners can spend on a holiday in the Bahamas. It would be quite nice for the owners to know at any moment whether they can go to the Bahamas or not, so the machine could keep a record of sums in both departments and subtract one from the other.

Of course, accounting gets a lot more elaborate than this, and a glance at any accountancy handbook will show you that over the centuries accountants have managed to make what ought to be simple into a very complicated business. That may be a rather cynical view, because even a small company's financial affairs can get quite complicated.

The simplest way to look at any business is as a series of contracts. Each contract goes through a number of stages, each of which has to be recorded. The owner of the business has to make tax returns at various points – both sales tax and profits tax, which are calculated on different views of the business. It may be necessary to look at all the transactions the owner had with Mr Smith, or at everything sold in the fourth quarter of the year, or everything that was spent on wages or advertising.

All this is in principle quite easy for the computer if the data is stored in a sensibly computerish way. What you have to do is keep a record of each contract in the database. Having got all the information about the contract, everything the accountant wants can be extracted by processing the basic records. Sadly, this is not how accountants do accounting – and you can see why when you remember that they had to rely on ink-and-paper technology. This imposes two constraints: first, you can only look up a piece of information by one characteristic – the name of a supplier if the records are arranged alphabetically, or the date if they are arranged chronologically – but not both. Hence in paper systems you have both a 'daybook' and a 'nominal ledger'.

Secondly, with a paper system you have to allow for errors all through the process, which is why double-entry book-keeping was invented. In a computer system neither of these things should be necessary. The 'daybook' and the 'nominal ledger' are the result of different views of the same data – searching the database by date or by name. And so long as the initial data is entered correctly, there is no need for double entry, because the computer can be relied on to do its sums accurately.

Unhappily, the programmers who produced accounting packages started out with two disadvantages. They did not have databases and they did have accountants. The accountants wanted the thing to look at every stage – even internally, where it was invisible – just like the paper systems. Consequently computer systems tend to maintain files that correspond exactly with the various books and ledgers of the paper systems, even, in some ridiculous circumstances, making the user type the data in twice. This makes accounting software very expensive to write and maintain, very clumsy to use and very inflexible.

This spread sheet shows a business plan for an unnaturally simple enterprise. The whole thing has been set up to turn on the 'Units Sold' in Quarter 1. That quantity determines the number of employees, the cost of materials and postage, and – of course – the income. The 'bottom line' shows what is happening to Joe Soap's bank balance. It opens with a debit of 20,000 – his expenses in setting up the business. The spread sheet lets him experiment: if he starts out selling only 4500 units (Sheet A), he is destined for the tubes; if he can shift 8000 (Sheet B), things look good

A

Joe Soap Inc.				
Quarters:	1	2	3	4
EXPENSES				
Employees	6	6	6	7
Wages	38500	41650	45115	48927
Overheads	22000	23800	25780	27958
Materials	22500	24750	27225	29948
P & P	4500	4950	5445	5990
Total Paid	87500	95150	103565	112822
Units Sold	4500	4950	5445	5990
INCOME				
Sales	85500	94050	103455	113801
Quarterly movt.	–2000	–1100	–110	979
Bank Balance	–20000	–22000	–23100	–23210

B

Joe Soap Inc.				
Quarters:	1	2	3	4
EXPENSES				
Employees	9	10	11	12
Wages	63000	68600	74760	81536
Overheads	36000	39200	42720	46592
Materials	40000	44000	48400	53240
P & P	8000	8800	9680	10648
Total Paid	147000	160600	175560	192016
Units Sold	8000	8800	9680	10648
INCOME				
Sales	152000	167200	183920	202312
Quarterly movt.	5000	6600	8360	10296
Bank Balance	–20000	–15000	–8400	–40

Sheet C shows how the sheet was set up using Microsoft's Multiplan.
1 Row and column numbers, to identify the 'cells'.
2 The starting figure for sales. Everything else is calculated from this.
3 Sales for each subsequent quarter are predicted to be 10 per cent better than the last. The formula [RC −1] *1.1' means: enter the figure in this Row and the Column to the left, multiplied by 1.1. This formula is copied into each cell to the right to produce the same effect in subsequent quarters.
4 The number of employees is 1 + the number in Row 14 and the same Column (Units Sold) divided by a 1000; i.e. the business has one manager and each other employee can handle 1000 units a month.

5 Wages and overheads are calculated from the number of employees at 7000 and 4000 each a quarter.
6 Cost of materials, postage and packing, calculated from Units Sold.
7 Expenses totalled – the sum of Rows 7 to 10 in the same Column.

8 The income at 19 per unit.
9 The quarterly movement – income less expenses.
10 The bank balance opens with −20,000. Each subsequent balance is the previous balance plus the movement in the previous quarter

C

	1	2	3	4	5
1 "Joe Soap Inc"					
2					
3 "Quarters:"	"1"	"2"	"3"	"4"	
4 "EXPENSES"					
5 "Employers"	1+(R14 C)/1000	1+(R14 C)/1000	1+(R14 C)/1000	1+(R14 C)/1000	
6 "----------"	"----------"	"----------"	"----------"	"----------"	
7 "Wages"	(R5 C) *7000	(R5 C) *7000	(R5 C) *7000	(R5 C) *7000	
8 "Overheads"	(R5 C) *4000	(R5 C) *4000	(R5 C) *4000	(R5 C) *4000	
9 "Materials"	(R14 C) *5	(R14 C) *5	(R14 C) *5	(R14 C) *5	
10 "P&P"	(R14 C) *1	(R14 C) *1	(R14 C) *1	(R14 C) *1	
11 "----------"					
12 "Total Paid"	SUM(R7 C:R10 C)	SUM(R7 C:R10 C)	SUM(R7 C:R10 C)	SUM(R7 C:R10 C)	
13 "=========="	"=========="	"=========="	"=========="	"=========="	
14 "Units Sold"	8000	(RC[−1] *1.1)	(RC[−1]) *1.1	(RC[−1]) *1.1	
15 "----------"	"----------"	"----------"	"----------"	"----------"	
16 "INCOME"					
17 "Sales"	(R14 C) *19	(R14 C) *19	(R14 C) *19	(R14 C) *19	
18 "=========="	"=========="	"=========="	"=========="	"=========="	
19 "Quarterly movt."	R17 C–R12 C	R17 C–R12 C	R17 C–R12 C	R17 C–R12 C	
20 "Bank Balance"	–20000	R[−1]C[−1]+RC[−1]	R[−1]C[−1]+RC[−1]	R[−1]C[−1]+RC[−1]	

COMPUTERS AND PICTURES

A computer-aided design (CAD) work station. The operator has a conventional computer screen to display program listings and text (left), a high-quality colour graphics screen (right), a keyboard and a digitizing pad

Opposite

Top Computer graphics can be used to present otherwise indigestible information. Here are four views of light intensity (plotted as mountains) in the double galaxy M51, known as the Whirlpool nebula. The relative density of 4 million pixels for each of five long-exposure photographs were transformed by computer graphics into the images shown here. Each pixel was colour-coded and stretched upwards to represent its brightness, the individual stars showing up as spikes

Below left From different views of a part in an engineering drawing, the CAD computer can create a view of the complete system, both assembled and exploded, and generate instructions for machine tools to make the parts. The information can then be used in maintenance manuals, parts catalogues and sales literature

Below right Not only can a CAD simulation show the parts in an engineering design, it can also calculate loads, show deflections, assess safety margins in use, producing information that would otherwise have to come from a prototype. It can also help work out the amounts of materials needed to manufacture the complete article

A fascinating and rapidly growing field of application for computers lies in the area of pictures and vision. This started out as a large number of disconnected areas. Computers were being used to help engineering draftsmen, to produce simulated pictures to train airline pilots, to help with drawing cartoon films and to edit ordinary ones. Computers were helping to produce special effects for television, to analyse satellite photographs of the earth's surface, to help astronomers analyse images of distant galaxies, to design textiles and to show clients how architects' designs would turn out. Computers were helping doctors make better sense of X-ray pictures, brain scans and films of athletes running and jumping. They were helping ergonomists to fit the human frame into all sorts of likely and unlikely machines.

In another line of development, people were trying to build machines and write programs to make computers 'see' through television cameras. The aim was to show the machine a room or a machine and get it to identify the furniture or the parts that make up the whole.

For a while, all these areas seemed quite separate, but now the boundaries are blurring, and in the seventeen pages that follow we try to give some impression of the wide and fascinating area embraced by computer-aided design and computer vision.

Unfortunately for the amateur, the first requirement in most of this work is some powerful hardware. To do good visual work you need high-resolution graphics. High-resolution graphics means at least lots of RAM, high-resolution screens and powerful processors. (It may be that the next generation of vision machines will use the parallel processing techniques described on pages 174-5.) The first micro that comes near to fitting this bill is Apple's Lisa and even that is not really powerful or cheap enough to bring vision into the micro marketplace. But without doubt we shall see suitable machines within the next five years.

There are two main divisions in this field: those applications that build up a picture within the computer by starting with an engineering drawing, a cartoon or a photograph – applications which use the computer as an aid to the artist or draftsman – and those which try to make the computer 'see' in the way we do. To prove that it has actually seen, it may be made to produce a picture of the scene it is looking at.

Within these divisions we also have to recognize another distinction: what the computer prints on the screen may be a long way from what it is 'really' doing. For instance, a computer-aided design (CAD) machine in an engineering factory might be used to help design a gearbox. The draftsman uses the machine to draw the detail of the cogs, to make sure they mesh properly and one part does not foul another. If necessary, the computer will do a stress analysis on the design so far to make sure that each part is strong enough for the job it has to do, but not so strong that it wastes material and machining time.

The machine so far has acted as a draftsman's assistant – executing orders such as 'draw a circle here, a line there, calculate the stresses on this part and that'. Then it 'makes a model' of the design and tries it out for fit, as if in wood. Having done that, the machine will produce instructions for computer-driven machine tools to make the individual parts: 'turn here to this radius, mill this part flat, drill a hole here 9 mm diameter ... '. It will work out the instructions for individual work stations in an automated factory (see pp. 136-7).

The machine will also calculate the sizes and shapes of the metal blanks that will be needed for machining. In a sophisticated system it will pass details of the amounts of material needed to the computer that keeps the firm's books and orders materials.

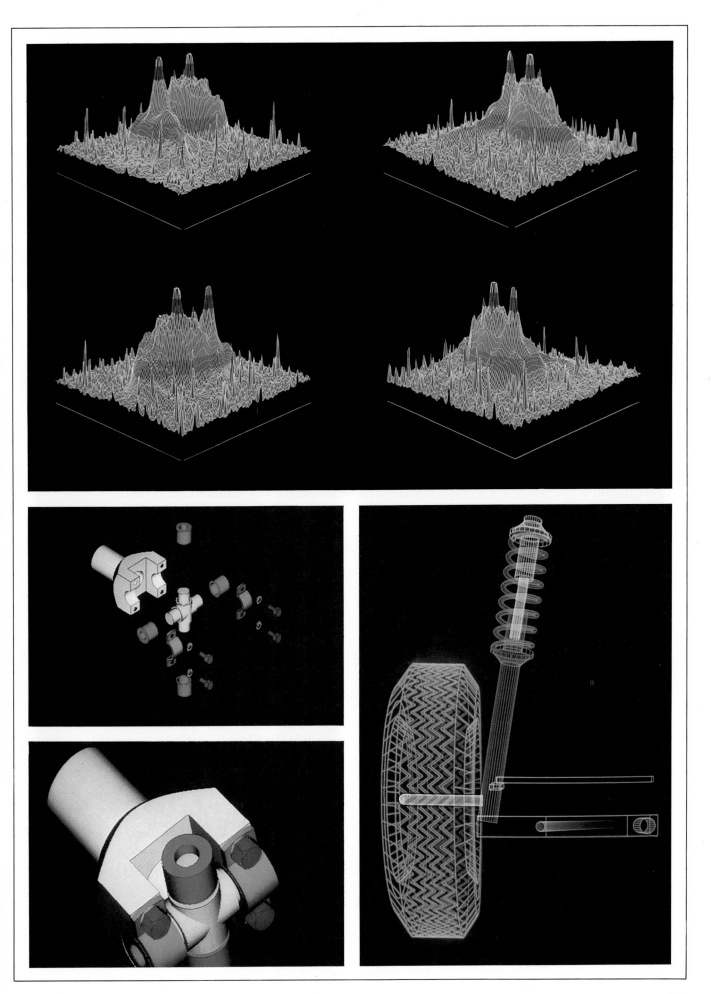

CAD

This page

The computer's ability to change colours at the press of a button is very useful in specialities like carpet design.

Clarks Shoes of England and the Computer Aided Design Centre, Cambridge, have perfected a technique for producing pictures of the finished shoe from design drawings that are hardly different from the manufactured article. This vastly reduces the time, cost and uncertainty of producing prototypes of new fashions. Notice how the faceting, characteristic of early computer-generated 3D images and clearly visible in the Harrier simulation on p. 106, has completely disappeared.

Engineering drawings of a chemical plant are quickly turned into a perspective view, saving hundreds of hours of tedious work for the draftsman.

A coloured, perspective view of a new building generated from the architectural drawings is almost indistinguishable from the finished structure

Opposite

This structural view of the US Navy's Tomcat fighter is almost as beautiful as the machine itself. It shows the aircraft's five main subassemblies: radar – pink; fuselage – blue; wings – yellow; engines – green; and tail – red.

Ergonomic human dummies, which exist inside the machine just as program subroutines, are as essential a part of the new design studio as the boxwood models they replace.

Scientists studying the movements of athletes digitize a film of a runing man, and then draw in by hand this stickman simplification so that the machine can then calculate the dynamics of his movements

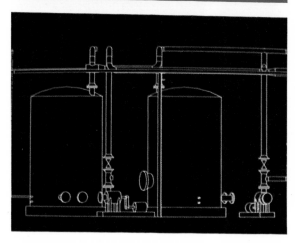
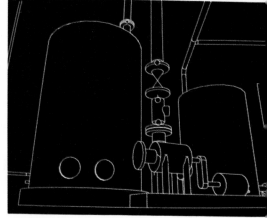

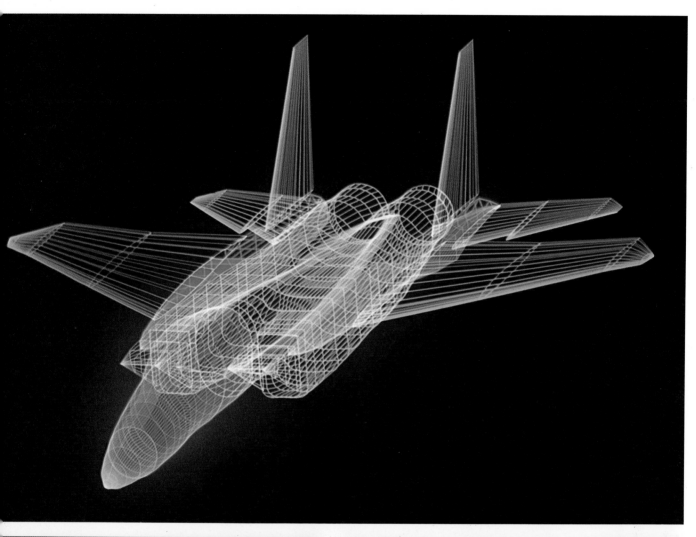

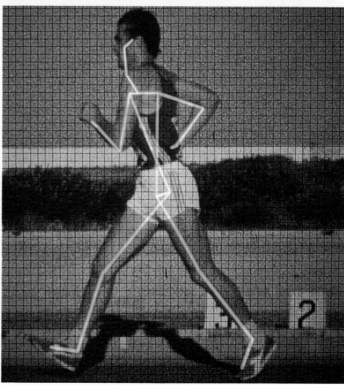

SIMULATION

Top left A more purely visual application for the computer's ability to draw lies in simulation. Airlines, air forces, navies and armies find it increasingly expensive to use real ships, tanks, helicopters and aircraft to train their people. It is much better to use simulators, which are now tremendously realistic.
A simulation for a fighter pilot, for instance, has to mimic the whole behaviour of his aircraft. The computer must reproduce the handling characteristics of the machine at different heights and speeds, with different loads of fuel and weapons. It must show the ground and other aircraft according to the height and attitude of the machine. The positions and attitudes of the aircraft in the scene must be correctly calculated.
This magnificent simulation of a US Marine Corps Harrier by Rediffusion, as seen from another aircraft, flies and fights just like the real thing. Notice the realistic shading on the underside, and the disappearance into the desert haze of the ground features beneath. However, the demands of real-time processing have forced the programmers to put up with faceting on the curved surfaces (as on the cockpit), which could be improved if there was more than 1/25 second available to produce each frame

Below Realistic computer simulations are being used by airlines to train their aircrews. These three views of an airport show it at touchdown in clear weather; from the same position in fog; and as it would look several miles away at night. There are programs of this kind for all the world's major airports

Top right It is quicker and cheaper by far to try out a new road layout on the computer than to build it and then decide you do not like it

Centre and below right Computer simulations are applied to unlikely looking problems. Here the British government's Road Research Laboratory experiments with a street lighting scheme – much more cheaply than building the real thing.
A change in lighting fixtures – simulated by a slight program change – produces a far better result

IMAGE PROCESSING

A most useful role for computers, halfway into real computer vision, lies in the enhancement and manipulation of photographs. Computers can now take blurred photos and make them sharp, take real colours and make them fantastic, take minutely detailed satellite views and search them for oil-bearing rocks or missile sites. Much of this work is founded on a mathematical discovery made by Baron Jean Baptiste Joseph Fourier (1768-1830).

Before we can appreciate what Fourier did, we have to understand how a computer can be made to 'see'. The business starts with the problem of converting a picture into bits – 0s and 1s. The easiest way is to take a television picture of the scene and then to *digitize* it. This involves dividing it up into pixels (see pp. 30-31) and then measuring the light intensity in each one. If you are doing colour work, you would also measure the intensity of each of the three primary colours in it too, but to keep things simple, we will assume for the moment that we are only interested in black and white pictures. Since the light intensity at each point in the scene is turned into a voltage by the television camera, all we have to do is turn that voltage into a number using an analogue-to-digital convertor (ADC).

A television camera scans its picture in parallel lines. To make things simple, let us imagine that we are going to have as many rows of pixels as there are lines in the television picture (about 200 in an industrial-quality television camera). If the ADC works at such a speed that it does 200 conversions a line, then we end up with a 200 × 200 cell picture.

The next question to consider is how many light levels we want. The ADC measures a light intensity and turns it into bits, the accuracy of the

measurement depending on how many bits it produces. The simplest possible measurement produces 1 bit – '0' meaning dark or '1' meaning light. A 4-bit conversion gives 16 light levels; an 8-bit conversion gives 256 – the system designer has to choose the accuracy he or she needs, trading processing speed and storage space against accuracy.

By putting a picture into memory, we have, in effect, converted it from two dimensions into one.

It is easiest to understand Fourier's insight in relation to music – which is also one-dimensional. A pure musical note consists of a sine wave at a particular frequency, and a tuning fork produces it reasonably well.

If you listen to two tuning forks together, you hear two notes, although the actual air pressure at your ear can only take one value at a time. Your ear can perform a Fourier analysis on the complex waveform and sort out the two original sine waves. Listening to an orchestra, it can sort out several dozen pure notes.

It is fairly obvious that the complicated sound of an orchestra could be resolved into a whole lot of pure notes; less obvious perhaps is the fact that any sound, or indeed any shape, can be. Fourier tells us that any function $F(x)$ can be transformed into simple sine and cosine waves by an equation like this:

$$F(x) = a_0 + a_1\cos(x) + b_1\sin(x) + \dots a_n\cos(nx) + b_n\sin(nx) \dots$$

where a_n and b_n are the Fourier coefficients. A particularly unobvious example is a square wave – a train of binary 1s. It is hard to see how square waves like those below can be made up by adding any number of continuous sine waves – but in fact they can be. The Fourier analysis of the

Sounds consist of many simple sine waves added together. Here two waves combine to make something quite complex. However, the ear can separate them again because different elements in the cochlea respond to each ingredient. Mathematicians would say that the ear performs a 'Fourier analysis' of the sound.
Below Surprising as it may seem, a square wave or pulse can be built up from enough sine waves. A single sine, plus 1/3rd of a sine at 3 times the frequency, plus 1/5th of a wave at 5 times the frequency plus . . . leads eventually to a square wave. The reverse process can be performed by a computer and means that, for example, sharp edges in digitized photographs can be broken down into sine waves on which simple calculations can be done. The way is then open for computer enhancement and processing of images

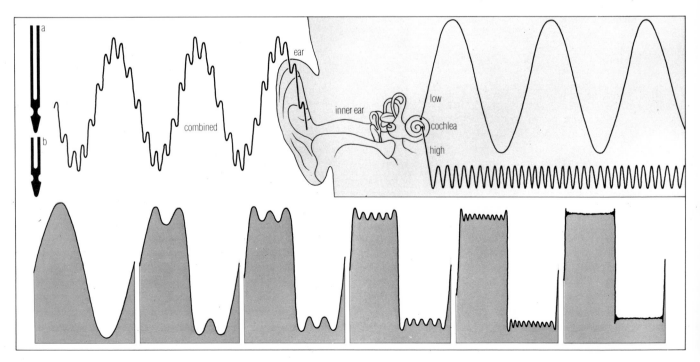

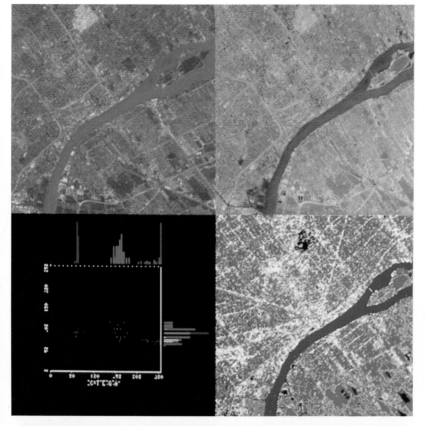

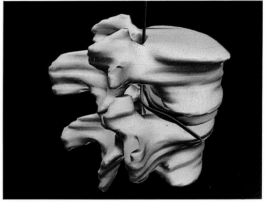

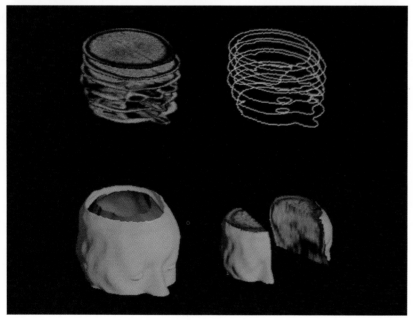

Top left Aerial and satellite survey photographs can be digitized and enhanced by the computer to reveal far more detail than was apparent in the first place. The two upper images are photographs taken at different wavelengths; at bottom right the computer has deduced and classified different land uses. Bottom left the computer has done some statistical analyses of land use in different areas of the city

Left This simulation of the inside of a patient's head by David Hogg of Sussex University uses brain scan 'slices' (top left) for its inputs. The program knows

about the structure of the skull, brain, eyes, etc., and looks for unusual objects which might be cancers

Above Research into back trouble produced this immaculate image of two human vertebrae with nerves and a not-yet-slipped disk

Top The snapshot of a sunny day on a beach on Mars comes to us through the hands of several computers. The original TV image is transmitted by radio. On earth it is collected in a huge satellite dish, stored, enhanced, printed on a computer screen and photographed

pulse says that it is made up of a basic wave, whose half length is the width of the pulse, plus a wave of $\frac{1}{3}$ the amplitude and $\frac{1}{3}$ the length, plus a wave of $\frac{1}{5}$ the amplitude and $\frac{1}{5}$ the length ... and so on.

The mathematics of Fourier transforms makes it possible to do operations like frequency filtering on any digitized information. It need not be confined to one-dimensional signals like sounds; the same operations can be applied to two-dimensional things like photographs. Once they have been digitized a number of operations based on their Fourier transforms can be done to enhance their images. A simple one is to amplify the high frequencies – in audio terms, raising the treble boost. High frequencies in a picture occur at the edges of objects, where intensity levels are changing fast. If these high frequencies are amplified, then the edges are made more visible and the picture is 'crispened'.

PAINTING BY NUMBERS

A painter takes colour out of tubes and puts it where he thinks best on a canvas. A computer takes colour from palette tables and puts them were the program thinks best on the screen. There is no reason why the computer should not act as a sort of intelligent canvas for artists.

Most paintings consist of outlines and colour patches within the outlines. At its crudest, this produces a 'painting by numbers' effect, but ultimately this is how most works of art in the European tradition are produced. The first step, getting the outlines into the machine, is the hardest. Admittedly, the artist has the keyboard at his disposal, and with it he can steer his 'pencil' around the screen. But, one might ask, how high would Leonardo's reputation stand if he had had to do his drawings the way a teenager chases Klingons? You *can* draw with the keyboard if you are masochistic enough, but a better alternative is the digitizing pad. You draw on that – often

The computer offers artists completely new methods and materials. They can 'paint' as if with brushes and colours. They may use images already inside the machine to change and improve what they have entered. Once a picture is established, the machine can be made to alter the colours and shading in an infinite number of ways

Right The illustrations at the beginning of each section of this book were created using Flair, one of the video-painting systems by which images are produced by drawing on a data tablet with an electronic stylus. Areas of the tablet are assigned to various functions such as 'Select colour' (from 256 mixable colours displayed on a screen palette), 'Select brush' (shape, size, etc.), 'Draw circle, ellipse…' The specialised software offers a wide range of facilities for modifying the image. Here the artist has enlarged a section of the illustration to work on in more detail. The palette can be seen at the bottom of the screen.
The finished picture, or various stages of it, is run-length encoded and stored on floppy disk from which it can be recalled and displayed. The system can also operate as a high-resolution character generator with the ability to 'cut and paste' type and adjust the inter-character spacing.

with a wired-up biro – you get a picture on the paper in the ordinary way, plus a picture in the screen.

Having got an outline into the machine, you can colour it in by steering the cursor to an area and telling the machine to paint it in magenta with speckles of green and puce. If that does not look right (as well it might not) you can instantly change the colour to orange with speckles of grey and violet.

So far so good, but this hardly scratches the potential of the computer. A decent graphics package should allow you to build up a library of sub-images which can be called up in the final work in the position, size and colouring you want. This is very useful for architects who have to present perspective impressions of their buildings with street accessories such as cars, lamp-

posts, mums pushing prams, trees and dogs.

There is no need to rely on your own skills as a draftsman. The computer, with a TV camera and a digitizer, can accept existing images. The New York subway scene on this page might have begun as a photograph. Having captured the image, the artist can then alter its texture, perspective, colouring. He can blend it with other images, repeat it in patterns and make it so its own mother would not know it.

It is easy to imagine that in a few years time when systems like this are common, high street art and graphics supplies shops will be selling digitized versions of standard images. You will be able to go out, buy the *Mona Lisa* or several underdressed young women on a floppy disk, take them home and conflate them into a most surprisingly automated piece of visual fantasy

PROFESSIONAL ANIMATION

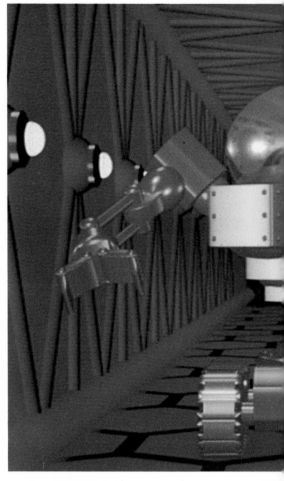

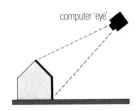

computer 'eye'

The best way to use computers is to make them do the stupid, boring jobs. If they do those well, it may be sensible to let them do something more interesting later – but, remember, always start with the dull stuff.

One of the dullest jobs in the world must be the drawing of cartoon films. One minute of film needs 1500 drawings; a whole movie, several hundred thousand. Watching film cartoonists work is like watching the grass grow. Not surprisingly, as soon as computers could produce reasonable drawings, they were pressed into service to make cartoons.

In a cartoon studio the best artists draw the peaks of the action – Tom draws his foot back; Tom kicks Jerry – and the lesser talents draw the many frames in between, showing Tom's foot getting nearer and nearer to poor Jerry's bottom. This process is called 'in-betweening' and is a natural use for computers.

Suppose we have a head-on view of a bulldog who has got himself attached – the way these characters do – to an air pump. Rather than draw the successive stages of his inflation, the animation system will in-between the start and finish drawings, producing the intermediate images by calculating proportionate points.

To save labour and to ensure consistency, film animators do not draw each frame of an animated film. The backgrounds are drawn once and used over and over again. The characters that move in front of them are drawn on sheets of transparent plastic and laid in the correct places for each frame to be photographed. The computer is perfectly equipped to handle this sort of thing – and several home computers have facilities for doing just this – though at a lower resolution than professional machines would need.

The computer can be very helpful with colouring: it can paint and repaint scenes instantly, allowing the artist to try out far more combinations than he or she possibly could on paper.

3D graphics

The computer really comes into its own, however, when it comes to drawing three-dimensional objects. This is a lot harder and a lot more interesting. In many ways the computer is ideally suited for work as the draftsman's assistant, since it can easily and rapidly do the very tedious calculations necessary for producing perspective drawings.

On the left we have an outline drawing of a house seen in perspective – that is, all horizontal parallel lines are shown as spreading out from one point on the horizon. The effect this has on the shape of the house is easily calculated and its elements can be plotted in the right position.

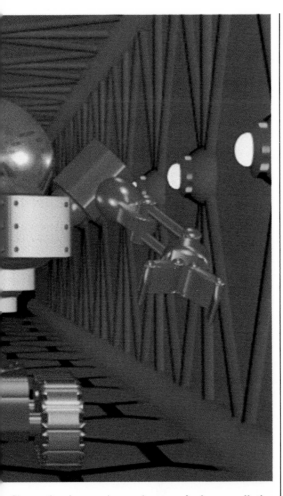

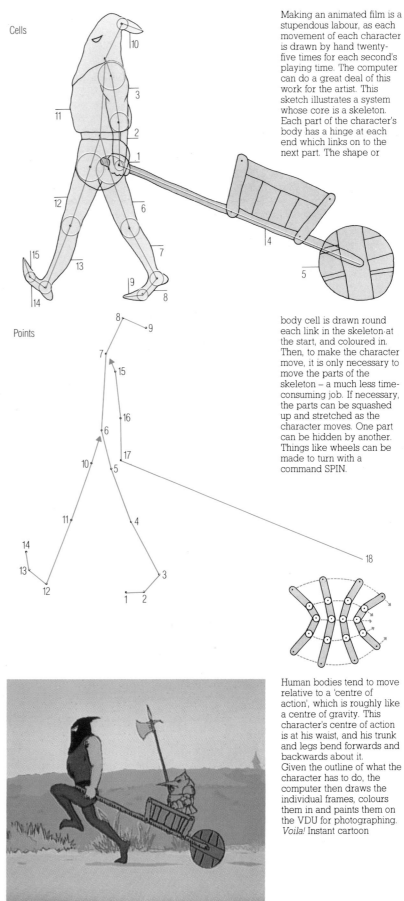

Making an animated film is a stupendous labour, as each movement of each character is drawn by hand twenty-five times for each second's playing time. The computer can do a great deal of this work for the artist. This sketch illustrates a system whose core is a skeleton. Each part of the character's body has a hinge at each end which links on to the next part. The shape or

Points

body cell is drawn round each link in the skeleton at the start, and coloured in. Then, to make the character move, it is only necessary to move the parts of the skeleton – a much less time-consuming job. If necessary, the parts can be squashed up and stretched as the character moves. One part can be hidden by another. Things like wheels can be made to turn with a command SPIN.

Since the house is made up of planes, all the computer needs to store are the coordinates of the surfaces, and this too makes things easy.

However, to make a realistic 3D image, we have to stop the house being transparent. This is done by 'hidden line removal', as shown on the right. This is the result of a process in which the computer calculates which elements come in front of others, and removes them. It is far from simple, and a lot of hard work has been expended on making efficient programs to do the job.

A house is not a very typical shape in nature or even industry. Most things tend to be curved in various complicated ways. The designer of software to handle 3D graphics has a choice: to calculate every point on the objects to be shown and store the points' coordinates, or to represent small bits of surface and store those. It turns out that storing points on memory is impossibly expensive. It is much better – though even this requires vast amounts to do a good job – to break each curved surface down into small flat polygons and to store them. No real Harrier ever looked just like the one on page 106, and there is a further software process used to smooth the polygons to get a natural-looking curve, but it takes a long time to run and cannot be used in real-time simulations.

Human bodies tend to move relative to a 'centre of action', which is roughly like a centre of gravity. This character's centre of action is at his waist, and his trunk and legs bend forwards and backwards about it.
Given the outline of what the character has to do, the computer then draws the individual frames, colours them in and paints them on the VDU for photographing. *Voila!* Instant cartoon

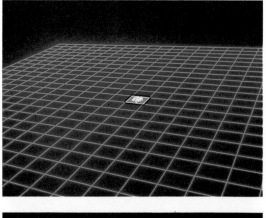

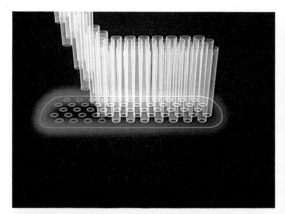

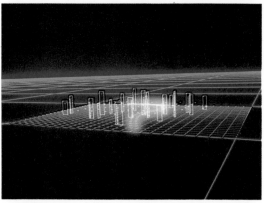

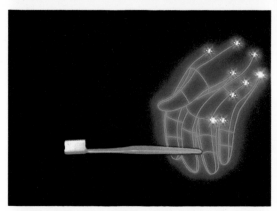

Right Computer graphics let modern artists create magical fantasy cities, here seen as if from a swooping helicopter

Centre Computer-simulated graphics are now being used for television advertising to give ordinary products an aura of high technology. This toothbrush becomes a marvel of space science

Opposite Advanced graphics machines make it possible to take imaginative leaps into worlds that never were. This Escher-like globe of springs was probably generated by a very simple algorithm, and startled its creator as much as it does us

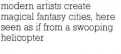

There is more to a picture than just shape. Real objects show texture, light and shade, colour and reflections of other objects. All these things can be calculated and the appropriate effects painted on the image. For instance, the texture of brick is quite different from that of glass. To produce a perfect effect the 3D graphics program has to calculate where the light is coming from, how it will bounce off the surface, what else it will fall on. Furthermore, the picture may be in motion. The computer should be able to calculate the movements of things in it – waves behave according to physical laws, and the program should be able to give the water in the waves 'weight' so that they behave properly. People move in particular ways and here too the machine should be able to calculate their proper movements.

It is not surprising that pictures as complicated

as this can take several hours of processing.

The upshot of all this is that computers are giving their assistance at higher and higher levels in the artistic process. To begin with, like a dumb assistant, they could change green to blue or sketch in a drawing if they had been given the rough. Now they can take over much of the artist's function. He or she can specify a landscape in general terms: a mountain there, a valley here, a rolling plain over there and a lake to round it off. The machine will then create the land contours – bearing in mind the laws of geology – clothe them in appropriate vegetation, coloured for the right time of year, put in the weather and the right light for the time of day and time of year and – what is left for the artist to do? Presumably the interesting part – thinking up the whole thing in the first place.

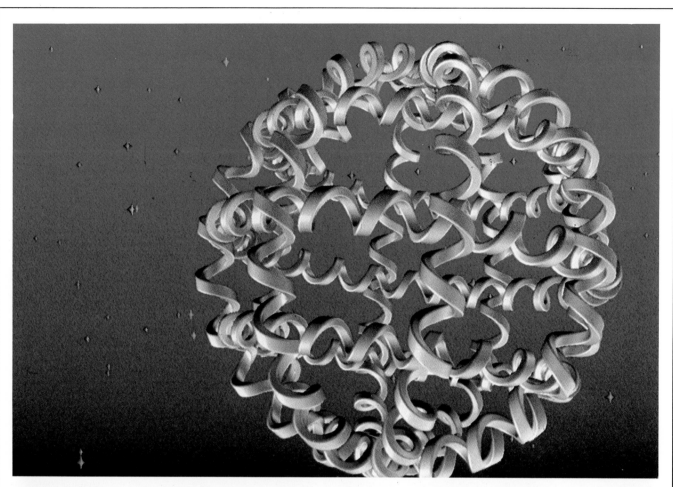

COMPUTER VISION

We have seen on pages 108-9 how a picture can be reduced to pixels and stored in a computer's memory. The hard work of computer vision lies in trying to make sense of the picture, and after a while it becomes clear that the human brain is a very great deal cleverer than the best computers.

The first problem an image analyst has to contend with is electrical noise. Even if the camera were shown a perfectly even grey sheet, which should produce a memory full of pixels with the value, say, of 127, it would actually be uneven. The average value might well be 127, but individual cells would fluctuate about that value. Some would be 126, others 128. Some might be as far out as 130 or 124. These variations are caused by atomic uncertainties in the camera, its amplifiers and the analogue-to-digital convertor. To combat noise, the system first has to run through the picture, comparing each cell with its eight immediate neighbours. If a cell is too different, then it is replaced with the average value.

The human eye and brain seem to analyse pictures by several processes. They extract outlines; they find areas of similar tone; they use shadows and a lot of basic physics – or common sense. We also have the advantage over computers of being able to compare the slightly different views from two eyes to get stereoscopic vision – but this is of little use until each eye working on its own has built up some idea of the masses in front of it.

The first thing a computer must do to make sense of what it 'sees' is an outline analysis. The object of this is to turn the picture into a line drawing. It is done by going through the pixels again, looking for cells that differ markedly from the average of their neighbours. Those cells are kept and the rest eliminated. The result is (or would be, in a perfect world) an outline drawing of the objects in the scene. The object of the exercise is to produce closed loops – each solid object in the scene ought to have an outline that goes right round it, returning to the starting point.

Unfortunately, in real life the outline breaks up and wanders about. It breaks up when the intensities on the two sides of the line are similar, so that the averaging process cannot find a difference; it wanders off when reflections produce meaningless intensity differences. Shadows present horrible problems because they cannot be analysed without knowing where the sun is. These difficulties are in addition to the ones you would expect of the outlines of faraway objects being broken by nearer ones.

However, let us assume that we have a good outline picture. It still will not have complete outlines of all the objects in the scene, because the far side of each object is hidden by its near side and the nearer ones will hide the farther ones. Not much can be done about the first problem because we cannot see the far side of any object. Something can be done about the second through a technique called 'vertex analysis'.

These eight photographs show various stages in digitizing a photograph of Kenilworth Castle as a preliminary to using the data for computer vision work. A shows the castle at a resolution of 2★2 pixels, B at 8★8, C at 32★32 and D at 256★256.
D has 64-K pixels, and each one can take one of 256 grey levels, so they require a byte of memory each. Full TV resolution is about 600★600 and would require 360,000 bytes in black and white; more than half a million in colour

E and F show the process of edge finding. The small white square in E is enlarged in F to show the change of intensity between grass and wall. By comparing the grey level of each pixel with its neighbour, the computer can deduce an edge running down to the left

G shows edge finding on the whole picture. The result, even on a fairly boxy image like this, is surprisingly messy

Another technique to help the computer resolve the scene into three-dimensional shapes is to look for regions of similar tone – for pixels which are near their neighbours in grey level. The result is shown in H

The next step is to try to join up broken, straight lines into continuous ones.
At this point the program to check vertices (see pp. 118–19) would take over and try to decide what was happening at each of the edges and angles.
Once the program has some idea of the three-dimensional shape of the object, it can go back and make allowances for shadows – which would otherwise be interpreted as objects.
While the human eye can make sense of an image like this in a fraction of a second, computer vision systems can only work with much simpler pictures in laboratory conditions, and can take minutes or hours to run, even on big machines. True computer vision may not come until we have vastly more powerful parallel processors (see pp. 174–5) to play with

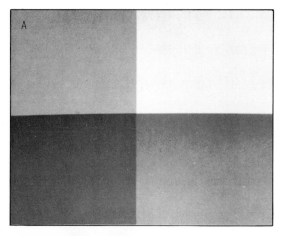

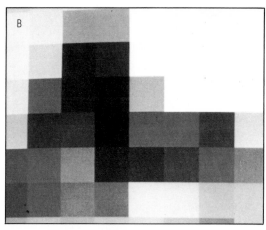

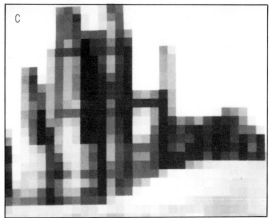

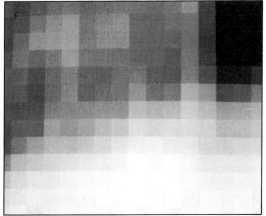

Vertex analysis exploits the fact that many things you would want to look at with a computer system have straight edges and corners. The laws of geometry control the ways vertices work: by looking at edges and corners the computer can sort out which are real corners and which are accidents caused by the overlapping of two different objects.

Using edge and vertex analysis, the machine can go some way towards filling in the gaps in its outlines, and distinguishing the outlines of one object from those of another.

A second technique for making sense of a picture is finding areas of similar tone. One method is picking a pixel at random and then seeing if the cells round it are reasonably near to it in value. If they are, the processor marks them. This process 'grows' areas which have similar intensities and are, presumably, part of the same objects. When the program can find no more matching cells, it picks another starting point and tries to grow another area. A program which used both of these techniques could try to match areas of similar tone with outlines, using the tone information to join up gaps in the outlines.

Another way that we sort out what we see is by applying very crude, basic physics. We know that things have to have supports, they cannot be top heavy. We have some idea about the proper thicknesses for walls, trees, branches. Things that are too low and flat or too tall and thin look odd – we assume that they must be the result of an optical illusion – a mistaken analysis of the scene.

When things move we know that they tend to move in straight lines, that if they turn corners they have to go round fairly gentle bends. If we see a bright blob vertically over a dark blob some distance away down a road, we might assume it was a woman wearing a light hat and a dark dress. If the two blobs separated, or they both started to move at great speed, we should be very surprised.

We also have a huge library of stock images. We know very well what people look like and how they are jointed. We know about all sorts of objects – tables, chairs, cars, bottles, oil refineries, ships, flowers, insects – and we draw on these stock images all the time to make sense of what we see. When people cry out, 'It's a bird. It's a plane. No, it's Superman!' they are applying stock images to a moving speck in the sky to try to make sense of it. As it gets closer and more information becomes available, they have to revise their estimates.

Unfortunately the computer is miles – light years – from this sort of processing ability. Each time it looks at the world it has to start afresh, as if it had never seen anything before. One potentially big area of application for computer vision would be in industry, working in factories, mines or inside nuclear reactors.

An apparently simple but useful task is to identify the parts needed for a particular machine so that each one can be picked up and inserted at the right moment. Even this is difficult. The first problem is that the computer can deal only with a two-dimensional picture. To avoid problems of dirt, shading and different coloured metals, it is usually presented with an outline – the part is put on a illuminated background and shown to a television camera. Many machine parts, such as gear wheels, are essentially flat, but there are many others that are solid shapes which could be put on the light table in several different ways and present several different outlines to the computer. One, crude, way to deal with this is to treat each orientation as a different part that has to be picked up and turned about differently in order to be properly assembled.

When the computer has been given an outline it sets about recognizing it in a number of different ways. First, it can measure how big the thing is. Then it can be made to calculate a number of indices about the thing's shape. In a recent program from the Machine Intelligence Unit at Edinburgh University, the machine set about recognizing chocolates (chosen as being simple shapes with subtle differences) by measuring things like the area of the shape, its perimeter, its maximum and minimum widths and so on. It was shown examples of caramel, cherry, montelimar, butter, orange and brandy chocolates and an expert system (see p. 86) worked out a rule for identifying the different flavours from various permutations of the measurements.

The human eye can easily recognize another human walking and deduce – roughly – the size, shape and position of his limbs from the way he moves. It may seem simple, but a program to do the same thing on a computer can take hours to process just a few seconds of film. Here a program written at Sussex University replaces the limbs and trunk of a walking man with 'tin cans' to show that it has properly analysed his movements

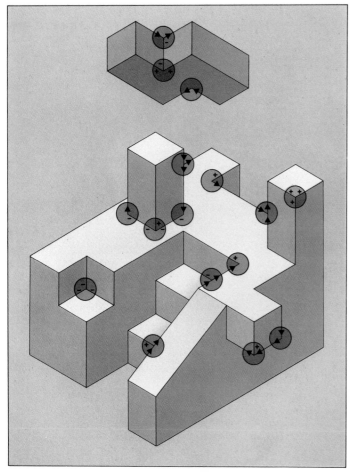

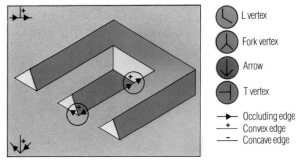

L vertex		
Fork vertex		
Arrow		
T vertex		

→ Occluding edge
+ Convex edge
— Concave edge

Left A proper vision system has to be able to turn a 2D image into a 3D object. Since such systems tend to be used in factories, the things they are looking at are often made up of lines and angles. The diagram on the left shows all the possible vertices and edges – convex, concave and occluding – that can occur in real objects. The computer goes round the two-dimensional image labelling the edges in accordance with the possible types. When it has gone all round, the labelling of the first edge should be consistent with the last one. If not, then the object is 'impossible', like the Devil's Pitchfork above. One of the twelve ways in which labelling might start is shown

Below left A simple way of getting a computer to recognize a machine part that might lie in one of many

orientations is to set the part on a light table in all the ways it might fall, so that the machine can recognize the different shapes that result

Bottom left In order to tell one shape from another, the machine can only work with simple measures. Here, trying to tell chocolates apart in an experiment at Edinburgh University, it measures a dozen parameters, among which are: maximum length and width and the diameter of the smallest circle that can be drawn inside the outline

Below The image of an object is focused on a digitizer. Each cell reports the intensity of light that it 'sees'. The computer finds edges by comparing the intensity in each cell with those of its neighbours. If there is a large difference, the machine deduces an edge

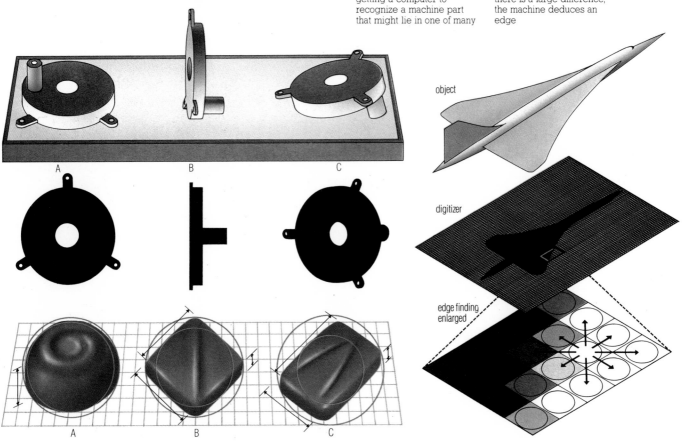

object

digitizer

edge finding enlarged

TALKING COMPUTERS

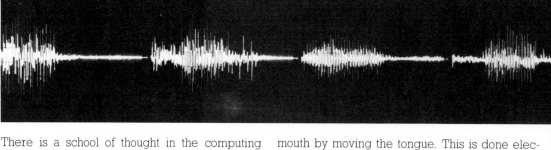

The complex wave forms of speech: the words 'The Joy of Computers' spoken into a microphone produced this trace on a cathode-ray screen. Computer systems that try to understand speech have to analyse these traces into various frequency bands and then try to match stored values for words they 'know' with what comes in from the microphone

There is a school of thought in the computing world which holds that computers will be no use to anyone until they talk and understand speech. The second part is, as we shall see, not so easy; the first part is possible. Talking computers have an obvious use in situations where their users cannot read because they are blind or too young; or where they do not want to have to read because they are doing something else – such as flying an aircraft, driving a car, walking round a storeroom checking stock.

In all these cases it would be useful if the machine could speak – perhaps reading aloud from its built-in instruction book in the first two cases and just giving comments, warnings or confirmations in the third.

There are two ways of tackling the digital recording and reproduction of speech. The first is simply to take the varying voltage levels produced by a microphone, to sample them at about 8 kHz, digitize the results and store them as a series of bytes. This works perfectly well, but requires about 8 kilobytes of memory for every second of speech. A 5-MB floppy dish would store only ten minutes' worth.

This is not really practicable. To understand how to do better, we first have to look at the mechanics of the mouth. Many years of research have produced a reliable conceptual model for the basic sound-producing mechanisms of the human mouth and throat. The human vocal tract consists of a sort of variable tube – the mouth,

mouth by moving the tongue. This is done electronically by altering the formant frequency in the middle of the vowel.

The consonant sounds consist mostly of pops, hisses and stops imposed on the vibrations of the oscillator or air column. To model this we only need a source of 'white' noise – that is, noise which consists of equal amounts of all audible frequencies. This is easily produced electronically by amplifying the output of a Zener diode.

There are also some nasal sounds – m, ng, n tapering down to the throat. Muscles in the throat and tongue can alter the size and therefore the resonant frequency of this space.

There are two noise-producing devices: the vocal cords (which are really folds of skin) in the larynx, which can be made tighter or looser so that they buzz at different frequencies when air from the lungs flows over them; and the hissing as air flows past the tongue and teeth. These two components can easily be modelled in an electronic system. The vocal cords buzz at preferred frequencies, which are set by the varying size and shape of the rest of the mouth.

This part of the system can be modelled by a variable frequency generator to play the part of the vocal cords; and a set of three digitally controlled filters to stand in for the effects of the different resonant cavities that can be formed by the mouth. These account for all the vowels – though words like 'bay' and 'boy' require a rapid change in formant frequency – produced in the

Below right Speech can be broken up into a number of frequency bands. The 'shape' of the sounds in each band can then be recognized by a computer program. Here, a system by Logica analyses the word 'zero'. In practice, such a system can only recognize a hundred or so different words spoken by one person who has 'trained' it by repeating the words into a microphone

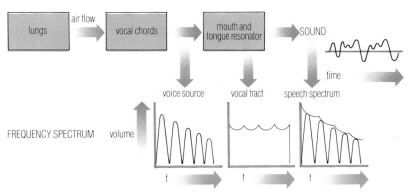

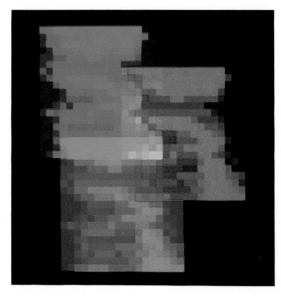

Human speech is a complicated thing. The vocal chords contribute a number of bands of tone of rising frequency and

decreasing intensity. The mouth and tongue form an 'organ pipe' of variable size that encourages some frequencies in the tone

bands or 'formants'. The result, shown on the right, shows large, low-frequency components and small high-frequency ones

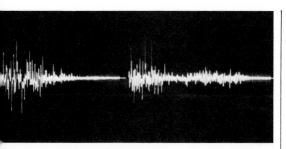

– which are produced by the characteristic resonance of the nose at about 1400 Hz. In a computer they need their own filter. And finally there are the fricatives – s, sh, z, th and f – which are produced by the tongue and teeth without resonance in the vocal tract. A good deal of skill is necessary to turn text into speech because it has to produce the particular throbs, clicks, whistles and psssts that are necessary to say, for example, 'How's your father?' in terms of the commands that would be issued by the nervous system to the muscles in a speaker's throat rather than storing the sounds spoken during the time it would take to say them. Once that is done, the saving in data is spectacular. People usually talk at about 100 words a minute and the average word is 6 letters long, so speech coded this way requires about 10 bytes per second – a six hundredth of the data required for directly digitized speech.

There are several chips available for this sort of job: one, the SC-01, offers consonants – f, g, k, t, z, b, d, j, p, h, m, n, l, r, w, th, sh, ch – and vowels – a, ah, ae, aw, e, eh, i, o, oo, u, uh, y – which all come in two or more lengths commanded by subscripts. For instance, there are four eh sounds, ranging in length from 59 to 185 milliseconds and three pauses also of different lengths. If you simply feed the SC-01 English text as printed, the results are usually garbage. 'Writing' with this stuff is not simple. 'Computer' needs to be: 'K UH₃ M P U₁ T ER'. 'Good afternoon' is 'G OO D AH₁ F T UH₃ NU U₁ N'.

Another problem is presented by regional accents. What sounds fine to a Texan will often be gibberish to a Scotsman (Texas Instruments' Speak and Spell toy, which uses a slightly different technology, was not a great success in Britain because no one could understand the American accent of the beast).

The final difficulty, which has not yet been satisfactorily tackled, is that much of the meaning in conversation is carried in the emphasis and intonation of what people say. Very often, in fact, we do not need to hear the words, we only have to listen to how they are said. To cope with this properly would mean that the computer should 'understand' from the general trend of the conversation that it should be being aggressive, reassuring, affectionate, bored and so on and put the right intonation into its speech. This is another problem which no one begins to know how to tackle.

Music Software

If speech turns out to have subtleties which the computer cannot handle, it also emerges, perhaps surprisingly, that the machine is an ideal assistant to a composer of music.

It looks after the tedious jobs of writing down the music, transposing keys, keeping track of the versions of a composition, and so on.

A number of machines that do all this are becoming available. One of them is called the Synclavier. It gives the composer a number of useful facilities. First, he has a synthesizer keyboard on which he can play the music he is composing. At the same time the notes he plays are displayed on the computer screen on music staves. He can write music for sixteen instruments at once (although an 'instrument' may just be a different timbre on the synthesizer). He can save written music on the disk, call it back and 'play' it through the synthesizer. He can redesign the sound and shape of any of his instruments' notes – the computer will display the volume and harmonic envelopes of the sound, together with a Fourier analysis* of it.

In many ways music and

computer programs are much the same. A piece of music is built up of complex layers of subroutines that specify timings, harmonies, keys, and so on. A motif may come into a piece many times in different ways; there is no reason why the composer should write it more than once. After that he calls it up – like a subroutine – with different parameters.

All this makes the conventional composer's life

much easier. But the Synclavier can also integrate his work with the strict timekeeping of film or video material. He can set the number of frames per second that his medium demands, and he can build synchronization cues into the score that will tie up with electronic vision control gear.

Not surprisingly, all this needs a 16-bit machine, and it is far from cheap. But when one reflects on the amount of specially composed music that the pop industry, film and television consume, it is a very useful application of the chore-eating ability of the computer.

*The principle of Fourier analysis is that any sound – or indeed any graphical shape – can be made up of a number of sine waves, and the point of that is that sine waves are easy to handle mathematically and to generate electronically (see pp. 108-9).

VOICE INPUT

We have seen how computers can be made to talk, though not very well. That is hard enough; but making them hear and understand is ten – a hundred – times harder. Just how much harder no one knows, because no one has done it.

Language is so easy for us that we underestimate the problems it causes for machines. There are layers and layers of these which all react on one another. The first is to turn the slurred and sloppy noises we make with our mouths into the relatively clear representation of letters. If you have ever tried to make a transcript of a tape-recorded conversation you will know how hard it is to sort out what people are saying – yet listeners actually on the spot probably had no difficulty. Speech is full of 'ums' and 'ers'; words that should be separated by a space on the page are run together; others have spaces in the middle where they should run on. This is not just a simple problem. Deciding what sounds go together to make up a word needs a lot of knowledge about the subject of the conversation. For instance, you might hear the same sounds in the adjective 'abominable' as in the phrase 'a bomb in a bull', depending on the context. A computer program that is to try to transcribe speech has to be able to 'understand' what the speech is about.

This understanding is one of the great problems of our time. It is quite clear that you need more than a dictionary. When someone says, 'I'll meet you at the same place', how do you know they do not mean the fish 'plaice'? When someone else says, 'Did they put the thing on the whatsit the same way they did last time?' you have no hope of understanding what is meant unless you have been paying attention to their preceding remarks. And that assumes that everything you need to understand the conversation has already been explained – that by ear alone you can follow people's thoughts. But of course this is seldom so. Very often people point and say 'that one over there – no, not that one, that other one' in a way that leaves a transcriber breathless.

But of course people do not use verbal shorthand only about things they can see, they assume all sorts of knowledge about things that have happened in the past. Some of this knowledge is so general that everyone knows it – for instance, that 'plaice' are not to be found at every street corner, and a conversation about a rendezvous probably uses the word 'place'. But a lot of meaning is carried forward from the speakers' experiences together that outsiders cannot share.

Even if the problem of giving the computer enough knowledge to understand conversations had been solved, we still should not know how to make the machine try out various possibilities of meaning as it attacks each new sound. What we want is an elaborate processing structure that offers possible interpretations of sounds up to a higher processor, which is building up a picture of the conversation – it will accept or reject in-

terpretations as they fit or clash with what has gone before.

The best we can do at the moment is a system prototyped by Bell Laboratories, which talks to people on the telephone about flight reservations. It does not have to have a lot of knowledge about the world outside airline timetables and the structures of simple English sentences. When a voice on the end of the telephone says to it 'I want to fly to San Francisco on Saturday' it does not have to do a lot of searching to establish what is going on. It will divide the speech up into words by listening for pauses. It also divides the words up into 'frames' 15 milliseconds long. Within a frame the frequency and volume of sound remains substantially constant, so the machine can describe the word in terms of these samples.

It divides the sounds into frequency bands each one octave (a doubling of the frequency) wide – 100-200, 200-400, 400-800, 800-1600, 1600-3200 Hz – and notes the intensity of sound in each

As part of research into the way the brain might work, workers at Brunel University, London, have built a machine that seems to imitate some aspects of a neural net. It is shown TV pictures of faces, digitizes them and makes its own connections among the pixels. It can then be trained to recognize various people and whether they are smiling or frowning. Such systems pose a serious problem because although they can work out for themselves how to identify someone, we cannot discover how they do it or comment if they seem to be doing it wrong

band in each frame. Having reduced each word in this way to a set of numbers, the machine can try to match them against stored words. These stored words may not be identical, but because there are not very many of them needed to converse about airline timetables, it is able to match each spoken word to a small number of candidates.

Having got the candidates, it can then try to fit them into the sentence structure. In the sentence we started with, 'I' and 'to' might have been clear, but the word in between not so good. However, a check with the system's knowledge of English syntax will show that the likely phrases starting with 'w' in that position are 'would like to' or 'want to', and there is not room for the first, so the word must be 'want'.

Transferring this technology to more general subjects raises more problems than the explosion of possible meaning for each uncertain word. In order to restrict the words searched, the system

assumes a grammar – a set of rules – that the speaker has used to string his or her words together. This works well enough for very simple sentences such as 'Mary (the agent) had (verb) a little lamb (object)'. The same structures works for 'I (the agent) gave (verb) her a kiss (object)'. The trouble is that many years' work on English grammar has shown that the simple appearance of rules like this is an illusion.

As you get deeper and deeper in, it seems that each word has its own individual set of grammatical rules, and this complicates the search problem horribly. You can no longer say 'the next word must be a verb, so I shall only search for words in my dictionary that I know are verbs' because there may just be one or two nouns that can fit into that place. Many hearts have been broken by computational linguistics.

So remember, the next time you see a conversing android on the screen – he comes into the category of 'wouldn't it be nice if ... '.

SENSORS

Computers interact with the world outside them in a wide variety of ways and through many different devices

Right The shape of a model is transferred to the machine by a digitizing arm. Accurate angle-measuring devices in the joints keep track of the position of the tip

Below right A computer does not care at all what it is working with. The ease with which quantities of liquid can be measured by level sensors in tanks, and moved about by operating valves and pumps, makes any sort of liquid process a natural for machine handling. Here is the control room of a large waterworks and (below centre) a brewery

Centre The sensors may be radars, miles away from the computer. Here an air traffic controller watches over a computer-painted portrait of 30,000 square miles of airspace. The machine draws streets in the sky; with the joystick in his hand the traffic-cop controller can run down the fastest jet

Far right This satellite dish on an oil rig is like a wire direct to the company's head office – which may be thousands of miles away. Remote spots like this in the global village will be served by satellite; in densely populated areas the links are likely to be by fibre optic

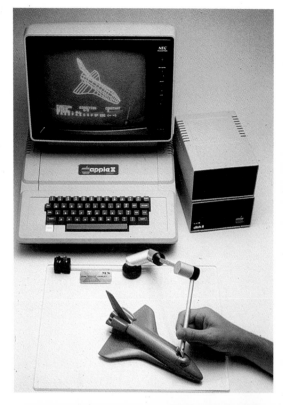

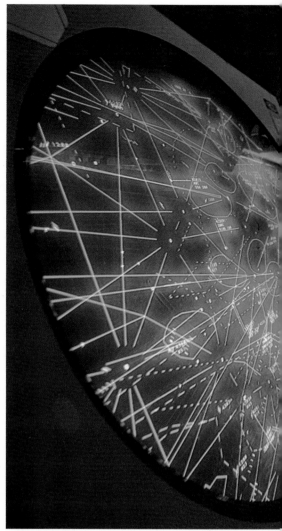

If the computer is to do anything useful in the world, it has to be provided with means to get information from it. The techniques for this are known as sensors. Most of them rely on some sort of electrical device to turn the physical effect to be measured into a voltage, which can then be converted to binary format by an analogue-to-digital convertor (see pp. 12-13).

The most important techniques – used in industry, science and the military – are concerned with measuring position, distance, speed and acceleration, and force.

Position

It is very often necessary to measure the position of some object or machine part. In the simplest case, we may want to know whether a door or a window is shut or open for a burglar alarm system. This can be done by a microswitch which touches the door or window. However, such switches are very liable to error and damage, so it is more usual to use a contactless device. A light beam can be broken by a little paddle when the window is shut. Better still, because the lenses may get dirty, is a magnetic sensor. This uses the

Hall Effect, relying on the fact that a magnetic field alters the properties of a transistor. So, to detect the closing of the window, a magnet is mounted in the window and a detector in the frame. A little electronic circuit detects when the window is shut and signals the computer.

In many cases the system may need to know

how far a part of a machine has moved along its possible course. The simplest solution is to attach the moving part to the slider of a variable resistance and then to measure the resistance (as in the joystick shown on pages 12-13).

However, a resistance can wear out, so a better solution is to use an optical system which pulls a grating past a light source and detector: whenever the moving thing shifts a distance equal to the width of one line in the grating, the system sends a pulse to the computer. The same sort of device can measure rotations as well.

Remote sensing

Often distances and thicknesses have to be measured without anything being able to touch the object being measured. An example would be the steel coming from the rolling mill described on pages 136-7. One solution might be to bounce a pulse of ultrasonic sound off the top surface and to measure the time delay – the thicker the steel, the shorter the delay. Another method might be to send a beam of X-rays through the steel and to measure the intensity on the other side – the thicker the steel, the less

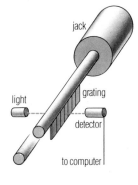

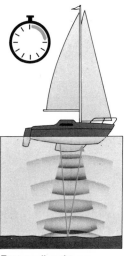

A computer to run a home energy management and security system needs to know whether doors and windows are open or closed. A magnet in the window affects the flow of current through a Hall Effect transistor in the window jamb if the window is closed, and does not if it is open. A little circuitry can then send an 'open/closed' signal to the computer

Measuring the position of a jack in a mechanical system – which might be the control flaps of an aircraft or the leg in the hopper (see pp. 132-3). The jack has a comb or grating attached to it whose teeth break a light beam as it moves. The computer counts the pulses in the light signal and so can measure the position of the jack

Even small yachts can measure the depth of water beneath their keels by timing the return of an echo from the sea floor. Modern navigation computers take this as an input and can use it with stored tide tables to improve in-shore navigation and to allow for currents

An example of digitized data making the invisible visible. The colours show the temperature of different parts of this rheumatic sufferer's hand (right, below). The computer converts infrared intensities to colour, showing the difference from the healthy hand (top)

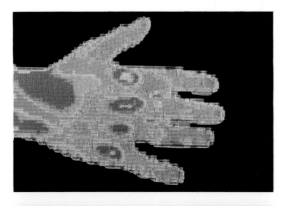

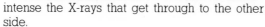

intense the X-rays that get through to the other side.

Ships and yachts have for many years used ultrasound to measure water depth, simply by timing the return of a pulse reflected from the sea bottom. The same system can be used to measure the contents of large vats of chemicals, petrol or oil. Geologists use explosions to make sense of the structure of rocks beneath the earth, in order to find oil.

The principle of time delay in the travel of radio signals is used for navigation. In modern civil and military systems a ship or an aircraft can calculate its position from the differing time delays in signals from a number of satellites.

Although computers cannot 'see' properly, they can be used to great effect to improve human vision. Earth-mapping satellites nowadays look at the ground with a number of cameras adjusted for different frequency bands. The resulting pictures can be analysed and combined by computer to produce very much more information than any of them would yield alone. Computer techniques can also be used to extract much more information from a photograph than it appears, at first sight, to contain (see pp. 108-9).

Speed and acceleration

It is not very difficult to measure speed. In a rolling vehicle an angular position sensor can be used to count bars per second to measure the rate of rotation of a road wheel and therefore the speed of the car. In aircraft, the pressure of the air stream can be measured, or a radar signal can be bounced off the ground and the Doppler shift, caused by the aircraft's forward motion,

Ships at sea can find their positions by timing signals from satellites

Below Oil prospectors need to discover the arrangement of rocks underground. One way of doing this is to lay out a line of microphones to listen to the echoes of an explosion, reflected from different rock layers. A recording is made of the signals. Back at the office, a computer program can reconstruct the rock strata

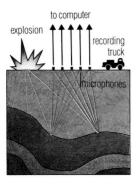

measured in the returned signal. A tiny propellor is often used to measure the rate of flow of liquid in a tube, and a magnet in one blade can trip a Hall sensor on each rotation.

There is no way of measuring speed without referring to the outside world. However, it is possible to measure acceleration using instruments that are completely contained within the vehicle, and from the acceleration it is easy to calculate the speed after a given time. Accelerometers come in two sorts: those that measure linear accelerations and those that measure angular ones.

Linear acceleration is easy: you just need a weighing machine. Imagine such a machine with a 10-pound weight in the pan, standing on the floor of a lift. As the lift starts to move upwards, the scale will read, say, 12 pounds for a little while. As the lift slows down at the top of its travel, the scale will read 8 pounds. A computer can be connected to the weighing machine and calculate from these measurements what the accelerations were, what the speeds were and where the lift was at any moment.

Measurements of angular acceleration are made with gyroscopes. As you will know if you have played with a spinning top, the thing resists attempts to turn it out of the position of its axis. These resisting forces can be measured and provide an indication of angular acceleration. In more sophisticated gyros, light beams are used. A pulse from a laser is sent round a closed path between three mirrors. It is detected after several turns. If the device – or the vehicle in which it is mounted – has turned while the light was in flight, the pulse will arrive sooner or later at the detector and the rate of turn can be calculated. Once you know that, you can work out how far you have rotated – if you know the direction you were heading at the beginning of a flight, you now know the direction in which you are pointing.

Linear and angular accelerometers like these are used to measure the speed and position of intercontinental ballistic missiles. They can be made so accurate that after a flight of several thousand miles, the warhead will land within a few hundred yards of its intended target.

Force

The easiest way to measure a force is to make it compress a spring and then to measure the length of the spring. Imagine that you want to measure the thrust of a jet engine. The simplest spring to choose is a strut taking the thrust of the engine to the aircraft. It is compressible – like a spring – but of course only to a microscopic degree. The way to do this electronically is to glue a thin strip of metal foil to the strut and use it as an electrical resistance. As the strut compresses and gets shorter, so the resistance of the foil decreases. The computer can measure this and calculate the thrust of the engine.

In the supermarket

bar-code reader

The computerized supermarket starts with bar codes on the products. The bar code is read by a light beam and sensor, and sent to the computer. The computer sends the price of the item and its description to the till for printing on the receipt. The customer pays in the normal way, but the computer also uses this information to update the stock records and do the business's accounts. It can re-order more quickly than is possible with a manual system. Also, by keeping an item-by-item control on stock, it makes pilfering more difficult. In the next development of the system, the customer's credit card will be put in the till and will allow the computer to send a message to his bank to debit his account by the amount of the bill. Shops and banks are working together in the UK to eliminate cash – which is expensive and easy to lose – from many daily transactions

Down on the farm

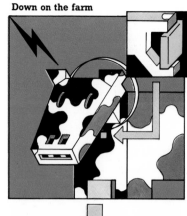

Computerized dairy farms are beginning to prove their worth. Each cow carries a small, passive radio transponder around her neck. When she enters the milking parlour it identifies her to the computer, which can then record her milk yield and issue the correct amount of feed. The computer can also do stock control on the milk collected and sold and so do the farm's accounts. Given information about the field in which the animals have been grazing, it can monitor grass growth and help to optimize the use of expensive fertilizers

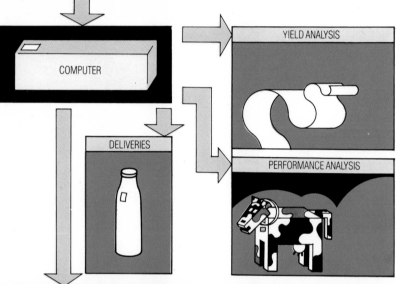

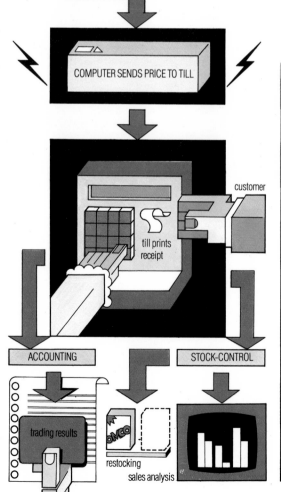

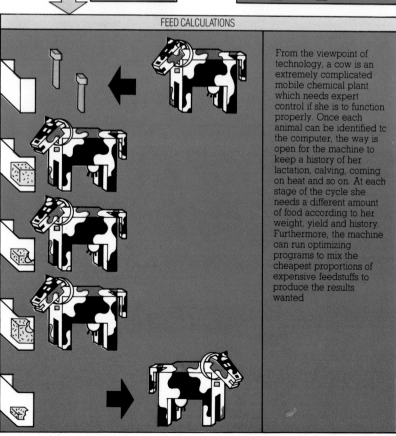

From the viewpoint of technology, a cow is an extremely complicated mobile chemical plant which needs expert control if she is to function properly. Once each animal can be identified to the computer, the way is open for the machine to keep a history of her lactation, calving, coming on heat and so on. At each stage of the cycle she needs a different amount of food according to her weight, yield and history. Furthermore, the machine can run optimizing programs to mix the cheapest proportions of expensive feedstuffs to produce the results wanted

A revolution is taking place in aircraft which – although it leaves them looking much the same from the outside – is profoundly changing the way they appear to their pilots.

This cockpit in a British Aerospace 1-11 test aircraft shows the new displays on the left-hand side.

Instead of the traditional dial and pointer displays (on the right), there are two large, colour CRTs driven by the aircraft's flight computer.

See the large artificial horizon in the centre of the left-hand display. Around are simulations of an altimeter and a rate-of-climb instrument.

In military aircraft, the same sort of display is often projected on the windscreen so that it appears to the pilot to be hanging in space in front of him – a 'head-up display' (HUD). The HUD display can paint otherwise invisible features on the land- and skyscape outside, like radar indications of hostile aircraft that are yet invisible, or stored targets over camouflaged positions on the ground.

The same principle has been used in civil aviation to project a 3D radar image of a real but invisible airstrip in front of the pilot so that he can land in fog

An airliner is an immensely complicated mix of machines which must be carefully managed to get to the right place at the right time while spending the minimum in fuel and wear and tear. At the start of the flight the crew input their flight and fuel plan. After take-off, the computer manages the climb-out.

The computer then manages the cruise phase, working out the optimum height and speed. If it is necessary to increase height, the machine works out the best moment to climb.

At the same time the computer checks the waypoints, showing predicted ETAs, speeds and heights. On arrival, the system commands the best point to start the aircraft's descent

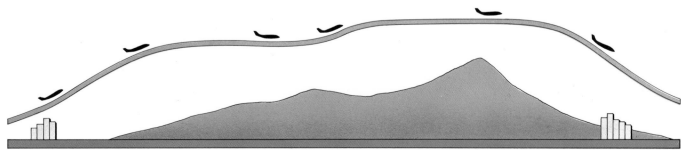

At least half of the mystery of the sea has been the complicated arithmetic that was needed to navigate a ship's way round the world. With the advent of computers that mystery is disappearing.

There are a number of calculations that a sea-borne computer can usefully do in a yacht, but before it can do them, it has to have input. The obvious things to measure are: speed through the water; compass heading of the boat; relative wind speed; and direction. Having collected these values, using the instruments shown on the right, there are several useful things that can be done with them. Navigators' first concern is with their position. They can find this out by taking bearings on lighthouses and landmarks, but there might be none above the horizon or it might be night or foggy, so they must always keep a 'dead reckoning' position – that is, a plot of the course and speed from where they started to where they ought to be now. A computer fed with compass course and speed through the water can do this without trouble. A dead reckoning facility would be extremely useful in the emergency of a man overboard – the helmsman would just have to push a reset button when the alarm was given, and sail back until the dead reckoning from that position was zero.

The next thing the navigators would like to know is the true wind speed and direction, and that too is not difficult to calculate, given speed through the water, compass heading and apparent wind speed and direction.

Murphy's Law, when applied to sailing boats, says that you spend threequarters of your time at sea beating slowly and uncomfortably to windward. It depends very much on your helmsman's skill whether or not you are going as fast to windward as possible – and it is not an easy thing to check – except by discovering at the end of several cold, miserable hours that you have not made as much progress as you would have liked. The computer can calculate the boat's speed upwind and display the result as a percentage of possible performance.

Racing enthusiasts can use the device as a stopwatch to tell them when the start gun is going to fire, and can record all the four variables, plus the helm movements, on tape for analysis afterwards.

However, the computer's uses are not yet exhausted. Out of sight of land, the navigators have to find their way by measuring the height of sun.

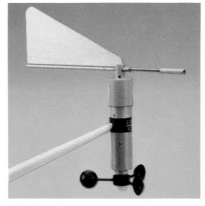

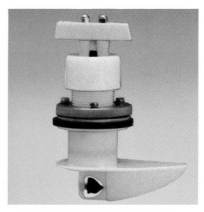

and stars above the horizon. Having measured these angles with a sextant, the navigators have to do some quite complicated arithmetic – using bulky published tables – to find out where they are. The computer can easily do these calculations for them.

Left The yacht computer needs to know the wind's speed and direction, signalled to it by this small sensor mounted on the masthead

Above The computer also needs to know the water speed, measured by this little propellor sticking out of the boat's bottom

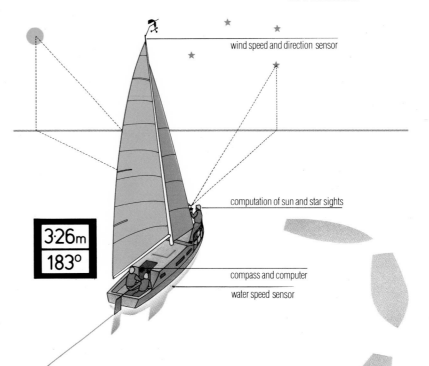

wind speed and direction sensor

computation of sun and star sights

compass and computer

water speed sensor

3·26m
183°

0·01m
276°

If you fall overboard from a small yacht at sea, you are apt to drown just because it is so hard for the people still on board to keep track of where you are. If a computer-driven navigation device is fitted, the helmsman simply has to reset the log to 0 when he

hears the yell 'Man overboard!' Then, the log starts to show the distance and bearing away from the man in the water. The helmsman only has to steer back until the log reads 0 again and he should be beside the swimmer

SERVOS

The detail of measuring the outside world is important but not all that crucial to the role of the computer in controlling machines. The central place has to go to the idea of the 'servo loop'. To understand this, let us take a simple example: you, driving a car down a straight road.

There are many things that can prevent you driving in a straight line: the steering may be set up with a pull to one side or another; there may be bumps in the road that throw you off course; passing lorries may suck you to one side or another; you may look away from the road so that your hand on the wheel inadvertently follows your eyes; there may be gusts of wind that blow the car across the road.

Quite clearly, you could not write a program to steer the car without also having precise knowledge of the actions of all other road users. If a passing lorry arrives a fraction of a second too early or too late, the program could be lethal. Even if you could write it, such a program would be useless. What's wanted is something much more flexible, that can adapt to varying and unpredictable conditions. Let's look at what it has to work with.

Your aim is to drive the car in a straight line down the middle of your lane. The only input we will consider is the evidence of your eyes. You can measure, in some way, how far the car is from the line you want it to take.

To make it cope with such a problem, the computer must work in the same way that a human does: it must do little experiments as it goes along. When one gets in a strange car, one tries out the steering and the brakes to see how they work. The machine must do the same – if the wind changes, it must notice and adapt. The technique for doing this is the 'servo loop'.

The servo loop that controls the car is very simple. You look at the road and work out from cues such as the edge of the road, the line down the centre, and other traffic, where you want to go. You calculate the *difference* between where you are and where you want to be and turn the wheel in such a way as to reduce the difference to zero. In other words, if you have drifted a little to the left you turn the wheel a little to the right. If you have drifted a lot to the left (or the road is curving to the right) you turn the wheel a lot to the right. Here is a simple program in Microsoft BASIC to simulate this problem.*

```
5 K1=.05:K2=-2:K3=.8:K4=.210: INPUT "WIND, MPH";W
20 PRINT "WHEEL ANGLE, DEGREES";
40 PRINT TAB(25);"CAR DEVIATION, FEET";
50 FOR J=1 TO 20
60 PRINT USING "###∅#";A*10;
70 PRINT TAB(25);:PRINT USING "###∅#";I
80 D=K1*W+A
```

*William T. Powers,*Byte*, June 1979, p.132.

```
90 I=I+D
100 A1=K2*(I+K3*D)
110 A=A+K4*(A1-A)
120 NEXT J
130 GOTO 10
140 END
```

When the program runs, it starts by setting four constants. K1 is to do with the car's streamlining and the grip the wind can get on it. K2 and K3 are to do with the driver's perceptions of the error signal. K4 is to do with his reaction time. The program then asks you to enter a wind speed in miles per hour. This is a notional gust from one side – say the left. To make it come from the other side, you would enter a negative number.

The program then prints out a table of wheel angles and the distance of the car from the desired track. There has been no attempt to get the physics right – the real calculation (see opposite) would be much more complicated.

It is assumed that each loop, as J increments, corresponds to a time interval – say $1/10$ second. Line 60 prints the wheel angle multiplied by 10 to make it a sensible figure. Line 70 prints the deviation I from the desired track. Line 80 calculates D, the extra deviation that has occurred since the last run through the loop. D is proportional to a constant, K1, times the wind speed, W, added to the angle of the wheels, A (which will usually have the opposite sign).

Line 90 adds the new deviation D to the old total I. The program now assumes that you, the driver, have noticed what is going on, and do something about it. Unfortunately there is a definite lag in the operation of your eye, brain and muscles, so you cannot alter A immediately to cope with the new conditions. To simulate this, the program calculates an intermediate angle A1 in line 100. Studies of human reactions show that the size of people's reactions to this sort of situation is proportional (via the constant K2) to the deviation I plus some more (that is, dependent on the rate of change of I). This is effectively D, the amount I has changed since the last loop, and is multiplied by the constant K3.

Line 110 then alters A by an amount proportional to the difference between A and A1 – to allow for the lag in your own internal servos – using the constant K4. A printout of this program starting with the car on track, hit by a gust of 30 m.p.h. is shown on the right. The car is very quickly blown as far as 1.9 feet downwind. However, in the next loop, the wheels are turned 19.9 degrees in the other direction, bringing the car back to within .5 feet of the desired track. It then swings away again, but soon settles down to a steady .8-foot deviation.

This behaviour is typical of many servo systems. There is an initial 'hunting' around the end position, followed by a stable condition with a small amount of error. There has to be some error

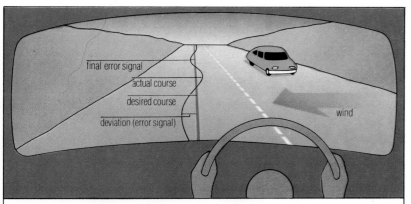

WHEEL ANGLE, DEGREES	CAR DEVIATION, FEET
0.0	0.0
−11.3	1.5
−18.0	1.9
−19.8	1.6
−18.6	1.1
−16.5	0.7
−15.0	0.6
−14.3	0.6
−14.3	0.7
−14.6	0.7
−14.9	0.8
−15.1	0.8
−15.1	0.8
−15.1	0.8
−15.0	0.7
−15.0	0.7
−15.0	0.7
−15.0	0.7
−15.0	0.7
−15.0	0.8

signal otherwise the wheels would not be turned to windward and there would be nothing to stop the car drifting downwind into the oncoming traffic. It is also interesting to notice that the system is relatively insensitive to changes in the constants. Try different values for K4, which corresponds to the driver's reaction time. If K4 is set to .4 (Grand Prix standard reactions), the gust is instantly corrected for. If it is increased to .5, the car never settles down but always swerves nervously from side to side. With K4=.6 the driver overcorrects, the car's swerves get bigger and bigger, and it is soon up the bank or under the wheels of the oncoming lorry.

By using a servo loop the computer can ignore great masses of fact about the outside world. In effect it does a little experiment every time it has to issue a control command. It just needs to know roughly, before it starts, the sort of control force it should use. Otherwise it might turn the wheel so hard that the car rolls over.

A servo loop depends on negative feedback – on an amplification of the error signal between what is happening and what ought to happen. If it were not for the servo loop concept, which in this example automatically includes the car and the road and the atmosphere, with all their quirks and imperfections, in the sensing and control system, it would not be practicable to make computers control machinery.

William Powers went on to propose a new theory of control, in which the servo loops do not look to see what has happened – i.e. where the car is – but what the system's sensors say about the position of the car. The object of the servo loop is to reduce the data input about the car's deviation to as small a value as possible.

The beauty about a servo loop is that it works without knowing anything about the world outside. You can think of it as a black box with two inputs – the error signal and the control signal – one output, and some dials on the side to set the constants. This box – or, rather, program subroutine – will then control anything. Here we have been steering a car, but the same sort of loop will control the accelerator as well. A car-driving program could use the servo subroutine, with different constants, for both purposes.

But the lowest-level routines such as these can be controlled by higher-level ones still. For instance, the target speed on an empty road is set by the distance of the horizon. If you have ten miles of straight freeway, you can drive at 180 m.p.h.; if the road disappears round a bend, you had better slow down to 10 m.p.h. In real life, of course, there will be other vehicles on the road, and their distances and speeds will also affect the target speed of the lowest level servo.

At a higher level still, a servo will control the purpose of the journey. We want to drive from New York to Troy to visit an aged aunt. So long as the aunt's house is not in sight, the second level servo sets the speed, and its control input is logical: '0' means 'Not there yet'; '1' means 'We have arrived; stop the car!'

The next level servo could decide whether we want to set out on this journey at all. It would take for its control signal various rules about 'good' behaviour that say the aged aunts should be visited, and feed an error signal into the system if they are not. Or a higher-level servo might be one to do with cash flow, and take for its error signal the difference between the aged aunt's bank balance and your own.

THE HOPPER

The availability of cheap, powerful microcomputers makes it possible to build machines that would have been quite impossible before. One example is the single-leg hopper,* a sort of mechanical kangaroo, which was built to study the way in which humans and animals move, and also to explore the possibilities of making vehicles that do not move on wheels or tracks.

By using a micro, the designers of this machine were able to produce a device that did not rely on its geometry to stay upright. Instead, like an animal, if it stops concentrating it falls over. It consists of a 'body' – a frame that holds various sensing instruments, jacks and the computers – and a 'leg' – a fast-acting, low-friction pneumatic jack with a non-slip foot on the end.

Since human ingenuity cannot yet match the power-to-weight ratio of muscle, the machine's energy comes from outside in the form of compressed oil and air through a lightweight hose pipe. The single leg is gimballed in the middle of the body. It can be made to swing fore and aft or from side to side by sets of jacks. Conversely, the angular position of the leg is signalled to the computer by length sensors attached to these same jacks. The driving power of the machine is the main jack in the leg. By lengthening it suddenly, the machine can be made to hop up in the air. When it comes down it compresses the jack again and will bounce. Only a little air needs to be let into the jack to overcome the energy lost to friction and the machine will hop in one place at its natural resonant frequency.

The designers found that if they could make it hop in one place without falling over, it was not hard to make it move about. To make it hop

*Marc H. Raibert and Ivan E. Sutherland, *Scientific American*, January 1983, pp. 32-41.

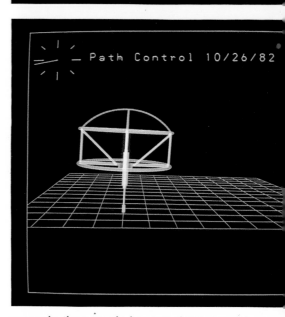

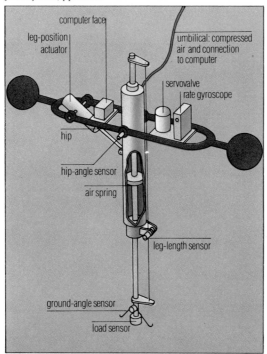

Detail of an early version of the hopper, which required lateral support in order to operate

computer face
leg-position actuator
umbilical: compressed air and connection to computer
servovalve
rate gyroscope
hip
hip-angle sensor
air spring
leg-length sensor
ground-angle sensor
load sensor

properly they needed to run three servo loops (see pp. 130-31). The first loop controls the hopping height by adding or releasing air from the air spring in the main jack. Obviously, the weight of the machine and the capacity of the jack make up a resonant system. Most of the energy needed for a hop is provided by the rebound from the previous hop. The servo loop starts with a height sensor in the main jack, goes to the computer, is compared with a preset, ideal, hopping height. If necessary, the computer issues commands to air valves to let air into or out of the jack.

The second loop calculates the proper angle for the leg while the machine is in flight so that it lands in balance. This takes into consideration the forward speed of the machine and the inclination of the body – forwards or to the side. It turns out that a single computer program will work whether the machine is hopping on the spot, moving off to a run, moving at constant speed, leaping over obstacles or slowing down. This

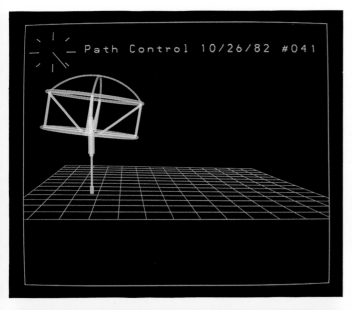

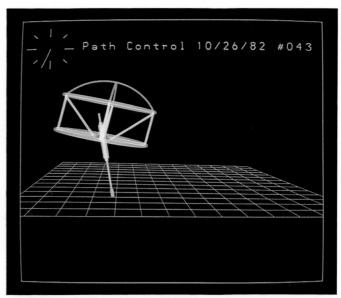

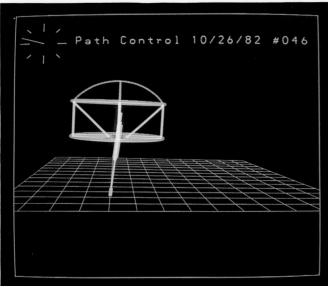

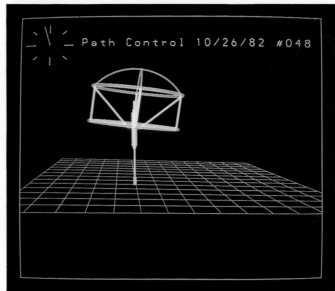

loop takes for its inputs the gyroscope signals that provide information about angular accelerations and the relative position of the jack and body. When the hopper is hopping in one place, this loop will correct for small imbalances as the body starts to fall over one way or another. When the machine is to start running, say, to the left, the leg is moved to the right to make the whole hopper tip to the left so that the next jump will move it to the left as well as upwards. The third loop stabilizes the device while it is on the ground.

Once these three loops are running properly, the machine imitates the loping run of the kangaroo very well. The hopper swings its leg forwards and backwards through a large angle just as the animal does — it has to in order to keep balanced in the air. The designers of the hopper intend to extend their ideas to a four- or six-legged machine that might well be very useful in country too rough for wheels or hovercraft. However, as we saw on pages 116-19, computer vision is not yet good enough to give the mechanical animal 'eyes'. It would need a human driver to tell it where to put its feet.

These six photographs show a computer simulation of the then unbuilt hopper (see text). The simulation can verify design principles and allows changes to be made quickly and easily. Building the machine was only necessary to make sure there were no bugs in the simulation

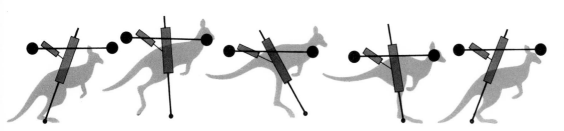

The action of the hopper superimposed on the shape of a kangaroo

ROBOTS

An artist's magical evocation of the Android-Builders. In reality, the attempts to create mechanical simulations of the human body are proving far more difficult than anyone had guessed.

The photograph below shows the late Chris Evans with 'Freddy' at Edinburgh University. Though primitive, Freddy represents a more likely ancestor of the robots of the future. This picture was taken in 1975, shortly before UK government funding for robotics research was cut in favour of nuclear physics. As a result of that rather short-sighted economy, we are now buying Freddy's descendants from the Japanese

Although few of us have met a free-moving, tin-suited robot in the metal, like R2D2 of *Star Wars*, we all know perfectly well how it should behave. Every respectable work of science fiction has robots in profusion: pedantically correct robots, pathetic broken robots, spy robots that pretend to be pedantic, and mad robots that have to be sent to the breaker's yard because they have forgotten Asimov's three Laws of Robotics.

As we shall see, the engineering in a classical tin robot is beyond us and looks as though it will stay that way for some decades to come. No one has the faintest idea how to set about building a human-looking robot – an android like those in *Blade Runner*. What we have all seen is robots built into other kinds of machinery.

Once we can make the computer get its inputs from the 'real world' with sensors, we can get it to do many jobs that would otherwise have to be done by people. This is nothing new. From the beginning of the machine age, steam engines needed continuous control of the supply of steam to the cylinder: when the piston is at the top of its stroke, steam must be let in from the boiler; when it is at the bottom, the used steam must be let out to the atmosphere. Engine-builders provided two taps and expected the operator to hire a small boy to open and shut them at the correct moments.

Legend tells that one of these small boys saw that he could rig up some string to do the job automatically so he could doze the afternoons

away. He had built the first robot – a robot valve opener and closer. This robot illustrates the three problems of robotics that are still with us: detection, intelligence and execution.

The robot has to detect cues from the real world and work out what to do about them. In this case it had to detect the right moments to open and close the two valves. It then had to apply the necessary force to do what was wanted – turn the valves. This very primitive robot did both functions in one, because the beam of the engine had so much force, strings tied to it at the right places could easily pull the valves round. In many cases sensing and execution are completely separate functions – and in between them nowadays often comes a microprocessor.

ROBOTS IN INDUSTRY

We saw on pages 124-9 how computers can get input from the real world – from a multitude of different sensors, ranging from a simple contact switch on a window, to a nationwide chain of radars. Having got the input, the computer has to work out what is wanted. Since, as we saw on pages 116-17 and 122-3, we do not yet know how to make computers see or hear the way we can, a crucial part of the art of robotics is to get inputs that the computer can make sense of.

If a robot is running a steel-rolling mill, it is no good just pointing a television camera at the white-hot steel coming out of the rollers and expecting the computer to work out from the picture the thickness of the steel plate. Special devices have to be installed to measure the thickness with the required accuracy and feed the results in a suitable form to the computer's interface.

Right This time-delay shot of robot welders at work at a Chrysler plant shows an environment where man cleary has no place

Below In a Japanese robot-making factory a self-absorbed, low-IQ robot tractor bustles along looking for a load

Below An automated production line. The purpose of the line is to cut gear wheels and shafts from metal blanks, which can be seen on the conveyor belt that delivers them to the appropriate machines in the right order. Ranged along the far side of the belt are the machine tools that do the actual shaping. Each machine is served by a robot which takes the metal blanks from the belt, loads them into the machine tool and, once the parts are shaped, replaces them on the belt. The control stations for each stage of the process can be seen in the foreground. The computer which controls the production line is kept in another room

Once the computer is set up to interpret the input from that device as steel thickness, it cannot be expected to realize if someone connects it to a thermometer instead. Having measured the thickness of the steel, the computer then makes a decision and outputs the result by operating huge screw jacks to alter the spacing of the rollers. The whole system is a perfectly good robot, which can replace Old Harry, the skilled workman who used to adjust the rollers by hand; but it looks nothing like our preconception of a robot.

There are a vast number of robots like this in modern industry, many of them specialized and capable of adaptation over a very small range. The steel-rolling robot, for instance, can probably only be adapted to produce different thicknesses of sheet. If you wanted to alter its function, say, to make railway rails, you would probably have to get in a team of engineers to redesign the thing. It has none of the flexibility of the human it replaced. But, on the other hand, it has none of his proneness to error, fallibility, fatigue, bad temper – or his expense.

The challenge for the robot designer is to pro-

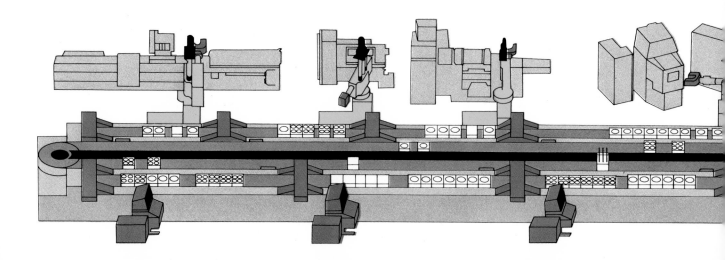

duce a machine that is sufficiently specialized to do its work well, and yet is flexible enough to be reprogrammed without redesign. This problem is particularly acute in robots with vision. Production-line robots that are expected to 'see' when the next part arrives have to be provided with very specialized sensors, such as light beams which are broken by the arriving part. If the part changes shape then the sensors have to be set up again and the machine reprogrammed. Another problem is that we are still unable to make devices as sensitive and versatile as the human hand. You can give a robot a spray gun or a welding head or a drill, but it is not possible to make a device that will hold all three.

Robots are, however, beginning to replace human workers in jobs that are heavy and repetitive or that have to be carried out in uncomfortable and dangerous surroundings. An excellent site for a robot is in the welding section of a car production line and that is usually where they are to be found. They are beginning to creep into coal mines, freeing men from a job that is quite unsuited to the human frame.

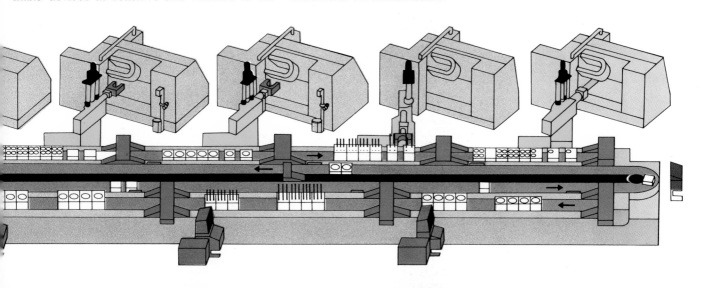

HOW A ROBOT WORKS

Any competent workman could assemble a machine, given a box of the necessary parts and a drawing. Yet consider the appalling complications of trying to build a robot to do the same job. It would need a vision system that could identify individual parts within a heap of other parts. Then it would have to have a wildly intelligent expert system that could work out from the drawings the order in which the parts should be put together. Finally, a 'hand' would have to be built that could use all sorts of tools; that had the delicacy to assemble clockwork and the strength to break rocks.

The whole thing would have to be cheaper than a workman and as easy to reprogram. A skilled man earns about £15,000 or $30,000 a year in the West. This represents the interest and amortization over five years on a machine costing $85,000 and that is roughly what it is worth paying for a robot. The sum is more complicated, of course, because it may be worth paying more for a machine that will work longer hours than humans or will do heavier or more dangerous jobs than they can. But there is not a lot of money available to produce a synthetic human. Using today's technology, it is out of the question to produce an all-purpose, humanoid robot that can be stood in place of Old Harry at the rolling mill controls. What we now call a 'robot' is just a computer peripheral which can pick things up or manoeuvre a tool on a production line.

The robot consists of a single arm, whose end can be moved anywhere within a radius of about 10 feet. On the end of the arm will be a wrist joint which can rotate and angle up, down and sideways. Instead of a general-purpose hand, the robot will often be given specialized tools – a welding gun, suction pads or a paint spray.

The task of the programmer is to provide a language which will allow the end-user of the arm to program it simply. The user must be able to tell the robot to wait, say, until a car body comes down the assembly line. When the breaking of a light beam tells the robot that the body is in position, it is told to move its hand to the start of a roof seam and then to weld it shut. This

The whole point of an industrial robot is to move its 'hand', and whatever is attached to it, to anywhere in a hemisphere around the pedestal. Since it has to move fast and accurately and may have to pick up quite heavy loads, the robot has to be a solid piece of engineering.
The normal robot has six 'degrees of freedom' (as shown by the arrows) – that is, it can rotate round six joints. They are: waist, shoulder, elbow, and two at the wrist, and the tool-holder, which can spin round. Four of the many tools that can be attached are shown: an electric seam-welding head, a spot welder, a small-part gripper and a suction pad for handling large flat objects. The arm is controlled by the computer on the left

There are four fundamental
ways of articulating the joints
to move the hand. The
machine below uses the
scheme in the bottom right-
hand box

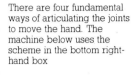

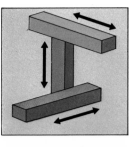
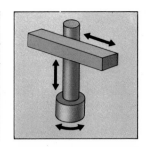
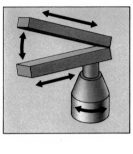
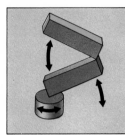

involves commands like: 'Go from Park to Start-seam. Move to Endseam, Welding as you go. Go to Park.'

'Weld' is a subroutine which detects the distance of the welding head from the body of the car, monitors the flow of current and the length of the welding rod and does all the right things. 'Startseam' and 'Endseam' are positions in space that are preprogrammed into the computer from the design of the car body. The programmer of the robot can either type in these two positions as coordinates, or put the robot into 'learning' mode and steer the head by hand. The language should have routines to smooth out the wiggles of the manual demonstration.

It should be possible to give the robot any subroutines – little sets of movements the programmer wants performed in different places. Suppose the robot is being used to load bottles into a crate and then to screw lids on them. The movement necessary to screw each lid on is the same, but it has to be performed in a different place each time.

When sensors become more sophisticated it will be possible to program robots in a more general way, by giving them the same sort of instructions one would give a stupid human. 'Take the bottles off the production line, screw a lid on each one and fill the crates.'

TRAINING ROBOTS

An interesting, if rather exotic, peripheral for a micro is a training robot – a small, table-top version of the monsters found on the factory floor. In fact, much of the function of the microcomputer industry is to spread computeracy in all its forms, so this is not as useless as it might sound. And, if you had a business handling large quantities of very small objects, you might even build a production line with such machines.

The machine shown here is made – and very solidly made – by Mitsubishi of Tokyo. It comes with its own CP/M micro, but could be connected easily enough to any machine with a serial port.

The robot arm has six small drive motors. In common with many industrial robots, these are all 'stepper' motors which are driven by a series of electrical pulses, and turn a small fixed amount for each pulse. The output of the motors is geared down so that the limbs of the robot move between

.04 degrees and .08 degrees per pulse. This makes it possible for the controlling computer to 'know' where each joint is by counting the pulses sent to it. Without that feature, the robot would have to have a complicated and expensive set of sensors to measure and report the positions of its joints.

One motor in the base plate turns the whole robot on a vertical axis from side to side. The shoulder, elbow and wrist joints work horizontally so that the grippers can be put anywhere in a hemisphere around the machine. The wrist can spin round and round – unlike its human counterpart. A sixth motor closes the grippers by pulling on a wire.

Commands are sent to the robot much as they

would be to a printer: as a series of strings. For instance the line of BASIC

LPRINT "H"

when the robot is attached to the printer port will make it go 'Home' – curl up – with all its motors at one end of their travel. This is so that the controlling micro knows where they all started from and can keep track of where they are at any moment during operation.

The micro in the base is programmed to allow for the time need to accelerate and decelerate the joints, so that movements are performed smoothly and accurately.

The machine responds to fifteen different commands. These come in two levels. At the lower level, each joint can be rotated a specified number of steps. This could be commanded by keyboard input, or through a touchpad, so that the machine could be taught. For instance, at the start of the draughts-playing program illustrated on this page, the arm would reach out to show where it expected the centre of the board to be, and where it would look for the two piles of chips. The human operator has to adjust the position of the robot and the playing pieces so that the blind machine can find them during play.

Once a position is established – as, for instance, over the pile of white chips – it can then be given a number which is stored in the robot's RAM. As long as the power is kept on, it will remember this position, and will go to it on the command

LPRINT 'M3'

Having got to the right position, the grippers can be closed to pick up the draught which can then be moved to another position and released. It would not be hard to write a program to pick small objects like test tubes off a belt and put them into a box. The offsets needed to put each tube in its appropriate position in the box would be built into the program.

The controlling computer's program can, of course, initiate the robot for a particular job by sending it a whole list of positions in the form of specified numbers of steps for each motor from the 'nest' position. For example, the program to play draughts starts out by commanding a range of positions:

10 LPRINT "P1,0,372,–958,592,–592,0"
20 LPRINT "P5.739,–707,–431,–86,–1114,0"

and so on. The grippers can be moved to these positions during the run of a program simply by specifying the appropriate number.

ANDROIDS

The idea of making a machine that behaves like a human – an android – is fascinating. From one point of view, every computer is a sort of android, in that it mimics and improves on human mental processes. But it certainly does not look human and it lacks all of a human's ability to move about, handle objects, see, hear and feel. The hope of creating such a machine, or a major part of one, has been the inspiration of many leaders in computer science and engineering, as well as in the arts. In fact, the most successful android builders have been the film makers (as in *Blade Runner*) who can use human beings to stand in for their otherwise inoperative creations. A vast amount of work has been done, but at the end of it all we have to admit that, compared with Mother Nature, we know very little about either computing or engineering. Let us look at the major problems one at a time.

We need a machine that is capable of moving itself about over rough ground, up stairs, up trees and even cliffs for several days before its batteries run down. It should be able to pick up the equivalent of its own weight and stagger with it. The same hands and arms must be capable of picking up and threading a needle. We have nothing remotely capable of this sort of performance. A machine using electric motors and batteries would go, on the flat, for less than an hour before running down – one flight of stairs would exhaust it. A mechanical arm strong enough to use for a tug-of-war would weigh nearly 100 pounds. Even if we knew how to build walking

legs (which we do not yet), they would come out weighing more in the region of tons than tens of pounds.

The human eye has the equivalent of some 3 million pixels; the best available televisions have 1 million. But even if we had a suitably sensitive mechanical eye, we could not process its information in less than hours – as against the eye and brain's $1/25$ second – and we still do not know how to do more than 1 per cent of the necessary processing.

The human brain contains some 10,000 million neurons. Each neuron is attached to many others and has an unknown value in terms of byte storage, but we might assume that it can store 100 bytes. The brain is then equivalent to a million million bytes or the contents of a 100-foot cube full of today's memory chips. And that again assumes that we would know how to organize the memory if we had it. One of today's 16-bit micros would take more than three weeks to search that much memory for one four-letter word.

So, we have to accept that the science-fiction android is very far in the future. Curiously enough, the serious attempts to build an android were made some ten years ago or more. The designers used what would be considered today to be excessively massive computers, but that is not important. The software is what matters and that has not changed very much – those early experiments showed that there was such a gap between the performance of machines and humans that there was no real point in trying to bridge it at this stage in development. The two experimental androids were called Shakey – built at Stanford University – and Freddy – built at Edinburgh University.

Shakey was a mobile robot with an arm, grippers and a television camera which trundled rather shakily around a small world of five rooms, a ramp and various boxes that it could manipulate. Its computer was static,

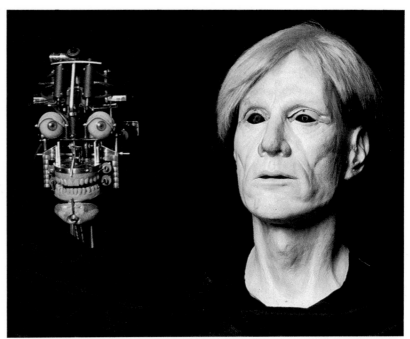

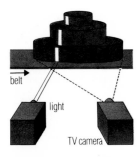

Industrial vision problems are often solved by cruder methods than artificial eyes. Here a thin vertical beam of light shined obliquely is played on engine parts on a conveyor belt. The pattern of stripes 'seen' by the TV camera gives a good indication of the type, position and size of the part being illuminated

There have been many attempts down the ages to create androids

Below right 'Mlle Claire', built by Dr Hardner at l'Hôpital Bretonnaise, Paris, in 1912, hands out surgical instruments on a ward round

Below A computerized, moderately human-looking dummy helps medical students learn their craft

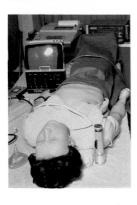

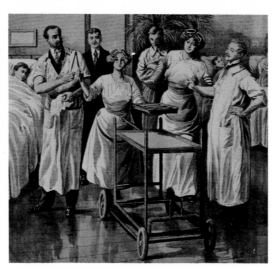

connected to it by way of a cable. Freddy was a static device, consisting of a gripper on an arm suspended from the ceiling. It looked at objects spread on a table below it that could be moved in two directions by electric motors.

Freddy was an attempt to combine visual sensing, machine intelligence and a robot arm into a mechanical assembly-line worker. Although Freddy has been dismantled for a decade now, it is likely that the first more intelligent shopfloor robots will work very much as Freddy did. It was programmed to assemble small toys from wooden parts tipped out in a heap on its work table. Before a run began, the human operator had to go through two sets of training exercises. First, he had to show Freddy all the parts of the toy in all the positions in which they could come to rest on the flat work surface (see pp. 118-19). He then had to tell the robot how to grip each part and put it into a standard position. Finally, he had to program the machine to assemble the parts in the right order. Having done these things, Freddy would then behave in a remarkably intelligent manner.

It would try to pick out bits it needed from the heap of parts and put them to one side in the standard positions they would have to be in for assembly to begin. If no individual parts were visible as separate entities, Freddy would attack the heap of bits and try to pull items out of it. If that did not work, Freddy would swing its arm through the heap in an attempt to break it up.

As we have seen, existing robots are long on brawn but very, very short on brain. They cannot do anything very much in the way of sensing. A robot welder on a car line, for example, will be told by the closing of a switch that the next chassis has arrived. It sets to, like a blind man, to weld where it has been shown, and if the car is not where it should be, then the thin air gets a seam of hot metal put into it.

This case is not too bad, because the description of the end condition contains some clear clues about what to do first. However, in real life,

one would like the answers to questions like: 'How can I become rich and famous?' If there were any clues in the question you would not be asking the computer for the answer.

We saw on pages 116-19 the impossibility of imitating full human vision. Even much simpler schemes are not a great success. It is one thing to make a machine recognize a few wooden blocks in the laboratory, when conditions can be made just right, but quite another to produce a piece of equipment which can be installed in any old factory and work reliably. There the vision system has to contend with vibration, noise, dirt and quite unpredictable lighting. An unexpected shadow, a smear of grease or a reflection off a shiny machine part could all make the object look completely different to a simple-minded vision scheme.

Even with perfect lighting it is still very hard to work out what it is that the camera is looking at. One simple but effective scheme is to illuminate objects with a very thin bar of light falling obliquely across the scene viewed by the camera. To check that the object to be handled is in the right position, the vision system now has to compare the bright bar seen by the camera with a remembered version.

We said glibly, above, that the computer just has to compare the shape of the bar, as the object moves through the light beam, with a remembered version. This is not at all easy, particularly as the object may be in a random orientation, and programmers have to reduce the computer description of an object to a set of apparently irrelevant numbers, such as the ratio of its length to its circumference (see p. 119).

Even touch is very demanding on processing time. It is not very difficult to provide robot grippers with contact switches or pressure pads that can signal whether a gripper has gripped something and if so how hard, but even for so simple a thing the processing required is immense. A few sensors really need the continuous attention of a computer if it is not to miss the transitory bumps that may signal vital information such as 'I tried to pick up the cog but it slipped out of my hand'. If a single computer is to do everything, the production line must be slowed down to crawling pace; if multiple computers are to be used, the designer is faced with as yet unsolved problems of parallel processing (see p. 174).

All industrial robots have to be told how to set about their tasks, just as Freddy was told. A human has to work out a strategy for them, and program it in: 'First you do this and then you do that....' If robots are to fulfil the potential we think we can see in them, they will have to be able to work out for themselves what to do.

Shakey was an experiment in decision making as much as anything else. Shakey moved about in its little world of rooms, doors and boxes that it could push about. To make things simple, it would be given tasks like 'Put purple box next to red box in room 2'. First, Shakey had to explore its world to find out where the boxes were to begin with. The computer program (called STRIPS) then had to work out the necessary steps to produce the desired result. It had available various actions that Shakey could perform. It could move itself about. It could get next to boxes. It could push boxes. It could go through doors.

It is easy for us to see that there are two ways to do this task:

Push purple box to room 2, then fetch red box from room 4

Push red box to room 2, then fetch purple box

Knowing where the red box is to begin with, it is not hard to work out that it should be pushed into room 5 and then into room 2. And so on. But even so, there is a lot of computing to do here. The basic problem is that at each stage there are a number of things the computer can do next. It starts out in room 5: what should it do? It can stay put or move to rooms 1, 2, 3 or 4. In room 4 it can push the red box either to somewhere else in the same room, or out of the door. Once the purple box is in room 5, it can be pushed into rooms 1, 2, 3, 4, or left in 5.... It soon gets too complicated to explain in words, so it is better to draw a diagram like the one shown on the right.

But even this is far from complete. Anyone who tries to draw all the things Shakey can do before it has moved all the boxes into all the rooms will have used about an acre of paper. And even this diagram cheats, because it ignores whole masses of decisions about pushing boxes. So any program that proceeds simply by running through – even if only in its 'imagination' – every step that can be taken from every other step will soon be defeated by a 'combinatorial explosion' (see p. 175). It must do better than that.

Even much simpler questions such as 'How do I get to the airport for the 9 o'clock flight to Chicago?' may involve complicated deductions from a lot of knowledge about cars, bicycles, taxis, buses, trains, commuter airlines and where it is nice to wait and where it is not.

There is something in the human brain that is very good at this kind of stuff – if there were not, the human race would have disappeared down the gullet of a sabre-tooth tiger long ago – but computers are not at all good at it.

However, a lot of the difficulties in this field can be put down to excessive ambition on the part of computer designers. If we keep firmly in mind that a computer is just a complicated electric typewriter that can do a lot of boring and dangerous jobs, then it will be seen as the great success it is.

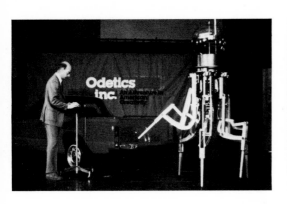

An idea whose time had gone before it had even come. Back in the sixties, an ingenious American company demonstrated this robot whose sole function was to get its six legs out of the truck, stand on the floor and then get back in again. Encore!

NETWORKS

Two methods of linking
long-distance networks on a
national or international
scale are by fibre optic
cable or by satellite. On the
right British Telecom
technicians lay an
experimental cable between
London and Birmingham.
Although the actual fibres in
the glass cable are very
thin, they need to be
wrapped and armoured to
withstand life in the world
outside the laboratory. On
the far right, engineers
maintain a satellite dish at
Goonhilly, the British end of
the transatlantic satellite
link. Because satellites are
36,000 kilometres away and
have rather low-powered
transmitters, the dishes have
to be big to collect enough
energy for reliable data
transmission. However,
advances in technology are
now making it possible to
have smaller dishes, which
can be mounted on the roof
of an office

The whole of business – and, one might even say, a large part of civilization – is about sending messages to each other. We send letters, telephone calls, newspapers, TV programs, bills, invoices, reports, books, plays, and notes left on the kitchen table. At the moment we use dozens of different technologies to carry these messages to each other, from pencil and paper to satellite radio.

As computers infiltrate our daily life, so the opportunity arises for connecting them up in networks – from ones which are intimately close to where the flow of data is densest, as for example in a single building, to long-distance ones which transmit modest data flows across half the world.

Multi-user Networks

The possibility of linking personal computers together immediately opens up the idea of an electronic office. People have been talking about this for years now, and in some places it is beginning to happen. However, before we get too embroiled in the subject, let us just look at the ways in which computers can be linked together.

Crudely speaking, there are three levels of linking. Machines can send messages to each other over serial speed lines (see pp. 22-3). Alternatively, they can share the same disk, swapping data to and fro through the files on it, at normal disk access speeds. Finally, they can share each other's processors and memory.

The usefulness of the first possibility is severely limited by the speed of the lines. The whole point of a computer is that it should do jobs quicker than its human operator can; if it cannot, then there is no point going through the agony of using it. Telephone-line speeds transmit a screenful of information in about 10 seconds. That is all right for short messages like invoices or hotel bookings, but would not be adequate if you were trying to edit a book-sized text file.

This level of interconnection is suitable for a lot of routine transactions between businesses,

where the messages are short and formal; but not rich enough for what goes on inside a business, where people may be sending each other memos, reports, letters, cash-flow projections or lists of invoices. Electronics is only some help here; it cannot change the fundamentals of what is happening.

Zipf's Law (see p. 87) comes in here again, because it says, roughly, that the volume of information two people need to exchange is inversely proportional to the distance between them. This is very convenient, because the cost of communication rises steeply with distance.

The second level – sharing disk files – means that people can have the electronic analogue of a shared filing cabinet. This is how offices actually work now: each person does his or her job by taking a document, processing it in some way and putting it back in the file so that other people can use it when they need to.

Of course, once the system is computerized it offers two great advantages over its paper predecessor. In the first place, everyone can see instantly what is happening. In a theatrical agent's office, for instance, if all the executives used terminals into a shared file system, they could all know instantly what was happening to all their clients. Without it, they would have to keep passing each other notes. Secondly, they could all get at information in the database by asking for it in a number of ways. 'Find a red-haired, one-legged French-speaking dwarf' would be no problem with a well-designed database manager.

In this sort of installation it is necessary to provide the individual user's micro with access to a shared disk where it can find all the computer files it needs. In the paper system, two people cannot work independently on the same file at the same time, because the first user has removed it from the filing cabinet. You need some electronic equivalent in the computer: this is normally achieved by locking individual Records in the database (see pp. 94-7) when the first user

Opposite Three levels of
networking: a multi-user
network in an office (below);
a local network in a factory
or on a university campus
(centre); and a long-distance
network between towns
within one country or
between countries, linked
by satellite or cable (top)

147

Today's office (left) and the electronic, paperless office of the future (right). Files are stored in the computer and memos are sent through the network that links the machines. Information comes down the telephone and is fed in through the modem (foreground). In the paperless office the tedious, low-skilled job of physically conveying paperwork has been eliminated

takes them. Latecomers get a message on their screens saying something like 'Record locked', so they know that someone else has got there first.

This problem is known in the trade under a variety of terms: 'file contestations' or 'record collisions'. It is essential that software for use in a network system can sort out collisions, otherwise the most fearful foul-ups can happen as two people alter the same record in ignorance of each other. A simple solution is to use single-user software managed by a multi-user database such as Superfile, which automatically takes care of collisions. This scheme, allowing several micros to get at the same disk files, works quite well and, now that disks with up to 30 MB of storage are quite cheap, shows real promise.

There are essentially three ways of arranging the sharing. In a 'multi-user' system, several people share the same processor. In a 'multi-processor' system, each person has his own computer, but they are intimately linked to a central master which controls the disk. In a 'ring', individual computers are connected by a high-capacity data link so they can swap data to and fro.

In the first scheme, each user has a chunk of memory and the processor attends to each in turn. This is how main-frames do multi-user processing – they had to because the processors used to be so expensive, you could not possibly give each user one of them. Moreover, they were powerful enough to get round a large number of users quickly enough to give each one satisfactory service. Unfortunately, some of the designers of 8-bit multi-user micro systems have unhesitatingly copied the main-frame solution without realizing that there is little point in making several people share a processor chip that costs only $5.

The main 8-bit multi-user operating system is a derivative of CP/M called MP/M. It uses bank-

switched memory to give each user some 48 K of space to run his programs. That in itself is a severe limitation. The processor then has to switch from bank to bank, doing whatever processing needs doing for each user. While an 8-bit processor like the Z80 is powerful for most office workers' jobs, it is not up to servicing half a dozen of them. Performance is 'degraded', as the technical term has it, if more than a couple of people are using the system.

The more powerful 16-bit machines, particularly those using the 68000 processor and its upwards derivatives, can cope much better. They are powerful enough to work in the same way that minis and main-frames do, often using the same operating system, Unix. Several users can be served by the same processor and each user may possibly run several different programs at once. This is called 'multi-tasking' and is available on single-user 16-bit machines under the 'Concurrent CP/M' operating system.

However, on 8-bit machines, which are still much cheaper, a much more sensible scheme is to give each person a single micro with a full 64 K of memory, a screen and a keyboard, and let everyone share the same disks. This is usually called a 'multi-processor' system. In practice users get at the disks through a central master micro that does nothing else but service the users and the disks – it is often called a 'file server'. The master, which may be a 16-bit machine, runs some suitable multi-processor operating system. One of the best known is CP/Net – each user thinks he has CP/M. There are also Turbodos, McNos, Hi-Net and many others. There are again two ways of doing this trick. One way is to put the several users' computers in the same box with the disk and the master, and giving each one a terminal. The other is to give each one a complete computer, with high-speed links to the master and the disk.

The advantage of the first is that you can have slow lines to the users' terminals since you only need to transmit a screenful of data every so often. The lines can be cheap and relatively long – up to a few hundred metres. The disadvantage is that you have to buy each user a separate terminal to display and accept the data. This could have been part of the user's processor, at much less cost.

The other method is to put each user's processor in his terminal – to give him a complete micro, which saves money – and to provide high-speed links back from each micro to the master. The individual micros will normally have been built by the same manufacturer to ensure compatability, though there are networks available which purport to link dissimilar micros together.

The third scheme, the ring, uses special interface hardware to connect each computer to the ring, and then a high-speed link between the interfaces – usually co-axial cable. (The name 'ring' can be misleading because the connecting cable need not join back onto itself.) So far rings have been rather slow to gain acceptance in the micro world. They do, however, make it possible in principle to link computers made by different manufacturers to the same master, and this in turn allows organizations that have acquired computers piecemeal from different sources to join them all together to make an electronic office.

The difficulty with rings so far seems (to me, at any rate) that they try to be too clever. Various systems offered on the market purport to allow the user of one micro to take over the screen of the other; to use spare memory on another machine to process his programs and so on. This sort of thing is useful and practical when linking main-frames and minis, particularly when there is a large and well-trained staff of professionals to maintain the whole delicate structure. It provides endless hours of fun for academics in computer science laboratories, but is all much too complicated for ordinary users.

The third way of interlinking micros is to make them separate parts of the same big computer. This means that all the processors share the work, that all the memory is accessible to all the processors. The idea is that if, for instance, your processor is idle because you are running a word-processing package to write a letter and at this precise moment you are looking at the ceiling wondering whether to call your correspondent a 'flaming liar', or the 'victim of a terminological inexactitude', and your neighbour's processor is overworked because it's sorting a big file, your processor should chip in and help.

We shall look (on pp. 174-5) at how the next generation of computers might use many processors in parallel, but the proper container for such a thing is a chip, not an office full of ordinary, non-crazy people.

There are several ways of making computers serve several people at once. A single machine (top left) can service the disks and all the users' terminals, apparently simultaneously. In fact, it deals with each in turn, but so fast that the delays should be unnoticeable. This is called 'multi-tasking', and is how main-frames, minis and the more powerful 16-bit machines work.

Another scheme (top right), more often found in 8-bit systems, gives each user access through a terminal to his own computer. An extra machine handles the disks, giving each user access to them when needed. This is called a 'multi-processor system'.

Alternatively, the individual processors may be in the users' terminals, connected to the central 'file-server' by a high-speed cable (below left). A fourth variant (below right) is to link separate computers – which may be from different manufacturers – through small add-on machines and a 'ring' of special fibre optic cable. This is often called a 'local area network' or LAN. Finally, a single computer can run several programs at once for a single user (below). This is called 'concurrent processing'

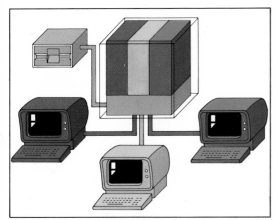

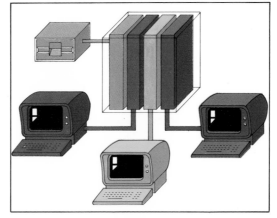

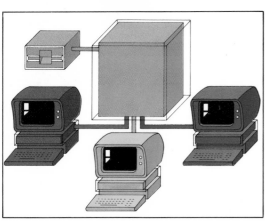

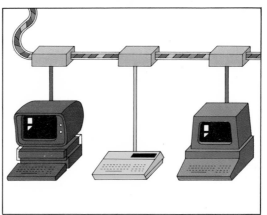

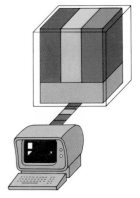

THE ELECTRONIC OFFICE

We have seen on the last two pages how micros can be linked together to allow people to share the same files. An obvious arena for such technology is a small business. There are an awful lot of them in the Western world, and they do mostly standard things that are reasonably amenable to automation. Let us look at such an outfit – a couture business which designs, makes and markets high-fashion hats for smart ladies. It has eight departments, and for simplicity, we shall give each one a single employee:

Managing Director
Assistant/Secretary
Salesman
Designer
Warehouse/Dispatch Person
Manufacturer
Book-keeper
Accountant

All eight have micros linked to a master with a hard disk. They all access a database manager on the central hard disk which maintains the company's records. Some of the micros have their own printer or other peripheral, others use the central printer on the master. To see what happens, let us trace the day's work through the network.

The whole object of the exercise is to make money, and the front end in that laudable endeavour is the Salesman **1**. He telephones people – usually the owners or buyers of dress shops – and persuades them to buy the firm's wonderful hats. He either rings up new people, whose telephone numbers he has found somewhere, or old customers and persuades them to buy. He has a telephone modem so he can take orders and messages directly from his clients' computers.

Imagine him ringing up new people. He gets them on the phone and persuades them to take some interest in the firm's products. If he is given an order, he has to get it into the system. He will enter the customer's name, address, the sort of shop and so on in a standard form that appears on his screen. The information he enters is stored on the hard disk and is available to everyone else.

Suppose now that the telephone rings. It is

someone he already knows, who wants to place a further order. He keys her name into the form on his screen, and types her order into the form. This creates a new Record on the disk, which has the customer's name, the customer's unique identification number to link her to a separate Record with her address, and a description of her order. In this case it is half a dozen each of the firm's tremendously successful 'Punk Bubbles' and 'Tarzan's Dream' numbers – how much they cost, what discount the customer gets, where she wants them sent and any other relevant details.

The Dispatch Person **2** is now the one to watch. She has a program that scans the database looking for Records such as the Salesman has just created,

which have an order but no indication that they have been processed. When the program finds such a Record, it checks against the stock list to see whether the firm has actually got what is wanted on the shelf.

In fact, they are three Tarzan's Dreams short, so the program creates a new Record to say how many hats need to be made to keep stock levels up. The Dispatcher then enters how many she has got on to her screen. The program checks to see whether there is a discrepancy between the stock list and what she

actually has on the shelf. It then does several things. It creates a Record that shows Mrs Johnson has been sent 6 Punk Bubbles and 3 Tarzan's Dreams. It creates a Record that says Mrs Johnson would like 3 more Tarzan's Dreams when they are in stock. It prints out a dispatch note on the printer beside her with what is being sent and an address label with Mrs

Johnson's address on it. The Packer **3** can then make up the parcel. The program will add the 3 Tarzan's Dreams that are needed to a list for the factory to make.

When the manufacturer has made the wanted hats, they are added to the stock list and physically put on the shelf. This program also makes a note of the materials that have been used to make up the new stock. This is necessary for the Accountant, and for other programs that order more materials.

The database now has a Record that Mrs Johnson has been sent some of the things she ordered. The Book-keeper **4** is now the star of the show. Her program scans the database for order Records and makes a note that today Mrs Johnson became a debtor for the cost of the goods she had. The Book-keeper's program creates an invoice to be sent to Mrs Johnson, and makes a note that the goods have been dispatched.

At the same time, a payment arrives from Petit Pierre of Dallas for some fripperies they had six months ago. The Book-keeper enters this into her machine. The system finds the Record in the database that holds the debt and eliminates it. There is now no need to keep any computer Record of that particular transaction, so it will be erased, the total merely appearing in the sales ledger.

From time to time the Accountant **5** needs to see what has been happening – what has been bought, what is owed, what has been paid. His programs will tear around the database finding out these things and presenting them in a way that accountants like – and usually no one else can understand.

The Managing Director **6** needs to see some of all this too. He wants to know if the Salesman is keeping up a satisfactory turnover of calls. Does the company often lack stock – as in Mrs Johnson's case – to fill an order? If so, why? Should he go to a brisker manufacturer? He needs to know what is being ordered – is there enough business in those exotic fur caps made by Nepalese hill women to justify the Designer's very expensive trips to that part of the world? How long are customers taking to pay? Is the business becoming a moneylender rather than a hatter? How many bad debts does he have? How did sales improve after last month's advertising campaign? When his rival, Miss Chou Chou, introduced her new range at the beginning of the year, did it make any great impression on sales? What sort of people buy what? Should he be trying to sell into a different market altogether?

To make these decisions

he needs a lot of information which is often best presented in the form of graphs, pie charts, histograms. He has at his disposal a range of software which will pull information out of the database in just these forms. He also has financial planning packages that will do discounted cash flows and produce debtor profiles.

His Assistant **7** is more of an office manager. She produces most of the documents that the company sends out, such as brochures and price lists, and to do this she uses a special word-processing terminal and a high-quality printer. Like many people coming into business in the mid-eighties, she has a minor qualification in computing, and is capable of writing small programs in Pascal or BASIC for use in the system. Her secretarial function has almost disappeared since all those who need to write letters are expected to do it themselves on their own terminals, using a word-processing package.

The Designer **8** uses a standalone graphics machine with a digitizing pad, which is linked to the main computer. He uses it to try out new shapes in 3D, to specify and quantify the materials needed for the firm's creations.

The computer **9** is linked to everyone's terminal. It is a 16-bit machine running a multi-user, multi-tasking operating system, and has a couple of 40-MB hard disks. It also has a high-speed dot-matrix printer for internal documents. Because it does so much of the donkey work, it leaves the office juniors **10** plenty of time to tell each other the old, old story.

Finally, of course, there is the most important function of backup. Once a day, or once a week, depending on how paranoid everyone is, the whole contents of both hard disks must be copied onto tape and the tape taken away to be stored in a safe place, so that if the office burns down, or gets wrecked by an angry customer, the essential programs and files are still available. It is much easier to replace the hardware than the data the software has created.

LONG-DISTANCE NETWORKS

A classic star telephone network. Subscribers' telephones are connected to a local exchange. These are connected in turn to trunk exchanges, which are linked to international exchanges. Although this design of network is not really suited to computers, it has to be used simply because there is such a vast capital investment in equipment

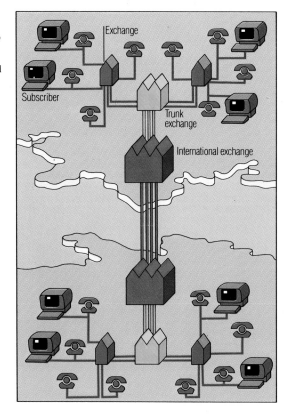

As computers spread through the world, we shall see them taking over many of the functions of telephone, telex and particularly the postal services. They will be used for exchanging invoices, bills, delivery notes, memoranda, reports and documents of all sorts.

The postal service does, slowly and by hand, more or less what you would want done electronically and fast. You can concoct any sort of message you want – it can be a bill or a love letter or a pair of socks – wrap it up pretty well as you like and address it as seems best. History tells us that letters to 'Fred, One Eye Road, Yorkshire' got delivered to the right man in Nelson Road, Burnley. It would be nice if you could treat computer messages in the same informal way. You ought to be able to find people from part addresses. You ought to be able to find them as they move about the country – in a proper data network people could have mobile addresses. You ought to be able to address people not just by their locations but by their businesses, politics and interests, so that you could send a message to everyone with a Timex-Sinclair computer, to all farmers in west Somerset, or to all members of the Democratic Party. A person's data address would tell you a lot about him or her.

As Ghandi said about Western civilization: 'It would be very nice', and it has not happened yet.

The first model people look at for any sort of electronic network must be the telephone system, simply because it has been around so long and is so successful. In the telephone system, up to 9999 subscribers are connected in a 'star' system to a telephone exchange (there cannot be more because an individual telephone number is limited to four digits). Exchanges themselves are generally connected in stars to trunk exchanges; and trunk exchanges in different contries are connected in stars to international exchanges.

It is easy to see how to find a particular subscriber – you find the right country, the right area or trunk exchange, the right local exchange and the right pair of wires leading to the person you want. It only takes a dozen or so digits to specify any one of the several thousand million people in the world connected to the international trunk dialling system. The system has its advantages: it concentrates all the 'intelligence' the system needs in the exchanges where the PTT can maintain and protect them (telephone exchanges are natural targets for terrorists and revolutionaries). Conversely, the telephone sets that are supplied to subscribers can be simple and therefore cheap. In the days when intelligence had to be mechanical, this was a good idea. The star system also corresponds to traffic flow. Although you can telephone anywhere in the world from any telephone, people tend to make far more calls to other people nearby. The density of traffic in a telephone system tends to follow Zipf's Law (see p. 87).

However, the star system also has disadvantages. It uses a terrific amount of wire since each subscriber must, at least, be connected back to the exchange. It is difficult to add a new subscriber since you have to install new machinery in the exchange and a new pair of wires out to the house. Although we have been talking about telephone calls using voice signals, we can use just the same terminology to talk about computer data since data can be turned into sound signals and sound can be turned into data (see pp. 120-23).

For many years now, computers have been linked one to one through long-distance channels. More recently they have been connected in networks around single processors. Then the processors were themselves networked together. One of the best known of these was the American ARPA (Advanced Projects Research Agency) net. Getting into the system required connection to the proper processor, knowledge of the proper protocols and was generally complicated. It was also very expensive and was usually only available to people working for universities and the military.

Data on these networks is usually gathered into 'packets' of standard length which are sent off down the line one after the other like railway wagons. The whole process is very cumbersome. The post offices of the industrialized countries mostly have plans to offer data highways through their own computers. However, access to these systems is difficult and expensive and nowhere near as flexible as, say, the mail service. At the

grassroots level people started – particularly in America – improvising networks using the telephone system.

As we saw above, data transmission by telephone is slow and unreliable. Moreover, it is very rigid. Something can be done about this by writing software that will handle the business of dialling, listening for the different tones, checking that one has got through to the right computer (or person). For instance, a man installing an automatic system to control fifty or so remote, unmanned television stations in the Midwest of America will get his microcomputer to ring each of them up during the night, and load what tele-

vision channels the station should broadcast the next day at what times.

In Britain British Telecom's Prestel offered a network of data – you could put up a screen's worth – which is accessible to anyone connected to the system who could be bothered trudging through it, but the screens are so crude and so hard to find that it has failed to gain any general acceptance. British Telecom then offered a 'gateway' service which would link any computer by telephone with any other – through their own. But that too was very expensive and hard to work. So far the possibilities of the computer in mass communications have not begun to be reached.

Above Two examples of electronic information distribution. The first shows a British Telecom Prestel restaurant guide; the second a BBC Ceefax program listing in BASIC for microcomputer enthusiasts.

Right A modem takes input from the computer in the form of bits, turns the '0's and '1's into tones of different frequency, and sends them down the telephone line. A simple, amateur modem like this encloses the transmitter and receiver of the telephone handset in two little rubber cups. More professional modems dispense with the speakers and are connected directly to the telephone line

Below Some manufacturers are experimenting with combined telephones and VDUs to access Prestel and other videotext systems

Below right Here a customer examines his bank account in the experimental Homelink system. Terminals in shops could debit customers' bank accounts directly

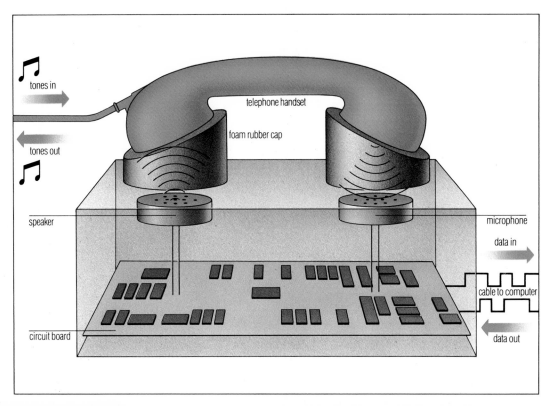

A decade or more ago Britain's Post Office experimented with 'tele-conferencing'. Studios were set up in big cities: groups of businessmen who wanted to meet would go to the nearest studio to be connected by television and document copiers. It foreshadowed the electronic 'global village' (see pp. 178-9), but was limited and ahead of its time. However, these facilities and more will soon be provided by computer links

Technically speaking, we should want any one of millions of computers, anywhere in the world, to be able to transmit data to any other. That is rather a tall order, so let us first consider how you might allow a smaller number of machines to communicate with each other. There are essentially two ways. The first is switching, in which the star network of the telephone system is reproduced, so that each terminal is connected to an exchange, and each exchange is connected to a higher-level exchange, and so on. The second way is by bussing (see pp. 22-3). All users are connected to a stream of data and allowed to fish out whatever is addressed to them.

In the long run the first system is probably no good. It is too cumbersome and limited, and the exchanges are too complicated. Furthermore, why build exchanges to switch data when the intelligence to do it is already in the individual microcomputers? The second method makes much simpler demands on the technical infrastructure. You just need to present all the signals in the system to each terminal. The signals can get there in several different ways. In one system a central master controls the network, which might best consist of a single strand of glass fibre.

The network of fibres simply has to connect everyone together. It is rather as if they all were using radios: anything anyone transmits can be picked up by all the others. There is no need, at least in the simple system, for switching centres like telephone exchanges. All that is done by the individual terminals. If we take a network covering the British Isles and offshore islands as an example, no one would be more than 1000 miles from anyone else by fibre. This means that to get a signal to the farthest part of the network and back would take only half a millisecond.

If no one has anything to say, there are no transmissions. Suppose that terminal A wants to send a message to terminal B. Each one has a unique identifying number – rather like a telephone number. A first has to get the attention of the master. It transmits its number followed by

B's number. The master does a check sum on the numbers (see pp. 12-13) to make sure that the numbers are valid – they have not got scrambled – and retransmits the call. A listens to see that its call has been properly retransmitted. Everyone listens to the master all the time. Since this call is for B, all the others keep quiet. If the terminal B is alive and well, it transmits its number as an acknowledgement. The master checks to see that there is no scrambling – which could be caused by a fault in B's equipment – and tells A to go ahead. A then transmits his message to B. When A has finished, it sends a 'clear' signal, which the master retransmits to the whole network to tell them that they can now send their 'I've a message for so-and-so' signals if they want.

The perceptive reader will wonder what happens if A and, say, C both send 'I want to send a message' signals at the same time. There is a collision. The master gets the two signals superimposed on each other. It tries to do its check sum on the mess, fails, and says nothing. Neither A nor C hears its signal retransmitted, so they both try again. To prevent a further collision, they each wait a random amount of time – calculated statistically from the traffic density – and retransmit. Since the delay is random, they probably will not both retransmit at once. Whichever gets in first causes the other to shut up until it has finished.

This system was first developed for the Aloha ('hello' in Polynesian) network of computers in Hawaii in the mid-seventies. Aloha used cable rather than glass fibre, but the principle is just the same. You might think that the system would spend its whole time sorting out collisions. However, it turns out that if the data-handling capacity is high enough this is not a problem since the 'I've got a message' signals are so short the chance of one colliding with another is small. The network can handle about 80 per cent of its theoretical capacity – which would, of course, mean that everyone transmitted exactly in step, one after the other without breaks.

The alternative would be to poll (see pp. 28-9) every station in turn to see whether it had a message. This wastes time on the inactive stations and starves the active ones. Moreover, the master has to know who is on the network and who is not. In the Aloha scheme people can leave and join as they wish.

This sort of system has an enormous data capacity. Fibre optics now can carry some 300 Mb/s. At a realistic load factor of 80 per cent, that gives 240 Mb/s or 30 MB/s. One way of thinking about this capacity is to look at the slowest part of the information interface: the human eye for reading, the human finger for typing. Sooner or later everything on the network has to pass through both of these channels. Few people can read and absorb more than, say, 5000 words a day. Few professional writers produce more than

 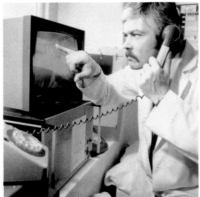 

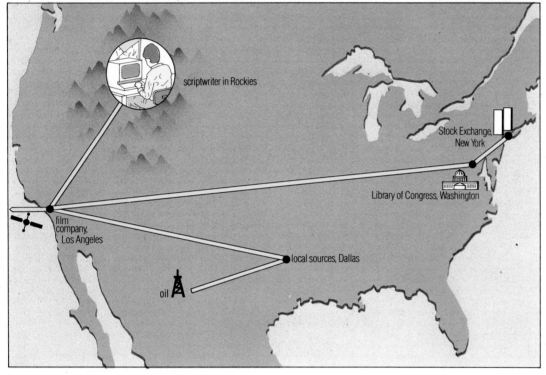

scriptwriter in Rockies

Stock Exchange, New York

Library of Congress, Washington

film company, Los Angeles

local sources, Dallas

oil

1000 words of finished text a day, but we also have to consider commercial documents and 'junk mail'. On average, 5000 words of text a day will be a generous allowance for each user of the network. So we have a working figure of 5000 words or 30,000 characters (a text word averages 6 characters) per user per working day. That averages $1/3$ B/s, so a single glass fibre trailing round the country would serve the data needs of some 90 million people.

In practice, people in London seldom want to send messages to people in Orkney (see Zipf's Law, p. 87), so it would probably be better to have networks confined to geographical areas, with switching centres to route messages between them. Over longer distances, data networks will probably use either glass fibre cable under the oceans, satellite or microwave radio. These high-capacity channels will be rather expensive to provide, so they will have to operate on less informal lines. Data will have to be col-

lected, compacted and forwarded in packets as it is now in big computer systems.

However, the beauty of the Aloha system is that addresses do not have to be geographical. When we ring a telephone number we actually call a house or an office – an inanimate thing which cannot talk to us. We hope that the human being we want to talk to will actually be there, but most of the time he or she is not.

What we want is to be able to ring a particular person without necessarily knowing where he or she is. In the star system this is very difficult to arrange; everyone would have to leave forwarding addresses with their home exchanges as they move about. Life being what it is, you might say you were going to be at Sally's for the afternoon and find that in fact you had to go to Johnny's, so you would have to leave a reforwarding number on Sally's number. The whole thing would get out of hand, particularly if you tried to move from one exchange in a star system to another.

Left A geostationary data relay satellite. The wings are covered in solar cells for power; the dishes focus radio signals on single countries or continents on earth. The satellite hovers over a fixed spot on the equator

Top left Glass rod for drawing into fibre optic for information transmission is pulled from a furnace under surgically clean conditions

Top centre The fibre optic – a hair-thin strand drawn from glass rod. The glass has to be spectacularly pure, a thousand times purer than ordinary glass

Top right Information is sent down the fibre optic as pulses of laser light

Right For multimode transmission over short distances, larger core fibre is used, made up of two types of glass: the core, along which the light travels, and the cladding, which steers the light rays down the central core by refraction. This picture of the rods before drawing, taken at Bell Laboratories, clearly shows the different types of glass

In the Aloha system, where all the intelligence is in the terminals, addressing becomes very easy. A terminal might have a fixed number corresponding to its address, but it might also have numbers corresponding to the people near it. So, when you arrived at Sally's, you would program her terminal to accept your calls. When you moved on to Johnny's you would do the same thing. Miss Wonderful's telephone call or computer text message would wing its way infallibly to you. Your computerized bills would find your debtors wherever they were. The addressing system could be even more generalized, so that you could belong to special interest groups – either recreational or professional. You might want to get all messages for members of your amateur dramatic society. You might well subscribe to magazines, newspapers, journals or news sheets that are distributed in digital form through your computer. They too would follow you about if you wanted – you would just have to tell the machine where you were to ask for them off the network. The possibilities are staggering.

Optical fibre

During the 1980s we shall see a rapid transition from copper cable and radio links, either direct or via satellites, to optical fibre. Thousands of miles of fibre optic are being laid in America and Europe, and the first fibre underwater cable is due for completion in 1988, as is a link from Japan to Hawaii. An optical fibre consists of a minute thread of very pure glass through which a light signal can be flashed. The light is generated by a laser or a laser diode and is pulsed digitally to encode the information, which may be computer data, voice or television.

The glass is so pure that the signal can go up to 35 kilometres (or 20 miles) before it has to be reamplified (current copper cable needs an amplifier every kilometre or less). The data capacity of a fibre is limited by the semiconductors used to generate and detect the light pulses, to some 300 Mb/s. As semiconductor technology improves, so the data capacity of existing links can easily be increased. And as glass replaces copper, so the world's store of the red metal will be mined again from beneath the city streets.

HUGE DATABASES

It seems very likely that the spread of computers into offices and homes, and the installation of high-speed data links by the telecommunications authorities of the world, will have a dramatic effect on the storage and retrieval of information. At the moment, if you want to find out some fact you do not know, you have to search for it in a library. You might go to your neighbourhood library and look first in the *Encyclopaedia Britannica*. If that does not work you would look in other encyclopedias there, and then start to search the section shelves. You might want some piece of information that changes fast, such as a railway timetable, and then you would consult a book that is republished much more frequently than an encyclopedia. You might want to know how to advertise animal feed in the Philippines, or look up the suppliers of cast-iron pipe in Bolivia – you would have to consult a trade directory.

These are all items of information that have been gathered together by someone or other and published – all you have to do is find the right publication. But there are other things you might need to know very badly which may well not have been collected and published, for example, the average share price of Hong Kong companies trading with mainland China, or the average profitability (based on tax returns) of computer companies in West Germany.

These technical possibilities will inevitably revolutionize the world's stocks of information. There will be – and is already – a trend towards electronic publishing of 'hot' information, such as share prices, sports results, entertainments listings, air, rail and road timetables.

This process will continue. Already people are beginning to see that information which has traditionally been published on paper, such as economic indicators and forecasts, could more easily be issued as data for personal computers to be run under a database manager. For example a news sheet about the economies of Africa would be much more useful to its subscribers as a database running on their desk-top micros so that they could ask it questions like 'Who is the Finance Minister of Kenya?' or 'What is the value of The Gambia's fish exports?' New editions of the news sheet would be sent out as floppy disks or data by telephone to update each user's database.

Before this can happen it will be necessary to convert the world's stock of printed information to digital form. This is quite an undertaking.

In the second stage we can expect that this process will itself be automated, and that intelligent software tools will become available to do the work of research assistants. When all the major information sources of the world are on line, it will be possible to say to your software assistant, running on your personal computer (which by then will be as powerful as today's main-frames), 'Go and find out everything you can

about the painter Turner'; or 'Prepare a report on the world's jute market'. The clever little thing will presumably consult a wide array of secondary databases that will catalogue the major data sources. It will then ring them up and send them messages with its requests. 'Tell me this?' 'Where can I find that?' Having got the answers, it will collate and sort them into a usable form. It may well not print out a complete report, but again present the results as a mini database which the human inquirer can consult.

This software will be a long way beyond current database managers. It will have to have a good deal of intelligence – to be able to take an overview of a subject and work out the best strategies for finding out more detail. It will have to be able to run about in the information world like a dog chasing sticks and bringing them back to its master.

There will also be a huge requirement for automatic reading equipment, because the world's stock of paper information will have to be transcribed into electronic form. The British Library holds about 13 million books, and the average is probably is 60,000 words or 360,000 characters long. There might be another twenty such centres in the world, making about 93 million million characters to be transcribed from books. To those you must add the daily papers, of which there are 5000 published in the world, each about 100,000 words or 600,000 characters long. Treble this for the daily output of scientific and technical magazines, and allow that there is a hundred-year backlog to be transcribed. That gives another 54 million million bytes to be turned into ASCII format before the world's stocks of knowledge are fully automated. This job will have to be done by machines – and as yet these machines do not exist in the numbers, or with the power, that will be needed. And we shall need software that can translate from one language into another.

There is a flaw in this wonderful prospect of the knowledge of the ages being available at the push of a button. The problem is that knowledge is power, and free access to it is not in everyone's interest. An example is the state archive of Spain, which include the records of sunken treasure galleons. While no one knew about them researchers were allowed free access. Few people knew how to work the archive or how to read the ancient, handwritten documents in it. Now that the secret is out, the archive is a treasure hunter's Mecca. Many other lodes of valuable information lie undisturbed because they are too hard to work and no one knows they are there. When automated researchers can go burrowing wherever they like there may well be great pressure to restrict access by encrypting the database and giving the keys only to approved people. This would be a great pity and a sad reversal of a tradition of academic freedom that is many hundreds of years old.

Coding

There is already a need for encryption and coding, of course. The trouble with electronic data is that it can be copied in the twinkle of a transistor. Paper has its virtues: the uniqueness and durability of documents is one of them. There is no electronic equivalent of a banknote that can be passed from computer to computer without being copied. Instead you have to have some scheme for making sure that messages can only pass between two people and that outsiders cannot interfere. In this way one bank can tell another to pay a sum of money to one of its clients. Both ends keep a log of the messages and a check can be made that the right thing has happened.

Given the power of computers there is no problem about scrambling text and numbers up so thoroughly that it would take many years' work on the largest machines to unscramble them by random procedures. However, there is a more interesting alternative, which has come out of the world of mathematics in the last ten years. This is a type of encryption called 'trap-door coding', which relies on mathematical procedures that are easy to do one way but very hard in reverse. An example is finding the prime factors of a large number (200-300 digits). This can take an enormously long time to do, but if you know the factors, it is child's play to multiply them together to get the number. This principle can be used to construct a coding system in which, paradoxically, the code can be published, but only the person who devised it can read messages encrypted in it. If two such codes are interlocked, the parties in correspondence – a bank and its clients, for instance – can be sure that the messages they read can only have come from each other.

A REVOLUTION IN THINKING

One of the reasons why computing is difficult is that it incorporates some radical shifts in intellectual perspective from the 'commonsense' view of the world that we have inherited from the brash, self-confident scientists of the last century. These shifts are now built into the traditions of computing. People in the industry have absorbed them unconsciously; people outside are repelled without knowing what it is that puzzles them. The mental struggle required to become computerate mimics the convulsions that revolutionized mathematics in the first half of this century.

The proximate cause of the upheaval was three questions put to the world of mathematics by David Hilbert in 1900: is mathematics *complete* in the sense that every statement in it can be either proved or disproved? Is mathematics *consistent* in the sense that no 'wrong' statement can ever be arrived at by a series of valid steps? Is mathematics *decidable* – is there a definite method which can, in principle at least, be applied to any statement to see whether it is true?

Kurt Gödel, a young Hungarian mathematician, answered the first two in 1929. In the process of answering them, he invented what seemed to many people at the time to be a mad way of coding mathematical rules and formulae as numbers. He gave every mathematical statement a code number and then showed that whatever system of rules was adopted for the mathematics, there would always be extra code numbers – that is, statements – that could not be derived from those that already existed. In other words, there would always be statements in any logical system (not just our own everyday mathematics) that could be neither proved nor disproved from what had gone before. He also showed that no mathematics could be proved consistent without drawing in extra rules from outside.

This was pretty bad for mathematics, but good for the computing that was to come, because in the process Gödel drove a pickaxe through the wall that had seemed to separate mathematical rules and formulae from the numbers they generated. He simply said, 'Every rule is also a number.' At the time this seemed weird to a fault; now we take it for granted. When you write the line in MBASIC:

100 IF A > 34 THEN C=COS(K) ELSE C=SIN(K)

the computer just sees the Hex number (see pp. 12-13):

FF D 60 64 0 8B 20 41 EF F 22 20 CF 20 43 FO FF 8C 28 4B 29 20 3A A2 20 43 FO FF 89 28 4B 20 0 0 0

Every formula you can write corresponds to a different Hex number, and if you want to do sums on those numbers, or arrange them in order of size, there is nothing to stop you.

This cavalier attitude to symbols was one of the essential changes in thought that had to happen before computing could begin.

The second necessary precondition was to get rid of the idea of the 'calculating machine'. Almost as soon as man learned to count (and that was as big an intellectual achievement as anything that has come after), he seems to have tried to automate the processes of arithmetic. As engineers grew more skilful, calculating machines became more complicated. But, like scientists, they got better and better at less and less. Any change in the way a machine worked necessitated elaborate rebuilding.

This step too arose out of Hilbert's challenge. Alan Turing, a shy, gauche young mathematician at King's College, Cambridge, in the mid-1930s, tackled the third problem. Gödel had cracked the wall, Turing was to push it over. He argued that if there were a method for proving any theo-

rem, one would just have to set a human mathematician (a 'calculator', as he would then be called) to apply the rules. To see what would happen next, Turing eliminated the human mathematician and substituted an imaginary machine to do the job. It might have been more stupid than any human, but in the end, it would have come to the same result.

The machine would take a mathematical theorem – a string of symbols – and work away at it in a perfectly mechanical way to find out whether it was provable or not. In other words, it was to do computing, though that was not how it was seen at the time.

Without, perhaps, knowing what a far-reaching innovation he was making, Turing threw out from his design the rat's nest of cogs, levers and shafts that earlier designers of calculating machines had been forced to use. His notional device was simple to the point of imbecility.' All the cunning was to go in what we would now call the software.

The Turing machine consists of an infinitely long paper tape divided into squares. The machine has a mechanical head which can move square by square indefinitely in either direction. It can read, erase and write symbols into the

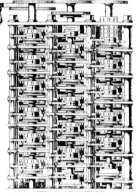

Above Charles Babbage (1792–1871) tried to build the first computer out of mechanical components

Right Mechanical calculating devices reached the limit of complexity in differential analysers. Here, a machine made by Vannevar Bush at MIT in 1935

Below Turing's endless – and completely imaginary – tape machine that led to the computer as we know it today

squares under it. According to the symbol it reads, it can change its 'state' – we would now say, it would set or reset one of a bunch of internal flag registers. In accordance with its state, it reacts differently to the next symbol it reads. This ability of a program to test some data and branch on the result was an essential idea which Turing got, from Babbage's ill-fated Analytical Engine.

Once there is a 'program' to determine the provability of any mathematical theorem, the machine will trundle to and fro, working away at the problem. If the theorem can be proved, the machine will stop; if it cannot it will not.

Turing went on to use his conceptual machine – in conjunction with an earlier result of Cantor's – to prove that there could be no definitive method for solving all mathematical questions.

In a way this was good for mathematics, because it made mathematicians feel that there was still a job for them. But its real importance – of course, quite unappreciated at the time – was to set the shape of the computers we use today. The paper tape is the one-dimensional string of memory that can contain both data and program. The head that crawls along it is the processor. The only difference – and this is not fundamental – is that the processor can get to any memory location directly, rather than having to crawl step by step along a tape. All the cleverness of the machine goes into the instructions on the tape.

The logicians of the nineteenth century had shown that all mathematical processes could be built up from simple logical steps. Turing's second major contribution – which we now take completely for granted – was to show that a machine which could do simple logic could do all mathematics and therefore could imitate any other machine at all. With such simple and apparently unpromising materials, he had built – in his mind – a universal machine.

Alan Turing (1912–54), the
British mathematician whose
conceptual tape machine of
1936 was the theoretical
forerunner of today's
computers. During the
Second World War, he
worked at the heart of the
Allied code-breaking effort,
Ultra. He died of poisoning in
1954. Some people think he
was murdered by the
Security Service as a
homosexual security risk

The mental stage was now set for computing. It had on it two very simple props. The first was a big square slab that had written on it the uncompromising slogan: *Everything in the universe can be reduced to a meaningless string of symbols* . The second prop was another slab which said: *Every process in the universe can be reduced to a meaningless string of symbols*. Everyone who has got used to computers has, consciously or unconsciously, absorbed these two propositions. They make it rather hard for the rest of the world to sympathize.

Turing worked with von Neumann at Princeton and there met Claude Shannon, whose slim book, *The Mathematical Theory of Communication*, is one of the classics of the twentieth century. Shannon invented the irreducible unit of information: the bit, the answer to a Yes or No question. That was another essential step which made it possible to do computing on electronic machines.

A German engineer called Konrad Zuse built the first binary calculating machine in 1937. Turing independently used the same idea to build a multiplying machine using electromechanical relays in the same year. Then the war intervened. Zuse and his calculators got drawn into the V rocket projects; Turing became one of the mathematicians at the heart of the intensely secret Anglo-American code-breaking effort of the early years of the Second World War.

Code-breaking in 1939 was done with pencil and paper in a quiet room. The volume of material which had to be handled at the British centre at Bletchley Park made automation essential. Turing and his colleagues soon built electromechanical machines to test possible decryptions of German signals and, by the middle of the war, had a device which did indeed do the magical test and branch instruction, the first sign of an authentic computer.

In America similar hybrid machines were built for code-breaking and the calculation of the paths of artillery shells (see pp. 88-9).

Turing then drifted away from code-breaking and built a completely electronic voice scrambler, which may well have been the first useful machine using binary methods.

Immediately after the war America had ENIAC, a machine which used 18,000 electronic valves to store 20 numbers. The race was on to develop this technology, but the competitors ran suprisingly slowly. The war had left much of civilization in rubble; the 'winners' had more urgent problems on their plates than realizing the dreams of eccentric mathematicians. Britain, very slowly, built a straggly, jumbled machine at Manchester, whose great breakthrough was the storage of current data on the screens of cathode-ray tubes (see pp. 30-31). The electron gun would 'write' a spot of charge at a particular position on the screen to store a bit. The charge would take some time to leak away and could be refreshed before it had completely gone. America struggled with the same problems but with less immediate success. Well-informed people on both sides of the Atlantic thought there

might be work for perhaps five or even six of these machines in the whole world.

The history of computing since then has been much less clear cut. There have been few dramatic flashes of inspiration: progress has come through relentless improvement in the detail of engineering, leading to cheaper machines and more of them. Increasingly it is the user who designs the machines he uses. To see why this is, we have to look back again, but not so far.

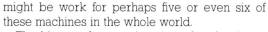

Current Trends

The present, even in these modern times, only makes sense when we look at it in the light of the past. Computing is no different: it is an immensely interesting, rewarding activity which has drawn in much of the best intellectual talent of the last forty years. Like any other scene of rapid growth, it has matured in a haphazard way. People have tried to plan it, but the usual experience is that

by the time a plan has been agreed and published, reality has moved off somewhere else. Out of this vigorous growth, though, have emerged many basic concepts, devices, interconnections, languages. Anyone who wants to swim with confidence in the sea of computing needs to have some idea about these things.

Had the transistor not been invented, it is likely that computers would still be awe-inspiring curiosities. However, it was, and because a transistor is very much smaller, cooler and more reliable than a radio valve, computers began to shrink in size and price and grow in power, so that we can now put substantial computing power on anyone's desk for the cost of a mechanical typewriter.

At the same time as transistors became smaller and cheaper so too did the storage devices that computers use as filing cabinets. While this book was being written, the first 5$\frac{1}{4}$-inch Winchester hard disk drives were appearing on the market: giving – affordably and on a desk top – storage for 2 or 3 million words of text in each machine. Laser disks currently under development look like giving each user several thousand million words of storage at the same sort of price in a few years.

This process of miniaturization and cheapening has gone on for twenty years in the manufacture of chips. Since computers are no more than great heaps of transistors bundled together in chips which are properly (one hopes) connected together on circuit boards, it means that computers have become smaller and cheaper – or

Top left America's first valve computer, the ENIAC, 1946

Left Professor F. C. Williams and Tom Kilburn at the control panel of the British Mark 1 which they developed at Manchester University. The Mark 1 is claimed to have run the world's first stored program on 21 June 1948. It was programmed by setting switches on the front panel in 32-bit code entered backwards. This system was perhaps the ultimate in 'user unfriendliness'

Inset John von Neumann (1903–57), the elegant refugee from Hungary, who led the early development of computers in America

Above Claude Shannon (1916–) of the US Bell Laboratories, the inventor – or discoverer – of the 'bit', the irreducible unit of information, the answer to a yes or no question. Here, in 1952, he demonstrates the first computer-driven maze-running mouse

more powerful for the same price. This trend has followed such a steady path that it has been elevated into a law of Nature: every ten years you get 100 times more transistors on a chip. This means that computers increase in power by a factor of 1,000,000 every decade for the same price. What looked at first like a simple, if rather remote, technological trend has had a most important and unexpected human result. For an example, look at the variants of the personal computer you can buy today. Babbage, Gödel and von Neumann would have been staggered.

Each machine has its own BASIC. Everyone who writes a BASIC Interpreter thinks he can improve on the original scheme. Each machine has different screen handling, and many have idiosyncratic disk drives. One would think that there is not much room for eccentricity in the design of a keyboard, but no – it is very hard to predict what keys will be on or off a keyboard you have not inspected. Even something so simple as 'delete' varies from one machine to the other – to write a routine that will always delete the character to the left of the cursor is far from simple.

Anyone who has spent more than half an hour with a computer knows that when you have typed something in, you hit RETURN to make it take effect. Well, do you? On many machines the return key is labelled 'NEWLINE' or 'ENTER'. On some machines, for good measure, there are two, one for each name. Deeper in, one assumes that every key on the keyboard sends a single character to the machine. This is almost true, but RETURN, NEWLINE or ENTER sends one that is actually interpreted as two: a line feed (ASCII 10) and carriage return or 'go to left-hand margin' (ASCII 13). This can cause a lot of confusion if you are writing a program that expects only one. Another historical oddity hangs over from the days when VDUs were unknown and people communicated with their machines through a teletype – rather like a telex machine. You typed a message to the computer; the computer typed a message back. This caused some problems. If, for instance, you wanted to delete some characters from your message – which might be a program line – you obviously could not step the print head back along the paper the way that you can move a cursor on the screen. Instead, the computer repeated the deleted letters enclosed in backslashes to show they had been removed. Thus you might ask the machine, 'How's your father/rehtaf/mother?' Although no one has used a teletype in the microcomputing world for years, you can still find languages and operating systems that carry on like this. A more insidious relic is the continuing use of editors that will look at only one line at a time. And there are other jokes so deeply embedded in the woodwork that hardly anyone suspects they are there.

The difficulty with personal computing today,

and for some years to come, is that we are caught up in the blizzard of Darwinian selection. The capitalist system excels in drawing forth all manner of solutions to a sufficiently paying problem. Eventually the best – or perhaps the least bad – will be selected and become the standard. Unhappily we, the users, have to play the part of Nature and winnow out the failures. This is hard work and tearful at times.

The Caxton Analogy

The first computers were feeble, hugely expensive and very difficult to program. As the years went by, they became more powerful or less expensive – and only slightly easier to use. The only people who could afford them and their very expensive staffs of attendants were governments, armies and huge commercial organizations – such as banks – with fairly mundane problems.

A computer is no more than a machine for running a program, just as a printing press is no more than a way of reproducing an author's words. Mass-produced programs used by vast numbers of people on cheap personal micros are very similar to mass-produced books read by vast numbers of people. In the early days of computing, programs were created by a small, extremely well-paid elite, whose main interest was in preserving their jobs. Programs and computers were bought by people who did not understand them and did not want to. The whole thing was rather like the situation that must have existed at the start of printing.

Before Caxton set up shop, books were – and had been since long before the Romans – extremely expensive objects produced by hand for a very limited elite. If you were rich enough to afford a book, the chances were you could not read it because you were a king or duke and had spent your youth in the arts of war. When you wanted a book read you hired some recluse in a black frock to read it. You were like the managing director of a big company which buys a computer and its programmers. He does not understand computing, he wants results. (Very often the result was just the prestige of owning a computer, for recent research has shown that only half the processes computerized over the last ten years or so benefited by the change from manual working.)

If you wanted a book (a computer program) in the days of Caxton you went to the local monastery (IBM, ICL, etc.) and asked the good abbot to get one written for you. He would call Brother Jerome (the programmer) from his cell and set him to work. The whole job would take several years and cost 20,000 crowns.

Then Caxton set up in business. In the time it takes Brother Jerome to sharpen his quill, Caxton has printed a couple of pages. By the time B.J. has illuminated the first initial letter, Caxton has run off a complete edition of a hundred copies and has them on sale at 4/- or 50 cents each (the actual cost of the first *Canterbury Tales*).

The good abbot is appalled, and with reason. He would say, if asked, that no real book can ever cost less than 20,000 crowns and it is the most arrant folly to think that it ever could. Caxton's so-called 'books' are mere toys. No gentleman need read, for heaven's sake. If he wants a book read, the abbot will be happy to send a clerk round (for a fee).

But that is not how it turned out. The duke and his descendants found that they had to learn to read after all. The abbot and his monks, as producers of amazingly expensive literature, joined the dinosaurs. Until recently, this was how the big computer world viewed the micro. Although this attitude is changing fast, we have to live with the results of decades of development under the old system, whose most important single feature was the distinction between those who paid but did not understand, and those who were paid and did. The people who actually built and programmed computers had a very strong incentive to make a mystery of their art. To be fair, this was not hard for them, because computers are quite different from ordinary life and take some getting used to. But as well as the natural difficulties of the new medium, we also have to surmount, or tear down, quite artificial barriers that have been built up over the years to keep outsiders definitely out.

Furthermore, we have to take into account a much more complex community. Before the micro there were only a few thousand computers in the world, and a few tens of thousands of people interested in them. A small, highly paid, self-absorbed group of professionals found it relatively easy to adopt common standards for languages, communications protocols, disk formats and so on. Usually everyone did what IBM did, but whatever happened, there were fairly well-defined and well-understood standards.

Things have changed radically in the last five years. There are now some million microcomputers in the world, built by more than a hundred different companies. Few of the builders or the users were brought up in 'big computing'. Very often they invented and re-invented the standards they needed as they went along – sometimes they bore some resemblance to the traditional versions, sometimes not.

This again is very like the early days of printing. No one knew what a book ought to look like. Often the title page was at the back, not at the front where we now expect it. It was a matter of chance whether the three important contributors to a book – the author, the printer and the publisher – all got their names on the thing. In fact, for a long time, these three quite separate functions had not established themselves.

Most serious of all, there was no reading public. Instead of the millions of literate people that there are now who will buy good books, rewarding in the process all the people who helped to make them, Caxton looked out on a world where only a handful of people could read. Imagine his feelings when he had a stack of new *Canterbury Tales* behind the counter and no one in the street who could begin to appreciate them.

In the early days of printing, it was enough to have a press. Almost anyone could write an adequate manuscript, and you sold the finished books at the door of your workshop. It took many years before control of the press stopped being the bottleneck in book production, and for the twin trades of author and publisher to emerge. Today, in the Western world, there are printing presses on every corner, but very few people who can write an interesting book and even fewer who know how to produce it, advertise it, distribute it and generally turn a good idea into a profitable venture.

In computing we are just emerging from the Caxton stage. The hardware (the press) is decreasing in importance. A computerate public is emerging who can tell good software (manuscripts) from bad. The new profession of software publisher is emerging – a person whose job is to select software, present it properly (compare an author's typescript with the finished book), get it reproduced in bulk, advertise it and distribute it. It is all very different from the way it seemed back in 1940.

CHIP MANUFACTURE

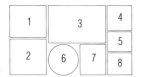

Chip manufacture is a curious blend of the highest technology and a country kitchen. When you visit such a plant, you are dressed in lint-free overalls, propelled through airlocks, past radiation scanners, into rooms cleaner than any you have entered in your life. There, mysteriously attractive women, masked and gum-booted, whose eyes only are visible – like the members of a hi-tech harem – carry little trays of chips and wafers about. They slide them under microscopes and fuss over the pictures on the TV screens; they carry little baking dishes of silicon to and from the computer-controlled doping ovens. In this kitchen the scullion has a PhD; the cucumber being sliced over there is a single, vast crystal of silicon and the sections are polished optically flat – to within a fraction of a micron. The sandwiches at Blandings Castle were never that fine.

1 Since computers are practically blind, it is always a problem to get visual data into them. Here a technician is using a digitizer – the ring in her left hand – to enter amendments to a fairly simple integrated circuit design

2 Workers in a clean room at an integrated circuit factory lining up masks before the next stage of lithography. Although chip making uses very expensive and sophisticated tools, it is essentially a labour-intensive cottage industry

3 Once a layer of resist has been laid on the silicon wafers, they are transferred to vacuum ovens and 'sputtered' with atoms of metal or dopant spat out by a white-hot source (top)

4 A quartz tray of silicon wafers goes into an oven for a high-temperature treatment. This picture clearly illustrates the limited amount of 'real estate' – the area of silicon – that a chip factory can process daily. Since the cost of a chip is its share of the overheads, it is most important to maximize this amount

5 At each stage of the chip-making process, a new photographic mask has to be laid over the structure that is being built up. Here a technician in an integrated circuit factory uses a high-powered binocular and TV microscope to check a mask for alignment

6 Chips are made several hundred at a time on thin silicon wafers like this. They are tested in place with probes connected to a computer, and then broken into separate chips. A few of the locations on the wafer are test spots

7 The microprocessor chip is glued to the lower half of its plastic case, in the middle of the lead frame. The contact pads on the chip are hand-connected by tiny wires to the appropriate lead

8 Once the wafer has been broken into chips, the individual devices are bonded into their conductor frames. Technicians using microscopes will then connect the terminal pads on the chips to the integrated circuit package pins with hair-thin wires

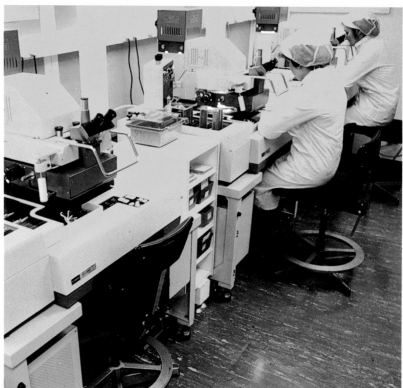

Instead of a bread-slicing machine, they have a diamond saw to cut the wafers into chips. When the hair-fine cuts are made, a bold man hits each wafer with a mallet to break the chips apart. Little objects fall from this woman's fingers – she is not shelling peas, she is sorting processors.

A long line of workers with microscopes and soldering irons look as though they are making jewellery – but no, they are mounting the chips in their cases and connecting the hair-thin conductors to the pads on the integrated circuits.

This cross lady attends a mechanical spider: integrated circuits fly from her fingers into this basket if they pass the tests; into that if they fail. The quality-control man hovers nearby, anxious to count the proportions because, like a kitchen, this factory makes its living by serving up acceptable silicon meals.

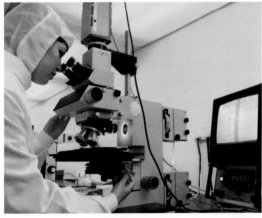

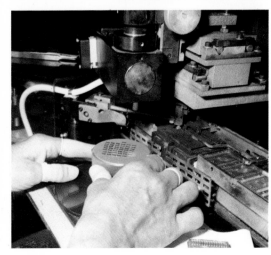

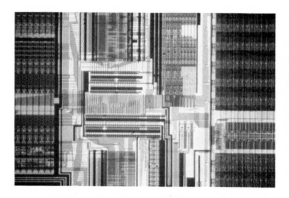

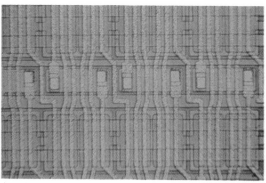

Right Hewlett-Packard, the doyen of manufacturers, startled the computer industry in 1983 by announcing the 32-bit micro. This literally put main-frame power on a user's desk and offered more computing power than anyone knew what to do with. Compare the regularity of the structure with Texas Instruments' rather messy 16-bit chip on page 19

Far right An early experimental integrated circuit composed of Josephson junctions – a super-fast switching circuit cooled to within a few degrees of absolute zero

Opposite Circuitry diagrams of a microprocessor chip enlarged about 300 times. Each layer in the final chip is represented by a different colour, and all the connections must be right before the chip goes into production. As line widths decrease and circuits become more complex, the job of design and checking gets much more difficult. Already, computer-aided design systems are used to produce the first versions of these drawings. The CAD system need only be told what the circuit is to do and it will select the right combination of gates and lay them out in (nearly) the most efficient way

The third generation of micros will have RAM measured in millions of bytes (MB). If each memory location in 1 MB of RAM were written on an index card and the cards laid end to end along the Thames they would reach from London to beyond Oxford, some 63 miles

The chips in the machine used to write this book – and almost certainly those in your computer if you have an ordinary micro – are at the '6-micron' level. This means that the conductors used to make the transistors inside them are 6 microns wide (a micron is a millionth of a metre and about a twentieth of the thickness of the paper on which this book is printed). This 'line width' is a most important measure, because it tells you immediately a lot of information about the performance of the chip itself.

At the time of writing, the better commercially available chips were made with lines about 2.5 microns across. That means a single transistor will take up a 40-micron square and you can get some 24,000 of them on a chip. Even though the eye can only see a vague blur on even a 6-micron chip, there is a mad scramble among manufacturers to get smaller line widths. The reason is – as we saw on pages 165-6 – that the cost of a chip is pretty well unaffected by what is on it. If you can reduce the line width you get more, smaller and faster transistors.

In fact the improvement in performance is pretty spectacular. If the line width is halved, the number of transistors on the chip is multiplied by four. Furthermore, the number of electrons contained by each conductor is also divided by four, so they move four times as fast. This increases the speed by a total factor of 16. However, the supply voltage has to be halved because the conductors are twice as close together.

The end effect is that the chip works eight times as fast for the same money. This must be a good thing, since it means that you can make a computer with the same power as before, but for one eighth of the cost. And because you then sell many more computers – since a law of marketing says that if you halve the cost of an item you quadruple its sales – this means that you can make the computers even cheaper because you are making very many more of them.

The American Department of Defense can see the benefits of miniaturization as well as anyone else, and it has, for a few years now, been encouraging the chip-manufacturing industry to try even harder for small line widths in its VLSI (Very Large-Scale Integrated Circuit) programme. Chips with line widths as small as .5 micron have been made in quantity, and if a processor using them could be brought to the market, it would be as powerful as some twenty of IBM's 370 series main-frames. Hewlett-Packard have recently announced a 1-micron, 32-bit processor chip that effectively puts a main-frame computer on the top of a desk.

The drawback to small line widths is that it gets very much more difficult to manufacture a good chip. A fault that could be ignored on a 5-micron chip can well disable a 2.5-micron one. Chip manufacturers reckon that they need a yield of about 30 per cent good chips per wafer to make a profit. The new, high-density chips may produce an agonizing yield of only one good chip from several wafers.

There are all manner of disorders dense chips are heir to. The masks used to make them shrink and expand, throwing out the registration. Dust particles so small that they will go 'through the finest filters settle on the masks and chips and wreck them. Even the wavelength of the light beams used to print the resists gets long enough to bend round the thin lines, so that the needle-sharp patterns degenerate into a fuzzy muddle.

Limitations of the laws of Nature

As we saw at the beginning of this section, if you can make the line width used to draw the micro circuits on a chip smaller, you can in principle make the machine work very much faster. A faster machine means either the same power for less money or more power for the same money

Oxford   London

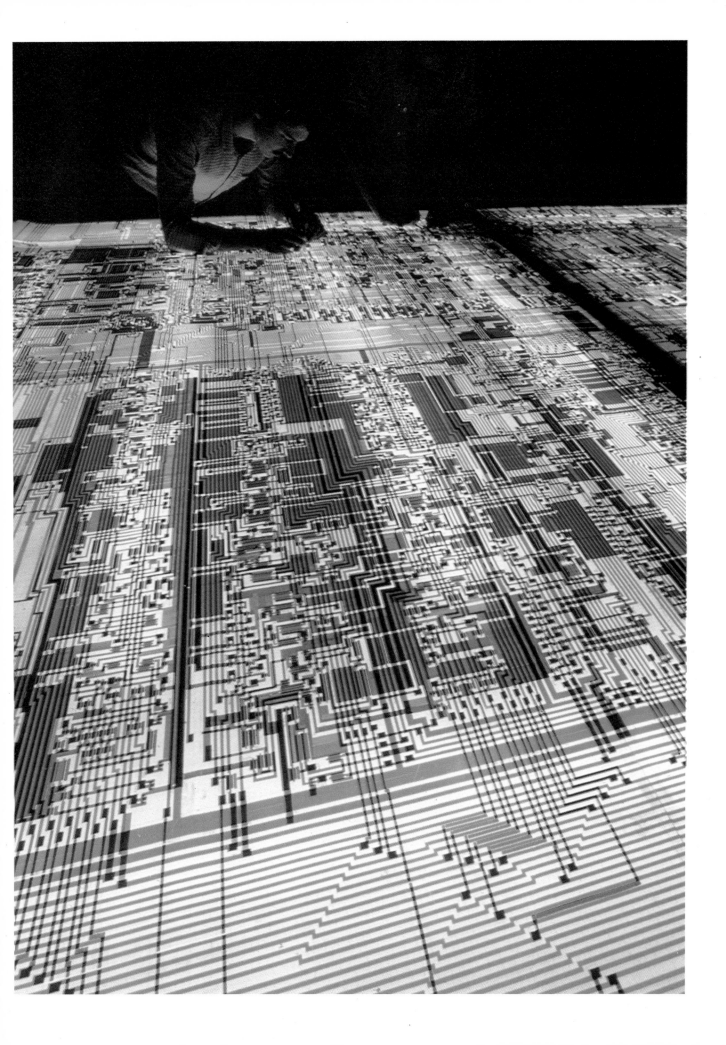

and is (so everyone will tell you) a Very Good Thing. However, you may be sure that sooner or later Nature will halt this desirable progress. It is interesting to try to see some limits to shrinkage.

The first problem, which is causing grave concern even now, arises from the fact that chip making is essentially a printing process. Several layers of very complicated patterns have to be accurately printed on top of one another in a very small space. The obvious way to do this is photographically. The masks are drawn up human size (see pp. 168-9) and then shrunk photographically to the minute proportions necessary for the chip. They are transferred to the chip by coating the silicon with a resist – a light-sensitive varnish – which is exposed to light through the mask. The parts that are exposed become hard; the rest of the mask can be washed away. This makes it possible to etch some parts of the chip and not others, to deposit conductors in this place and not that.

As long as line widths were no smaller than a few microns, this worked quite well. The trouble sets in when line widths fall to less than a micron, because the wavelength of visible light is about the same as the conductor widths. This means that the lines no longer cast sharp shadows, and the chip begins to look like a street map seen through a thick fog. The answer is to move to shorter wavelengths for the reproduction process. The designers of chip-making machines can use ultraviolet, with wavelengths ranging from one tenth to one thousandth of a micron, or X-rays, with wavelengths down to 10^{-14} micron. But as wavelengths get shorter, so the radiation gets harder to handle, and photographic processes get more difficult.

One answer is to abandon light and masks altogether, and move to electron beams. Energetic enough electrons have short enough wavelengths, and can be steered about neatly by electric fields. In fact, the whole technology is well understood by the makers of electron microscopes, so it is possible to make chips by drawing a computer-generated pattern of conductors straight onto the silicon. This works quite well, but is awfully slow, as we can easily see when we remember that a modern VLSI chip may have a dozen layers, each one as complex as the street plan of a capital city. The advantage of the old photographic process was that you could make up negatives to print off 400 chips on one wafer by repeating the masks for a single chip – just like printing a sheet of postage stamps. The electron-beam process means printing each stamp individually.

This is slow, and slowness matters, because the whole point of making chips smaller is to make them cheaper. If they end up being slower to make, then they become more expensive again. Secondly, there are problems about the conductors and electrons in the lines themselves. As

lines get smaller, so they come nearer to the width of the actual atoms of the conductor material. It does not much matter which metal is used as the conductor, because atoms are all about the same size – roughly 10^{-10} metres across. When a conductor gets so small that it is only a few atoms across, it is likely to evaporate within the lifetime of the computer. A reasonable estimate is that you cannot make a permanent conductor less than 20 atoms wide, which sets a lower limit of a five hundredth of a micron – fifty times smaller than today's chips. If a machine using such a line width could be made, it would be a thousand million times more powerful than today's micros. But, there are other problems that appear long before lines are small enough to disappear.

A major problem even with 1-micron lines lies in the uncertain position of electrons. As Werner Karl Heisenberg told an unwilling world in 1927, you cannot discover both an electron's position and speed. If you know how fast it is going – because it is sauntering along one of the conductors in your ultramicroscopic chip – you cannot know where it is. You think and hope it is in one of the conductors or a transistor or wherever its duty in the interests of computing may call for it to be, but Heisenberg's uncertainty principle tells us that it is only a ball of probability. It may be where you think it is, but it may equally well be elsewhere – notably in the next-door conductor where it should not be. This kind of thing can

make a mess of the best-designed chip. It is said that probability effects like this are already causing trouble in 64-K RAMs.

A solution to this problem may be to use a smaller and more precise bead in our electronic abacus. The electron, although minute by human standards, is quite heavy and lumpy. A better bead would be a particle of light – a photon – which is more precisely positioned and weighs nothing. This means that it can be shunted around using less energy. And that means in turn that computers can run smaller and cooler – which, as we shall see in a moment, is a very good idea indeed.

A computer using photons would replace transistors by semiconductor lasers. Workers at Edinburgh University have had a device for some time which lets one beam of light switch another, just as a transistor lets one electrical current switch another. If such devices can be made small enough, it should be possible to translate the architecture of today's machines directly from electrons to photons.

However, even supposing that smaller chips can be made – and knowing the ingenuity of mankind, there is little doubt they will be one way or another – there are more difficulties. The first, and most fundamental, is concerned with the speed of signals. Einstein discovered that nothing can travel faster than light – which goes about its business at 300 million metres a second. This may sound so fast that it does not matter, but in fact it does.

A computer takes its time from a central clock: 'tick', everything sucks in a new bit of data; 'tock', they process it; 'tick' the data gets moved on. If the machine is to work properly, the clock pulses must arrive everywhere in the computer at the same time, or at least within one tenth of a clock pulse of each other. This means that the longest dimension of the computer must not be more than the distance light can travel in one tenth of a clock pulse.

Today's micros work at clock speeds of 4–10 MHz. One tenth of that is $^1/_{40}$–$^1/_{100}$ millionth of a second. In that time light moves between 7.5 and 18 metres and this – surprisingly – is how big you can make a computer. If you want to speed things up by increasing the clock rate – and that is an obvious strategy – then you have to make your machine smaller. A 100-MHz machine could be no bigger than 1.5 metres across. This seems to be no problem if you are at the same time making your devices smaller – as you would have to to make them run at that speed. The problem arises in trying to get rid of the waste heat from millions of transistors crammed into such a tiny volume. As a computer is made smaller and faster, it must also get hotter. Ultimately it will explode when switched on.

The elegant way out seems to be the superconducting computer, which runs in a bath of liquid helium. At one stroke the two main problems are solved: since electric currents flow without resistance in superconductors there is little waste heat to get rid of; and because of the refrigeration needed to get the machine down to 4 degrees above absolute zero, what heat there is can easily be disposed of. Of course, this argument assumes that today's superconductors have to be used; it would be inconvenient to have to keep your computer in a bath of liquid helium. It seems that there are substances – though no one is quite sure what they are – which will act as superconductors at much higher temperatures.

There are two devices that might be used to construct a superconducting computer. One is the Josephson junction, which depends for its working on two effects. The first is electron tunnelling. We are used to things being either electrical conductors or electrical insulators: copper conducts electricity; polythene does not. As so often in physics, these facts are only true when you consider masses of material that are large by atomic standards. If you can make a thin enough layer of insulator, separating two conductors, a small number of electrons will 'tunnel' through. The reason is essentially Heisenberg's uncertainty principle again – some of the electrons just happen to be uncertainly on the far side of the insulating barrier at the crucial moment, and therefore behave as if it were not there. The second effect is that if such a thin barrier between two conductors is cooled to a point where they become superconductors, the barrier stops being an insulator. Electrons flow unimpeded across it – until a magnetic field is applied. Then it becomes an insulator again.

Here, as Brian Josephson noticed in 1962 (he was awarded a Nobel Prize ten years later), we have the ingredients needed for an electronic switch. The current you want to control flows through the Josephson junction; the current that is to control it flows in a coil nearby so it forms a

The central processor of a Cray 1, the world's fastest and most powerful computer. The processor has to be small to prevent speed-of-light synchronization errors. It also generates so much heat that it must be water-cooled. The cabinets in the background contain memory and subordinate computers to handle input and output

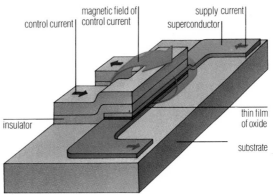

Low-temperature devices offer tremendous switching speeds. The hypercomputers of a decade hence may live in a bath of liquid helium. One of the devices being investigated is the Josephson junction. Current flows in the superconductor and through the thin oxide film as if it were not there, as long as there is no magnetic field. The current can be switched off by running a control current, to generate a field, in the top conductor

The Quiteron is more like a conventional transistor, but again relies for its switching effect on being knocked in and out of the superconducting state. A rapid rise in voltage between S1 (blue) and S2 (green) lets a current flow from S2 to S3 (purple)

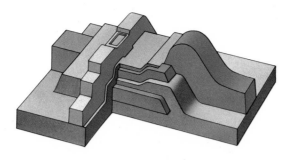

magnetic field. If the controlling current is small or off, there is no field and the Josephson current flows normally. If the controlling current increases so that it creates a magnetic field, a point will come where the junction switches, the insulator re-establishes itself and the controlled current stops.

Josephson junctions switch really fast – in about 10–15 picoseconds, which implies a clock speed of something like 50,000 million cycles a second. Of course, as we saw above, a computer running that fast would have to be no wider than .06 centimetres. In fact, the whole thing would have to be built on a single chip if signals moving at the speed of light were to get from one side to the other quickly enough. Unfortunately, Josephson junctions take up a lot more space than transistors, so the possibilities do not seem immediate. So far, a few big companies like IBM have experimented with these devices, but no one has yet built a serious commercial computer with them.

Researchers, also at IBM, recently announced a new device, the Quiteron. This works more like a transistor, in that a voltage on one terminal turns a superconducting current on or off between the other two terminals. A voltage-controlled device is more desirable than one controlled by current because it is easier to chain many of them together. The Quiteron is also said to take up less room on the chip, so it is more suitable for densely packed circuits.

Parallel processing

It is, however, beginning to dawn on people that more and more powerful single processors are not the whole answer. Many computing problems would still be too big even if you had processors a thousand times faster than the best we can foresee today.

To understand why, you have only to go back to the description of making a computer 'see' on pages 116-17. We had to get the processor to scan the whole visual field many times, comparing each pixel with its neighbours. The best current vision systems have perhaps 100,000 pixels, and even using main-frame power, programs to recognize people walking can take hours to run. Compare that with the human eye, which has some 3 million pixels (rods and cones) and can do all its processing comfortably in $1/25$ second.

What is wanted in computing is not so much faster processors as many more of them. This is, after all, how the eye works. Light falls on the rods and cones; they send signals to the brain about the colour and intensity of the light they detect, but they also do a lot of low-level processing among themselves – averaging out noise, adjusting for light and shade, detecting simple shapes and movement. What is wanted in computing is just this 'parallel processing'.

Imagine a machine which had simple processors attached to each light-sensitive cell. The very first stage of vision – averaging with neighbouring cells to eliminate noise – could be done by all the processor cells in half a dozen machine cycles, as against the millions it would take a central processor to get around them all.

Similarly, the individual processors can all detect edges by asking their neighbours: 'Do you see the same colour and intensity that I see?' Those that do not tend to lie on or near an edge of something in the scene. The same sort of process can construct regions of similar tone all over the picture simultaneously. When processing has reached the level of 'Is it a bird? Is it a plane?', the same multiple architecture can operate as a database, looking up many possible identifications simultaneously.

Several companies and institutions are working on the problems of processing in parallel. Britain's GEC has a device for vision processing called the Grid chip, where many processors are joined to each other and each to its own little bit of memory where it can store data and program. To make a practical machine, this memory also needs to be accessible to a master processor which can load each element with the appropriate bit of program: do noise averaging; do edge finding; do region growing; look in your database to see what you have got....

Another scheme, from Stanford University, is to have a more general-purpose arrangement.

Right One possible scheme for linking processors: a single processor (1) is connected to the outside world and also to two others (2). They are each connected to four (3s), and those to eight (4s). These lowest-level processors are connected to eight small segments of memory which hold program and data. The whole thing can be made on one chip, and can be configured to behave in many different ways. If levels 2, 3 and 4 are told to be quiet, we have processor 1 connected to its memory, like today's chips. If 1, 2 and 3 are quiet, we have eight processors running in parallel. And there can be any combination in between

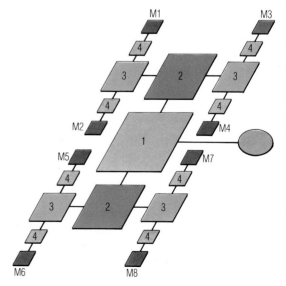

There are four levels of processor. Each processor at one level controls two on the level below, so that there are eight processors at the bottom level. They have control of all the memory. Since any of the processors can be set to be 'transparent' – to pass on instructions without doing anything to them – this hierarchy gives a number of possibilities. At one extreme the single high-level processor has control of all the lowest-level memory and works just like one of today's processors. At the other extreme all the higher-level processors become transparent, leaving the eight at the lowest level to work in parallel. And of course any combination in between is equally possible.

The difficulty is that until the hardware is available for people to play with, they will not really know what they actually need. And until people have a fairly clear idea of what they need, no one in either government or industry is keen to spend the billions of dollars necessary to make it. At the moment, although people can see vaguely what is wanted in hardware, no one has much idea about writing software to control parallel tasks. It is easy enough when you want a lot of simple processors to do something in unison – as we did in the vision machine. But it gets very much more difficult when you want a number of different jobs done at once, as, for instance, with a large amount of numerical information. One processor might be calculating averages while another does mean variations. But the second could use the first's results to speed up its own work. People are beginning to tinker with parallel processing languages, but no one has got very far as yet, partly because they can only simulate parallel processing on single processor machines. Certainly we have not seen the explosive growth in techniques that occurred as soon as conventional computers were thrown on the mass market. At the moment parallel processing is a damp, unhatched embryo lurking in the egg of the future.

The transcomputational

So far we have been looking – in a rather dilettante way – at possible increases in the power and speed of computers. It is quite interesting to look at the problem from the other end by asking: 'Are there are any problems that no conceivable computer, however powerful, could solve?' Indeed there are. The familiar game of chess is one. Bearing in mind that computers are good at being pedantic, you might think that the way to get one to play chess is to tell it all the laws of the game, and let it work out all the posibilities in turn. Having done that, it ought to be able to select the best set of moves and play them to an assured win.

But it is not that easy. On average, at each turn in a game of chess, there are some 30 possible, distinct, moves. Each one of those leads to 30 more in the second turn, and each of those to 30 more in the third. So the machine has to explore

30, 900, 27,000, 24,300,000,... positions. This soon gets out of hand, and it is quite easy to see why the complete game of chess will never be searched by any computer likely to be built in our lifetime.

The same sort of difficulty arises in many other searching problems. Imagine that you are a travelling salesman with a hundred cities to visit. In what order should you tackle them so as to travel the least distance? On page 145 we looked at the difficulties of making a computer 'think' how to solve a problem. The only way we can tackle this problem is to make the machine do one of its repertoire of actions, and then another and another, and see if, at the end of it all, it has happened to hit on the desired solution. It is like the monkeys typing Shakespeare, and you certainly need eternity to get results.

Eternity means longer than we have had since the beginning of the universe. Hans J.Bremmermann, a man with a taste for the unanswerable argument, tackled the chess problem – and the travelling salesman problem and a lot more of the same sort – like this. He shows that the maximum data-processing rate of a computer that weighs m grams is mc^2/h, where c is the speed of light and h is Planck's constant. This comes out to be about 10^{47} b/s per gram, which either seems a lot, if you are thinking about word processing, or not very much, if you are thinking about playing chess. To stop any arguments about how much a computer might weigh, Bremmermann simply supposes we have one made from all the matter in the universe, weighing 10^{55} grams. The universe has been in existence for 20 billion years or 6.3×10^{17} seconds. In that time, with a computer of that size you could not possibly process more than 10^{120} bits. Bremmermann says that any problem which requires more data processing for its solution than that generous allowance is 'transcomputational'.

A total of 10^{120} bits might seem enough, but in fact a dozen or so chess moves uses it up. The universe as a computer running from the beginning of time could not solve the travelling salesman problem for a hundred cities either. A lot of artificial intelligence problems look as though they will be transcomputational too.

This may sound depressing, but all it really tells us is that brute force is not the way to solve problems. We know that perfectly well by watching ourselves do this sort of thing, particularly playing chess. Faced with a difficulty, only the most pedestrian person methodically lists all the possible actions and then eliminates the duff ones. We feel our way to a goal, led on by some mysterious light that tells us we are on the right road. But just how to program that light has so far escaped the brightest minds.

Perhaps you, gentle reader, will find the answer, and become the hero of the twentieth century.

MASS STORAGE

Smaller, faster, more powerful chips are only part of the story. What holds personal computing back more than anything else is the paucity of backing storage on today's machines. A few years ago 240 kilobytes of data on a single disk was thought to be riches beyond the dreams of avarice; now, 10 megabytes (40 times as much) is fairly ordinary. But even that is small compared to people's real storage needs.

A 12-foot bookshelf can can easily hold 100 books, each containing 50,000 words – a data storage of some 30 megabytes. A drawer in a standard filing cabinet might hold 50 files, each containing 100 sheets of paper and each sheet with 300 text words: a total of 9 megabytes. Most office workers soon accumulate one full filing drawer each. A working group of half a dozen would need a total storage of some 100 or 200 megabytes if they were to dispense totally with paper in their daily work. They would, of course, need long-term archival storage, which might still be best on paper.

This sort of argument points up the need for backing storage devices with far greater capacity than today's hard disks. One possibility (see pp. 42-3) is vertical magnetic recording. It is claimed that by magnetizing a disk in rodlike regions through the disk, with a recording head on either side, rather than in flat patches on only one side as is done today, it will be possible to increase storage by a factor of 40. And that would mean Winchester disks with storage capacities of 1500 million bytes (1.5 gigabytes).

Another, more immediate, possibility is the laser disk. This device was originally invented for the storage of television programmes, which demand vast amounts of data. A colour television signal has a band width of some 8 MHz and can hardly be digitally coded into less than 8 Mb/s or 1 MB/s. That means one hour's programme must take up 3600 megabytes (3.6 gigabytes), more than twice as much as the best possible Winchesters, and that is the sort of storage which a laser disk must have if it is to be useful.

A laser disk encodes digital data through a pattern of tiny pits etched in a spiral, rather like a gramophone record. The pits are read by a low-power, finely focused laser. Because nothing physically touches the disk, it cannot wear out; because the access is done by rotating the disk and tracking the head in and out, the technology could, in principle, give the kind of random access needed for computing.

The difficulty, until recently, was that laser disks were read-only. The data to record a television programme was printed into each disk in manufacture and could not thereafter be altered. This was not much use for computing – and, as the indifference of the customers showed, was not much good for video recording either. However, a recent development looks as though it will change that. Sony Corporation have announced a new type of laser disk which can be written to as well as read. The essential ingredient is a metallic antimony-selenide film, laid down on top of a bismuth-telluride film, which is in turn carried by a plastic disk. When a reasonably powerful laser hits the surface, its energy passes through the antimony-selenide film to be absorbed in the layer underneath, where it turns to heat. The outer layer is changed by the heat from an amorphous structure to a crystalline, and this makes it reflective rather than matt. Consequently, the write process produces a digital signal in the form of shiny dots on a grey background which can be read by a low-power laser.

One drawback is that data cannot be unwritten, but since such a disk would hold the output of a fast typist working for 700 years, this might be tolerable. In fact, as anyone who has had a precious file eaten by a wayward computer knows, it would be very soothing to have an unerasable copy of every file you ever made. However, Matsushita have announced a similar sort of device in which the disk *can* be erased and made ready for rerecording by the application of an even higher-powered laser.

The uncertain thing about using laser disks for computing is the error rate. Disk manufacturers reckon that their equipment must produce one bit in error in less than 1000 million. Recording for television is far less rigorous, since a bit in error just produces a spot on the picture for $1/_{25}$ second, and the eye easily adjusts. It may be necessary to record computer data many times over on laser disks, with some elaborate checking mechanism to make sure that the error rate is held down low enough.

A further point, which has not yet become a problem in personal computing, is how a file that big can be searched. The speed at which data can be read off a disk is limited by the speed of the chips used to process it, and ultimately by laws of physics (see pp. 171-4). Imagine that we are looking for the word 'hippopotamus' on a full 4000-MB disk. Even if we had one of the imminent 32-bit super microprocessors, it would still take an hour to read the whole disk – and an 8-bit micro would take a day. We shall have to devise much more sophisticated methods of indexing stored information than we use today.

At first sight, either of these technologies appears to provide far more storage than any individual or even a fairly large group could possibly need. Remember, though, that it may be necessary to encode the data several times to get an acceptably low error rate. Furthermore, people will probably want software using these disks to keep two or three copies of earlier states of their files as backups. Finally, it is likely that the indexes necessary to find anything again will take up quite large amounts of the available space. All in all, the improvement will not be as spectacular as it might at first seem.

An enlargement of a segment of a laser disk, showing the microscopic pits that are read by the tiny laser beam. Such a disk, when used for computer data, ought to be able to store several years' worth of continuous typing

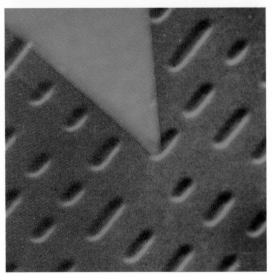

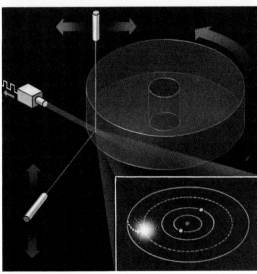

Far left Laser disks for use by computers will need to be writable by the laser as well as readable. This simulated enlargement of such a device by some 10,000 times shows the laser beam cutting out a pit to record a '1'

Left Gigantic amounts – hundreds of thousands of megabytes (gigabytes) – of data can be kept in a small space once it can be written in three dimensions rather than two. A promising technique, using existing technologies, writes data bit by bit into a wheel of transparent material with two lasers that overlap in a small data cell.
The atoms of material in the cell are excited by the laser energy so that the outermost electrons jump to higher orbits and stay there for a short time. This process records a '1' in the cell, which is read by re-exciting the cell with the lasers at lower power. If a '1' is there, some of the electrons fall back into lower orbits, emitting a flash of light which is picked up by the detector. If a '0' is stored in it, no flash occurs. As with RAM, the data evaporates fairly quickly and has to be refreshed by reading and re-writing it

However, on the horizon are storage technologies that will put the volume question firmly on the shelf. One method uses a principle fundamental to lasers: if you excite an atom of almost anything by biffing it with light of an appropriate wavelength, some of its outermost electrons get excited and jump into orbits farther out. After a while they will decay and fall back to where they were, emitting a photon of light. This emission can be stimulated by a further small smack from the laser. This second emission is detected by a photoelectric cell and reads the data bit written or not written by the original laser pulse.

A solid disk storage could be made with two low-powered lasers at right angles, whose beams add up to one of the right power only within the small volume where they cross. That volume forms a data cell. One laser would point down into the disk and be moved in and out from the centre like the read/write head on a conventional disk drive. The second would point radially into the centre and move vertically to access data cells at different levels. The two lasers firing strongly together would excite atoms in a data cell and write a '1' there. The two again, crossing in only one place, would fire less strongly to stimulate an emission which would be detected by the photoelectric cell.

THE ELECTRONIC VILLAGE

'The Electronic Village' is an evocative phrase coined by the computer guru James Martin in his book *The Wired Society*. What he meant by it was that when (and if) the trends in cheap computing hardware and broadband data links mature, people will be able to use electronics to link themselves into a worldwide community as casual, intimate and informal as a village.

Before this can work, we need cheap personal computers able to display and manipulate high-quality four-colour pictures and with enough data storage to hold all an individual's personal and business records. We also need high-capacity data links capable of transmitting vast amounts of information very cheaply. The British Post Office is already installing a national network of fibre optics which will eventually penetrate to every home and office, linked to networks abroad by satellite radio. Big computers will act as exchanges, picking messages off the high-speed data busses and switching them to their destinations. Any two computers anywhere can be connected through the network so that two people working together – on opposite sides of the world – can share the same information. This information would consist not just of the text files (see pp. 146-9) of today's computers, but of photographs, film, animated plans and drawings.

The network can carry not only text typed at the keyboard or drawn from a data file, but also voice and four-colour pictures and diagrams. These pictures might be sketches, plans, drawings – which might change as the two people doodle at the computers. The network could also carry colour television – part of each computer station will be a television camera so that users of the network can see each other. It also gives its users access to bigger computers and databanks. Much of the information stored in today's libraries will be held in big computers, accessible to inquirers on the network.

The network will be used by almost anyone who needs to communicate with another individual: for example, executives and their personal assistants (the computer will do most of what secretaries used to do), architects and their clients, salesmen and their customers, authors and their editors, doctors and their patients, a general and his colonel. The effect of the electronic village on these people is that they can live where they like, but work together as closely as if they were in the same room. Furthermore, the computer acts as an intelligent personal assistant at either end, storing and retrieving information either from their own or larger national data banks.

There is no reason why communication on the network should be limited to pairs of people. The computers can be used as a means of broadcasting – probably much entertainment, both sound and picture, will come down the data links (see pp. 158-9). But because the network can pick people out intelligently, it will be used as a medium for group activities: schools, universities, clubs, political groups, trade unions. Children using the home computer station can attend classes with others from many hundreds of miles around, conducted by a teacher who might live in another continent.

Effects on society

As the physicist Heisenberg said, 'Prediction is difficult, especially about the future', but we can be pretty sure that the electronic village will have some profound effects on the organization of advanced countries. Today about half the workers in the West live in cities and are employed in handling information. They crowd into the cities to spend their days in office buildings which are, in effect, vast filing cabinets for the millions of pieces of paper they produce. The proportion of office workers must increase as factories are automated; and an increasing proportion of national resources will have to be devoted to moving these workers in and out of their cities.

There is little point in moving the workers bodily to the information if you can move the information to them at a fraction of the cost.

Of course, people will still need to meet, to discuss their plans and share their experiences, and they can do this in settings different from today's offices. Most of their work they can do from home – or near it, for many people will not want to stay at home twenty-four hours a day. They will probably travel a short distance to a communal office space where they get on with their own work while enjoying the sociability of other workers. Of course, people who want to retreat to the wilds can do so and carry on a brisk professional life at the same time. So we can expect electronic networks to have a profound effect on cities – very much reducing commuting, reducing office space, producing small village communities of office workers in the countryside. They will go into the city occasionally to meet their colleagues face to face, but most of the time they will get on with their routine tasks by computer.

Rush hour of the future? In the electronic village commuting may no longer be necessary

WHAT NEXT?

Quite early in the Industrial Revolution people could foresee telephones, steamships, airships, flights to the moon and the planets. The Western world was embarked on a course of development which was far away from these things, but whose path clearly led in that direction. In the same way we can see how the present helter-skelter development of computing might end up.

First, the miniaturization of chips – which means more power for less cost – will continue until there is no real hardware limit to what computers can do. Machines small enough to fit in a pocket will have the computing power of today's Crays and more; data storage will hold the equivalent of several million text volumes in an equally small space. High-speed data links will enlarge everyone's huge personal databases to include all the world's knowledge, efficiently indexed and served by software assistants, so that anyone, anywhere, any time, can find out anything.

One tremendous application of this technology will be in the arts. There seems no reason why animation, database management, vision and artificial intelligence should not fuse to produce an amazing new sort of art which combines film, novel and computer game. Presented perhaps in holograms, this entertainment will produce stories in the form of plays with realistic, lifesize, three-dimensional settings, in which the characters are constructed afresh each time. The plot and the appearance and behaviour of the characters can be changed, either randomly or by the intervention of the watchers – who might themselves be actors.

It would presumably be possible to let people insert themselves into stories – either as main characters or bystanders, according to temperament. Once they are in the story, the machine will reproduce them alongside the fictional characters, and their decisions and reactions will influence the flow of events. If you think *Gone with the Wind* would look better with you as Scarlett O'Hara or as Rhett Butler, then you are at perfect liberty to insert yourself in the plot. Or, if you prefer more modern havoc, you can flee a devastated earth to stand alone, the last of your race, on a deserted planet.

This sort of thing running on a network opens up another vast area of entertainment and social action. Instead of one or two people running a script to amuse themselves, many people can play in the same arena – an arena that exists only in the computer's imagination. This might entirely replace spectator sports, turning them into multi-user interactive hyper-video games. If people begin to take this sort of thing seriously, it could spill over into business and politics. If computers can produce a more interesting and tractable world than the real one, there is no valid reason why people should stay out in the rain. There is no reason why interaction with the computer should not be made much more physical

than it is today, so that runners, for instance, might have their own little treadmills connected to the network and compete in an electronic Olympic Games.

A great many businesses will be run completely automatically by machines. Computers will be able to see and reason at least to the standard of something like a literate sheepdog. It is doubtful, however, that all this intelligence will be matched by equal development in hardware engineering.

The main application of this may well be in warfare. It could be that by the end of the century

there will be few jobs for fighting men. Warfare may become a symbolic contest of economies and machines. And that can only be for the good.

The development of massive machine intelligence and high-powered communications will effectively free users of the system from their physical locations. They will be able to carry on an economic and intellectual life equally well from almost any point on the surface of the globe. The consequence of this, though, is that people who do not make it into the electronic world – either because they personally, or their societies, are not up to the intellectual challenges – will be

at a desperate disadvantage. It is hard to see how this process will not produce two worlds – an immensely well-served intellectual elite who control information, politics, war, production; and an incomputerate peasant mass.

But this is no new thing. It was how all the developed nations worked until the Industrial Revolution, by the development of stupid machines that each needed a more or less intelligent and responsible master, produced mass democracy. It is ironic that technical sophistication looks likely to reproduce the slave states of ancient Egypt and Rome.

WHERE WILL IT END?

The great issue in computing is whether machines can be made as clever – or even cleverer – than man. There are those who say that within a century machines will be far quicker and brighter than humans; machines will know infinitely more, work far faster, and be immune to those distressingly human foibles of love and hate that so hold back human progress. They will be able to make and maintain themselves and will have no use at all for people. In effect human intelligence will have evolved into a new silicon home, shedding our limitations and leaving its original dwelling of flesh and blood as far behind as we have left the lizards.

A recent television programme on developments in computing opened with a grey-haired professor asking whether, when computers had far outstripped man in their power and intelligence, they would be kind to us. There are really two questions here. The first is can a computer be made as powerful, or even more powerful than the human brain? Secondly, if such a computer could be built, would it be the same as a human or would there still be some essential difference?

It is not easy to reply to either question. It is hard to answer the first because we do not really have any idea how the brain works. It consists of about a hundred thousand million neurons. A neuron's job seems to be to do with signal processing, and nerve signals consist of more or less rapid streams of pulses. Signals are transmitted from neuron to neuron through synapses where they seem to be carried by various exotic and illegal chemicals. All in all, a neuron seems to work something like a transistor, but one with ten or fifty inputs and outputs rather than one of each. Despite many decades of work, no one yet knows what a neuron does or how it does it. Even if we understood the individual neuron's function, we have little idea of how the huge number of neurons in the brain might be connected together to produce the terrific computing power of humans in terms of vision, language, and association.

It has always been fashionable to model the human body and brain in terms of the most up-to-date technology. When I was small I had a (not very modern) book that described the human body as a factory, with boilers, pistons and a managing director in top hat and tails controlling the whole enterprise. Today the fashion is to see the brain in terms of computing.

We looked at the brain as electronics on pages 142-3. Another way is to start with games like 'Twenty Questions'. The theory of this entertainment is that, by asking twenty yes or no questions, a skilful player can guess any simple phrase, such as 'the President's right ear'. Two multiplied by itself twenty times is about a million, so the popularity of this game and the fact that it is twenty rather than thirty or fifteen questions suggest that the human brain can store about a million ideas. If we allowed that everyone has vastly more memories that they cannot describe in words

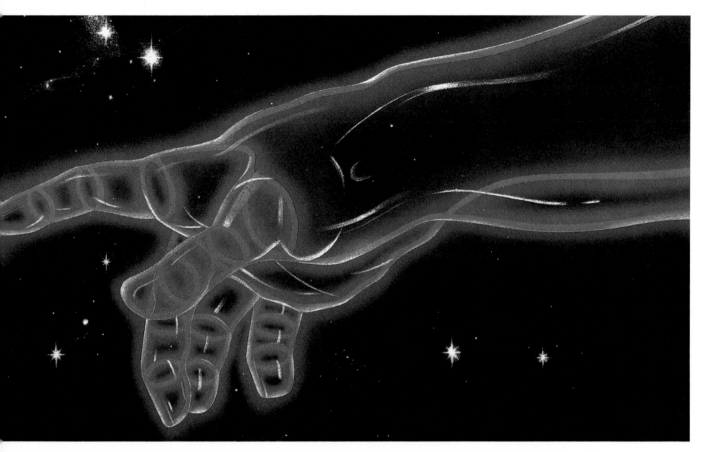

than those that they can – memories about the appearance of their friends and family, how to drive a car, the feel of cat's fur, the taste of wine, the smell of a coat – then we have to find room in the brain for some thousand million 'ideas' – whatever they are. Perhaps each neuron – whatever that is – stores one.

But, for what it is worth, there seems no barrier but ignorance to our ability to build a machine a million times more powerful than anything we have now, that works in a way we do not begin to understand. That will have to do as an answer to the first question.

If computers can be made to mimic every function of human behaviour, can they be considered alive? From one point of view anything that behaves like a human is a human. The nearest person to you could be an android – one that is apparently made in a most artful way of flesh and blood, but is still a machine. If Nature can evolve a humanlike android, then surely so can the computer scientist. Or is there something essentially different between a machine and a human being?

This is not a terribly new question. For a long time those who believed that living things were not machines could point to the vast areas of our ignorance and say that lurking in them was something completely non-mechanical. However, as our understanding of animate and inanimate nature progresses it becomes harder and harder to believe that there is any point in the inward voyage of science where the laws of Nature give up.

And if there is no particular structure which distinguishes men from machines, then one has to look elsewhere for the difference.

Some people have proposed that the freedom of the will resides in the randomness of the subatomic world (see pp. 60-61). Perhaps the brain is just a huge amplifier to bring the 'life' of subatomic particles up to human scale. This 'life' – which we perceive as random and unpredictable behaviour – presumably reflects laws and events in some universe 'at right angles' to this one which we cannot see. But even if this were so, there is no apparent reason to prefer neurons to transistors as crossover points for this random behaviour. Alternatively, 'life' consists in the sheer complexity of organisms – in the hundred thousand million neurons rather than the mere megabytes of RAM that we can deploy.

A third suggestion is that the laws of physics, which seem so inexorable, are like the statistical laws that govern the appearance of letters on this page – they are accidental and have very little to do with the real meaning of the text.

But ultimately, as far as we can see, the brain consists of ordinary molecules arranged in a complex way, obeying logical laws. If we can understand what those laws are, everything we now know about computing says that a machine can be made to obey the same laws. And if it can, then, presumably, we have a living computer. Whether that will be good or bad is hard to say. It certainly is not a problem we are going to have to worry about this decade, or even this century.

ASCII CODE CHART

	0000 0	0001 1	0010 2	0011 3	0100 4	0101 5	0110 6	0111 7	1000 8	1001 9	1010 A	1011 B	1100 C	1101 D	1110 E	1111 F
000 0	↑@ 0 NUL	↑A 1 SOH	↑B 2 STX	↑C 3 ETX	↑D 4 EOT	↑E 5 ENQ	↑F 6 ACK	↑G 7 BEL	↑H 8 BS	↑I 9 HT	↑J 10 LF	↑K 11 VT	↑L 12 FF	↑M 13 CR	↑N 14 SO	↑O 15 SI
001 1	↑P 16 DLE	↑Q 17 DC1	↑R 18 DC2	↑S 19 DC3	↑T 20 DC4	↑U 21 NAK	↑V 22 SYN	↑W 23 ETB	↑X 24 CAN	↑Y 25 EM	↑Z 26 SUB	↑[27 ESC	↑\ 28 FS	↑] 29 GS	↑↑ 30 RS	↑← 31 VS
010 2	32 SP	33 !	34 "	35 #/£	36 $	37 %	38 &	39 '	40 (	41)	42 *	43 +	44 ,	45 -	46 .	47 /
011 3	48 ∅	49 1	50 2	51 3	52 4	53 5	54 6	55 7	56 8	57 9	58 :	59 ;	60 <	61 =	62 >	63 ?
100 4	64 @	65 A	66 B	67 C	68 D	69 E	70 F	71 G	72 H	73 I	74 J	75 K	76 L	77 M	78 N	79 O
101 5	80 P	81 Q	82 R	83 S	84 T	85 U	86 V	87 W	88 X	89 Y	90 Z	91 [	92 \	93]	94 ↑	95 ↓
110 6	96	97 a	98 b	99 c	100 d	101 e	102 f	103 g	104 h	105 i	106 j	107 k	108 l	109 m	110 n	111 o
111 7	112 p	113 q	114 r	115 s	116 t	117 u	118 v	119 w	120 x	121 y	122 z	123 {	124 |	125 }	126 ~	127 DEL

185

BASIC COMMANDS

A simplified guide to the BASIC language, based on Microsoft's MBASIC 80

Operators

A=B	make A equal to B
C↑D	raise C to Dth power
−X	Make X negative
K+L	add K to L
M−N	subtract N from M
E∗F	multiply E by F
G/H	divide G by H
P\$+R\$	tack R\$ to the end of P\$

Relational operators test two values: the expression is replaced by −1 if true, 0 if not. Try: PRINT (1=1). You should get −1. PRINT (1=2) should produce 0.

Why does PRINT (A=B) produce −1?

A=B	A equals B
A<>B	A does not equal B
A>B	A greater than B
A<B	A less than B
A>=B	A greater than or equals B
A<=B	A less than or equals B

Logical operators do bitwise comparisons on two bytes (see pp. 20-21): NOT, AND, OR, XOR.

Basic commands

AUTO (m,n): used when entering programs. Numbers each new line written from m, incrementing by n. If m and n are omitted, both are 10

CALL (variable name) (argument list): calls a machine code subroutine at the address (variable name) and passes arguments to it

CHAIN (filename): loads and runs the program in (filename)

CLEAR m,n: sets all variables to 0 or null. If m and n are present, sets highest memory location used by BASIC to m (so that machine code can be loaded above it) and the stack space to n

CLOAD (filename): loads and runs (filename) from cassette tape

CLOSE #m, #n . . . : closes files numbered m, n . . . in an OPEN statement

COMMON (list of variables): passes variables to a CHAINed program

CONT: to continue execution after a ↑C to break, a STOP or END. Used in debugging

CSAVE (string expression): saves the current program called (string expression) on tape

DATA, m,n,o,p . . . : Gives a list of constants – which may be string. They are transferred to program variables by READ a,b,c . . .

DEF FN(name) (parameter list) = (function): to define your own functions. For instance: DEF FNADD (X,Y) = X+Y. Later in the program you can write Z=FN(A,B). Z will become the sum of A and B

DEFINT /SNG/DBL/STR (range of letters): defines variables starting with the range of letters as integer, single or double precision numbers

DEF USR (digit)=(integer expression): specifies the starting address of an assembly language subroutine. (CALL is much better)

DELETE m–n: erase program lines from m to n

DIM (list of arrays): specifies maximum sizes for numeric or string arrays

EDIT n: edits line number n. The programmer can move the cursor, insert, delete, find and replace text in the line

END: stops the program, closes all the files and returns to immediate mode

ERASE (list of array variables): eliminates the arrays in the list and frees the storage they occupy

FIELD #n,p AS R\$, r AS T\$ . . . : sets up fields in a random file (see below). The first field is R\$ and is p bytes long, the second T\$ and is r bytes long, etc. . . .

FOR K=n TO r (STEP p) . . . NEXT K: executes the program lines in between the two statements, adding p to K each time until it becomes equal to r. If 'STEP p' is omitted, the increment is 1

GET #n,p: reads the pth record from the file n into the structure set up by the appropriate FIELD command

GOSUB n . . . RETURN: transfers program execution to line n. When RETURN is executed, execution goes back to the statement after the GOSUB

GOTO m: Transfers execution to line m

IF . . . THEN . . . ELSE: evaluates the expression after IF. If it comes to −1 (see relational operators above), the commands after THEN are executed. If not, the commands after ELSE are executed. If there is no ELSE, execution 'falls through' to the next program statement. However, a statement on the same line – IF . . . THEN: (statement) – will only be executed if the test *succeeded*. This is rather illogical, but useful

INPUT "prompt"; A,B . . . : prints the 'prompt' if present and waits for the user to type in the variables A,B, etc., separated by commas. Can be used with strings or numbers

INPUT #n,A,B . . . : as above, but gets variables from file n

KILL (filename): erases filename from the current disk

LET A=B: puts A equal to B ('LET' is optional)

LINE INPUT "prompt"; A\$: gets a complete line with commas, quotes, etc.

LINE INPUT #n,A\$: as above from disk

LIST m–n: list program lines m to n

LLIST m–n: prints lines m to n on the printer

LOAD "filename": loads filename from disk

LPRINT USING "##.##"; A,B . . . : prints the variables A,B, etc., on the printer, formatting them with the USING expression if present. Printing these variables would produce this result:

23.456	23.45
1.6	1.6
100	0.0 (with an overflow error)

LSET(string) ... RSET(string): moves a variable into a field preparatory to PUT to write it to a random file

MERGE "filename": reads in filename from disk (which must be in ASCII – see SAVE) and merges it with the current program

MID$(A$,m,n)=B$: takes n characters from B$ and overwrites them into A$ staring at the mth, i.e.: MID$ ("CONCATENATE",4,3)="DOG" produces "CONDOGENATE"

NAME "old filename" AS "newfilename": renames file

NEW: deletes the program in memory

ON ERROR GOTO m: a sort of GOSUB. When an error occurs, execution goes to line m. The error number is written into the variable ERR, and the line on which it occurs into ERL. The subroutine at line m can test the error, do something useful and RESUME execution at some appropriate line

ON A GOSUB/GOTO m,n,o,p, ... : evaluates A to a digit r and goes to the rth line number in the list m,n,o,p ...

OPEN "m", #n, "filename": opens the file and gives it the number n. The mode m can be 'I' for serial input to the program, 'O' for output, 'R' for random.

OUT i,j: sends the integer i to the port j

POKE i,j: Pokes the integer i into the memory address j

?/PRINT USING "exp", a,b,c, ... : prints a list of variables on the screen. "?" is shorthand for PRINT. See LPRINT for USING. If the variables are separated by commas, they are tabbed; if by semicolons, they run on. A linefeed is printed at the end unless there is a comma or semicolon

PRINT #n,a,b,c ... : prints variables to file number n

PUT #n,K: writes the data in the appropriate field – put there by LSET or RSET, to the kth record in random file number n

RANDOMIZE (n): restarts the randomizing process with the number n as a seed. If the seed is not changed, the same random numbers will be produced. If n is omitted, the program stops and asks for a seed from the keyboard

READ a,b,c ... : transfers the next items in a DATA statement to the variables a,b,c. ... See RESTORE

REM: what follows is a remark

RENUM m,n,o: renumbers program lines to start with m, from n in the old numbers, incrementing by o

RESTORE m: makes the next READ look at the DATA statement on line m

RUN m: starts program execution at line m. If m omitted, at the beginning

SAVE "filename", A: saves the current program under 'filename'. If followed by ',A', the file is saved in text format. It can then be text edited, compiled or merged

STOP: stops the program. CONT resumes execution

SWAP A,B, A$, B$: exchanges the two string or numeric variables

TRON/TROFF: for debugging: prints the line numbers as the program executes them. TROFF turns the facility off again

WHILE (exp) ... WEND: as long as the expression after WHILE is true, the program lines down to WEND are executed. Like a FOR ... NEXT loop

WRITE (#n): like PRINT, but puts quotation marks round strings and commas between items

Functions return a variable:

ABS(X): the absolute value of the expression X: PRINT ABS(7*(−5)) will produce 35

ASC (X$): the ASCII value of the character in X$

ATN(X): the arctangent of X (in radians)

CHR$(I): the character whose ASCII code is I

COS(X): the cosine of X (in radians)

EXP(X): e to the power X

FRE(X): the amount of free memory

HEX$(X): the hexadecimal version of a decimal number X, i.e. HEX$(32)=20

INPUT$(m,n): the next m characters typed at the keyboard, or, if n is present, from file n

INSTR(i,A$,B$): searches for the first occurrence of B$ in A$ (starting at the ith character if i is present) and returns the number of the character at which it is found. For instance: INSTR(4,"A fine romance in the summer"," ") will return 7 – the position of the first space after the 4th character

INT(X): the largest integer less than X

LEFT$ (A$,i): the leftmost i characters of A$

LEN(A$): the length of A$ in characters

LOG(X): the natural logarithm of X

MID$(A$,i,j): the string j characters long starting at the ith in A$

OCT$(A): the octal value of decimal A

PEEK(i): the byte stored at memory location i

RIGHT$$($,i): the rightmost i characters in A$

RND(X): the next random number in the sequence. X is a dummy variable

SGN(X): the sign of X. If X>0   SGN(X)= 1
                              X=0   SGN(X)= 0
                              X<0   SGN(X)=−1

SIN(X): the sine of X (in radians)

SPACE$(X): X spaces

SQR(X): the square root of X

STR$(X): turns the number X into a string

STRING$(i,j): a string length i, repeating the first character in J$,

TAB(I): moves the cursor on I characters

TAN(X): the tangent of X (in radians)

VAL(X$): turns X$ into a number

ACKNOWLEDGEMENTS

The authors and publishers would like to thank the editor of *Practical Computing* for permission to reproduce the program listings on pages 62–76.

Thanks are also due to the following for providing photographs and illustrations:

Photographs

Abacus, University of Strathclyde 104 *bottom*
Ann Ronan Picture Library 144 *bottom right*, 163 *bottom left*
Apple Computer Ltd 35 *top*, 46-7
Art Directors Photo Library 105 *bottom right*, 124 *bottom left*, 137 *top*
Atari 48 *top and bottom left*, 49 *bottom*, 50 *bottom*
Franklin L. Avery 48 *right*, 51 *top right*
BBC/Ceefax 153 *top*
Bell Laboratories 155 *right*, 156-7 *bottom*, 165 *right*
Benson UK 4-5
Chris Bidmead 32
Paul Brierley 18 *top right*, 25, 177 *bottom left*
British Aerospace 156 *left*
British Telecom 125 *top right*, 146 *top and right*, 153 *bottom left*, 154, 155 *left and centre*, 156-7 *top*
British Telecom/Prestel 153 *top*
Brookes & Gatehouse Ltd 129 *top left and right*
CAD Centre, Cambridge 104 *top, and centre below*
Calcomp Sanders 39 *top*
Calma 102
Cambridge Instruments 86 *bottom*
Commodore 36 *top*
Columbia–EMI–Warner 143 *bottom centre*
Casio Electronics Company Ltd 14 *bottom*, 31 *bottom left*
Computervision 103 *bottom left*
Control Data Ltd 105 *bottom left*
Courage 124 *bottom right*
Cray Research 173 *top*
Datini Archives 100 *top*
DEI/Mark Lindquist 111 *top and bottom*
DEI/Dr Steiner Rutgers Medical School 109 *bottom right*
Department of Computer Science, University of Manchester 14 *top*, 165 *centre left*
Department of Trade and Industry 10
Digital Effects Inc. 115
Elliot & Fry 164 *left*
Jeremy Enness, 15 49 *top*, 77, 120 *top and below right*, 140-41
Evans & Sutherland 103 *bottom right*, 104 *top*
Evans & Sutherland and Rediffusion Simulation 106 *top*, 107 *top*
Ferranti Electronics Ltd 18 *top centre*
Gamma 136 *left*, 143 *top right*, 144 *bottom left*
General Electric Company PLC 18 *bottom left and right*
Grove Park Studios Animations 113
Hewlett Packard 170 *left*
David Hogg, University of Sussex 109 *bottom left*
IBM 40 *top*, 169 *4 and 6*, 170 *right*
Image Bank 124-5 *top centre*, 165 *bottom left*
International Imaging Systems 109 *top left*
Intertrade Scientific Ltd/ACT 38
Jorge Lewinski 116
Logica 110 *left and bottom*, 120 *bottom left*
Lucasfilm Ltd 143 *bottom left*
Micro Control Systems 124 *top left*
Microsoft 51 *bottom right*
MIT Museum 163 *right*
Moving Picture Company 114
Myriad Audio Visual Sales 100 *bottom*
National Academy of Sciences 165 *right, inset*
National Film Archive 143 *top left*

Nelson Max, Lawrence Livermore National Laboratory 112 *left*
New England Digital/Jonathan Sadah 121 *bottom*
New Scientist/Jerry Mason 104 *centre above*
New York Institute of Technology/Lance Williams 112-13
Nottingham Building Society 153 *bottom right*
Odetics Inc. 140-41
Philips 177 *top*
Plessey Semiconductors Ltd 43, 168-9 *2 and 7*
Popperfoto 178
Qume Corporation 36 *bottom left and right*
Redifon Simulation/Evans & Sutherland 106 *bottom*
Rheumatology Research Unit, Addenbrook's Hospital, Cambridge/CAD Centre 126
Richfield Graphics 18 *top left*, 169 *5*
Rodime 42
Rutherford Appleton Laboratory 172
Red Saunders 50 *top*
Schaefer Instruments 109 *top right*
Science Museum, London 163 *top left*
Science Photo Library 88, 103 *top*, 168 *1*
Scientific American/Robert F. Bonifield 132-3
Scott, Brownrigg and Turner 39 *bottom*
Sharp Electronics Ltd 39 *centre*
Sierra On-Line Inc. 51 *left*
Sinclair Research 22, 27, 31 *centre*
Smiths Industries 128
Sperry Univac 165 *top left*
Stanford Research Institute 86 *top*, 142 *right*
Tate Gallery, London 143 *bottom right*
Texas Instruments Ltd 19
Transport and Road Research Laboratory 107 *centre and bottom right*
University of Edinburgh 135 *bottom*
Richard F. Voss/IBM Research 90-91
Laurel Wade 16
Walt Disney Productions © 1982 89

Diagrams and Illustrations

Bob Chapman, 12, 16, 17, 20, 21, 24, 25, 32, 33, 34, 35, 40, 41 *top*, 42, 42-3, 44, 45, 60, 80, 81 *bottom*, 83, 84, 88, 89, 91, 108, 112, 113, 119, 120, 124, 125, 126, 128, 129, 131, 132, 133, 136-7, 138-9, 144, 145, 153, 155, 170, 173, 174, 177
Les Edwards/Young Artists 134-5 *top*
Bob Ford 159
Peter Goodfellow/Young Artists 180-81, 182-3
Grundy & Northedge 13 *top*, 22, 23, 27, 31 *left and bottom right*, 57, 127, 148, 149, 152, 179
Hayward & Martin 26, 30, 31 *top right*, 36, 37, 41 *bottom*
Val Hill 121
Peter Holt/Ian Fleming Associates 13 *bottom*
Peter Knock 54-5
Gordon Lawson/Ian Fleming Associates 150-51
Graham McCallum 8-9, 52-3, 92-3, 160-61
Tony McSweeney 95
Chris Moore/Artist Partners 142 *left*
Ingram Pinn 87, 90, 162-3, 164, 167
Max Rutherford 116
John Thompson 11, 28-9, 147
Jonathan Wolstenholme 97

Grateful thanks are also due to Professor Alexander and Dr Stonham, Brunel University, Old Oak Primary School, London, and Mitsubishi Electric (UK) Limited for providing facilities for photography.